Philosophies of Education

from the standpoint of the
Philosophy of Experimentalism

Philosophies of Education

from the standpoint of the

Philosophy of Experimentalism

BY

JOHN P. WYNNE, PH.D.

State Teachers College
Farmville, Virginia

GREENWOOD PRESS, PUBLISHERS
WESTPORT, CONNECTICUT

To

JOHN DEWEY
WILLIAM HEARD KILPATRICK

and

BOYD HENRY BODE
*The three experimentalists in philosophy
who have achieved most in
philosophy of education*

Preface

From the standpoint of the philosophy of experimentalism, education consists of desirable experience. All important philosophies of education may be reduced to three general positions. First, of the people who are interested in education, many are primarily interested in the maintenance and extension of order and authority. Since some of these seek such ends through external dictation and imposition, their position may probably be designated as *educational authoritarianism*. Second, there are always people who are primarily interested in the maintenance and extension of individual freedom. Since some of this group seek these ends through direct self-development, expansion, or expression of the powers of the individual as they are prior to experience, their position may properly be designated as *educational laissez faire*. Third, there are those who reject, not only the extremes of educational authoritarianism and educational laissez faire, but any eclectic or middle-of-the-road position which seeks a compromise between them. They find their standards neither in external authority nor in the individual apart from experience, but in experience itself. Since those who adopt this attitude toward desirable experience — education — in recent years have been given the intellectual support of the movement in philosophy now usually called experimentalism, their position may properly be designated as *educational experimentalism*.

During the period between the close of World War I and the outbreak of World War II, there was a tendency in many quarters to swing away from educational authoritarianism toward educational laissez faire. In other quarters there was a tendency to abandon both of these extreme positions, adopt educational experimentalism, and attempt to cause the pendulum to swing in a new direction. But the public and the teaching profession in general usually confuse the position of the educational experimentalists with that of the adherents of educational laissez faire. This confusion has resulted partly from the fact that the proponents of both educational laissez faire and educational experimentalism have subjected authoritarian principles and

practices to constant criticism, and also from the fact that these principles and practices have been combined in the public mind under the
head of progressive education.

At the outbreak of World War II when people everywhere, including
pupils and school authorities, were already disappointed with their
new freedom, they were ready to look again to external authority for
control and direction. Moreover, the prosecution of the war in democratic countries depended upon rapid educational results that could be
achieved only through authoritarian drill. The educational authoritarians were quick to take advantage of the conditions provided by the
reaction against laissez-faire principles and practices and by the successful results achieved under the pressure of war through the application
of authoritarian principles and practices.

With renewed energy this group is now urging the general adoption
of these authoritarian principles and procedures as a policy and a program especially in school education, although this movement is by no
means confined to the schools. They complain of the inadequacy of
progressive education which, they say, failed to prepare youth for the
war; they commend the quick results of the educational authoritarian
program adopted during the war. They now advocate formal and
systematic procedures, seeking to establish intellectual justification for
them based on philosophical foundations. Various elements of many
authoritarian groups having little in common except their antipathy
to progressive education are now banding together to fight it and
establish old principles and practices under new names.

The present study is designed to help clarify the situation so that the
public, as well as school people, may better understand the issues involved. When the three philosophies of education here under consideration are defined so that the layman as well as the professional school
worker can understand them, interest in the controversy between traditional and progressive education should decline. We should have less
name-calling and more intelligent examination of principles. This
book is designed to describe these three different positions clearly
enough for the average educated individual to understand and apply
them in his effort at the educational improvement of himself and others
with whom he deals, and also clearly enough for those directly responsible for school education to see the various alternative positions.

These three tendencies in educational theory and practice are always
with us. The problems to which they are applied in this study are
relatively permanent and enduring, but the tendency in much current

educational discussion is to consider only two alternatives — the authoritarian and the laissez-faire positions. This study is intended to contribute to the clarification of the issues between educational authoritarianism and educational laissez faire, at the same time stating in comparable terms educational experimentalism as a third position.

Since the topics considered are those with respect to which teachers, supervisors, and administrators usually have to take some stand in practical situations, the book is designed also as a text for students — both graduate and undergraduate — who are taking their first course in the philosophy and principles of education. The first part, devoted to experience, is designed primarily for the general reader interested in dealing with himself as well as with others, whether in the school, the home, the church, the state, business and industry, or anywhere else. The second part, devoted to school practice, is designed primarily for those responsible for the control and direction of the school. Those who have any responsibility for school education should, however, be interested in education in its wider aspects as well as in the activities of the school. Some such general orientation among the conflicting philosophies of education seems indispensable at any time but more particularly at present, not only for members of the teaching profession who already occupy positions in the schools, but for every student who contemplates entering the teaching profession in any capacity. It is the purpose of this book to help provide such an orientation for those engaged in teaching, supervision, and administration on all educational levels, and for others who contemplate entering these fields of service.

There is no way in which I can express my obligation specifically to the many philosophers and students of education, representing a multiplicity of points of view, who have influenced the interpretations of experience contained in the pages that follow. However, I owe so much to Professor John Dewey, Professor William Heard Kilpatrick, and Professor Boyd Henry Bode that I must acknowledge my indebtedness to them particularly. Had they and their students failed to develop the philosophy of experimentalism in terms of education, a work like this might not have been possible at all. I had the good fortune to study for several years under the direction of Professor Dewey and Professor Kilpatrick and to confer with the latter and also with Professor Bode on problems connected with the development of this study. For the assistance they have given me I am deeply grateful. They are in no way responsible, however, for the theories and principles here developed. These are the results of my own analyses and interpretations of the three philosophies of education considered most important by educational representatives of the movement in philosophy variously known as pragmatism, instrumentalism, humanism, and experimentalism.

For the stimulation necessary to get the study clearly formulated, I am indebted to the summer school authorities of the University of Pittsburgh and of the University of Pennsylvania, who provided me with opportunities for making public presentations of the theories and principles here developed. From time to time during the study I have secured valuable criticism and suggestions from Dr. William H. Burton, of the Graduate School of Education, Harvard University, who is especially interested in the application of philosophies of education to the problems of the teacher. In like manner I have had several stimulating conferences on various phases of the study with Dr. Fred M. Alexander, State Department of Education, Richmond, Virginia, who is particularly interested in the in-service education of teachers. Administrators of several teachers' colleges and university schools of education have offered pertinent criticism and advice.

Dr. Evan R. Collins, Dean of the College of Education, Ohio University, provided the opportunity for me to try out the book in manuscript form with two summer school classes in which both graduates and undergraduates were enrolled. During the years in which the study has been in progress through the co-operation of my colleagues in Farmville State Teachers College, every part of the manuscript has been used in many ways. Finally, the ruthless criticism and constant encouragement of my wife, Alice Curry Wynne, have always been freely given. All these and many more have contributed to my effort to make these philosophies of education available to teachers and to those who assume responsibility for their pre-service and in-service education.

JOHN P. WYNNE

FARMVILLE, VIRGINIA
JULY, 1947

Editor's Introduction

The question that will arise at once is — Why another philosophy of education since we have many distinguished writers and many books already available? There is no use for just another book on the philosophy of education. There is, however, desperate need for a book that will interpret and explain the various philosophies of education and their value in determining educational policies, programs, and methods. This is just what the author of this book has done.

Throughout the early history of education, philosophy was regarded as a basic subject in the education of the personnel of the educational profession, but in recent years it has not been so regarded, and has been reduced to a minor place in the curriculum or dropped altogether. The decline of the importance attached to philosophy in the curriculum has resulted from confusion among educators about the various philosophies basic to educational interpretation.

In this book the author has explained the various philosophies and indicated the educational practices required by each. This procedure makes the book indispensable to the teaching profession. There is no longer need for confusion. Therefore, this book will meet an urgent need in teachers' colleges, schools of education, and the educational profession. I have read the book with genuine interest and predict that it will rapidly become an essential text wherever educators are seriously concerned with the vital problems of education in the postwar world.

E. George Payne

Table of Contents

PART II

THEORIES OF SCHOOL PRACTICE

Philosophies of Education

from the standpoint of the
Philosophy of Experimentalism

CHAPTER I

Introduction:
Philosophies of Education

EDUCATION IS PERHAPS THE ONLY OCCUPATION in which everyone is constantly engaged, for it includes all activities that influence subsequent conduct in either desirable or undesirable ways. All of us, therefore, are engaged in education every day of our lives, because the things we do affect someone favorably or unfavorably. For the most part, they affect others, but they at least affect us. Education is then not confined to the school. It occurs almost everywhere, for virtually anything we do influences someone. Education as a process, therefore, consists of activity, and as a product, it consists of the effects of activity. From the standpoint of the philosophy of experimentalism, philosophy of education consists of the different attitudes which people consciously or unconsciously assume as to what educational activities are desirable. Everyone who maintains any consistency in his thought and conduct in dealing with himself and others has some kind of philosophy of education. Whenever he undertakes to justify this attitude intellectually, he is already engaged in the philosophy of education.[1] But just as education is not confined to the school, so the philosophy of education is not just a study of school education. Nor is it merely a part of professional education. The philosophy of education is of concern to people everywhere who are interested in the influences that affect behavior or conduct, either their own or that of others, for good or for ill. *Just as education is a universal occupation, so the philosophy of education should be a universal study. It is an indispensable factor in general education as well as in professional education.*

DEMAND FOR INTEGRATION

Although education is much more inclusive than schooling — in fact, it is as broad as human experience itself — illustrations and

---

[1] L. Thomas Hopkins, *Interaction: The Democratic Process*. D. C. Heath and Company, New York, 1941. Pp. 173–197.

1

examples of different attitudes, theories, or philosophies of education are perhaps easiest to find in discussions of the school. Students of education have little difficulty in pointing out two extreme views that may properly be considered philosophies of education and which are applicable not only to activities of the school but to activities of people everywhere.

The first view has often been called *traditionalism, conservatism,* and *essentialism* — terms that emphasize the importance of authority, order, and control by fixed standards. The second view is usually called *progressive education.* To many people it is the direct opposite of the principles and practices constituting the first view. But happily even some traditionalists recognize some good in progressive education, which, on the whole, they condemn. In recent years, some of their more liberal leaders have come to the conclusion that their traditionalist views, as well as the progressive education they condemn, represent important points of emphasis, but not an adequate philosophy of education. In other words, the conflict between conservative education, whatever it may be called, and the progressive education they condemn can never be settled through argument, nor even through experimentation, because both philosophies contain valuable elements.

Both the conservatives and the progressives need to go further afield to develop some other point of view that will combine the valid elements of both conservativism and progressivism. This demand has been so clearly stated by the late Professor W. C. Bagley, one of the recognized leaders of that form of conservatism in education which he called *essentialism,* that it may be quoted here to represent the present attitude of all broad-minded and liberal conservatives everywhere. He says: "Now that the war is over, there may be both an opportunity and a stimulus to develop an educational theory that will effect a true integration of those elements of both Essentialism and Progressivism that are most worthy of survival." [2] In other words, Dr. Bagley admits that there is something in progressivism over and beyond what many conservatives condemn, and he likewise admits that there are certain elements in conservatism that may well be discarded. He sees the need of developing a different philosophy of education that is not merely a compromise. Something in the two extremes must be discarded in favor of some new position which the proponents of both can accept.

Some years ago, Professor Dewey made a similar statement, although

---

[2] W. C. Bagley, Editorial, *School and Society,* 62:150, September 8, 1945.

he did not use the terms *essentialism* or *progressivism*. By using a figure of speech, he describes the same two extreme attitudes toward education. Apparently, he avoids such terms as *essentialism* and *progressivism* because he, like Professor Bagley, recognizes that there is much good in the theory and practice of both views. He describes the two extremes, whatever they may be called, and, in the following words, states his demands for their integration: "The history of schools not only in art but in all lines shows a swing of the pendulum between extremes, though it must be admitted that the simile of the pendulum is not a good one, for the schools remain, most of them, most of the time, near one extreme, instead of swinging periodically and evenly between the two. Anyway, the two extremes are external imposition and dictation and 'free expression.' Revolt from the costly, nerve-taxing, and inadequate results of mechanical control from without creates an enthusiasm for spontaneity and 'development from within,' as it is often phrased. It is found that children at first are then much happier in their work — but gradually tend to become listless and finally bored, while there is an absence of cumulative, progressive development of power and of actual achievements in results. Then the pendulum swings back to regulation by the ideas, rules, and orders of someone else, who being maturer, better informed, and more experienced, is supposed to know what should be done and how to do it.

"The metaphor of the pendulum is faulty in another respect. It seems to suggest that the solution lies in finding a mid-point between the two extremes which would be at rest. But what is really wanted is a change in the direction of movement." [3]

Apparently, Professor Dewey and Professor Bagley, whatever terms they use, are thinking of the same extremes. They are certainly both asking for the development of another point of view. Apparently, they both wish to integrate the two extremes to cause the pendulum to swing in a new direction. This is what experimentalists have been working for and are still working for today. The purpose of this book is to elaborate the two theories which Dewey, representing what some people call progressivism, and Bagley, representing what some people call conservatism, condemn; and also to indicate and elaborate the new position which both anticipate.

To do this it is necessary to give each of these philosophies of education a name. To call them *essentialism* and *progressivism* would be to

[3] John Dewey, "Individuality and Experience," *Journal of the Barnes Foundation,* 2:1–6, January, 1926.

miss the point of Professor Bagley's statement. He is not interested in the maintenance of essentialism, but rather in the maintenance of its valid elements. He is not interested in discarding progressivism, but in discarding its invalid elements. Certain things in both essentialism and progressivism he condemns. The same is true of Professor Dewey. He does not condemn all the system, order, and fundamentals that the essentialists idealize, and he does not approve everything that every so-called progressive idealizes. We need new names, therefore, for the two views condemned by both "conservatives" and "progressives." Moreover, we also need a name for a new philosophy that both Dewey and Bagley advocate. The one extreme of "external imposition and dictation" we may designate as *educational authoritarianism,* and the other extreme of "free expression" as *educational laissez faire.* Since this idea of integrating these two philosophies, or of causing the pendulum to swing in a new direction, is approached from the standpoint of the general philosophy of experimentalism, it seems quite appropriate to call this philosophy of education *educational experimentalism.* In fact, it is the philosophy of experimentalism in its educational aspects.

EDUCATIONAL AUTHORITARIANISM

Educational authoritarianism signifies the attitude assumed by all those who think and act as though education were determined in all important respects by influences outside the individual as well as by all those who deliberately defend and support theories that justify such external control and direction. Many people who have never taken courses or studied books in philosophy of education are educational authoritarians. They include not only those who have direct control of the schools but also people in all walks of life, it matters not what their occupations may be. They include pupils as well as teachers, children as well as parents, the young as well as the old. Educational authoritarianism is adopted perhaps by most people most of the time, and perhaps by everyone at some time with respect to a particular situation.

But educational authoritarianism is not just an unconscious attitude which uninformed people assume in the way they think, feel, and act with regard to influences that affect the behavior and conduct of people. It is an attitude which has intellectual support in many historical philosophies and theories of education — an attitude which recognized students of philosophy and education have deliberately sought to justify. In our effort to explain the meaning and significance of educational authoritarianism, we shall, therefore, give some attention to both the attitude of the unsophisticated rank and file and the more deliberate and reflective theories of the sophisticated intellectuals. Educational authoritarianism is a body of educational attitudes, practices, and doctrines derived from a variety of sources, and yet so similar that they may be considered as constituting a general educational point of view or philosophy of education.

Some readers who are familiar with many philosophies of education may wonder just which of these are here considered authoritarian. As already indicated, this philosophy of education includes elements that are not derived from any particular historical theory of education. It contains theories concerning the ways people think, feel, act, and speak in many situations. Such theories pertaining to thinking, feeling, acting, and speaking are influenced by factors derived from many sources. Some of the more important of them consist of recognized philosophies of education and the application of general philosophies to education. Some are derived from the theory of formal discipline, the so-called scientific movement in education, the educational applications of objective idealism, neo-humanism, neo-scholasticism, mechanical materialism, neo-realism, and behaviorism. All these have influenced the development of educational authoritarianism as it actually exists today in the minds, hearts, and conduct of people everywhere.

EDUCATIONAL LAISSEZ FAIRE

Educational laissez faire signifies the attitude assumed by all those who think, feel, and act as though education were determined in all important respects by factors inherent within individuals themselves, as well as by all those who consciously defend and support theories that justify the direct expression, development, and realization of individual propensities. As in the case of educational authoritarians, not all exponents of educational laissez faire have arrived at their position through deliberate study and investigation. They include people in all walks of life, teachers and pupils, parents and children, people everywhere who consistently or even occasionally think, feel, and act as if the good life consists in the elaboration, development, realization, or expression of the inner life.

Perhaps there are no definitely formulated philosophies of education that lend logical support to educational laissez faire as there are in the case of educational authoritarianism. Still in the history of human thought, there are many intellectual slogans, principles, and theories which have been used to justify laissez-faire practices. Just as there are, perhaps, few people who adopt a consistent laissez-faire attitude in dealing both with themselves and with others, there are doubtless only a few recognized authorities who maintain a consistent laissez-faire position in the development of theories and principles. Nevertheless, many principles have been developed and supported by recognized students of education and philosophy which have been taken to justify laissez-faire programs and practices. Moreover, laissez-faire principles have often been used as standards by authorities who criticize unfavorably authoritarian principles and practices. Educational laissez faire, like educational authoritarianism, consists of a body of educational attitudes, practices, and doctrines derived from a variety of sources, and yet so similar in meaning and significance that they may be considered as representing a general point of view or philosophy of education — a philosophy of education that is in many respects the very opposite of educational authoritarianism, against which it may be conceived as a reaction and a protest.

This philosophy of education cannot be identified with any of the historical theories with which informed readers may be familiar. It includes educational applications of the Rousseau tradition, and certain aspects of the philosophy of Bergson, Romantic Idealism, and psychoanalysis. In addition, it contains other elements that cannot be definitely ascribed or attributed to any historical theory.[4]

EDUCATIONAL EXPERIMENTALISM

Educational experimentalism, like the other two philosophies of education whose importance leading experimentalists recognize, signifies an attitude that many people often assume in their thoughts, feelings, and actions in connection with educational matters, as well as the principles and theories which lend it intellectual support. Many educational experimentalists have never studied the philosophy of experimentalism or its educational principles and practices. There are strands of experimentalism in common-sense practices and principles everywhere, just as there are strands of authoritarian and laissez-faire principles and practices. There are educational experimentalists among people in general, just as there are representatives of educational authoritarianism and educational laissez faire. Just as there are experi-

---

[4] William F. Drake, "Progressive Education: A Dichotomy," *School and Society,* 53:508–509, April 19, 1941.

mentalists among pupils, teachers, school administrators, and parents, so there are experimentalists among employees and employers, buyers and sellers, and people in all walks of life. There are perhaps strands of educational experimentalism, along with strands of educational authoritarianism and educational laissez faire, inextricably intertwined and interwoven in most of us.

But educational experimentalism is not simply an unconscious philosophy which people assume on occasions. It also includes theories, principles, and practices which educational representatives of the philosophy of experimentalism have defined, developed, and elaborated. There are many philosophical proponents of educational experimentalism, but, as already suggested, when we speak of the more intellectual and reasoned aspects of this philosophy of education, we have in mind primarily the teachings of Dewey, Bode, and Kilpatrick, and their students, although we recognize elements from others like Charles Sanders Peirce, F. C. S. Schiller, William James, and George H. Mead.

Educational experimentalism, whether conceived in terms of an unconscious attitude or in terms of philosophical theories intellectually determined, differs in important respects from both educational authoritarianism and educational laissez faire. It rejects the position that education is an either-or affair. From this point of view, education does not get its direction from the environment in isolation from the individual or from the individual in isolation from the environment. It gets its direction from factors that arise within experiences in which both the individual and the environment are functionally combined. Moreover, it is not a middle-of-the-road position. It is not just a compromise between educational authoritarianism and educational laissez faire; it is not dedicated to maintaining a midway position between the two extremes. It is dedicated to giving educational policies, programs, and activities a new direction.

EXPERIMENTALISM AND PROGRESSIVE EDUCATION

One way — perhaps the best way — of suggesting the general meaning of experimentalism is to consider it in its relationship to a school movement generally known as progressive education. For a generation, progressive education has been variously understood and misunderstood, approved and condemned by practical schoolworkers, students of education, and the general public. Students of education who have developed the educational implications of the philosophy of experimentalism, whether designated as pragmatism, instrumentalism, or humanism, are usually considered progressives as contrasted with the traditionalists, whose theories and practices they have not hesitated to criticize and condemn. Identification of the educational teachings of the experimentalists with progressive education is perhaps inevitable. Still there is an important difference between progressive education as it has been sponsored by the Progressive Education Association, which has recently become the American Education Fellowship, and educational experimentalism, which may be considered the educational equivalent of the philosophy of experimentalism.

Strictly speaking, then, the philosophy of educational experimentalism cannot be logically identified with any school movement such as progressive education. Such movements, however they may be designated, represent a reaction against current principles and practices, and they attempt to develop better schools along lines different from the traditional schools against which they are raising a protest. The leaders in such movements naturally seek theoretical support in any philosophy of education which assumes the role of criticizing the traditional school and its underlying philosophy. The experimentalists — particularly Dewey, Kilpatrick, and Bode, and their students — have, like Rousseau and other naturalists and romanticists, not hesitated to subject the philosophy and practice of the traditional school to severe criticism. Furthermore, these experimentalists have looked to the progressive movement and to the Progressive Education Association to develop a school in which the constructive principles they advocate can be effectively applied. From their point of view, the traditional school is so controlled by custom, tradition, and habit that it has been almost impossible to get it to adopt new methods of improvement. Thus, the experimentalists have relied more and more on the development of a new school that was not bound to the past.

Experimentalists have never identified their philosophy with the principles underlying the progressive school or the Progressive Education Association, by whatever name it may be called. Experimentalists look upon the function of philosophy as mainly that of criticism. From their point of view, the business of a philosophy of education is to criticize various practices and their underlying principles so as to render them intelligible and consistent in so far as possible. Experimentalists have never considered progressive education to be a systematic application of their philosophy. They have, however, sought to criticize progressive schools to direct them toward the practical application of their philosophy in whatever system might be developed. The progressive schools thus need the experimentalists and the experimentalists in turn need the progressive schools. Any progressive movement in education needs a philosophy of education. Established institutions usually do not need a philosophy. The less they say about theory the better for them. Their philosophies as clearly defined systems may have long since been forgotten, having become imbedded in the methods, the forms of organization, and the customs and traditions of people. But those who wish to change the habitual ways of doing things require some theoretical justification for doing so. The exponents of the progressive schools look to the critics of the traditional school — the experimentalists — to supply them such theoretical justification.

On the other hand, the experimentalists have sought above everything else to influence current practice. They have looked upon the school as the means by which the meaning and significance of their philosophy could be expressed and tested best in terms of practical experience. But the ordinary schools whose principles and practices they criticize do not readily adopt the experimentalists' philosophy of education. The experimentalists, therefore, sought to help the progressive schools, which needed and welcomed their support, and became members and leaders in the associations and movements designed to develop a new school. They assumed that they could work more effectively inside such groups than outside them. The influence of the progressive movement has demonstrated that the experimentalists were right in their decision.

The result, however, has not been entirely satisfactory. There were many progressives who agreed with the experimentalists with respect to the defects of the traditional schools and who were unable to adopt the educational philosophy of experimentalism. Some progressives adopted this position, but others adopted the opposite of whatever they condemned in the traditional school. Some were influenced by the philosophy of Rousseau and other naturalists and Romanticists, and still others by the psychoanalysts. Many progressives have not understood the philosophy of experimentalism, or its educational principles, and have adopted interpretations of this philosophy provided by others who are not experimentalists, or even by philosophers and students of education who oppose experimentalism. The progressive school does not represent a systematic interpretation of the educational principles of the philosophy of experimentalism. It contains many elements which the experimentalists condemn as strongly as do the authoritarian critics of progressive education who represent the philosophies underlying the traditional school.

The experimentalists now, as understood by the public, by many students of education, and by many members of the teaching profession, are responsible for the progressive-school movement, including its so-called "lunatic fringe." Many people condemn the defects of the progressive school, which they identify with the teachings of the experimentalists. These attacks on progressive education and on the educational philosophy of the experimentalists, which mean the same thing to most people, are widespread. They come from many sources. The neo-scholastics and the so-called cultural humanists, who are fundamentally opposed to one another in the traditions they wish to promote, are aggressive in their attack on progressive education. The apparent educational deficiencies of our youth who have attended the public schools are blamed on the progressives, even though most schools have scarcely felt the influence of the progressive-school movement. The general movement to improve the public schools in the name of progressive education in consequence of many unsound principles and practices that have been advocated has contributed to further condemnation of progressive education. Consequently, when the Progressive Education Association decided to change its name to the American Education Fellowship, the step was hailed in some quarters as an indication that the organization's fight to develop and apply its principles had been abandoned.[5]

The attack on progressive education seems to many to be at the same time an attack on the philosophy of experimentalism. But from the standpoint of experimentalism, there is much in what is called progressive education that should be condemned. However, the experimentalists, since they are working from the inside and understand progressive education, do not join in a wholesale condemnation of it. They see the progressive-school movement as an effort to improve current educational practice, and they are trying to help it develop a philosophy to guide and direct its efforts. Some of its principles and practices are sound and some of them are unsound. It has not yet developed a consistent theory of education and thus represents a mixture of conflicting points of view which the experimentalists would like to see integrated into a set of principles and practices consistent with

---

[5] Harold Rugg, "Harold Rugg Comments on the Policies of the PEA Director," *School and Society*, 59: 230–231, April 1, 1944.

their own philosophy of education. Least of all do the experimentalists see the condemnation of progressive education as a condemnation of their own philosophy. Since they know the situation from the inside, they not only refuse to condemn the progressive movement in many of its aspects but they condemn the wholesale attack which its opponents have leveled against it. As for their own philosophy of education, the experimentalists are glad to see it exemplified in any school or school system anywhere. Any effective attack on experimentalism must be made in terms of its own theory and application and not in terms of principles and practices that are attributed to it in the name of any school movement, whether designated as progressive, traditional, or something else.[6]

WAYS OF STATING PHILOSOPHIES OF EDUCATION

Any philosophy of education to be rendered most intelligible must be stated systematically in terms of theories or principles. Such theories or principles to be meaningful and significant must be stated with respect to certain pertinent topics which people consider in reflective discourse, or with respect to which they assume some position in thought or practice. Now, there are three groups of people, although overlapping in some respects, that should be interested in philosophy of education.

The first group consists of those primarily interested in general philosophy; that is, education in its most general aspects. The topics which they particularly like to consider are those widely recognized as fundamental in the general field of philosophy, such as the nature of mind, knowledge, reality, and value. Since experimentalists interested in education have already treated these topics rather systematically, and since it is necessary to keep this volume within reasonable bounds, in this study these subjects are considered only in relation to topics of especial interest to the other two groups.[7]

---

[6] John T. Wahlquist, *The Philosophy of American Education.* The Ronald Press Company, New York, 1942. Pp. 84–138.

[7] Experimentalists have stated rather systematically educational authoritarianism and educational experimentalism in terms of mind, knowledge, reality, and value. Dewey gives considerable attention to mind, knowledge, and value as related to education in his *Democracy and Education;* Bode defines historical philosophies of education in terms of mind in his *How We Learn;* Brubacher defines education in terms of reality, knowledge, value, and mind in his *Modern Philosophies of Education;* and Kilpatrick has elaborated rather fully the educational implications of his conception of mind in his *Foundations of Method,* in *A Reconstructed Theory of the*

The second group consists of those interested in educational principles and practices in general which affect people in all walks of life. Most people, whether they are directly interested in the schools and in philosophy or not, are interested in the effect of policies, programs, and practices on their own behavior and conduct and on the behavior and conduct of those for whom they assume any responsibility. Experience is a topic with respect to which people everywhere assume some position; and experience and education are so closely related that an explanation of the one involves an explanation of the other, and a theory of the one is also a theory of the other. Moreover, any effort toward educational reform requires the development of a theory of experience in which proposals projected for the improvement of conditions have their intellectual justifications. Since the experimentalists are interested in instituting educational reform rather than in maintaining the *status quo*, they should welcome any effort to state their philosophy of education in terms of experience. We are interested here not only in doing this but also in comparing the experimentalists' philosophy of education with the two other philosophies of education which they consider particularly significant. Consequently, in Part I of this study we shall state systematically educational authoritarianism, educational laissez faire, and educational experimentalism in terms of comparable theories of the same important features of experience.

The third group of people who are interested in philosophies of education are included in the second group, but they have a specialized professional interest that should be considered. Reference is here made to teachers, supervisors, administrators, and others who have the direct responsibility of operating the schools and colleges. They are interested not only in principles and practices which are of concern to people in general, but also especially in the policies, programs, and activities of the school. School practice is, therefore, the one topic that should seem most immediately and directly significant to them. Consequently, in Part II of this study we shall state systematically the three philosophies of education to be considered in terms of comparable theories of the same important features of school practice.

Educative Process, and in *Remaking the Curriculum*. With the exception of brief discussions of the educational theory of Rousseau by Bode, Dewey, and Kilpatrick, with some slight attention to the psychoanalysts, the experimentalists have not defined educational laissez faire in terms of philosophy, although a basis for such treatment is provided in certain theories which are stated and combated in Dewey's *Experience and Nature* and *The Quest for Certainty* and in Dewey and Tufts' *Ethics*.

PART I

Theories of Educative Experience

CHAPTER 2

Education and Experience

WHENEVER WE REFLECT seriously on the meaning and significance of human existence, we recognize the possibility of a better life than we have known. We dedicate ourselves to its realization, at first for ourselves, then for our children, and finally for all men. That is the dream which gives meaning to "life, liberty, and the pursuit of happiness." That is the vision which gives meaning to "freedom, equality, and fraternity." That is the ideal which gives meaning to "of the people, for the people, and by the people." That vision is "America," "the West," "democracy." It is the ideal which fires imagination, inspires struggle, and sustains hope. It is the function of philosophy of education to analyze and define this dream, vision, or ideal of reflective humanity and to suggest means for its fuller realization. For this ideal of humanity is the educational ideal. From the standpoint of the philosophy of experimentalism, the nature of the good life — the nature of education — which all men desire in their serious and reflective moments, can best be explained in terms of experience. But we must define experience — actual education — as a preliminary step in defining desirable experience or desirable education. Experience consists of interactions that are continuous in the life of individuals and in the social groups to which they belong. Interactivity and continuity thus constitute the fundamental features or dimensions of experience. When these features are defined, experience is defined. A definition of experience, which is a definition of education as it actually takes place, constitutes the first step in defining education as it should be. Education is experience and the essential features of experience are interactivity and continuity.

INTERACTIVITY OF EXPERIENCE

Interactivity consists of interactions or transactions that take place among things. But since there are many kinds of things, there are many kinds of interactions. The interactions of grains of sand on the seashore are different from the interactions of chemical elements in a test tube or chemical elements in the world of nature. The interactions of plants with inorganic matter are different from the interactions of chemical elements. The interactions of plants with inorganic materials are different from the interactions of animals with one another and with inorganic things. The interactions of human personalities are different from the interactions of physical things, from the interactions of plants, or even from the interactions of the lower animals with one another and with other things.

We have, of course, been speaking in general terms; for some human interactions are very similar to those interactions of inorganic things, plants, and animals. But, on the other hand, some of the interactions of human beings are very different from the interactions of other things. Some human interactions contain factors that are not found in the physical or organic world, factors certainly not found below the higher primates and probably not below man himself. These higher interactions are continuous with interactions on the lower levels in that they include them, but the interactions of the human being are peculiar in that they contain factors not found in any other interactions.

These higher human interactions are experiences or aspects of experiences. They have a physical basis, undoubtedly. They involve sense organs, the nervous system, and physical stimuli. They certainly involve living matter, which is always different from inorganic matter, or the merely physical. But they involve much more. They involve feeling, impulse, and memory that are in evidence among the higher animals. They also involve forms of thought, feeling, and action beyond the level of the physical or organic world. Interactions that involve forms of thought, feeling, and action are experiences. Education consists, then, not in mere interactions, but in interactions involving such thought, feeling, and action as are unknown in the interactions of things and organisms below man.

However, because experiences are special kinds of interactions, they are nonetheless interactions. Such a conception has, of course, been clearly implicit in what has just been said. Nevertheless, the fact that this feature of interactivity has so often been neglected in philosophy, psychology, and educational theory, justifies giving it special attention here. Experience, as James and Dewey have indicated, is a double-barreled word. It involves not only a subject but also an object. It is not merely a mental process that takes place within the mind or head. It involves the mind, the self, or the individual, however they are defined, but it also involves the things with which the mind, the self, or the individual interacts. These things may be physical, mental, concrete objects, things in the physical environment, or ideas recalled in memory or projected in imagination. They may be near at hand or distant in time and space. Experiences are always transactions that occur in the actual world, the subject of which is some human personality.

CONTINUITY OF EXPERIENCE

Experience is also a peculiar kind of interaction, transaction, or activity in another way. It is continuous. Empirically considered, the self, the mind, the personality of each and every one of us is a stream of experience, whatever else it may be when considered in some other way. Within this stream there are high spots, events with a beginning, a development, and an ending. These are experiences. Those who assume responsibility for their own improvement or for the improvement of others are interested in these particular experiences, but they are interested also in the whole stream of experience in which particular experiences occur. In the words of William James, "Experience is without breach, break, or division." [1] Every part is related to every other part. The individual is not only aware of things in each experience; he is also aware of the connecting links that relate experiences to one another.

In this study we are thinking primarily of the continuity of experience in another sense. Such a conception was, of course, clearly recognized by James, and has been rendered more explicit by Dewey, Bode, Kilpatrick, and others. We refer to the continuity underlying experience, or perhaps better, to experience in the more inclusive sense, involving both the conscious and the unconscious. Such continuity is a function of physiological habit consisting of the effects of experiences. It involves the continuity of consciousness which James emphasized, but it includes the enduring factor that is unconscious.

James himself had a great deal to say about the physiological basis of experience, and he even defined education in terms of habit. "Education," he says, "in short, cannot be better described than by calling it *the organization of acquired habits of conduct and tendencies to behavior.*" [2] Nevertheless, in his discussion of continuity James had in mind the

---

[1] William James, *Psychology: Briefer Course.* Henry Holt and Company, New York, 1892. Pp. 157–159.

[2] William James, *Talks to Teachers.* Henry Holt and Company, New York, 1899. P. 83.

continuity of consciousness. To him all conscious activity had its physical correlate in the nervous system. Moreover, he assumed the operation of physiological conditions underlying consciousness.

While recognizing the continuity of consciousness, which James emphasized, Dewey has attached special importance in his discussion of experience to the continuity of habit and has rendered this more explicit. Every experience affects the individual who has it. The effect, sometimes called the residue, outcome, result, or learning, is preserved in the form of some physiological change, which is habit in its most generalized meaning. This physiological change, produced through interactions called experiences, is continuous with physiological changes produced in previous experiences and will be continuous with physiological effects produced in subsequent experiences.

Experience, which in a practical and psychological sense is education, is a process of habit-forming, whatever else it may be. Every experience modifies to some degree the effects of past experiences and the modification thus effected abides to be modified by later experience.

Education, which to James was a process of habit-forming, becomes to Dewey a process of growth. Habits are not only formed, but when formed they influence in important respects the habits that can later be formed. The quality of present habits affects the quality of future habits.[3] However, James speaks in terms of bundles of habits.[4] In Dewey's later discussion, habits, which are at bottom basal to continuity, are not conceived as mere bundles. Bundles imply separation of one habit from another. For Dewey, habits are conceived as all of a piece. Every habit interpenetrates with all other habits, which in combination constitute the whole personality, the whole self.

The continuity of experience consists not in a mere series of habits nor even in a sequence of habits. Each new habit grows out of the old habits as well as embodies the effects of the new experiences. In other words, experience which is educative is not only a process of growth, it is a process of growth of a special kind: it is a reconstruction of experience. In every experience, old habits are remade in terms of the demands of the new situation. Education in its practical, psychological, and existential sense is a process of habit-forming. But it is more than habit-forming. It is growth. But it is more than growth. It is that

---

[3] John Dewey, *Democracy and Education*. The Macmillan Company, New York, 1912. Pp. 54–62.

[4] William James, *Talks to Teachers*. Henry Holt and Company, New York, 1899. P. 66.

habit-forming and growth which may be best defined as the reconstruction of experience.

Reconstruction of experience involves both interactivity and continuity. The individual whose experiences are preserved, conserved, expanded, and extended through the continuity of habit interacts with other individuals and with other environmental factors. It is through this process of interactivity and continuity that the experience of the individual is reconstructed. Also, it is through this same interactivity and continuity that the experience of the group is reconstructed. As Dewey has pointed out, the individual passes but the group lives on. The reconstruction of the experience of the individual through his relationship with others reconstructs the experience of the group.

The experience of the group, however, is also reconstructed in another way. The changes in the individual affect his environment — the things with which he interacts. Not only are those with whom the individual interacts changed but the whole physical, social, and cultural environment with which he interacts is also changed. The funded experience of the race, consisting of habits, customs, traditions, ideas, ideals, and appreciations, is modified by experience of individuals. Education, as the reconstruction of experience, signifies not only the remaking of the experience of the individual but also the remaking of society.

DESIRABLE EXPERIENCE

Dewey has shown that education cannot be identified with experience, and has defined interactivity and continuity as principles on the basis of which the desirable qualities of experience may be determined. In this connection, however, it is very easy to misunderstand his position in regard to the meaning of both education and experience. Although to some he may seem to say so, Dewey does not mean that education in a practical, psychological, and existential sense is different from experience. He means that education in a desirable sense is quite different from education — experience — in a practical, psychological, and existential sense. Experiences whose effects are preserved through psychological or physiological continuity are educative to the degree that those who have them are thereby made different and to the degree that the group to which they belong and the environment in which they live are likewise made different. But such education, such experience, may be desirable or undesirable. Education in a desirable and constructive sense is not, then, identical with education or experience of just any kind. Although education as such may be identified with experience as such, education that is desirable cannot be identified with experience as such. Only desirable experiences are educative in this positive and constructive sense.[5] In fact, desirable experience and educative experience are the same.

Education is the reconstruction of experience. But any experience represents the reconstruction of experience. Just as we cannot help educating ourselves in some way, so we cannot help reconstructing our experiences. Experience and education are the same thing. However, some experiences are desirable and others are undesirable. Some may even be neutral in their constructive effect. In estimating the desirability of an experience, one must consider the features of interactivity and continuity. The quality of the experience in its relationship to subsequent experience must always be considered in judging its educational worth.

Dewey speaks of *interactivity* and *continuity* as principles. As a matter of fact, however, they are not principles in a positive and constructive sense. They are principles in a psychological and existential sense. They must be considered in evaluating, estimating, and appraising the educational worth of experiences. Neither interactivity nor continuity in and of itself enables one to distinguish the desirable from the undesirable, the approved from the disapproved, the constructive from the destructive. Both interactivity and continuity are as much in evidence in an undesirable as in a desirable experience. The fact that effects are produced through interactivity and are preserved through continuity suggests that the quality of the interaction must be judged not only with respect to present learning but also with respect to future learning. In a word, an educative experience in the desirable sense must be good. To be good it must be good in effect in the present and also be good in effect on subsequent experience. The principles of interactivity and continuity we have called features to distinguish them from principles in an ethical and constructive sense. They are principles to take into account, but they do not in and of themselves indicate what is desirable or undesirable.

James, Dewey, Kilpatrick, and Bode, as well as other students of education, whatever they have seemed to say on special occasions, have

---

[5] John Dewey, *Experience and Education.* The Macmillan Company, New York, 1938. Pp. 23–52.

John P. Wynne, *The Educative Experience.* Farmville Herald, Farmville, Virginia, 1940. Pp. 9–13.

contended that mere interactivity and continuity do not define education in a constructive and positive sense. James defined education in terms of habit, but he recognized that mere habits were insufficient. Education in a neutral and psychological sense could be defined as habit or tendencies to action. But the habits that constitute education in the sense of improvement must be useful.[6]

Dewey defines education as growth, reconstruction of experience, and even as life. At times, it is difficult to tell whether he is speaking of education, life, and growth in a psychological sense or in a constructive and positive sense. Nevertheless, an adequate interpretation of his theory requires taking into account the spirit of his whole position rather than any particular statement in isolation. He certainly is interested in a positive and constructive conception as well as in a merely formal, psychological, and existential description or explanation. He never stops with education as growth, reconstruction, or even life. He goes much further. The right kind of growth must be growth in democracy. The best kind of society is a democratic society. A group is democratic to the extent of the number and variety of the interests constantly shared in the group and to the extent of the freedom and fullness of the interplay of the group with other forms of association. Such a conception suggests a direction of growth.[7] He likewise gives reconstruction of experience a constructive interpretation. It becomes "that reconstruction or reorganization of experience which adds to the meaning of experience, and which increases ability to direct the control of subsequent experience."[8] The same is true of education as life. Any kind of education is life. But the kind of education Dewey seeks, as he repeatedly emphasizes, is that kind that expands and deepens the meaning of life.

Kilpatrick endorses the conception of growth, reconstruction, education as life, and the remaking of life. He does not stop with mere formal statements, however. He goes further; he proceeds to indicate lines of desirable growth, the kind of desirable reconstruction, the qualities of the good life, the factors that seem important in the desirable remaking of life.[9]

---

[6] William James, *Talks to Teachers*. Henry Holt and Company, New York, 1899. P. 67.

[7] John Dewey, *Democracy and Education*. The Macmillan Company, New York, 1912. Pp. 95–97.

[8] *Ibid*. Pp. 89–90.

[9] William H. Kilpatrick, *Foundations of Method*. The Macmillan Company, New York, 1925. Pp. 197–198.

Bode is disposed to refrain from speaking of education as growth and even objects to the conception. He recognizes both growth and reconstruction as psychological and existential conceptions, but rejects all interpretations that take such conceptions as supplying adequate direction. He seeks direction in democracy as a way of life, which he defines in terms of the continuous widening of the area of common interests and concerns.[10]

The experimentalists agree that education is a process of habit-forming, growth, reconstruction of experience, and remaking of life; but they also agree that such a conception is in itself insufficient. It is only a starting point. The experimentalists' conception signifies that education is a continuous process and that each period in life is of value and significance on its own account and not merely preparatory to some later period. But this conception of education does not indicate what kind of life is desirable. It does signify that the qualities of habit depend upon the qualities of experience, and that the qualities of present experience are continuous with the qualities of subsequent experience, but it does not indicate what qualities are desirable. The nature of such qualities may be implicit in Dewey's qualifications of the reconstruction of experience, in Kilpatrick's lines of desirable growth, or in Bode's democracy as a way of life and a continuous widening of the area of common interests and concerns. These three philosophers, however, have said much more about the desirable qualities of experience than can be embodied in a very simple definition or even in its brief elaboration. We shall, therefore, undertake to define the desirable qualities of experience, hoping that, if such qualities are not implicit in the formal definitions of education that the leading experimentalists have provided, they will be consistent with the trend of the philosophic spirit of experimentalism.

FEATURES OF EDUCATIVE EXPERIENCE

One way, perhaps the best way, of defining such qualities is to determine what features of experience are most important and then to translate them into the qualities that experience itself finds most desirable. Educative experiences have both horizontal and vertical dimensions. Horizontally, they involve the interaction of individual and environment. Vertically, they involve continuity in terms of the effects of experience on the individual. Interactivity and continuity

[10] Boyd H. Bode, *Progressive Education at the Cross Roads.* Newson and Company, New York, 1938. Pp. 108–109.

are features of all experience, but we need some finer analysis to discover other features that are educationally significant.

These features can be distinguished by asking certain questions that seem quite pertinent. Although it may be that the individual and his environment both enter into every experience, we want to know their relative importance. The *relativity of experience* thus becomes an essential feature of educative experience. Next, we want to know whether the experience is on the biological level, the mental level, or the social level. It is generally admitted that education occurs on a social level. We wish to know, then, what kind of sociality is most desirable. *Sociality* thus becomes a second essential feature of educative experience. We may point out that educative experience involves the interaction of the individual and his environment, and is on the social level, but we still wish to know what causes educative experience to begin and to keep going. If it be admitted that all educative activities arise from some motivating condition, we still wish to know what is the most desirable motivation. *Motivation of experience* thus becomes a third essential feature of educative experience. We also know that changes are produced in the individual through experience. The individual absorbs things, appropriates things, or expresses himself by means of things, or changes himself through the use of things. How does this productive or creative function operate and how should it operate to be most desirable? Thus, *creativity of experience* becomes a fourth essential feature of educative experience. Perhaps the most familiar feature of experience is its selectivity. Whether considered in terms of behavior, learning, or consciousness, experience is always selecting and choosing, emphasizing some things and neglecting others. We are therefore interested in determining the nature of desirable selectivity, and so *selectivity of experience* becomes a fifth essential feature of educative experience. We know that experiences involve thinking, feeling, and willing, and that these factors are often in conflict. We know that these factors must be somehow related, and we wish to know how this functional relationship that actually exists may be rendered most desirable. *Unity* thus becomes a sixth essential feature of educative experience.

We now have six features of educative experience that may be designated as follows:

1. Relativity of experience
2. Sociality of experience
3. Motivation of experience
4. Creativity of experience
5. Selectivity of experience
6. Unity of experience

There may be other important features of educative experience, and the ones we have selected may be given different names. Perhaps they may be classified or analyzed into more or fewer features. It appears, however, that they do constitute important points of emphasis and that, when interpreted or translated in consistency with one another, they constitute a philosophy of education.[11]

Perhaps an illustration may be helpful at this point. Suppose you have decided to give a friend of yours a necktie for a birthday present. You are not able to go shopping yourself, so you ask your brother to purchase the tie for you. Your brother, not knowing the friend and having little idea of the kind of clothes he usually wears, asks for some specifications. Since you have your mind pretty well made up as to what kind of tie you wish, you proceed to give some general suggestions. Knowing that your brother is a very good judge of men's clothing, you do not wish to be too specific because you do not know exactly what kind of tie he may find. You wish to give him some range of choice. Two kinds of ideas, very closely related, run through your mind. The first kind corresponds to what we call the features of experience. They perhaps include price, pattern, material, and color. But such factors are not self-explanatory; they are mere factors to take into account. You then proceed to state the price range, the pattern, the types of materials, and the color you prefer. If you specify too definitely, such criteria are rules to be followed and your brother may not be able to find the tie you wish. If you explain or interpret the several features in general terms, such criteria are principles and leave considerable room for individual judgment on the part of your brother. He will be almost sure to make a purchase which will approach the kind of tie you have in mind.

If it be clearly understood that the foregoing analogy is drawn not between the experience of purchasing a necktie and experience in general, but between the features of neckties in general and the features of educative experiences in general, the illustration, although overdrawn, indicates the kind of program we have before us in Part I of this study. Just as neckties have certain features with respect to which people may adopt different attitudes, so experiences have certain features with respect to which people may adopt different attitudes, principles, or theories. Those who are interested in securing desirable experiences for themselves and for others must be interested in the different atti-

---

[11] William H. Burton, *The Guidance of Learning Activities*. D. Appleton-Century Company, New York, 1944. Pp. 138–139.

tudes that people assume toward the nature of desirable experience. To compare these different attitudes — which are also called principles or theories — we shall state them with respect to the features of experience that we have designated as the relativity, sociality, motivation, creativity, selectivity, and unity of experience, analogous to certain features of neckties, such as price, pattern, material, and color.

Individuals are continually having experiences themselves, and they are continually influencing the experiences of others. The parent in the home has the responsibility of guiding and directing the experiences of his children. The teacher in the school has the responsibility of guiding and directing the experiences of his pupils. Leaders in church, state, business, industry, and organized labor have the responsibility of guiding and directing the experiences of many people. Leaders of social organizations, such as civic clubs, professional and vocational societies, and sororities and fraternities, and leaders of young people, even student leaders in various activities of our schools and colleges, have the responsibility of influencing the experiences of the membership of the groups they serve. Moreover, every one of us, old and young alike, has the responsibility of choosing desirable experiences for ourselves, as well as of influencing the experiences of those with whom we are associated in the activities of daily life. In other words, all of us are engaged all the time in education. Everyone should, therefore, be interested in the theories, principles, or qualities of desirable experience, or perhaps better, of educative experience.

As already indicated, from the standpoint of the philosophy of experimentalism there are three important attitudes toward life and education that may properly be designated as educational authoritarianism, educational laissez faire, and educational experimentalism. When stated in terms of three sets of principles governing the same six features of educative experience — relativity, sociality, motivation, creativity, selectivity, and unity — they may be readily compared.

To consider these three philosophies of education in terms of the theories they adopt with respect to the aforementioned features of experience is not to say that individuals often consciously and deliberately label themselves as exponents of authoritarian theories, laissez-faire theories, or experimentalist theories. It means rather that the experimentalist is able to distinguish these three attitudes and state them in terms of the positions they assume with respect to the foregoing features of educative experience. He notes authoritarian, laissez-faire, and experimentalist interpretations of these features implicit in current educational practices in our social and institutional life and the principles used to justify them. The theories or principles thus constituting these three philosophies of education are not merely explicit and logical formulations of authoritative students of education representing different historical schools of thought. They include many elements from many historical schools of thought and recognized philosophies of education. But such philosophies are best conceived as the theories or principles which the experimentalist attributes to certain people on the basis of the educational policies, programs, and activities for which these people are responsible.

The author, as an educational experimentalist, assumes the philosophy of experimentalism and is primarily interested in indicating its educational implications and applications. But he realizes that the best way for him to do this is to compare his philosophy of education with other philosophies of education. Perhaps the best way of making such comparisons is to contrast different interpretations which proponents of educational authoritarianism, educational laissez faire, and educational experimentalism place upon the features of relativity, sociality, motivation, creativity, selectivity, and unity. In explaining, elaborating, and criticizing the different theories of such features, the author adopts the general outlook of the movement known as the philosophy of experimentalism. In this way, he may clarify the meaning of the two extreme positions to which he objects and at the same time make some contribution toward integrating them into a new position, not only in the minds of those directly responsible for school education but in the minds of people in all walks of life.

CHAPTER 3

Relativity of Experience

DO WE MAKE OUR ENVIRONMENTS or do our environments make us? Do we find our ideals, values, and standards within ourselves, or do we find them in our surroundings? Should we look to ourselves for direction or to the authorities of the outside world? Are things inherently good or bad or only good or bad because of the way they affect us? Doubtless at one time or another each of us has asked himself such questions as these. Whenever we do so, we are dealing with the relativity of experience, which, as here conceived, means that experience involves the interaction of individuals with their environments. From the standpoint of the philosophy of experimentalism, the relativity of experience emphasizes the conviction that the way the individual and the environment are considered in their relationship constitutes a focal point of emphasis in social and educational theories.

That proponents of this philosophy consider relativity an important feature of educative experience is indicated in Dewey's statement to the effect that there always tend to be two schools of social reform, one emphasizing original and native human nature, the other emphasizing the influence of the social environment; and that the "difficulty persists in securing and maintaining an equilibrium with reference to intrinsic human nature on one side and social customs and institutions on the other." [1] It is also indicated in Kilpatrick's statement that "as we think thus of organism and environment, of the self and the environment and institutional life, the problem of interaction arises. Many see here only an interaction in which one factor must yield entirely to the other. Our historic past held in effect, if not in words, that the individual, particularly the child, must be adapted exactly to the institutional life about it. Education has traditionally been so conceived. As opposed to this view, a few extreme protestants on the other side have again in effect, if not in words, given the individual *carte blanche*. Institutions must yield. But our discussion leads

---

[1] John Dewey, *Human Nature and Conduct*. Modern Library, New York, 1929. Pp. vii-viii; 9-10.

rather to another position. Institutions are the ways in which we jointly conduct our 'shared interests.' " [2] Throughout his consideration of the theories of learning and their educational implications, Bode likewise recognizes these same theories of the relativity of experience.[3] An explanation and elaboration of these different attitudes assumed toward the relativity of experience is one way of explaining and elaborating educational authoritarianism, educational laissez faire, and educational experimentalism, which, from the standpoint of the philosophy of experimentalism, constitute the three philosophies of education that are most inclusive and influential. From the standpoint of the philosophy of experimentalism, there are three theories of relativity as a feature of educative experience, and they constitute respectively principles of these three philosophies of education.

THEORY OF OBJECTIVE CONTINGENCY
(EDUCATIONAL AUTHORITARIANISM)

Conceptions which emphasize the environment are usually designated as objective; those which emphasize the individual, as subjective. In educational authoritarianism, the emphasis in theory and practice is on the environment, and the standard of direction is found in the environment apart from experience. The nature of desirable experience is therefore relative to the environment. Since the term *contingency* is synonymous with relativity, this attitude toward the feature of relativity may be designated as the *theory of objective contingency*, and the attitude that places the emphasis on the individual, and that finds its standard of direction in him apart from experience, may be designated as *subjective contingency*. The theory of objective contingency constitutes one aspect of educational authoritarianism, just as other interpretations constitute aspects, respectively, of educational laissez faire, and of educational experimentalism. There are, of course, many different authoritarian philosophies of education, but, from the standpoint of the philosophy of experimentalism, the fact that they are authoritarian is the significant thing, and their differences in other respects are relatively unimportant. The authoritarians thus conceive the principle or theory of objective contingency in different ways, but the important

---

[2] William H. Kilpatrick, *A Reconstructed Theory of the Educative Process.* Bureau of Publications, Teachers College, Columbia University, New York City, 1935. P. 8.

[3] Boyd H. Bode, *How We Learn.* D. C. Heath and Company, New York, 1940.

thing is that all authoritarians place the emphasis on the environment rather than on the individual. Any reference, therefore, that we make, in the pages that follow, to different authoritarian philosophies of education is designed to explain and elaborate the theory of objective contingency rather than to explain and elaborate fully any of these philosophies of education as they have been developed historically.

The authoritarians of all schools of thought recognize the importance of both the individual and the environment in experience. They think of learning as involving response representing the individual as well as subject matter representing the environment. They think of knowledge as involving the operation of general principles supplied or produced by the mind as well as the facts supplied by the environment in direct experience. In education, they typically admit the fact that the acquisition of subject matter requires at least some activity on the part of the individual. But they are inclined to think of the environment as supplying not only a condition of education, of learning, and of knowledge, but also the standards of direction.

Perhaps the meaning of the theory of objective contingency may be suggested by reference to some of the well-known historical theories of education. These theories of education usually represent a combination of practical conditions involving economic, political, and educational factors in addition to developments in science and philosophy. For instance, the well-known theory of education usually called formal discipline represents a theoretical formulation of the interests of a feudalistic and aristocratic class and a psychology of learning that was at the time familiar. According to this theory, the implications of which still influence educational thought and practice, the mind consists of the faculties of feeling, willing, and thinking, including such sub-faculties as perception, memory, imagination, and reasoning. The main function of educative experience was thought to be the exercise of the so-called faculties. If a faculty was strengthened through exercise on one thing, it was strengthened to the same degree for dealing with everything else. For instance, if the memory was improved through learning the conjugation of Latin verbs, it was improved to the same extent for memorizing other things, such as the names of people. At first sight it seems that the differences in subjects are relatively unimportant. But the social class in control of social institutions always took the proper steps to see that those subjects were studied which contributed to their maintaining the superior social position which they had held under different conditions. In other words, standards of direction were determined by the subjects selected for study. Even now, certain subjects are emphasized in our schools and colleges primarily because they are thought to provide general training for certain faculties of the mind better than do other subjects.

The Herbartian theory of education, which, on the other hand, seemed to meet the needs of the middle class — merchants, manufacturers, and enterprisers of various types who had convictions they wished the people to believe — obviously placed the emphasis on the environment and on subject matter. From this point of view, experience is not a process of exercising faculties of the mind, whose existence the Herbartians denied, but a process of organizing ideas in the soul. In fact, for Herbart the system of ideas thus developed constituted the mind. Desirable experience, educative experience, consisted in learning the proper ideas. The proper ideas were always the convictions and beliefs of the class in power. These ideas were embodied in school subjects, particularly in literature and social studies. The problem of education thus became the organization of subjects and ideas in such a way that the individual understood, accepted, and applied them. Some consideration was given to the individual as a means of getting the proper things learned, but what should be learned was a question to be decided by those in charge of the schools. The principle or theory of objective contingency was assumed in this authoritarian theory of education, which dominated many schools a generation ago and which still is influencing them in many quarters today, since the direction of educative experience was clearly determined by the subject matter that embodied the values of an economic class.

The spiritual unfoldment theory of education, which is sometimes called adjustment to the spiritual environment, recognizes the importance of the individual as a factor in experience, but it looks to the environment for direction. Just as in the theory of formal discipline, thought, feeling, and willing are considered the essential aspects of experiencing. But those processes of individual experience are thought to correspond to aspects of the all-inclusive spiritual environment which include the individual. Stated in terms of subject matter, the curriculum consists of science, corresponding to thought; art, corresponding to feeling; and history and political science, corresponding to willing. The study of some science, some art, and some government is essential for the individual at every stage in his educational career. As a matter of fact, in practice the subject matter selected is designed primarily for the purpose of preserving the ideas and ideals of what has been called the great social and religious tradition.

The cultural adjustment theory of education consists of the educational implications of the so-called neo-humanism that Irving Babbitt, G. E. Moore, and others propounded and elaborated a few years ago, and the more important aspects of the theories that Robert M. Hutchins, Stringfellow Barr, and others are now popularizing. Recently, this last group has organized an association known as "Education for Freedom, Incorporated" for the purpose of making known the foundations and implications of their philosophy of education. From the standpoint of the philosophy of experimentalism, this theory of education constitutes another good illustration of educational authoritarianism; and its emphasis on the environment as the source of direction in desirable experience is a good example of the theory of objective contingency, which is one principle or theory of the authoritarian philosophy of education. As a practical program the constant core of subject matter — the proper educational environment — consists of certain selected books in which the ideals of civilization as the neo-humanists conceive them are embodied. Education consists primarily in the mastery of these so-called "best books."

The supernatural adjustment theory of education is now being constantly explained and elaborated by the educational leaders of the Catholic Church. Like the other two spiritual adjustment theories, this philosophy of education assumes that there is an environment superior to the individual and that it contains the standards to which men everywhere should be led to conform. This environment consists not in the general religious and social ideas, ideals, and beliefs of the past or the standards of the great cultural tradition. It consists in the dogmas of the church as they are defined by its recognized authorities. As in the other authoritarian philosophies of education, the standards of direction to be observed by the individual, by the school, and by the other educational institutions, are to be found in the environment, particularly in the powers and forces that supply them and give them meaning and significance. It thus assumes, as do the other authoritarian theories of education, the theory of objective contingency as the proper interpretation of relativity as a feature of educative experience.

Finally, the so-called scientific movement in education — also known as the mechanical-habits theory of education — assumes that the chief function of the school is to secure the mastery of desirable facts and skills. This theory represents a combination of philosophical and psychological principles and the apparent interests of a social class, as in the case of the theories of education already mentioned. With the constant development of business and industry, increasing emphasis was placed upon the definite and specific information and upon the mechanical and automatic skills most useful in economic production. Certain psychologists began to interpret all thought, feeling, and action in terms of mechanical response. According to this theory, only a study of the environment can supply the direction required for guidance in teaching, in curriculum-making, and in administration. The students of education who are scientifically trained study the demands of practical life scientifically and supply the aims to be sought and the methods by which they are to be secured. In this theory of education we have another illustration of educational authoritarianism and the theory of objective contingency since the subject matter thought to embody the new aims determines the direction of educative experience.

Such theories of education, which are now influencing current principles and practices of the school as well as those of other social institutions, are all forms of educational authoritarianism, but they conceive of the individual in different ways and of the environment in different ways. To some the individual is primarily spiritual, to others he is primarily physical, and to others he is a combination of the physical and the spiritual. To some the educational environment consists of one type of spiritual tradition, and to others it consists of other types, while to still others it consists primarily of the prevailing social and economic conditions. They are all agreed, however, that the standards to be sought in educational practice are to be found in some kind of environment that is prior and superior to the individual to be educated, whether in the school, the home, or in some other social institution.

The foregoing historical theories or philosophies of education embody in their applications varying theories of the mind, self, or individual, and the important points of emphasis arising out of varying social, economic, and educational conditions. They all have been consciously and deliberately applied to school education at one time or another. As theories of desirable experience, they have influenced ideas, beliefs, and activities in all fields of human relations. They now are influencing educational theory and practice in the school and outside the school. In some instances, they are still consciously and deliberately applied in the development of educational policies, programs, and activities. But most people who adopt the theory of objective contingency do so as a matter of course without explicit reference to these so-called historical theories of educative experience. These historical theories have been explained briefly here for two reasons. Doubtless, elements from some of them often influence those who adopt the principle of objective contingency; one or more of these historical theories may be used in an effort to justify intellectually the principles and practices which assume the theory of objective contingency. Moreover, the educational theory of the present is not separate and distinct from the educational theory of the past. Therefore, it will be necessary from time to time to refer to these historical philosophies of education in order to illustrate other principles in subsequent chapters, and apparently, they could be introduced most conveniently at this point.

From the point of view of this authoritarian theory of the relativity of experience, it matters not what form it assumes, the primary function of education in school and out of school is to mold childhood and youth in conformity with fixed standards that are good and right within themselves without reference to the present interests and needs of individuals. In other words, the chief function of the educational authorities is to decide what aims should be sought and what methods should be used in securing them, and it is the function of those directly responsible for practical programs and activities to see that these authoritative ends are secured according to authoritative methods as expeditiously and economically as possible under the conditions. The aims and methods may differ from place to place and from time to time, but whatever they are, they are in the last analysis prescribed by those who, in consequence of native genius, official power, or experience, hold positions of authority. Such ends and means may also be changed from time to time, but they are fixed until they are changed by those authorities. They are not to be changed by those who are directly responsible for educational activities. Some variety may even be allowed, but it is always a prescribed or limited variation. It is supplemental and subsidiary to the fundamentals which are prescribed for all.

The theory of objective contingency is often assumed by people in dealing with one another outside the schools. Most of us have been subject to the influence of the schools and directly or indirectly to the authoritarian philosophies underlying the various forms of educational authoritarianism to which we have referred. Many of us tend to place the responsibility for our shortcomings on the environment. We fail to catch the ball because of a hole in the glove or the sun in our eyes. Social groups often lay the responsibility for their plight on the inadequacy of social conditions. Even the most belligerent of nations, whenever they start a war, usually contend that they are fighting in self-defense. They are compelled to fight, so they say, because of the activities of neighboring nations.

Those who adopt the theory of objective contingency first isolate in thought the individual from his environment and then look to the environment to supply adequate stimulation and direction. In biological terms, they think of the environment as a comparatively powerful force ʻwhich, when combined with the relatively small force of heredity, produces the biological individual. In psychological terms, they think of the stimulus as more effective than the capacity and disposition of the individual in the production of experiences. In sociological terms, they think of individual achievement and success as primarily the effect of the opportunity supplied by social institutions and by the conditions of social life at particular times and places. In educational terms, they think of subject matter representing the environment as relatively superior to method representing the individual in determining the direction of educative experience.

It is, perhaps, impossible to separate those who place the primary emphasis upon the environment from those who place the primary emphasis upon the individual. There is an element of both attitudes in most of us. In reflecting upon their own successful achievements, most people give the credit to themselves, while in reflecting on the successful achievements of their neighbors, they give the credit to the favorable conditions. On the other hand, in reflecting on their own failures, they place the blame on the unfavorable conditions, while in reflecting on the failure of their neighbors, they place the blame squarely on their neighbors' shoulders. Such inconsistency represents not a reasoned theory, but a psychological tendency, which the study of philosophy of education should help to rectify. The environment is either superior to the individual as a determiner of his activities, or it is not. There is no class of activities for which the environment is entirely responsible, nor class for which the individual is wholly responsible. There is a tendency toward inconsistency in all of us, but those who consciously and deliberately adopt the principle of objective contingency in dealing with themselves, if they are logical, must also adopt it in dealing with others. If they adopt it in dealing with themselves in one class of activities, they must adopt it in dealing with others in the same class of activities. Those who adopt this theory of the relativity of experience unconsciously should adopt it deliberately and reflectively. If they cannot apply the theory in general, they should abandon it and adopt some other interpretation of the relativity of experience which they can so apply.

Those who adopt this interpretation of the feature of relativity tend to think in terms of absolute standards of conduct. Those who accept such standards consider some things as good and right within themselves independent of the individual. According to them, there are some ideals, ideas, and beliefs that are inherently good and that should be embodied in the hearts and minds of all. They believe that there are some best ways of doing particular things that should be observed in all situations. From their point of view, the business of those responsible for education — whether in the home, in the school, or in other social institutions — is to lead others to adopt and apply these standards and methods in all fields of human experience.

From the standpoint of the philosophy of experimentalism, such qualities as blind obedience, dependence, and subserviency, which suffuse the experiences of those who are engaged in the process of teaching and learning such absolutes as the foregoing, are undesirable. In consequence of such experiences, many of us as a matter of fact have certain ideas, ideals, and beliefs that are second nature to us. When we act upon them unconsciously, they serve as absolutes. When subjected to re-examination in particular situations, many of them, perhaps all of them, are open to question. Nevertheless, we are inclined to maintain our standards and do over and over again what we have done in the past. For instance, many people believe that they should keep their promises, whatever they are. In many situations the keeping of a promise is a disadvantage not only to the individual who makes it but to everybody else involved. Nevertheless, some of us are inclined to keep our word, even when doing so, on the basis of obvious consequences, is undesirable, all things considered. Even when we do decide to act on the basis of what seems most desirable under the conditions, we still have the feeling that we have done wrong and still hold that promises should be kept. Such an attitude or quality of personality represents the cumulative effect of the operation of the principle of objective contingency.

What has been said in regard to keeping promises might be said with respect to other ideals, beliefs, and attitudes. The same may be said also of the use of certain forms and procedures that we have learned. In other words, the adoption of the principle of objective contingency, whether by leaders or by followers, results in a kind of enslavement. From the standpoint of the philosophy of experimentalism there are few, if any, absolutes. Principles such as keeping one's word represent a point of emphasis that should be considered in all moral situations wherever they are involved. Far too few people consider such standards seriously enough, but there are others who hold them uncritically without regard to circumstances. The same applies to all methods and forms of procedure. There are typical forms and procedures of wide application. But often a combination of such forms and procedures in practical situations is better than any one authoritative scheme, however well established. In other words, the best plan of action under any particular set of conditions can often be determined only after one is confronted with the specific situation, although a consideration of typical authoritative methods may be very helpful, even indispensable.

Stated in a somewhat different way, the quality of experience involved in learning fixed standards and procedures is undesirable. The educator in any capacity who adopts absolutes as ends and means is constantly incapacitating himself for dealing with practical situations in which his beliefs and methods are inapplicable. The great Danish educator, Grundtvig, is reported to have said that it is impossible to decide what a child should learn before he is born. From the standpoint of the philosophy of experimentalism, it is impossible to tell exactly what should be done in any situation outside the situation itself. Those who are used to learning things as good or correct, independent of experience and in ways that are conceived as universally effective, are riding for a fall.

According to the experimentalists, the quality of blind faith and trust in the fixed standards to the development of which authoritarians are devoted leads to a false sense of security. It becomes a characteristic of the particular conceptions, convictions, and beliefs which are learned. They are conceived as absolutes, and it becomes impossible to abandon them in practical situations. It may be psychologically impossible to abandon them even in the face of destruction and catastrophe. Note the difficulty the American people have had in modifying the absolute of "avoiding entangling alliances," or now are having in changing the absolute of national sovereignty. Note the difficulties they have had in giving up the conception of the traditional two-term limit for president. Note also the influence of fixed barriers as a method of defensive warfare, symbolized by the Maginot Line of the French and by the Siegfried Line of the Germans. What is true for peoples and nations is true for every normal individual. Experiences that receive their guidance and direction from standards objectively determined by those in authority are pervaded with a quality of blind faith and assurance and belief in fixed standards, which at best is inadequate to the demands of life and at worst leads to pain and suffering. Rigidity as a quality of experience leads inevitably to rigidity of personality, and people who are inflexible in thought, feeling, and action, are incapable of dealing effectively with the new and the untried.

Of course, some may hesitate to reject absolutes. They may contend that everyone should tell the truth, be honest, pay his debts, and obey his parents. But our position here is not that such standards are unimportant. Such standards are important, and many people everywhere should give them much more weight in the practical affairs of life than they are accustomed to give them. If such ideals were trivial and irrelevant, they never would have been developed. They are exceedingly significant. These ideals are so significant, in fact, that they should be understood properly. They represent points of emphasis that have meant so much in the history of the human race that no one should neglect them in situations to which they are relevant. They are like traffic lights; they should always be considered even when they are not literally obeyed. The problem here is not one of holding such standards; it is a problem of how they are held. The contention of the experimentalists is that such ideals as truthfulness, honesty, and honoring one's parents, should be held as flexible standards; that is, be capable of modification and adaptation in practical situations where other standards must also be considered. In fact, only through such flexibility can the common ideals and beliefs receive the recognition they deserve. When held as absolutes, many people must find so many exceptions to the so-called ideals that their validity is undermined. In other words, flexibility in the use of standards is essential to the maintenance of the standards themselves. When the principle of objective contingency succeeds, authoritative standards enslave people, and when it fails, people are left without standards of any kind; and thus they fall back on their own inclinations and become slaves to personal impulse and desire.

Theory of Subjective Contingency
(Educational Laissez Faire)

In the laissez-faire philosophy of education the emphasis in both theory and practice is always upon the individual, and the standard of direction is found in the individual apart from experience. Therefore, we shall call this attitude *subjective contingency*, just as we have already designated as *objective contingency* the attitude that places the emphasis on the environment as the standard of direction. Subjective contingency constitutes an aspect of educational laissez faire in the same way that objective contingency constitutes an aspect of educational authoritarianism. Just as many different elements representing historical conceptions of life and education enter into the authoritarian attitude toward the feature of relativity, so different elements from many sources enter into the laissez-faire attitude toward it. Educational laissez faire contains elements that are attributed to Rousseau, elements that are attributed to the German Romanticists of the nineteenth century, and even elements that are often imputed to the experimentalists who reject it. But perhaps the most influential factor that enters into this theory of the relationship of the individual and his environment in experience arises from the social conditions, as in the case of the theory of objective contingency.

Doubtless, the most widely accepted belief supplying the historical background or theoretical justification of the theory of subjective contingency, as well as other laissez-faire principles, is the belief in the goodness of human nature in its pristine state before its interaction with the environment. In consequence of conflicts in social affairs, men have, from time to time, appealed to nature as a standard. But they have not found always the same standard. It appears that the kind of nature they discover invariably consists of factors, the direct opposite of those they find in ordinary experience. It is impossible to enter here into a consideration of all the theories of the goodness of nature. Our discussion must be limited to that theory which developed in Europe during the eighteenth century and in America during the nineteenth century.

The social conditions of the eighteenth century in Europe were not only almost unbearable, but they were shocking to the imagination of the more sensitive souls. Political tyranny, religious intolerance, economic distress, educational torture, and deadening formality in social relationships prevailed in the British Isles and on the continent. As sensitive and reflective leaders sought to bring about a change in this distressing state of affairs, they resorted to the criticism of social institutions. To make their appeals for reform effective, they had not only to point out the defects of civilization, but to point the way to a better life for all. To do this they had to have some kind of standard.

They found the suggestion of the kind of standard they required in the reports of explorers about primitive peoples in distant parts of the world. In literature the "noble savage" was romanticized. According to this conception, based upon the reports of journalists, who received their information from explorers in distant lands, primitive peoples, even savages, were good and kind. They were thought to have all the desirable qualities of personality that were so sadly lacking in the peoples of Europe. The conclusion was easily drawn that the difference between the savage and the civilized man was due to civilization. The activities of primitive man were based upon the inherent goodness of his nature, and the activities of civilized man were based upon artificialities of social institutions that civilization itself had produced. In other words, the social reformers used the goodness of nature, which they imputed to man, in isolation from civilization, as a standard in their criticism of social conditions, and in their projected policies and programs of reform. *Liberty, equality,* and *fraternity* — the slogans of the French Revolution — were derived from a consideration of the natural conditions of men outside the influence of civilization, and were hailed as standards of political reform. The so-called natural rights of men incorporated in the Federal Constitution of the United States reflect the conception that goodness of men is independent of the artificialities of the existing social arrangements. The conception of the individual as good until perverted not only was contrasted with the religious conception that the individual was bad until converted, but it served as a new standard of reform. It was a standard to which educational as well as political reformers could appeal.

The most influential leader among those who adopted the goodness of nature, particularly human nature, as the basis of social reform was Jean Jacques Rousseau. He may not have contributed much to the general idea of the goodness of nature, as some contend; but he did so elaborate the conception that it appealed to men everywhere. He defined and elaborated, in terms of politics, religion, and education, this conception of the goodness of nature or the world, which, at times, he seems to identify with God. There are many passages in Rousseau's writings which indicate that he attributed to human nature not only some desirable qualities but some undesirable ones as well. However, among educational reformers and practical workers who looked to Rousseau for theoretical leadership, it was the goodness-of-nature concept that attracted their attention, that controlled them in their formulation of principles and in their projection of programs. It makes little difference what interpretation scholars may place now upon Rousseau's theory of human nature derived from an analysis of his writings. It is certain that in the minds of his followers in Europe and America, human nature is good and should supply not only the means but also the ends of education. It was the obligation of parents and teachers everywhere to take the propensities of childhood as the starting point in education; to discover in them the conditions under which social aims were to be realized; and to find in them also the aims that were to determine all subject matter, methods, and organization.

From this point of view, educative experiences, desirable experiences, although they involved the use of the environment as an occasioning and contributing factor, were determined primarily by the expression, the realization, or the actualization of the native propensities or dispositions immanent in every individual. But apparently it was desirable to provide a scientific analysis of original human nature, if the social reformer and the educator were to receive specific suggestions from the general theory of the goodness of nature. Rousseau himself conceived human nature in terms of certain original dispositions, common to all men. However, the increasing interest of students of education and social workers in the origin, nature, and operation of native tendencies led biologists and psychologists to devote considerable study to their analysis and description. Recognized authorities analyzed, classified, and defined many different tendencies, which they usually called instincts. With the knowledge of the instincts constituting original nature, it seemed logical to expect educational workers to give scientific guidance to the unfoldment, realization, or actualization of human nature in its pristine goodness as it came from the hand of God.

The results of the development of the instinct theory of psychology proved that this expectation was not entirely warranted. There was considerable difference in the lists of instincts provided by recognized authorities. In the minds of some authorities, there were only a few instincts, while in the minds of others there were many. According to some authors, animals have more instincts than man, whereas according to William James, man has more instincts than animals. There has never been a satisfactory criterion by which an instinct may be distinguished from a habit. The wide variation in the classification of instincts and the difficulty of distinguishing instincts from habits led psychologists to abandon almost the entire conception of instincts.

The instinct theory of psychology had backfired. Instead of leading to a detailed and authoritative understanding of human nature that could be intelligently followed, it led to much confusion and misunderstanding. Obviously, if the educator attributed to pupils original tendencies that they did not have and prescribed activities corresponding to such fictitious tendencies, then he would miss the spirit of Rousseau. Instead of actually providing for the realization of nature, the educator was imposing certain social or cultural requirements on the individuals in the name of nature. Instead of treating people according to their natures, in practice he might be treating them according to social standards against which the theory of natural goodness was a reaction and a protest. In other words, as Bode says, this theory of nature isolated from environment is an absolute, and although it had the effect of arousing men to champion the cause of the individual, when specifically analyzed the natural individual is reduced to a bundle of instincts common to all. Obviously, such a fixed conception of the individual does not represent human nature as it actually is.

Gradually it dawned upon many students of human nature and of education that the individual and his environment are more closely related than it was once thought. They are in constant interaction, and the only place to determine the nature of the natural individual is in practical situations. From the standpoint of the parents or teachers, the nature of the child consists of his impulses and responses in the home and in the school where they actually occur. Members of the teaching profession are now not so much concerned with original nature as with the immediate desires, impulses, and interests of the individual, which, although they may be derived from nature, contain elements of habit and knowledge as well. What is important and fundamental is that these impulses and desires now take the place of the fixed instincts of the earlier day.

Nature is conceived to be just as good and perfect as it ever was, but it cannot be so formulated and classified in advance that parents and teachers can use it as a criterion of operations. They must find their criterion in nature, but they must find it in actual concrete situations rather than in authoritative studies of the biologists and the psychologists. From this point of view, lists of fixed tendencies, interests, and needs immanent in the individual apart from the environment and common to all men should be abandoned. They are, at best, merely social products, things that certain people unconsciously desire and impute to human nature. Nevertheless, human nature is still conceived by this group as inherently good and right.

Another conception that supplies the historical background and theoretical justification of subjective contingency, as well as other principles, is that of change. Change, along with substance, was early recognized among the philosophers of ancient Greece as an important feature of the world that required some kind of explanation. At first philosophers took change for granted. The substance of the world, whatever it might be, was conceived as lifelike. This dynamic character of the material of which the world was made was conceived as explaining the nature of things. Eventually, however, change was distinguished as a feature of things that required explanation even as did substance. By some, change was looked upon as merely a phenomenon, without any foundation in nature. By others it was considered a defect of ordinary experience and therefore not fundamentally real. By still others, like Heraclitus, it was considered to be a fundamental characteristic of reality or perhaps even reality itself. But however change may be conceived or explained, it has been long considered an important feature of nature that requires theoretical explanation.

In prevailing theories from ancient times until near the end of the nineteenth century, change was conceived as determined. The fact of change was, of course, recognized. Any event that occurred anywhere was attributed to some force outside the event itself. But whatever the nature of the force might be, it was thought to be occasioned by some other force. There had to be some final cause of movement. In other words, the events, occurrences, and variations in conditions were conceived as coming from some force lying outside experience and beyond it. The source of this force, whatever it might be, whether physical or spiritual, was itself fixed. Any movement or change of condition was conceived as occasioned by some fixed cause that did not itself change. In other words, the world was thought to be somehow determined in all parts by some fixed power that always remained the same.

On the other hand, the conception of Heraclitus that all things change, even reality itself, has gained wider and wider acceptance. The social institutions of the Eastern nations like China have remained virtually the same for some thousands of years. The mediaeval empire of the Catholic Church and the European emperors remained virtually the same for hundreds of years. But out of the religious revolution emerged various religious denominations; out of the political revolution emerged modern states; and out of the economic revolution emerged new methods of production and distribution. The development of science and technology produced social and economic changes, and these in turn produced other changes.

It became increasingly clear that the world — at least the human world — was on the move. It was difficult to tell in what direction the next change would occur. It seemed that there was no fixed order in which changes had to occur. They could apparently occur anywhere and in any shape. Moreover, science itself, which had replaced the fixed spiritual realities of the past with fixed material atoms, began to discover the radioactive substances which seem to act spontaneously. Even the atoms, and the electrons and protons which were embodied within them, were not conceived by the scientists as fixed. In the meantime, philosophers were reviving the teachings of Heraclitus. According to some, such as Bergson, not only were things changing but change was conceived as a fundamental feature of reality if not reality itself.

At the end of World War I, many people of the Western world did not have any clear idea as to what the future would be. They could not endorse the reactionary movement for the re-establishment of the old political, economic, and religious world that had been shaken to its foundations. The old world was passing before their very eyes, and they did not know what the new world would be. They had but one hope left to them. They could trust human nature. They adopted, consciously or unconsciously, the spirit of the Rousseau tradition. The nature of man was good, right, and infallible. But the old instinct psychology was gradually breaking down. The nature of human nature had to be discovered, if at all, in practical situations. Again they thought in terms of the young rather than in terms of the old. It was to childhood and youth that they looked for the solutions of the problems of the world. The new schools in Europe and the progressive schools in this country seemed to provide the institutions required for putting this theory into operation. In many of these schools the nature of children supplied suggestions not only as to materials and methods but also as to the aims of education. The belief that nature is changing, as well as the belief that nature is good, is implicit in many features of the new education. Desirable experience was thought to consist in the unfoldment or development of human nature itself as it is apart from experience. The desirable experience, so it was believed, had to find its standard of direction in the nature of the individual rather than in the environment with which he interacts.

Another movement which lends support to the principle of subjective contingency and other principles of educational laissez faire is what, for convenience of reference, may be designated as the waywardness of human nature. It contains many elements common to the conception of nature as good and dynamic. Yet it springs historically from a different source and contains a special emphasis of its own. It had its origin in Germany during the latter part of the eighteenth century and the first part of the nineteenth century. It is associated with the philosophic literary geniuses, Lessing, Goethe, Heine, and Schiller, and such poetic and literary philosophers as the two Schlegels, Novalis, and Schelling.

The great philosopher Kant had formulated the German traits of scientific and technical capacity and spiritual insight in two conceptions. The conception that the world of nature which science knows is only a world of appearances subjected to the laws of the mind seems to justify the German capacity for scientific research and technical efficiency. The noumenal world that lies beyond the phenomenal world, although unknown in the ordinary scientific sense, still reveals itself through the feeling of moral obligation and the practical reason. However, this noumenal world should, in the long run, give direction to the scientific and technical activities, and it is destined to overcome and regulate them in the distant future.

After the Prussian defeat at Jena in 1806, Fichte undertook to bridge the gap between the phenomenal world and the noumenal world. In this way he sought to unite the peoples of the German states that were only loosely associated economically and administratively. He conceived the noumenal world as spiritually capable of supplying an intellectual and moral direction to the German nation. The group of literary geniuses and poetic philosophers to whom we have referred developed what is known as the German Romantic Movement.

From this point of view, the spiritual and noumenal nature of the world conceived by Fichte was adopted in general outline. According to Fichte, the noumenal world, which Kant projected but failed to describe, is the world which each one of us knows directly in self-consciousness. In everything a man sees in the physical and social order there is a unification of the deeper self that he experiences in himself. We all see the same world because we are part and parcel of this more inclusive spiritual world, and our moral beings need and choose "common tasks." The real world, the spiritual world of which we are a part, is a moral order in which we realize our possibilities and to which we must conform.

The Romanticists accepted Fichte's conception that the world of reality is spiritual, but they rejected the conception that it determines our nature and our position in it. From this point of view, the world order, whatever it may be, is what human beings make it. We are not so much a reflection of the spiritual world as the spiritual world is the reflection of our own genius. Every genius thus makes his own spiritual world. What the world is for one man is decidedly different from what it is for another man. It is true that the world is essentially spiritual. The spirit which we express in self-consciousness pervades the physical, animal, and social world. The world as we experience it is a reflection of our own self-consciousness. Consequently, the world of the genius, the world of the Romanticist, is what he himself perceives in the objective world.

Here is where the idea of the waywardness of human nature appears. Every genius is different from every other genius. He thus constructs a spiritual world different from that of any other genius. Moreover, he differs from himself from time to time and, therefore, changes the spiritual world that he constructs. The break with the all-inclusive absolute world is almost complete. The fixed and inclusive world of which each one of us is a part becomes the spiritual world which everyone makes according to his own order. Man is a completely wayward being, without any fixed course of direction, order, or destination. He is governed by his own feeling as to what is the true nature of things. From this point of view, the man of genius is peculiar, unique, and inconsistent. He is different from other people. His vision of the world varies from time to time as his perceptive moods vary.

In the German Romanticism, however, it was the men of genius who had the self-consciousness that enabled them to construct their own world. The world was as unified, rich, and significant as the individual could make it. But the world, after all, was relative to him and dependent upon his own perceptions. His experiences, of course, involved a reference to objective nature, but nevertheless its character and quality were derived purely from his own inner nature.

This conception of the subjectivity of experience could not long be confined to the experience of the genius, however. If the world of the genius is relative to his own self-consciousness, it is a logical next step to conclude that the world of every man is relative to his own self-consciousness. The nature of the individual determines the nature of the world he perceives. Consequently, every individual has a different world. He is unique, peculiar, wayward, and inconsistent. This conception was easily believed applicable to men everywhere. The conception of Rousseau had done its work. All were by nature equal. Each, therefore, had the power to determine his own world.

This waywardness of human nature was adopted by leading thinkers in Europe and America. It influenced such English poets as Wordsworth, Coleridge, Byron, Keats, and Shelley. It influenced the great genius of American poetry, Walt Whitman, and that unique romantic transcendentalist man of literature and philosophy, Ralph Waldo Emerson. It was reflected, in combination with the influence of Rousseau, in the educational policies, programs, and activities of that peculiar, unique, and wayward schoolman, Bronson Alcott.[4]

This same spirit seems to pervade much of the literature, music, and fine arts of the present day. According to this point of view, every product of a creative genius represents a reality that is peculiar to him. Some of his work may be considered unintelligible and meaningless to others; but it is significant to the producer, it is a valid representation of reality. What is good to the man of genius is inherently good. But in a democracy everyone is created free and equal. Therefore, what is good to the individual man is inherently good.

This Romantic movement in literature and philosophy was bound to make itself felt in education. The way had already been paved for it by Rousseau and by the development of political democracy. The Romantic movement in education emphasized the element of change. It provided a form of intellectual justification for a spirit that was already commanding the respect of men. It represented a justification of a reaction against formality in social life, in the fine arts, and in education. Like the Romantic naturalism of Rousseau, it became not only an appeal to the waywardness of geniuses but to the unique and peculiar in all men. Romanticism supplied a theoretical basis for the effort to break the formality of the schoolroom through the adoption of the native propensities of childhood as the ends as well as the means of education. It assumed the goodness and dynamic character of human nature, and thus contributed to the tendency in many quarters to look to the individual for the standards of direction in situations where desirable experiences were generated. But its main contribution lay in the emphasis it placed on the manifestation of the true nature of the individual in specific situations.

As already suggested, the conceptions of human nature as good, the world as dynamic, and the individual as wayward are not responsible for the fact that many people often do, as a matter of course, use immediate personal disposition, impulse, and inclination as standards of

---

[4] Dorothy McCuskey, *Bronson Alcott, Teacher*. The Macmillan Company, New York, 1940.

direction in dealing with themselves as well as in dealing with others. Subjective contingency is effective as an operative principle among people who have never heard of such conceptions. It is exemplified in the activities of the young and the old, the ignorant and the learned, in all countries, and in all periods of human history. The authoritarians often attribute a belief in this theory to those who oppose them. Perhaps few individuals or groups have deliberately advocated such a theory as a guiding intellectual principle, although many people assume this principle or theory of the relativity of experience on many occasions. Nevertheless, it has been consistently rejected by the experimentalists, although it is still imputed to them by authoritarians. The foregoing conceptions of human nature, the world, and the individual supply the basis of the intellectual justification of the principle of subjective contingency, and those who unconsciously adopt it in practice are under the logical obligation to justify it in theory. Reference to these theoretical elements that have been used to justify this principle should, therefore, be suggestive to those who are interested in the foundation of a principle they often unconsciously take for granted.

This laissez-faire theory of the relativity of experience is exemplified in many activities of many people in all walks of life. It is implicit in their manner of dealing with others. We are all familiar with people who do not hesitate to try to do anything they wish. They do not seem to consider any traditional customs nor the standards of fair play. They do not hesitate to push in at the head of the line, rush for the best seat, purchase more than their share of a scarce commodity, or even violate the law in matters which, by common consent, serve the best interests of all. Even those people who take into account varying demands in most situations on occasion do many things which only their own propensities, or perhaps voices of their own consciences, dictate.

The parent who does not have any clear ideas concerning what his children should eat, how they should dress, what kind of recreation they should have, or how much they should work, permits them to do very much as they please. Such a parent, who does not have any standards of his own and who accepts the immediate wishes and wants of his children at face value as the source of direction in his dealings with them, is adopting the theory of subjective contingency.

The operation of the principle of subjective contingency in our schools and colleges can be seen by any qualified observer. The tendency of teachers to adopt it is indicated in many ways. Those who do not have any aims for their pupils may accept the direct proposals of the pupils themselves as the ends to be sought. Those who reject the conception of teaching subject matter without reference to the child may follow the lead of the child without reference to the subject matter. Those who reject the theory of logical organization may neglect the problem of organization entirely. Those who have suffered from the formality imposed by fixed methods may lose respect for recognized procedures. Those who have been responsible for using a curriculum determined in advance may leave the development of the curriculum entirely to the pupils. Those who do not know their subject matter may ask all kinds of questions and never commit themselves to any definite conclusions; so far as the pupils can tell, their own answers are all correct.

This laissez-faire interpretation of the feature of relativity is implicit in the activities of those school administrators and supervisors who fail to develop policies and programs of their own and who seek instead to secure all aims and procedures from the proposals of those whom they are expected to guide and direct. Student leaders in our schools and colleges often suggest programs of action merely because they think that such proposals will be immediately acceptable and appealing. Many teachers have had students in their classes who were considered leaders by the other students. Sometimes these leaders have made proposals in regard to the work merely because they thought those proposals would be just what the other students would like to hear.

Nor is the operation of the theory of subjective contingency confined to the school. It appears in the disposition of many leaders to do merely what their followers desire. The pastor of the church may seek merely to follow the disposition of his parishioners without any effort to change their attitudes and develop better procedures. The political leader may merely seek to follow the wishes of his constituents, even on issues about which they are uninformed. The merchant often tries to sell what people want, without any effort to influence them to buy products that will serve them better. Leaders in civic clubs and organizations often hesitate to propose new policies and programs that vary from the beaten paths, and when they do propose them, the group may reject the "new" idea without reflective consideration. Habit, as well as intuition and conscience, often controls the individual in practical situations and explains the tendency of most of us on many occasions to assume the principle of subjective contingency in dealing with ourselves and with others.

The conception of the continuity of experience leads the experimentalist to reject this laissez-faire interpretation of the relativity of experience. According to his point of view, the self or personality of each one of us is the product of habit. Habit is the foundation of the continuity of experience. It is always at work in the minds and hearts of people whose experiences are pervaded with the principle of subjective contingency. The person who merely lets himself go on occasion according to his disposition and inclination may let himself go more and more until he must have his own way or suffer tremendously from defeat and disappointment. The leader who takes his cues merely from the inclinations of those whom he guides and directs, must sooner or later become incapacitated for leadership. Those who have followed such leadership in the home, the school, and the community never grow up. Social maturity and responsibility become increasingly difficult for those who, with success and approval, take their own intuitions, consciences, and impulses as standards of thought, feeling, and action. Retardation in the development of social imagination, lack of consideration for others, and neglect of authoritative standards are cumulative. From the standpoint of the philosophy of experimentalism, those who adopt the laissez-faire theory of subjective contingency are adopting a policy of miseducation. We are not compelled to find our standards of direction in either the environment or the individual in isolation from each other. Neither is it necessary to assume a middle-of-the-road position and look to the one in some situations and to the other in other situations. The experimentalists have their own interpretation of the feature of relativity, which they assume in dealing with educational problems and which some of them are constantly seeking to formulate for the guidance and direction of people everywhere in dealing with themselves and with others.

THEORY OF FUNCTIONAL CONTINGENCY
(EDUCATIONAL EXPERIMENTALISM)

Like educational authoritarianism and educational laissez faire, educational experimentalism assumes that educative experience is a function of the interaction of individuals with their environments. In the experimentalist's conception of the interactivity of experience, both individual and environment are involved in every experience that ever occurs, although he places more emphasis on the influence of the individual than does the authoritarian and more emphasis on the environment than does the laissez-faire adherent. The experimentalist looks neither to the environment nor to the individual in isolation for a standard of direction in developing policies, programs, and activities. He thinks of individuals and environments as functional factors in an on-going process that change in meaning and significance in terms of each other. This attitude toward relativity as a feature of educative experience is designated as *functional contingency*, because it places the emphasis equally upon the individual and upon the environment and finds the standard of direction in experience in which they both function in terms of each other.

This theory of the relativity of experience has its basis in the experimentalist's conception of interaction in general. When two physical objects, such as things composed of earth, wood, or stone, strike against one another, we often think of one rather than the other as causing the collision. As a matter of fact, the interaction, when examined a little more closely, cannot be attributed entirely to the so-called causal object. The object that is struck is necessary in order to have a collision. Other objects may be responsible for the movement of the causal object, which, therefore, cannot be the sole cause in any final sense. Furthermore, additional objects enter into the situation.

Collisions, interactions, or transactions do not typically take place in a vacuum. They take place on surfaces composed of such substances as earth, metal, wood, or stone — all of which vary in their nature, and influence what takes place upon them. Interactions take place in water, in the air, or in the earth, or perhaps better, in space-time. The media in which events occur enter into the events. Even when events take place in a vacuum, they are different from other events. Any event involves much more than is evident from casual observation. In fact, every particular thing is an event that is entangled with other events — each with its own geography and history — which are in turn entangled with still other events. An interaction of any two observable objects embodies, then, much more than appears on the surface. It may not embody everything in the universe, as some have thought, but it certainly involves many things that do not immediately reveal themselves.

What is true of interactions on the common-sense, molar, or macroscopic level is likewise true in the physical universe as conceived in the physical sciences. Interactions here, too, are relative to the system in which they belong. In biology and psychology, behavior is not merely occasioned by something in the organism or in the individual or by something in the environment. Both the organism or the individual and certain features of the environment known as stimuli enter into these interactions; but many other things enter into them, also. Experience on any level whatever, ranging from the lowly amoeba to the most intelligent and spiritual among human kind, involves both the individual and the environment in many and varying combinations. Human experience is relative to many factors in the individual and in the environment with which he interacts. It has long been recognized in sociology that both the individual and the group to which he belongs affect his experience. The relative importance attached to the different factors in any given situation influences our attitude toward it, and the relative importance attached to certain types of factors which enter into experiences influence our attitudes toward experience. If education is "of, by, and for experience," as Dewey suggests, then one's attitude toward these different types of factors that enter into experience must influence one's theory of education.[5]

From ordinary observation, it is quite clear that the experience of an individual is influenced not only by what is obviously present in a particular situation but also by what the individual has experienced in the past. A person under a given set of conditions acts differently, feels differently, and thinks differently from the way one brought up under other circumstances acts, feels, and thinks. What one has been experiencing enters into the qualities of his present experiences. The person who has plenty of sweets available daily reacts quite differently to a chocolate bar from the soldier who has long been deprived of sweets. Rest, sleep, food, digestion, elimination, circulation, growth — all enter into the quality of our experience. The character of the activity in which one has just been engaged, such as strenuous physical exercise, intellectual concentration, or physical relaxation, listening to good music, or reading a story, enters into the qualities of one's experience when an opportunity presents itself to go swimming, to attend a circus, or to take a nap.

Things with which an individual apparently interacts in the process of experience always belong to a situation. A child may, when left alone, become frightened at the presence of a dog which delights him when he is taken into his mother's arms. The effect on the individual of such environmental factors as altitude, temperature, and humidity, is recognized by people everywhere. Other environmental influences

---

[5] John Dewey, *Experience and Education*. The Macmillan Company, New York, 1938. P. 19.

are part and parcel of the situations in which people and observable things are the obvious factors to which we are directing our attention, and the way they act, feel, and think is influenced by these more recondite factors as well as by those which are in the plain view of all.

In current educational theory and practice, some attitude is usually assumed with respect to the relation of the individual to his environment. That the ability and capacity of those being educated affect the kind of education they are able to receive is commonplace in educational theory everywhere. Scarcely any recognized student of education believes that all individuals should be treated alike in school or anywhere else. It may be necessary to treat them alike legally and economically, but when we have in mind their education, they must be treated differently. Different individuals cannot have exactly the same kind of experiences, and the greater their differences, the greater the differences in their experiences. The problem of individual differences thus looms large in current educational theory and practice. The scope, causes, and treatment of individual differences are central topics in educational psychology, curriculum-making, and methods of teaching. Attitudes toward individual differences are constantly influencing the curriculum, method, and administration of the schools.

It is also widely recognized that the conditions under which pupils and teachers work influence the character of the activities in which they engage, and the quality of the experiences they have. Scarcely anyone doubts the influence of the school grounds and the school building on the educational activities and experiences of the pupils. In fact, even the conditions under which the pupils live at home, the things they do in the fields, on the streets and playgrounds, affect what they do and experience in the schoolroom. The cultural frame of the community and its school enters into the experiences of the pupils and conditions what they can do and how they can do it. The availability of materials and equipment is recognized as a practical factor that must influence the experiences of pupils and that should be taken into account by educational workers. In the development of educational improvement programs, the ability and attitude of the teachers, as well as the capacity and attitude of the community, should be given some consideration. Even the teacher himself should recognize his own abilities and limitations. He cannot do exactly what others can do. He is also a part of the environment of the pupils and enters into their experiences even as does the subject matter of the curriculum. The importance of such factors is recognized in educational discussions everywhere.

Stated somewhat differently, the theory of functional contingency assumes that the individual and his environment are involved equally and mutually in all experience. One is no more important than the other. They are both indispensable. This theory of the relationship of the individual and environment is apparently taken for granted in such educational conceptions as "growth," "reconstruction of experience," "the remaking of life," which Dewey, Bode, and Kilpatrick have developed. In all these definitions of education it seems to be assumed that the individual and his environment are equal and mutual in every experience that occurs. Such a balance of the two sides of experience is sought in the philosophy of pragmatism, humanism, instrumentalism, or experimentalism wherever educational problems are under consideration. The leaders in these movements are so eager to maintain a proper balance that, paradoxical as it may seem, they are constantly overemphasizing first one and then the other. Such a situation is not difficult to understand, however, if we realize that in general there are always some people who overemphasize the individual and others who overemphasize the environment. In meeting these two extremes, the educational experimentalist seems to place the emphasis first on one factor and then on the other, for it is first one attitude and then the other that needs attention and correction. Consequently, the experimentalists are condemned by some for overemphasizing individual initiative and responsibility, and by others for overemphasizing routine habit. In other words, either emphasis may be discerned in the literature of this philosophy of life and education by those who wish to find it. When the educational literature of this philosophy is taken as a whole, however, there is maintained between the two factors a constant balance that we have designated as the theory of mutual or functional contingency.

Another difficulty that often leads to a misunderstanding of the theory of functional contingency assumed by the experimentalists is the conception of the meaning of both the individual and the environment and, consequently, of the relation between them, which is quite different from that assumed in both objective contingency and subjective contingency, the two other interpretations of the feature of relativity that we have considered. As already suggested, both these principles are alike in their conception of the relationship of the individual and the environment. In both theories, these two factors are conceived in terms of space, the one beginning where the other ends. Stated in a different way, this conception holds that the individual, who is external to the environment, is surrounded by it. As a consequence, we have such insoluble problems as the relative importance of heredity and environment, nature and nurture, intelligence and experience, to consider everywhere we turn in the social sciences and in educational discussion. According to the theory of functional contingency, these opposed influences are factors that enter into every experience, and these problems cannot be solved wholesale. Wherever experiences occur, both individual and environment enter into them and affect their quality. But this principle goes much further. Any experience leaves its effect in the individual. After each experience, the individual is changed in some way or other. He is in some respect a new person. Now, different people could not have the same environment, even if they could be surrounded by the same things. In other words, individual and environment are functional factors and each changes in terms of the other.

The individual is not merely in his environment; his environment is also in him. He is in his environment as flowers may be in the sunlight, not as fruit may be in a basket. The environment during any given experience consists of those things with which an individual interacts. He does not interact with everything that surrounds him, which is the kind of environment assumed in the other two principles. Everything that surrounds a person is not a part of his environment. Some of the things are not even included in his potential environment. Only the things with which he may interact constitute his potential environment, and only the things with which he does interact constitute his actual environment. Consequently, neither individual nor environment is fixed, and neither can be defined in structural terms. They change in terms of each other, and neither remains the same from one experience to the next.

In psychology, such factors as stimulus and response, situation and organism, representing respectively the environment and the individual, are functional conceptions and are meaningless without reference to each other. A change in the one signifies a change in the other. The situation includes the individual, and is itself a part of him. For instance, a boy, in building a model airplane for the first time, is building the concept of airplane into himself at the same time that he is building an actual model. Each changing part has both a subjective and an objective reference — it is both individual and environmental. In education, subject matter is not something external to the individual. It consists of those features of the situation which the individual uses. Things, whether definable in terms of objective things, data derived from things, or suggestions supplied from memory, are subject matter, not in consequence of their mere existence, but in consequence of their use in particular situations. For instance, written material in books, usually considered as subject matter, is not subject matter to the individual unless he uses it in dealing with an actual situation.

The individual and the environment are equally and mutually significant, the meaning of the one changing in terms of the meaning of the other. There are no individuals of predetermined potentialities that supply both the end and the method of experience and education. Nor can the individual, from the standpoint of the theory of functional contingency, be considered as mere putty to be molded by the environment that is external to him. There are doubtless such things as impulses, possibly even original tendencies, properly conceived. But although an act may be original the first time it occurs, whenever such an act is also an experience, it forthwith becomes a habit, and it is never entirely original again. In common with the other interpretations of the feature of relativity, the theory of functional contingency signifies that no act would occur in the first place if environmental factors did not provide the means of its occurrence. Impulses, whether considered as the manifestation of original nature or of acquired habit, require media for their expression. But the theory of functional contingency implies more than that the environment supplies the conditions of experience. The meaning and significance of experience depends upon what happens to responses and to the individual when they are expressed. An educative experience does not arise merely from the expression of some impulse or tendency. Neither does it arise merely from the impression of some kind of subject matter on a *tabula rasa*. It is a function of activities in which both factors — the impulsions and the effective surrounding situation — are equally, mutually, and inextricably interwoven and intertwined, the one changing in terms of the other.

The self as empirically conceived, however else it may be conceived in metaphysics, is nothing apart from its environment. It is the enduring effect of the continuous process of interaction. It is constantly in the making, emerging again and again from those events consisting of interactions called experiences. As the self emerges from each experience, it is not merely an enlarged edition of what it was before, as it might be according to some forms of the theory of objective contingency.

It is not merely the old self to which the environment has added some new substance, as it should be according to certain forms of the theory of subjective contingency. The old self has been transformed, remade, and reconstructed through the transaction that has occurred.

But such a transaction, such an experience, is not a one-way process. An experience is not merely a double-barreled word, having both a subject and an object. In experience both the subject and the object are affected. The individual is so reconstructed that his subsequent experiences are different. When the individual is reconstructed, his actual environment must also be different in his subsequent transactions. Both the subjective and the objective factors of experience have undergone reconstruction. Just as in a household of three children the oldest can never be an only child after the second is born and the younger can never be the youngest after the third is born, so an old self can never be the same again after an educative experience. With each addition to the family, the environment is changed in some respects as well as the children. Thus, after every experience, the actual and potential environment, as well as the individual, is changed in some respects.

This functional relationship of the individual and his environment is now widely accepted in those sciences that supply subject matter in dealing with educational problems. Stimulus and response in both biology and psychology are increasingly considered as functional rather than as structural conceptions. In sociology and social psychology, the individual is more and more conceived as an integral part of the group and the group is as much a part of him as he is a part of the group. For instance, the old conception of a group mind independent of members of the group is no longer acceptable in social psychology. The theory of functional contingency is, then, not contradictory to tendencies in those fields of thought from which students secure subject matter in dealing with educational problems, as are the theories of objective and subjective contingency.

The theory of functional contingency also seems more relevant to the social scene than do the other interpretations of the feature of relativity. According to this theory, the current disposition of the criminal, the indigent, and the derelict to place responsibility for their condition upon the environment cannot be justified. Neither can be justified the disposition of leaders in the state, the church, the schools, and business and industry to place the blame of these unfortunates squarely on their own shoulders. According to the theory of functional contingency, social policies, programs, and activities must not be based upon either individual or society in isolation. There are no such individuals and societies. Few individuals have made the best of their opportunities, and responsible social groups have not provided as favorable opportunities as they might provide. Both the individual and his potential environment enter into every experience. Both may be improved, and the improvement of the one implies an improvement of the other. But for the best results effort should be made both from the standpoint of the individual and from the standpoint of the social and economic conditions. The unfortunate individual cannot be rehabilitated and the more fortunate cannot be improved unless their environments are also improved. On the other hand, the individual who places all responsibility for his shortcomings on the environment is helpless and hopeless.

Absolute security is perhaps impossible in this life, and, could it be attained, it probably would not be either good for us or even good to us. Doubtless, many of us in such a perfect state, would, like William James, long for the real world where men have their ups and downs, their joys and their sorrows. The tendency of men to sell their liberty for a mess of pottage was never more in evidence than at the present time. The tendency to rely on others for security, protection, and support leads to slavery. The tendency to assert one's wishes and desires until prevented by outside force also leads to slavery. Slavery to impulse and caprice is different from slavery to domination and routine, but it is none the less slavery. These conflicting tendencies are to be found throughout the world, in every country, and even in many a human soul. The futility of both of them as they are working themselves out in practice before our very eyes is sufficient to justify the search for a different theory. It should be sufficient to lead men to the theory of functional contingency, which contradicts the opposing theories whose current application on such a large scale has justified the human disposition to do either as one is told or as one pleases. The quality of functional contingency seems to be in line with current developments in the field of science to meet the requirements of the social scene.

As we have already pointed out in connection with the theories of objective and subjective contingency, a positive and creative theory of education and experience has also its underlying practical, psychological, and existential principle. A theory of education or experience is a theory of what should be, but what should be depends somewhat upon what is. The educative process conceived in terms of the qualities of experience as they occur psychologically and practically, without regard to desirability, is known as the method of education in its broadest sense. The educative process conceived in terms of the desirable qualities of experience is the aim of education in its broadest sense. Any feature of educative experience when translated into a quality is in its first intent a principle of method and in its second intent an aim of education.

The theory of functional contingency is not only a principle of method, but it is also an educational aim. As a principle of method, it signifies that those who deal educationally with others shall know them. We must know them not merely in terms of psychology learned in books, though such studies are suggestive. We must know them in their actual environments. We should know something of the environment with which they have interacted, with which they are currently interacting, and with which they probably will interact in the not-too-distant future. We must know also how they have interacted, are interacting, and probably will interact under varying conditions. From this point of view, we should not expect to treat everybody alike. Even the Golden Rule, "Do unto others as you would have others do unto you," needs constant reinterpretation. "Even if all men agreed sincerely to act upon the principle of the Golden Rule as the supreme law of conduct, we should still need inquiry and thought to arrive at even a passable conception of what the Rule means in terms of concrete practice under mixed and changing social conditions." [6] When people are different in important respects, what would be agreeable to one person might be very disagreeable to another person. What is possible in the case of one person may not be possible in the case of another, and what is possible in the case of one person on one occasion may not be possible for that person on another occasion. We must take into account practical conditions involving our own capacity, the availability of tools and equipment, and the attitude of the community if we are to meet the insistent demand of actual conditions in the kind of world in which we live.

The same conception may be stated in another form. We must know the conditions that exist inside and outside individuals in their relationships. Only with such information can we deal with them intelligently, effectively, and sympathetically. We must go further and

---

[6] John Dewey and James H. Tufts, *Ethics*, Revised Edition. Henry Holt and Company, New York, 1933. P. 190.

prepare the environment with which they are now interacting in order to improve the quality of their experiences. Some activities are inadequate because of the nature of the individual who engages in them; others are inadequate because of the lack of certain materials and equipment with which to work; and still others are inadequate because of the capacity or disposition of the community. The educational significance of the activities of individuals depends, in part at least, upon the conditions under which they take place. In the selection of activities and experiences, the educator should choose either those that are practicable under existing conditions, or else so change the conditions that those selected become practicable.

As a constructive principle or aim of education the theory of functional contingency goes still further. It signifies that the experience of the individual engaged in educational activities should be colored, pervaded, and suffused with the quality of contingency. He should react to things as variable, changeable, and modifiable rather than as fixed, complete, and absolute. By comparison with other things we perceive things as long or short, large or small, heavy or light, dark or bright rather than as fixed, complete, and absolute. As an aim, the theory of functional contingency signifies that we should realize the relativity of our activities as well as of the activities of others. It is not enough to act relatively in regard to physical things and absolutely with respect to thoughts and ideals. It is not enough to act relatively with respect to ourselves and think of other people as acting absolutely. The relativity of things as perceived is a psychological fact that has been well established. At the same time, such a fact does not signify that people in general look upon concepts, such as good and bad, right and wrong, beautiful and ugly, as being affected by the situation in which they are experienced.

The lack of this quality of contingency in the experiences of our fathers probably accounts for the predicament in which we now find ourselves. Certain mental patterns developed by our ancestors in their tribal life in Europe and in the agricultural communities of rural America are now outmoded.[7] Some ways of thinking, feeling, and acting that have served isolated groups effectively are inadequate when those communities become interconnected physically, mechanically, and technologically with other communities throughout the world. The mentality of the horse-and-buggy days, to say nothing of the days

---

[7] J. K. Hart, *The Mind in Transition.* Covice Friede, Publishers, New York, 1938. Pp. 299–309.

of the oxcart and the stage coach, is obsolete in the days of the auto-mobile, the airplane, and the radio. Under static and fixed conditions over long periods of time, the development of mental patterns corre-sponding to the activities of circumscribed and fixed terrain of narrow range and scope may have been as desirable as it was inevitable, but the development of such patterns now is not desirable and need not be inevitable. The theory of functional contingency signifies that all patterns to be developed should embody an element of contingency, adaptiveness, and modifiability. Certain ways of thinking, feeling, and acting should not be learned as good or bad, right or wrong, beau-tiful or ugly within themselves without respect to circumstances and conditions. Such patterns should be learned as functions of particular situations and as subject to change as those situations change. They can be so learned only as the quality of contingency pervades the experi-ences through which they are learned. The theory of functional con-tingency is a theory of method since it suggests the quality of experience and of education in a practical and existential sense; but it is also an aim since it is a desirable quality of experience — education in a con-structive and ethical sense. Nor is it merely an aim, but a quality of all other aims that can be justified.

The theory of functional contingency, as an aspect of educational experimentalism, has far-reaching implications for educational practice everywhere. For parents it means that they must neither force their children to conform to values which they have learned as fixed criteria of activities, nor permit them to yield to immediate impulse in deciding what they shall do. They must be led to consider their impulses in the light of all available standards and then do what seems desirable in various practical situations. It means also that different pupils will be treated differently. For example, some parents insist on having their children receive high ratings in school. If an older child has demon-strated superiority in schoolwork, parents insist that the younger ones also achieve high ratings. Some children excel in some things, and others excel in other things. Some learn rapidly and others learn slowly. To insist that all do the same things equally well signifies that standards are taken from the environment. On the other hand, to permit children to attend school or not as they may be inclined or to pursue any course of activities without reference to conditions, present or prospective, is to seek standards in the individual without reference to his environment. The child should be considered in terms of both his capacity and his disposition, and the environment should be considered in terms of both its immediate demands and its future possibilities. Above all, the parent must look upon his values as relative and must also lead the child to look upon his values as relative. What each should do in a given situation depends upon what is required in the adjustment of a variety of standards to each other. Many situations require the development of new standards through a reconstruction of both impulse and past standards, and the doing of justice to both in the light of present conditions and probable consequences.

For leaders in practical affairs in all walks of life, the theory of functional contingency signifies that one should not try to enforce the impossible nor merely follow the crowd. The effort to impose authoritative standards on people who, because of inability or indisposition, are unable to meet these requirements cannot be justified. On the other hand, programs that the impulses and inclinations of individuals and groups suggest may be possible, but they are not always positively educative. The minister who lauds ideals that are impractical in modern life accepts by implication the theory of objective contingency, whereas the minister who idealizes merely what his church membership immediately likes to hear is adopting the theory of subjective contingency. According to the theory of functional contingency, he should emphasize standards that have a functional relationship to the conditions of the community and to the wishes of his parishioners. The political leader who supports only such measures as immediately appeal to his constituents, or who proposes only what their immediate desires dictate, may be a politician, but he is not an educational statesman. From the standpoint of the theory of functional contingency, measures that embody the impulses and desires of the people should be suggested and advocated, but these measures should, at the same time, require the consideration of authoritative standards and involve the reconstruction not only of the desires but of the standards themselves. What is true of the minister and the political leader is also true of leaders of all organizations and groups. The programs developed should not represent merely an elaboration of some authoritarian ideal. Nor should any program represent merely what appeals immediately to the group, taken individually or collectively. It should be sufficiently related to the impulses of the group to challenge consideration, but it should be on a level sufficiently beyond immediate impulse to require reconstruction of impulse.

In terms of the school, this theory of the relativity of experience requires that policies, programs, and activities take into account both the environment and the individuals involved. They must give consideration to past standards and present disposition and capacity. The only effective operative standards are those generated in each practical situation. It is impossible to tell what any particular youth should learn until we know him in his own particular environment. All youth is not to be expected to have the same curriculum, employ the same methods, and develop the same ideas and beliefs. The results of desirable experience vary with each individual, but they should be capable of modification and reconstruction with the development of experience. Things learned are to be conceived as tools to be used in dealing with practical situations and thus subject to change through use.

The individual who adopts the theory of functional contingency looks upon his impulses and inclinations as mere suggestions of possibilities. He stops, looks, and listens, and examines conditions with respect to possibilities and consequences. He considers suggestions with respect to himself and others. He considers them with respect to the future as well as to the present. Likewise, he thinks of his values not as criteria of judgment in all situations to which they are relevant; he looks upon recognized values not as indicating what should be done, but rather as factors to be considered. He may have moral standards, aesthetic standards, and intellectual standards that have become second nature to him. But he realizes, if he accepts the theory of functional contingency, that their consistent application in all situations to which they are relevant may cause pangs of conscience, practical inefficiency, and logical inconsistency. He therefore seeks to use these standards in dealing with situations in which they apply not as absolutes to which conditions of life must conform but as instruments for dealing with the problems of life. To revert to the disposition to keep one's word, any individual should look upon the value of keeping his promise as a standard to be considered in certain situations. He should stop, look, and listen before breaking faith; but he should also realize that there are occasions when certain other values are more important. Those who adopt the theory of functional contingency as a principle of educational experimentalism look upon their ideas, ideals, and beliefs as relative in meaning and application in dealing with themselves and with others. Experience is the original source and the final test of all values.

Perhaps in concluding this chapter it might be well to state, as definitely as possible, the qualities of experience that the three theories of the relativity of experience suggest, and indicate the nature of the program that lies before us in subsequent chapters. If the theory of objective contingency is conceived in terms of the quality of desirable experience, it may perhaps be adequately designated as *rigidity;* if the theory of subjective contingency is so conceived, it may perhaps be satisfactorily designated as *spontaneity;* and if the theory of functional contingency is so conceived, it may perhaps be properly designated as *flexibility.* These three qualities — rigidity, spontaneity, and flexibility — characterize respectively desirable experience implicit, respectively, in the authoritarian, laissez-faire, and experimentalist interpretation of the relativity of experience. Other principles of these different philosophies of education will be explained in succeeding chapters through consideration of different attitudes that their proponents assume toward the other five features of educative experience.

CHAPTER 4

Sociality of Experience

MOST OF US LIKE PEOPLE who are social-minded, and some of us try to be social-minded ourselves. Still, many of us admire the qualities of individual initiative, responsibility, self-reliance, and independence. In other words, we may approve, prize, and even idealize both socialization and individualization at the same time. Such seemingly conflicting theories and practices of individuals and institutions are reflected in current economic, political, ethical, and educational thought everywhere. To avoid logical inconsistency and practical inefficacy, some kind of reduction, compromise, or integration seems imperative. Perhaps the proper starting point in dealing with the problem is some widely recognized feature of experience.

From the standpoint of the philosophy of experimentalism, all educative experience is psychologically social. Some interactions are not experiences and some experiences may not be educative, but all educative experiences are as a matter of fact social. They all involve directly or indirectly not only an individual and an environment, but the interaction of a social individual with a social environment. Still the social quality of experiences as they actually occur may be either desirable or undesirable, educative or miseducative, in any positive and constructive sense. There are three different theories of the feature of sociality, just as there are three different theories of the feature of the relativity of experience, and like the latter they constitute principles, respectively, of educational authoritarianism, educational laissez faire, and educational experimentalism.

THEORY OF DOCTRINAIRE SOCIALITY
(EDUCATIONAL AUTHORITARIANISM)

In educational authoritarianism effective socialization is assumed to be a primary obligation of those responsible for educational policies, programs, and activities. From this point of view, desirable socialization consists in the achievement of enduring social values, whether defined in terms of abilities, knowledge, ideals, or attitudes, or in some other way. The form in which social values are expressed reflects the varying psychological positions of those who define them, and does not seem very significant with respect to socialization, however important it may be in other connections. The term "social values," therefore, may be used as a general conception to include changes of any kind to be produced in any individual for purposes of socializing him. According to educational authoritarianism, adequate socialization can be secured in only one way. The social values to be incorporated in the minds and hearts of people, particularly the young, must be determined in advance of practical educational situations and be taught as expeditiously and economically as possible under the conditions. Such a principle as an aspect of educational authoritarianism is here designated, for convenience of reference, as the theory of doctrinaire sociality. From the standpoint of this theory, indoctrination serves one or more of the following purposes: (1) to conserve the past; (2) to promote the interest of particular social groups; (3) to advance the general welfare; and (4) to facilitate human progress.

1. Some recognized authorities have insisted that the chief business of education is to transmit all the civilizing influences of the past to the rising generation. This position is also assumed by every teacher who tries to teach everything in the book, and by the student who undertakes to learn everything in the course without discrimination. It is implicit in the attitude of some who look to the past for fixed standards in dealing with the demands of current social situations. But the continuous accumulation of knowledge makes selection and discrimination imperative. We cannot learn everything and teach everything. Consequently, recognized authorities who now think of education as the transmission of social heritage and vicarious experience have in mind only the elements of the past that are socially desirable.

Such a conception thus establishes the basis for the belief in indoctrination. If certain elements of past civilizations are to be preserved, they must be learned by each generation. From this point of view, many things that should be transmitted have no meaning and significance in present experience. Nevertheless, if they are important and essential, they must be learned and learned well. The only way they can be learned is through the process of indoctrination — the acquisition of authoritative values without reflection or discrimination.

Selection and discrimination, of course, are necessary in deciding what social values are desirable, but this function is a responsibility of the educational authorities. It is the function of parents, teachers, and leaders in all social institutions, even the ministers of the church, to indoctrinate those whom they guide and direct with authoritative values. Practical conditions involving the capacity of individuals to meet these demands are irrelevant considerations in determining the ends to be sought. Everyone must learn the same things so far as possible. The indoctrinators, however, do not agree among themselves as to what elements of the past are desirable, much less as to what elements are essential. Consequently, any program of indoctrination involves the acceptance of some standard or criterion of selection.

2. As everyone knows, education is often used as a means of maintaining, safeguarding, and extending the interests of certain social groups. Since the ways of life of various groups are different, the social values with which they wish to indoctrinate their members are different. Social groups may fail to formulate deliberately any values at all, but, nevertheless, they seek to realize values in terms of changes in the thoughts, feelings, and actions of the members of their group as well as of members of the larger society. The formal disciplinarians in the past openly advocated strengthening the mental powers or faculties of the mind as their educational ideal, but actually they indoctrinated the young with conceptions that were favorable to the aristocratic class to which they belonged. The Herbartians would perhaps have been the last to say that they favored any particular social group, but the social conceptions with which they indoctrinated people often represented the interests and concerns of the so-called merchant class.

Those who today advocate the adjustment of individuals to the spiritual environment select for subject matter those elements of the spiritual environment whose study is expected to contribute most to the promotion of the interests of the social group that they represent. They advocate a balanced selection from the fields of science, art, and the social studies and typically use as criteria of selection the values advocated by the political and religious groups for whom they are consciously or unconsciously the spokesmen. Those who advocate spiritual adjustment through the use of the best books of their own selection as the core curriculum in the colleges use as their criteria of selection values that promote the interests of the social group that they represent. Those who advocate spiritual adjustment through conformity to the dogmas prescribed by the church use as their criteria of selection the values prescribed by their church. Those who advocate the adjustment of the individual to political demands of the state employ as criteria of selection the values that are thought to promote some dominant political group. Perhaps the best exemplification of indoctrination for political ends in modern times is that of Nazi Germany. But indoctrination has been openly advocated in all totalitarian states. The representatives of the so-called scientific movement in education who advocate the scientific determination of the aims of education, whether conceived in terms of skills or ideals, may unconsciously be adopting the values of the "economic royalists" whose interests require an abundance of loyal and efficient workers.

Besides these economic, religious, cultural, and political classes there are other occupational, civic, and professional groups which advocate indoctrination and which seek to socialize the people through indoctrination. Certain convictions and beliefs these groups wish to have developed and extended in the minds and hearts of men everywhere. Other convictions and beliefs they wish to undermine and destroy. They are not willing to let every belief and conviction compete with conflicting views, and thus be subjected to discussion and experimentation. Such groups, therefore, seek to indoctrinate for the kind of socialization they advocate and against the kind of socialization they reject.

The methods of indoctrination are many and varied. Various groups may indoctrinate and support legislation for the purpose of preserving freedom of the press, freedom of speech, or freedom of teaching. Some groups seek either by legislation or by social pressure to have certain possible social doctrines taught in the schools, and try to prevent the teaching of other viewpoints. Many individuals belonging to these groups are interested in formulating and making known their views to other people, but in their effort to get their values adopted they are unwilling to take unfair advantage of groups holding different views. They are not willing to engage in mere propaganda and indoctrination to achieve their ends. The tendency of many groups, however, is to seek in every way possible to circulate certain ideas and to prevent the circulation of other ideas. Such groups object to the teaching of some conceptions and advocate the teaching of others. They advocate the use of books that emphasize certain religious, political, and economic doctrines, and urge the elimination of ideas that support competing doctrines. They are continually worrying over what ideas teachers hold and what ideas they teach. They do not think socialization is the right kind unless it consists of indoctrinating people with certain conceptions and beliefs and eliminating all conflicting viewpoints.

3. However, most of those in democratic countries who advocate doctrinaire sociality as a principle do not do so in the name of any group interest. Perhaps most of them are influenced by the values cherished by many social groups. They are not supporting indoctrination deliberately as a means of advancing the interests of any particular class of society. They are advocating it rather as an indispensable means of promoting the general welfare. They are often opposed to indoctrinating children and youth with the convictions of special groups, and advocate indoctrinating them with convictions common to all groups. In other words, they are seeking to inculcate not merely beliefs that they think will serve the best interest of all groups, but rather the beliefs that are common to all groups.

Indoctrination of youth with values cherished by society as a whole is the kind of program usually advocated by recognized students of education. According to one approach, some set of authoritative objectives, aims, or values supplied by some authoritative individual, committee, or commission should be used as the basis for the program of indoctrination. According to another approach, the values common to a number of authoritative groups should be used.

There are many authoritative formulations of objectives, aims, or purposes of education, any one of which may be considered the proper basis of indoctrination. The three best known of these consist of the Report of the Committee of the National Education Association for the Reorganization of Secondary Education in 1918; the Report of the Committee of the National Education Association on Socio-Economic Goals of America in 1934; and the Report of the Educational Policies Commission of the National Education Association in 1938. For the convenience of some readers who may not be familiar with the values projected in these reports they are here briefly summarized.

The general objectives of education contained in the report of 1918 are as follows:

"*a*. Good health, including habits, understandings, and interests.

"*b*. Command of the fundamental processes, including those involved in reading, writing, arithmetical computations, and written and oral expression.

"*c*. Worthy home membership, involving the development of those qualities that make the individual a worthy member of a family, both contributing to and deriving benefit from that membership.

"*d*. Sound ethical character, involving the development, on the part of the pupils, of the sense of personal responsibility and initiative and, above all, of the spirit of service and the principles of true democracy.

"*e*. Good citizenship, involving the development in the individual of those qualities whereby he will act well his part as a member of the neighborhood, the town, the city, the state, and the nation, and those qualities that will give him a basis for understanding international problems.

"*f*. Worthy use of leisure time, involving the equipment of the individual to secure from his leisure recreation of body, mind, and spirit, and the enrichment and enlargement of his personality. ⸱

"*g*. Vocational fitness, involving equipment of the individual to secure a livelihood for himself and for those dependent upon him, to maintain the right relationships toward his fellow workers and society, and, as far as possible, to find in a vocation his own best interest." [1]

The general goals contained in the report of 1934 are as follows:

"*a*. Hereditary strength, involving the existing cultural influences on mating, and conscious control of reproduction instituted in such a way as to increase constantly the percentage of our people who are 'well-born,' and thereby to raise the average level of innate capacity.

"*b*. Physical security, involving the conservation and development of the superior innate capacities with which children are born.

"*c*. Participation in an evolving culture, involving (1) command of those skills that will enable the individual to use and enjoy, to the limit of his capacities, the culture of the group; and (2) provision by society for the proper derivation and utilization of values, standards, and outlooks in the enrichment of life.

"*d*. An active, flexible personality, motivated by intelligently chosen purposes, not by unguided impulse from within or casual pressure from without; capable of readapting flexibly to social change and to consequences of previous conduct; and disposed to express the individual differences in social ways.

"*e*. Suitable occupation, involving guidance, training, placement, and advancement.

"*f*. Economic security, involving the provision and employment of adequate devices and agencies.

---

[1] John P. Wynne, *The Teacher and the Curriculum*. Prentice-Hall, Inc., New York, 1937. Pp. 68–70.

"*g*. Mental security, involving bringing pure truth within reach of individuals in every case where non-social agencies are interested in hoodwinking them.

"*h*. Equality of opportunity, involving an equal chance for each to attain his fullest possible development; equality in rights and powers of the citizens to participate in the benefits of government and other institutions of society; equality in educational opportunities; and equality of opportunity to live a healthy, happy, satisfying life.

"*i*. Freedom, involving freedom of choice of mate, choice of occupation, movement of place of residence, manner of life, and choice of industrial, political, religious, and cultural affiliations; and the agitative liberties, such as freedom of speech, of the press, of the screen, etc., and freedom in research, in experimentation, and in teaching.

"*j*. Fair play, involving justice defined by the courts; sportsmanship of individuals constituting society; mutual respect for the rights of others, not only in the home and among neighbors but in the wider world society." [2]

The general purposes of education in American democracy proposed in the report of 1938 as goals to be approximated by every individual are designated as objectives. They are classified as follows:

a. The objectives of self-realization.

b. The objectives of human relationships.

c. The objectives of economic efficiency.

d. The objectives of civic responsibility.

The specific objectives into which the more general purposes are elaborated are stated as the traits of the educated person as conceived by the Commission:

a. From the standpoint of self-realization the educated person has an appetite for learning; can speak the native tongue clearly; reads the native tongue efficiently; writes the native tongue efficiently; solves his problems of counting and calculating; is skilled in listening and observing; understands the basic facts concerning health and disease; protects his own health and that of his dependents; works to improve the health of the community; is participant and spectator in many sports and pastimes; has mental resources for the use of leisure; appreciates beauty; and gives responsible direction to his own life.

b. From the standpoint of human relationships the educated person puts human relationships first; enjoys a rich, sincere, and varied social

---

[2] John P. Wynne, *The Teacher and the Curriculum*. Prentice-Hall, Inc., New York, 1937. Pp. 73–74.

life; can work and play with others; observes the amenities of social behavior; appreciates the family as a social institution; conserves family ideals; is skilled in homemaking; maintains family relationships.

c. From the standpoint of economic efficiency the educated person is both a producer and a consumer. As a producer he knows the satisfaction of good workmanship; understands the requirements of opportunities for various jobs; has selected his vocation; maintains and improves his efficiency; appreciates the social values of his work. As a consumer the educated person plans the economics of his own life; develops standards for guiding his expenditures; is an informed and skillful buyer; and takes appropriate measures to safeguard his interests.

d. From the standpoint of civic responsibility the educated person is sensitive to the disparities of human circumstance; acts to correct unsatisfactory conditions; seeks to understand social structures and social processes; has defenses against propaganda; respects honest difference of opinion; has regard for the nation's resources; measures scientific advance by its contribution to general welfare; is a co-operating member of the world community; respects the law; is economically literate; accepts his civic duties; and acts upon an unswerving loyalty to democratic ideals.[3]

Of course, the formulation of such values as are suggested in the foregoing brief summaries of three important authoritative reports does not in itself indicate that those who produce them or use them necessarily adopt the theory of doctrinaire sociality. All depends upon the way such objectives, aims, goals, or purposes are conceived and used. It is not always clear as to how they are conceived by those responsible for them. Doubtless, some members of such commissions and committees favor using standards to provoke suggestions and others favor using standards as ends to be achieved, goals toward which to direct educational policies, programs, and activities. Only this last attitude represents the theory of doctrinaire sociality. From this point of view, the only way that proper socialization can be realized is to have people accept social values that can be authoritatively determined outside actual educational situations.

There is no doubt that many people conceive of such reports as containing the values with which youth should be indoctrinated. For

---

[3] Educational Policies Commission, *The Purposes of Education in American Democracy*. National Education Association of the United States and the American Association of School Administrators, Washington, D. C., 1938. Pp. 47–123.

instance, the evidence contained in the report of the Educational Policies Commission cited above suggests the adoption of the principle of doctrinaire sociality. In the first place, the objectives are called "the purposes of education in American democracy," not merely some of the purposes. It is stated that these purposes are conceived as directives, since they "indicate the direction in which growth should occur" rather than the ends to be achieved by all. Nevertheless, it is made quite clear in the report that these objectives should be approximated. In other words, the only desirable education, the only desirable socialization, consists in moving toward the aims defined in this report. The administration, methods, materials, and testing procedures, so it is said, should be adjusted to contribute as much as possible to the realization of the ends proposed.[4]

Perhaps the outstanding evidence that the objectives into which the purposes of education are elaborated are conceived as values to be sought through indoctrination is suggested in the fact that all reference to the socio-economic goals proposed in the report of 1934 is neglected. Other formulations, including the formulation of 1918 and the analysis of several authoritative students of education, are considered. It is suggested that the analysis to be proposed by the Educational Policies Commission is similar to the preceding formulations. Only two explanations can be offered for the omission of references to the socio-economic goals proposed in the report of 1934. The members of the Policies Commission either were not acquainted with this report or else did not think that the points of emphasis it contained contributed anything to the analysis of the purposes proposed. The first explanation does not seem plausible, for the members of this commission certainly should have been acquainted with the earlier report. If the second explanation is correct, then it is quite apparent that the commission was unwilling to recognize the importance of the aims stated in this former report. Unless their own document is to be conceived as an instrument of indoctrination, why should no attention whatever be given to the socio-economic goals? It seems apparent that they did not recognize them as important. The socio-economic goals are different in important respects from the aims they are proposing. Indoctrination involves omission as well as inclusion. If the

---

[4] Educational Policies Commission, *The Purposes of Education in American Democracy*. National Education Association of the United States and the American Association of School Administrators, Washington, D. C., 1938. Pp. 127–128, 136–137, 146, 152–154.

purposes of education are not to constitute values with which youth is to be indoctrinated, emphasis on other conflicting purposes certainly should not be omitted.

Doubtless, sufficient evidence could be marshaled to prove that the values contained in the other two reports are conceived by some as directives in the process of socialization through indoctrination. But we have not been interested in proving the intention of the authors of any particular set of values with respect to indoctrination. We are not even interested in proving that any particular individual favors indoctrination. It is sufficient for our purposes if we have indicated that such authoritative reports may be conceived of as instruments of indoctrination. Insofar as they are thus conceived, these reports illustrate the theory of doctrinaire sociality.

When the three reports are considered together, the variations in emphasis are obvious and seem to require some explanation. In the report of 1918, the seven general objectives emphasize the defects in the economic, social, political, and educational situation to which the demands of World War I called the attention of educational leaders. The ten objectives in the report of 1934 emphasize the defects in the situation to which the economic depression beginning in 1929 called the attention of other educational leaders. The four purposes and their supporting objectives contained in the report of 1938 emphasize defects which the prevailing economic conditions, and the rise of totalitarian states and their challenge to democracy, called to the attention of still other educational leaders. Each of the three formulations emphasizes factors that are neglected by the others. If any one formulation is to be used alone as an instrument of indoctrination, then certain important points of emphasis will be neglected.

To overcome the foregoing difficulty, Professor Pittenger has proposed a second approach to the problem of indoctrination with values common to people of the United States. As he sees the situation, it is just as important for us to indoctrinate the youth of our country with "understandings, beliefs, and loyalties with respect to the basic and abiding principles of American Democracy" as it is for the totalitarian states to indoctrinate their people with understandings, beliefs, and loyalties with respect to the abiding principles of their way of life. Having accepted the principle of doctrinaire sociality with respect to common interests, Professor Pittenger is confronted with the problem of determining the understandings, beliefs, and loyalties to be used as a basis of indoctrination. He makes an intelligent approach to the problem with which he confronts himself. He seems to recognize the fact that a mere selection from various formulations of democratic values of those particular points of emphasis which seem to him most important would be eclectic in an undesirable sense. He therefore proposes to select the points of emphasis with respect to democracy contained in several of the more important authoritative statements. The four statements in which he finds these common factors are the report of the Educational Policies Commission to which we have already referred; the businessman's concept of democracy contained in a pamphlet by Philip D. Reed, Chairman of the Board of Directors of the General Electric Company; the concept of the more liberal group of educational and social leaders represented in the statement of George S. Counts in his *Dare the School Build a New Social Order;* and the "Manifesto" by members of the faculty of Teachers College, Columbia University.

Without examining here the four documents or the concepts which Professor Pittenger selects from them, for the purposes of comparison we shall state the conceptions which Professor Pittenger finds to be common to them all. He says: "Here, then, are suggestions of persistent basic principles of American democratic ideology which, if not exactly 'eternal virtues,' are universal in their applicability to all members of our society and apparently likely to continue so throughout the future. Democracy fundamentally respects the authority of truth rather than that of autocratic leaders or classes; it accepts compromise in the provisional adjustment of controversies to secure pragmatic ends; it believes in human equality as opposed to the fixed differentiations of hereditary castes, and it keeps open the avenues of progress for each individual citizen; it places the rights and responsibilities of individuals above those of any institution, including the state; it protects and aids individuals through proper provision for the general welfare; it accepts the principles of popular sovereignty and civil liberty; and it establishes the expansion and maintenance of human happiness as the criterion for judging the efficiency of social processes and institutions. Partisans of different ideal programs may interpret or weight these several concepts differently or they may give them different directions or applications; but none will take serious exception to any of them." [5]

The values of the democratic way of life thus proposed by Profes-

---

[5] Benjamin Floyd Pittenger, *Indoctrination for American Democracy.* The Macmillan Company, New York, 1941. Pp. 42–43.

sor Pittenger as a basis of indoctrination differ in important respects from the formulations of values contained in the reports of 1918, 1934, and 1938, to which we have referred. They are stated in more general terms. In fact, in the selection from the report of the Educational Policies Commission which he uses in comparing the four different statements, Professor Pittenger considers only the general principles of democracy stated in the document as a basis of the purposes and objectives to be defined rather than the more specific formulations themselves. He is interested in teaching general principles rather than in working toward specific ends definable in terms of concrete ways of behaving. Doubtless, common agreements as to the meaning of democracy must be stated in general terms if they are stated at all. Consequently, much latitude is left to those who subscribe to this program of socialization through indoctrination. In this respect Professor Pittenger's program has considerable advantage over other proposals. It also has the advantage of representing a wider consensus.

Nevertheless, even Professor Pittenger himself anticipates and answers the following objections to his plan of indoctrination: (1) American democracy does not have any significant ideology; (2) the growing child should be freed from all crystallizing adult influences; (3) indoctrination for democracy is just one form of necessary and desirable indoctrination; and (4) if the schools engage in indoctrination for democracy, they will inevitably engage in forms of undesirable indoctrination. Doubtless most people would agree with Dr. Pittenger's argument that American democracy does have a significant ideology, and that adults are responsible for the guidance, direction, and control of children. But there are many who are unable to agree with his argument in answering the last two objections to the effect that support of American ideals of democracy requires indoctrination.

In fact, some would insist that the freedom of intelligence, whether or not it is included in any consensus that may be secured from whatever source, is itself an ideal of democracy and any program of indoctrination contradicts the ideal of the freedom of intelligence. Of course, it may be said that the principles of democracy are so general and liable to so many interpretations and applications that the methods of indoctrination which they require emphasize rather than minimize the importance of intelligence as an aspect of the educative process. The rejoinder of those who oppose indoctrination of any kind is that wherever freedom of intelligence is recognized as an essential aspect of the educative process, indoctrination is impossible. Like other sets of aims or values, the ideals of democracy, such as those proposed by Professor Pittenger, may or may not be used as a basis of indoctrination. In fact, they may serve the useful purpose of supplying desirable emphases to which those entrusted with educational responsibility should be sensitive. When such ideals of democracy are used so as to emphasize intelligence, they should by all means be used along with other formulations of aims; but when so used, they are not instruments of indoctrination. When they are used as instruments of indoctrination, they disregard the importance of intelligence; thus, the process of indoctrination in the so-called ideals of democracy is itself undemocratic.

4. Indoctrination of any kind may be conceived of as a method of facilitating human progress. Even indoctrination for the conservation of the past may be considered as a means of progress. If the young learn the essential elements of civilization, they should be better prepared to cross the frontiers of civilization and make their own special contribution to the advancement of human culture. Certainly, if indoctrination for class interests may be conceived as promoting the progress of the group, then indoctrination for the common interest may be conceived as promoting the progress of society as a whole. But indoctrination for the facilitation of social progress is conceived in a somewhat different way from the types of indoctrination that have been considered. It is not merely progress that is to be sought, but the speeding up of progress. The promotion of group interests and of common interests may contribute considerably to progress, but those who emphasize speeding up progress have in mind making a new society quickly according to their own design. They are not satisfied to bring the young up in the tradition of their fathers; to teach them to do the things better that they will do, anyway; or to base the objectives of education upon demands which arise from other social institutions. In other words, the school is not to follow society but is to lead society. Its primary function is to build a new social order in accordance with ideals of the teaching profession, which has the interest of society at heart and a vision of the new world that may be brought and should be brought into existence through education.

The following quotation is from Professor Peters, who may be considered one of the scientific advocates of indoctrination as a method of facilitating human progress: "Our first step is to get a blueprint of the individual of the society we want — a detailed picture of the good citizen, the man of culture, the vocationally efficient person, etc. — indicating the specific ideals, skills, bodies of information, attitudes of mind, prepared judgments, abilities to reason, which are needed for getting on in his life. Our second step is, then, by using such instrumentalities as school subjects, discipline, and example as tools, to forge out individuals to conform to these blueprints. . . . We may as well recognize that one of the inevitable implications in the present trend of educational theory is indoctrination. The problems the individual will face in life are what they are, and one must become prepared to meet them as they exist. The individual needs, therefore, certain bodies of information and certain skills and perspectives and attitudes if he is to fit effectively into the world in which he will live. His training, if it is to be effective, must be directed toward these ends. . . .

"It is the business of the teacher to manipulate the learner's thinking, to lead him quickly against the snags toward which the false element of his notions will ultimately carry him, and to help him more speedily to swing into those currents of truth into which he would otherwise be destined to be drawn after long and costly fumbling. To start, thus, with the present interests and outlooks of the pupils and to manipulate these constantly and covertly toward ends that are known to be right, is one of the most delicate and challenging functions of a teacher. . . .

"It is well to remember that if we do not ourselves assume the responsibility of determining, by manipulation, what ideals children shall come to approve, they will get indoctrination from other sources — from the street, perhaps. They *will* be indoctrinated; all education must inevitably take the form of indoctrination, either by self or others, by the far-sighted or the foolish, since all education consists in a set of preadjustments for meeting the problems of life. . . .

"In order, therefore, to plan a functioning education we need to know what the preadjustments are that the individuals in question will need in order that we may make the attainment of them the objectives of this education. That necessitates 'blueprinting' the outcomes we want, just as the mechanical engineer blueprints the house or the electric transformer he wishes to build." [6]

The following quotation from Counts may be taken as representative of the more philosophical of the liberal group who think of indoctrination as a method of facilitating social progress. He says: "If the schools are to be really effective, they must become centers for the building, and not merely for the contemplation, of our civilization. This does not mean that we should endeavor to promote particular

---

[6] Charles C. Peters, *Objectives and Procedures in Civic Education.* Longmans, Green and Company, New York, 1940. Pp. 21–26.

reforms through the educational system. We should, however, give our children a vision of the possibilities which lie ahead and endeavor to enlist their loyalties and enthusiasms in the realization of the vision. Also our social institutions and practices, all of them, should be critically examined in the light of such a vision." [7]

The emphasis in both quotations is on the construction of a new social order according to specifications projected by educators. There is no intention in either case to neglect existing conditions. They are to be considered in the new society to be projected in imagination. It is a society that does not represent the narrow interests of special classes and groups. It is the social order that only the professional educator, free from the control of narrow interests, is able to conceive.

It appeals to those who recognize the dangers immanent in much of the so-called progressive education, which, to them, seems to be drifting from one thing to another without any clearly defined goals. They see the need for some standard of direction. They do not see how such a standard can be found in the spontaneous impulses of children and youth in which many teachers and some recognized students of education seem to be placing their faith. Furthermore, this conception of a new society, whether it can be definitely blueprinted, as the more scientific students of education believe, or merely stated in general principles, as the more philosophical believe, seems to supply not only a basis of progress in society as a whole, but also a means of efficiency and achievement in practical situations. It signifies the elimination of much lost motion. Children and youth are going to be indoctrinated, anyway, so it is contended by agencies outside the school. If the schools accept the principle of doctrinaire sociality, they can indoctrinate the pupils with the right values and thus counteract their inevitable indoctrination with the wrong values. Thus, much time and energy can be saved for the teacher and the learner. Moreover, all methods and procedures can be selected on the basis of their effectiveness in securing desired ends. Necessary knowledge and habits can be taught quickly, and, thus, the individual will have more opportunity to use his reflective capacities later. Indoctrination for the realization of a new social order, when clearly conceived, prevents forming habits in the wrong fields and developing procedures that must be eliminated, facilitates day-by-day achievement, relieves the mind from too much reflection on things that can

[7] George S. Counts, *Dare the School Build a New Social Order.* John Day Company, New York, 1932. P. 37.

be learned without it, and thus assures economy in action while moving toward clearly conceived ends that the teaching profession is best able to envision.

Perhaps a natural reaction of the reader to the foregoing consideration of doctrinaire sociality as an aspect of educational authoritarianism is that our discussion has been too general. What the reader wishes to know is what this theory of the sociality of experience means for him as a parent, citizen, community leader, teacher, or even as a person who assumes responsibility for his own educational development. For instance, the first impression of a member of the teaching profession may be that doctrinaire sociality is applicable to general policies and programs involving entire nations; that the individual or local group responsible for activities of limited scope in the schoolrooms of democratic countries like our own is quite beyond the reach of any systematic wholesale indoctrination; and that the individual teacher, administrator, or supervisor in local situations has little, if any, interest in the problem of indoctrination.

Such a natural response on the part of those responsible for educational activities is understandable. But the more general considerations pave the way for reference to things that seem more immediately and directly practical. Of course, indoctrination may represent a statewide policy of a nation and be used in all social institutions, as in the totalitarian states. But it can be adopted consciously by individuals and by groups in any field. Its application in the school illustrates its application in other fields and is of most concern to most teachers. We shall, therefore, give some attention to its implications with respect to certain features of school practice.

We have already seen that recognized authorities contend that people, especially youth, should be indoctrinated with some set of values that can be definitely stated. Now any school or unit of school administration may adopt such an authoritative set of aims and seek to use them as ends to which all activities of the school are to be directed. The adoption of such a policy assumes the validity of the theory of doctrinaire sociality. For instance, if the state department and local school systems adopt some such list of values as the Cardinal Principles, the Socio-Economic Goals, the Purposes of Education in American Democracy, build courses of study around them, and apply them directly or indirectly in the schools, they are observing the principle of doctrinaire sociality. If they formulate their own set of aims based upon the formulation of recognized authorities and available evidence from other sources, and cause every school to work toward these aims, they are still adopting the theory of doctrinaire sociality. They are not, to be sure, taking their aims ready-made from others, as in the case of those who adopt a single set of authoritative aims. But they are imposing their aims on the schools.

Any school staff which, in accord with the requirements of certain accrediting agencies, sets up its own aims may adopt the principle of doctrinaire sociality according to the way it uses these aims. If they are employed merely as means of causing the teachers to notice things that they would not otherwise notice, no imposition is necessarily involved; but if the teachers are expected to work toward the aims listed and none other, then indoctrination is involved. Even the teacher who sets up his own aims at the beginning of the year, or even at the beginning of the day, adopts the principle of doctrinaire sociality insofar as such a formulation renders him less sensitive to new points of emphasis that emerge in the actual process of operation. Any set of values that is formulated in advance of actual operations and used without modification involves indoctrination. Experience is too rich, deep, and meaningful in a changing world to be formulated completely at any place or time. New factors that cannot be taken into account in advance constantly emerge in the course of events. Any program that neglects the probability of such emergents assumes the theory of doctrinaire sociality.

The theory of doctrinaire sociality is often used as a basis of justifying academic freedom. According to some, the teacher is free only when he can state his own views and so maneuver the situation that they are accepted. But unless he adopts the principle of doctrinaire sociality, he cannot justify any effort to impose his views, either by the neglect of other views or by the overemphasis of his own. In fact, many teachers adopt the principle of doctrinaire sociality unconsciously. They do not mean to enforce their values upon other people but seem to do so in spite of themselves. Teachers with dominating and appealing personalities and teachers with strong convictions may enforce their values upon unsuspecting youth without any deliberate intention to do so. Insofar as pupils accept the beliefs of such teachers and instructors directly without thought, they are subjecting themselves to indoctrination. Those who sincerely emphasize the importance of the personality of the teacher as the most influential factor in the educative process may be subscribing to the principle of doctrinaire sociality. Insofar as the teacher imposes his own beliefs and reactions on his pupils through imitation and suggestion, he is adopting doctrinaire sociality as an operative principle.

Doubtless, the average individual is still puzzled about how indoctrination concerns him personally. As he sees the situation, the school officials are largely responsible for what goes on in the schools. He is mainly interested in looking out for himself and meeting his obligations as a citizen. Nevertheless, practically everyone is directly or indirectly involved in programs of indoctrination. In the first place, the responsible citizens of the community affect, according to the way they think about education, the activities of the schools and the educational influence exerted by other educational agencies of the community such as the home, the church, the local government, and business and industry. If the people of any given community look upon education as a process of indoctrination, the schools and other educational agencies must be influenced by this attitude.

In the second place, every one of us is constantly subjected to indoctrination policies and programs. Advertisers wheedle us daily over the radio and in the press. Politicians play down some ideas and play up others on almost every issue. Many publications promote special interests in a one-sided manner rather than publish impartially all available evidence or viewpoints on the problems being considered. Pressure groups are continually exerting their influence not only in legislation but on us and on our attitudes toward important social issues. In a word, propaganda is an agency of indoctrination, and most of us are subject to propaganda every day of our lives. Furthermore, most of us are inclined to look for evidence that supports our own prejudices and preconceptions. We attend the conferences, read the papers, and study the books that support our opinions. Insofar as our decisions are based upon insufficient information, suggestion, and imitation, we are adopting the theory of doctrinaire sociality in dealing with ourselves and supporting its use as an operative principle by all those who seek to influence the ideas, beliefs, and activities of others. Note how some daily papers, local weekly papers, even some college papers, resort to indoctrination, not only through the persons and things they emphasize, but through those they minimize; and note also how gullible people are taken in by what they read in print.

From the standpoint of the philosophy of experimentalism, this interpretation of sociality as a feature of educative experience must be rejected. As in the case of the principle of objective contingency, the quality of experience implicit in the operation of indoctrination is undesirable. The theory of doctrinaire sociality assumes the validity of the theory of objective contingency. It takes for granted that adequate controls of human conduct conceived as ways of behaving are fixed, stable, and certain. But the principle of objective contingency does not indicate what particular controls are desirable, or how they can be determined. It merely assures us that whatever changes are produced in individuals through experience must be determined by forces outside of him, and that when so determined and learned they are relatively permanent and enduring. While assuming that desirable ways of behaving are predetermined and fixed, the theory of doctrinaire sociality suggests a way of determining the content of the desirable ways of behaving. They are conceived not merely as any fixed controls of conduct but as those that are socially desirable.

According to the theory of doctrinaire sociality, the proper content of the aims or values to be learned must be determined on the basis of some particular frame of social reference. While the principle of objective contingency signifies that aims and values to be learned are determined outside of experience, the principle of doctrinaire sociality signifies that the aims and values that should be learned depend upon some particular frame of reference.

When the theory of doctrinaire sociality is thus expressed, policies, programs, and activities vary with the frame of reference which supplies the foundation for the determination of educational ends. Some find the frame of reference in the past, some in the present, and some in the future. Some find it in group interests and some find it in the general welfare. Consequently, in the development of any practical program there must be many conflicting opinions concerning what controls of conduct should be sought.

To overcome this difficulty, exponents of the theory of doctrinaire sociality have proposed plans for harmonizing the interests of all. According to one plan — that proposed by Professor Pittenger, which we have described — values common to the formulations of representatives of different social groups should be used as the basis of indoctrination. According to another plan, the teaching profession, which in reality represents the interests of all classes of society, should formulate the values with which the coming generation is to be indoctrinated.

The effective safeguard of education against indoctrination for group interests which these plans are designed to achieve is commendable. It is certainly not desirable to shape the minds and hearts of youth to serve the interests of any particular social group without reference to other groups. It does seem that the values held in common by all groups should be a primary consideration in any educational program.

On the other hand, it is not at all clear that either of the proposed plans could be so applied as to secure a set of democratic values with which our people should be indoctrinated. Indoctrination, as defined by experimentalists, consists of any method by which the learner accepts, without intelligent discrimination, certain ideals, beliefs, or standards and continues to hold them as reliable even under changed conditions.

From the standpoint of the philosophy of experimentalism, no such set of permanent and enduring values, which should be accepted on faith and retained intact without further critical examination, can be derived through discovering the common elements of existing formulations. To insist that only ideals common to certain authoritative reports and statements are the primary values of democracy does not leave any room for the incorporation of new values or for the use of intelligence on the part of the individual in practical situations. The ideals of democracy cannot be confined to fixed standards simply because many recognized groups subscribe to them. The acceptance of and devotion to such standards without intelligent discrimination as an aspect of the process through which they are acquired is undemocratic.

If we confine ourselves to a vision of a new society that is to be built through education, such as Peters and Counts propose, there is still considerable difference as to the kind of social order that is either possible or desirable. According to the educational scientist, the nature of the new society can be blueprinted in considerable detail, while according to the more philosophical members of this group, it can be envisaged only in general outline. Which program shall we follow? Shall we try to take factors from both groups? How shall we tell what factors to select? We are thus drawn into eclecticism in the objectionable sense inasmuch as we are not supplied with any standards of value by which to select the desirable elements from the conceptions of the different groups that seek to build a new social order. Authoritative students of education are subject to new visions and continue to make new analyses as conditions change. If they are able to modify their lists of values with which they would have their peoples indoctrinated, it seems that such values are not fixed. If they use intelligence and discrimination in the selection of the proposed ends of education, why cannot those directly responsible also use intelligent discrimination in the selection of their ends? Any educational program which does not encourage the exercise of intelligence and discrimination is undemocratic, even when its proposed ideals are derived from the vision of a new social order. Any program which does encourage the exercise of discrimination and intelligence is not a program of indoctrination. In other words, indoctrination and democracy are incompatible conceptions.

At this point, the question naturally arises as to what is the difference between this approach to socialization and that followed in totalitarian states. Of course, it may be said that the new social order to be projected by the teaching profession in this country is based upon democratic ideals. But here again the conception of what constitutes democratic ideals in the sense of controls of conduct, or in the sense of a set of general conceptions and loyalties, is not at all clear. The spokesmen for totalitarian states often contend that the new society which they have projected is the only real democracy and that the values with which they seek to indoctrinate the people are the only real democratic values.

Another objection to the program of indoctrinating the rising generation with any particular conceptions of a new social order is that it involves an attitude toward change that seems to contradict the facts of experience. For instance, any set of educational values that might be used as a basis of indoctrination soon becomes obsolete. A fixed set of educational aims represents the interests of some particular temporal and geographical situation. The cardinal principles or aims contained in the report of 1918 of the National Education Association Committee for the Reorganization of Secondary Education represent points of emphasis which emerged in this country during World War I; the goals or aims of the 1934 report of the NEA Committee on the Socio-Economic Goals for America represent points of emphasis which emerged during the great depression; and the purposes or aims of education in American democracy contained in the NEA Educational Policies Commission's report of 1938 represent points of emphasis which emerged in consequence of the pressure which the totalitarian states, through their propaganda agencies supported by military preparations during the years following Hitler's rise to power in Germany, were exerting against the ideas, beliefs, and loyalties of the way of life so long taken for granted in democratic countries. Any such formulation of values seems to represent no permanent or enduring characteristics of the world, of nature, or of society in the past, present, or future. It merely represents the reaction of more sensitive individuals and groups against some prevailing social situation.

However, this constant change in social values suggests a very serious objection to indoctrination of any kind. With the acceleration of change in the social scene, change in the social values and in their formulation should become increasingly rapid. By the time an indoctrination program is instituted for the imposition of one set of values, recognized educational leaders will have envisaged a different kind of social order and a new program will have to be instituted. Those who have been indoctrinated with one vision of a social order must have this vision blotted out and be subjected to indoctrination to establish beliefs in and loyalties to a new vision of another social order. Of course, it may be insisted that the values perceived in the various visions contain many elements in common. This observation is true enough. But the constant variation is the main thing. If conditions change — and they do — the system of indoctrination must lead to conflicts in society and in the minds and hearts of individuals. Indoctrination can be effective only where conditions remain practically the same over long periods of time.

Again, it may be pointed out that indoctrination is successful in the totalitarian states, which indoctrinate with one set of ideas and values during one year — even during one month — and then shift to another set. From one point of view, this program of indoctrination has proved successful. Hitler could hold Russia off while he tried his hand on England. When conditions changed he could lead his people against the "Communist menace." All he had to do was to shift the emphasis in his program of indoctrination. But it remains to be seen how such flexible policies of indoctrination will finally work out. The people may be trained to do as they are told, but the desirability of the effect of such constant shifts in conceptions and beliefs is doubtful. Furthermore, this kind of success is not contemplated in any of the programs designed for the indoctrination of youth with the ideals of democracy.

Unless we resort to more imposition than the exponents of doctrinaire sociality in democratic countries contemplate, no program of indoctrination in the ways of democracy is practical. The points of emphasis embodied in any formulation of social values should be taken into account in educational policies, programs, and activities. In a democracy a program designed to indoctrinate with one set of aims cannot be readily revised in order to indoctrinate with another set, as in the totalitarian states. Moreover, the changes in points of emphasis incorporated in each successive formulation of social ideals do not emerge suddenly. They are formulated for general use long after they have emerged in the experience of the people. It seems necessary, then, for teachers and pupils in practical situations to incorporate these emerging values in their activities long before they are incorporated in authoritative formulations.

As we have already noted, the operation of the principle of objective contingency generates for a time a sense of security, faith, trust, and assurance on the part of the people. Those who learn what they conceive to be right ways of thinking, feeling, and acting do not have to worry. Such a feeling of security in a world crumbling around us has its appeal. But the application of the theory of doctrinaire sociality is designed to give the leaders who are responsible for the programs of indoctrination some feeling of security. They decide the ends to be sought through indoctrination. The values to be imposed upon the people are all-important. If the leaders have the responsibility of selecting the values to be imposed, they can of course be certain that they teach the right things. They surely will impose, if they can, the ideas and sentiments that support the common interests, the general welfare, or the vision of a new social order. The operation of the principle of objective contingency gives people some feeling of security; the operation of the principle of doctrinaire sociality gives the leaders some sense of security.

Of course, the sense of security, trust, and confidence cannot be absolute for those who rely on authority, whether conceived in terms of custom and tradition, rules and regulations, or fixed ideas and beliefs deliberately selected. Experience involves both the individual and his environment, and occurrences in the latter that contradict established convictions and beliefs often lead to doubt and skepticism on the part of some, possibly on the part of all, in the course of events that vary widely from the usual. Changes in environment are embodied in experiences. When things are learned as fixed, the sense of security endures, at least for the multitude, so long as conditions change gradually and imperceptibly. But a day is sure to come when the cumulative effect of continuous and undetermined change will reveal itself. The sense of security which has enabled many to rest easy while the world is crumbling around them suddenly vanishes when they realize that destruction is impending. Some in whom authoritative values have been most securely fixed preach the old ideas and convictions with renewed energy. Others who suddenly sense the impending doom become frantic, and, having lost all sense of security, fear everything — even "fear itself." Those who, in spite of all the impositions of authority, whatever they may be, have preserved their own individuality and selected their own values and beliefs, now have the difficult and possibly the impossible task of getting the reactionaries, who preach the old convictions and beliefs with renewed energy, to see things as they are, and the equally difficult task of keeping the disillusioned blind followers from adopting any new set of beliefs with which opportunists may seek to indoctrinate them. People in general, having lost faith in the old standards, are prepared to attach themselves with equal devotion to the objectives of any new vision to which their attention may be directed. There is a vast difference between a sense of safety and security and the reality of safety and security.

The oscillation between faith and confidence and skepticism and despair — which must arise in a changing world in consequence of the operation of the principle of objective contingency in the minds and hearts of the people — shakes the confidence of the powers that be in the effectiveness of any particular application of the theory of doctrinaire sociality. They sense the oscillation of people between confidence and despair. They themselves realize that the fixed concepts and beliefs which they have generated in the minds of people through indoctrination are no longer tenable. Their only recourse is to change the ideas and beliefs that are to serve as a basis of indoctrination. They do not sense that the theory of indoctrination may be wrong in principle; they are committed to the theory of doctrinaire sociality. They change their set of values to which allegiance and devotion are to be attached through imposition, but they do not for a moment consider the possibility of any procedure other than that of indoctrination through which fixed ideas and beliefs are imposed upon those whom they guide and direct. The devotees of doctrinaire sociality attribute the unsatisfactory results arising from indoctrination to the values employed in indoctrination and not to indoctrination itself. But although the theory of indoctrination is still maintained, the faith of leaders themselves in the stability of any values must be eventually lost. Eventually, too, the faith of the people in their leaders must break down.

We have had ample evidence of the operation of the principle of doctrinaire sociality in both Europe and America during the last generation. In this country, educational agencies — including the school, the home, the church, the state, and business and industry — have indoctrinated people with a conception of the federal constitution as a fixed set of inflexible rules contained in a written document; with the conception that any kind of debt, regardless of the conditions under which it was incurred, is a just obligation; with the conception that our national security depends upon the avoidance of entangling alliances; and with many other similar ideas and beliefs. Such conceptions embody important points of emphasis and are at least partly valid. But they have been learned as definite and fixed. They have not been learned in terms of the conditions which produced them. Consequently, it is next to impossible to modify such conceptions in the face of threatened economic disaster and military ruin. Many people thus indoctrinated will sacrifice all they have, even life itself, rather than change their minds. Those who can change their minds often have to face the dreadful words: "Too little and too late." Only an impending doom can shake us from our beaten paths. These paths reflect the operation of the principles of objective contingency and doctrinaire sociality in the nervous system.

It should, of course, be evident even to isolationists by this time that we had to face the danger of a national catastrophe as a result of not being ready to meet the challenge of Germany and Japan. But the exponents of doctrinaire sociality have not yet seen that our plight was due in part to indoctrination. As they see it, our whole trouble was that we had not indoctrinated our youth with the right ideas systematically enough, that we had not indoctrinated ourselves in the good old American democratic tradition. The fact is quite the contrary, however. We had indoctrinated ourselves with good old American ideas to such a degree that we could not discard them when they were no longer valid. The advocates of indoctrination propose now that we shall enter upon a new systematic program of imposing ideas, beliefs, and loyalties. They would include values other than the ones which we have cited above, to be sure. But they would teach these values as being good, right, and true, not to be questioned. If any objection is raised, their reply will be that the nations with whom we have been at war came to power through indoctrination. The obvious logic, they say, is that we should indoctrinate our people with values we wish them to believe and cherish, just as Hitler, for example, indoctrinated his people with the principles of national socialism.

If the advocates of this point of view were not so completely indoctrinated with the principle of doctrinaire sociality, they would be able to see that our economic and political difficulties in recent years have been the outcome of a long period of indoctrination, and the result of the blind adoption of certain values as fixed. It is doubtful, however, if the situation would have been much improved had people been indoctrinated with any other set of values. A good, actually experienced, is unique. Values generated under one set of conditions do not endure forever without modification. Any set of values with which our people might have been indoctrinated would have become obsolete by this time.

Even some of the beliefs with which the people of democratic countries were indoctrinated during World War II became obsolete with the unconditional surrender of our enemies. Many ideas and beliefs which our people had to be taught in order to prepare them to fight the Germans and the Japanese could not have been used prior to the war as a basis of indoctrinating the youth who brought the Axis powers to their knees. Such ideas and beliefs did not then exist. Nevertheless, the youth of democratic countries who had been so inadequately indoctrinated have proved themselves more than a match for the most effectively indoctrinated youth the world has ever known. Many of the values with which we might now indoctrinate our youth, as well as those of the occupied countries, evolved during the war period. With the passing of the crisis and with the emergence of a new set of social conditions, we may expect new sets of social values to be formulated. Therefore, to indoctrinate our people or the peoples of the defeated countries with present, existing values would be to render them as incapable of dealing with a changing world as were their fathers, who have brought civilization close to death twice in a generation.

The fact seems to be that our embarrassment arose from the operation of certain of our fixed ideas and beliefs. But it was not a consequence of the content of these beliefs; it was a consequence of the way they were held. The way they were held was a consequence of how they were learned. They were learned as inherently true, right, and good. Any other set of values that could have been defined at any time in our history and deliberately imposed upon our people would have operated in the same way. Any set of values secured through the operation of the principles of objective contingency and doctrinaire sociality in any of their varied forms would have led to similar results. *Rigid ideas and beliefs, which are the only kind that can be imposed upon a people, must inevitably lead to dire consequences in a changing world.* If the early successes of the Axis powers were due partly to the effectiveness of indoctrination, as the authoritarians contend, then their ultimate defeat was also partly due to their effective indoctrination. If our early defeats were partly due to our ineffective indoctrination, our ultimate victory was partly due to this very same ineffective indoctrination.

There may be objections to the values used as a basis of indoctrination, but from the standpoint of the philosophy of experimentalism, indoctrination itself is always objectionable. Indoctrination is necessary in totalitarian states, but the social quality of experience thus fostered is undesirable. Whenever indoctrination is necessary to meet the requirements of a democratic country, that, too, will become totalitarian. Therefore, for any individual anywhere this quality of experience designated as doctrinaire sociality is not as desirable as some other social quality of experience.

From the standpoint of the philosophy of experimentalism, the problem of socialization is not how to indoctrinate people with democratic ideas, beliefs, and procedures, but how to provide the conditions for experiences pervaded with qualities that are as desirable from the standpoint of experience itself as the qualities of experience that totalitarian leaders have considered most desirable from the standpoint of the program of autocratic control. In the provision of these conditions all of us may have a part. The quality of flexibility implicit in the principle of functional contingency as an aspect of educational experimentalism has already been suggested. Perhaps some other interpretation of the feature of sociality will suggest other qualities of experience that seem more desirable from the standpoint of experience itself. To this problem we shall now devote our attention. In the meantime, we should try to avoid indoctrination in dealing with ourselves and with others.

THEORY OF INHERENT SOCIALITY
(EDUCATIONAL LAISSEZ FAIRE)

The proponents of educational laissez faire, the second philosophy of education here under consideration, identify sociality with desirable sociality, psychological sociality with ethical sociality. According to them, the process of socialization as it naturally occurs is socialization as it should occur. Therefore, the laissez-faire theory of sociality is here designated as *inherent sociality*. It is the exact opposite of the theory of doctrinaire sociality, which the authoritarians assume toward the same feature of experience. The adherents of both theories assume that socialization is an important consideration in the development of educational policies, programs, and activities, but they differ fundamentally with respect to the quality of experience that is socially desirable, and with respect to the way it may be secured.

As we have already indicated, the exponents of doctrinaire sociality think of socialization as a process of impressing upon people certain fixed social values authoritatively determined in advance. The exponents of inherent sociality, on the other hand, think that experiences which provide for the expression, realization, or actualization of the social impulses just as they occur are properly socializing.

Those who adopt in one form or another the theory of doctrinaire sociality seek to modify whatever inherent social qualities people already have so as to render them more satisfactory. They differ with one another as to the degree of sociality that is inherent and even as to whether there is such a thing as inherent sociality. But they are all agreed in principle that whatever sociality may in and of itself exist is insufficient. The proponents of inherent sociality, on the other hand, are content to let the social nature of man take its own course. To them the quality of sociality that, without cultivation, control, or direction, pervades the experience of all of us is in essence just what it should be. From this point of view, the duty of those who assume responsibility for influencing human beings is to provide an opportunity for the inherent quality of sociality to unfold, to develop, and to realize or actualize itself without constraint, obstruction, or hindrance.

The fact that an individual has potentialities of desirable sociality does not mean that he will certainly actualize or realize them. Much depends upon his environment. Those who are in control of the environment determine the degree to which stimuli are available for use in the development of the inherent potentialities of the individual. At the same time, however, these potentialities or predispositions themselves indicate the nature of the environment required. It is the duty of those in control to determine the direction social impulses are taking and to provide for them the subject matter they require for their expression and development.

Among the many characteristics which some biologists, psychologists, and sociologists have described, classified, and explained as native, or hereditary, some are social in quality. Among the more important of these social characteristics are imitation, gregariousness, co-operation, play, altruism, and sympathy. Those who assume that nature is good, right, and perfect in all respects until contaminated by the artificialities of civilization contend that these tendencies should be given freedom of opportunity to develop along with other native tendencies that are also good, such as acquisitiveness, constructiveness, pugnacity, and competition. From this viewpoint, apparently every innate tendency is good and constitutes not only the proper means but also the proper end of all social programs. The social quality of experience is desirable to the extent that every trait is given an opportunity for its freest and fullest development. Those who assume that human nature as a whole is neither good nor bad, right nor wrong, but contains some good tendencies as well as some bad ones, seek to root out the bad and preserve the good. They seek to give special opportunity to such tendencies as imitation, co-operation, play, sympathy, and altruism. Adequate development of these tendencies should, so it is thought, counteract the effect of the antisocial tendencies, such as the instincts to fight and to compete. But desirable sociality is inherent in human nature and needs only an opportunity to realize itself in experience.

From the standpoint of the philosophy of experimentalism, there are tremendous theoretical difficulties involved in the position of those who seek the actualization of inherent sociality through either the indiscriminate or the selective development of human propensities. In the first place, the existence of innate tendencies in any individual is now a controversial issue in the field of biology and psychology; the old notion of hereditary patterns finds little support in current studies in the field of genetics. The so-called instincts that have been defined and classified by psychologists and recommended by students of education as the means of motivating schoolwork are now considered as embodying environmental as well as hereditary factors. In other words, the so-called native tendencies, including those which are basal to any inherent sociality, are the result of the interaction of the individual with his environment. Many of the so-called instincts represent, in part at least, the effects of living in certain kinds of environment. To assume that any instinctive tendency is desirable mainly because it exists and then to seek to develop it is, in the last analysis, equivalent to seeking to maintain the existing social arrangements without modification.

The so-called instincts are not necessarily desirable human qualities; they are the qualities produced in social situations that have prevailed over long periods of time. What is true of the so-called native tendencies in general is also true of any particular tendencies in which inherent sociality may be supposed to reside. Any social policy or program, political, economic, religious, or educational, that assumes the desirability of the sociality inherent in native tendencies may turn out to be environmental and reactionary rather than naturalistic, progressive, or romantic, as at first sight it may seem to be.

The practical difficulties of those who seek to develop particular tendencies, such as imitation, gregariousness, play, and co-operation, are almost insurmountable. For instance, imitation, as everyone knows, is neither good nor bad, whether it be learned or unlearned. People should not, even if they are disposed to do so, imitate everything they perceive. By doing so they would place themselves on the same level of intelligence as the monkey, said to be the most imitative of animals. Likewise, gregariousness, whether instinctive or not, cannot be desirable in itself, however important getting together in numbers may be under certain circumstances and conditions. Even co-operation in the abstract without regard to its native or acquired features, without reference to consequences, is not desirable. Men co-operate for undesirable as well as for desirable ends. Playing, of course, whatever its basis in human nature may be, is good, but there are times to work as well as times to play, and mere play as it is manifested in the young is not as consistently and positively educational as it may be when subjected to organization and direction. Altruism itself, conceived by some as the one tendency whose operation supplies adequate balance and direction to the more individualistic tendencies, degenerates into mere sentimentalism when it is left without guidance and control. We are thus forced to conclude that inherent sociality, whether it is conceived as residing in human nature as a whole or in certain social tendencies, is neither theoretically nor practically desirable.

The theory of inherent sociality seems to be exemplified in the disposition of many people to neglect in their activities, policies, and programs recognized social standards. All of us are acquainted with people who neglect the accepted customs, courtesies, and amenities of social life. Some of them do so because they have never learned any better. They have simply been brought up under conditions where only very limited social standards prevail. They are not aware of the fact that in conversation, in dress, or in table manners, they are offensive, disagreeable, and discourteous. Others neglect those things deliberately and congratulate themselves on being different and superior. They are not only self-conscious, but also self-righteous. They not only refuse to conform to customary morals, manners, and courtesies, but look upon those who do conform to them as mere slaves to artificialities that are without foundation. They take pride in following their impulses and inclinations, whether or not their activities meet with social approval. Some may go so far as to feel that whatever is customary must be wrong, and they try to be different.

The desirability of the social quality inherent in such practices is questionable to say the least. If desirable sociality were inherent, people who are lacking in wide social experience would be able to adjust themselves readily to all social demands that confront them. But, as a matter of fact, all of us know people who do and say things that are positively annoying and disgusting to their friends without ever sensing that anything is wrong.

From the standpoint of the philosophy of experimentalism, those who disregard the customs and ways of what to them are the artificialities of civilization are confronted with almost insurmountable difficulties. Reliance only on native impulses as the standard of right and wrong is not sufficient. In the last analysis, those impulses may not, in fact probably do not, reflect original human nature. Rather they may reflect habits that have been formed under conditions of a narrow and limited social life. Such impulses may bring people in conflict with standards that cannot be readily flaunted with impunity. Impulses may be good, right, and effective under prescribed conditions where the habits and customs which support them were formed, but in the larger life of society they are bad, wrong, and ineffective. The pride of the nonconformists and the self-righteous does not guarantee security in this world or salvation in the next. It represents a kind of intellectual rationalization of conduct that is impractical in the world of human affairs. The social quality of such activities is not inherent in human nature and any principle in which they find intellectual justification is inadequate.

The theory of inherent sociality also seems to be exemplified in the tendency of certain people to avoid taking a public position on important social issues. All of us are acquainted with individuals who seem to be constitutionally opposed to stating their position in regard to social problems. They question others about their positions but never state their own convictions. In matters of practical public concern, some are not even willing to vote their convictions, while others wait to see what the general will may be and cast their vote with the majority. Such an attitude may find justification in one of two assumptions. First, it is easier and second, statement of conviction leads to indoctrination, which, to those who adopt the principle of inherent sociality, is a vicious doctrine.

From the standpoint of the philosophy of experimentalism, such an attitude is faced with objections. There is no reason to believe that the majority is always right, and the statement of convictions need not involve indoctrination. If one is such a social conformist that he fears to be different and must always seem to agree with the crowd, he cannot make any contribution to the solution of important social problems. Moreover, one individual is just as much a member of the group as any other. If everyone waited to see what stand others take, judgment, conclusion, and action would be impossible. The disposition to entertain only such ideas and have only such convictions as are immediately acceptable to one's fellows may be inherent in some individuals, but in practice it cannot be regularly desirable. There may be times when it is more expedient to conform without doing any damage to a cause, but there are other times when it is more expedient as well as more important to take a stand. Merely to follow the crowd in public is a vicious policy that undermines the character of the individual and prevents those interested in improving social life from rendering the help they might. It is possible to be sensitive to the ideas and feelings of others without endorsing them. Those who are so inherently social that they cannot bear to disagree do not demonstrate the desirability of the quality of inherent sociality. Such a quality, if it exists, is undesirable when it assumes the form of mere social conformity.

If there is one thing that our social institutions need more than any other, it is people with convictions who are capable of expressing them and unafraid to do so. The tendency in many quarters to endorse any point of view merely to save energy and conform to the opinions of authorities or of the public is dangerous. People often think what others think, do what others do, and believe what others believe. Often they pretend to conform when they have no thought or disposition one way or the other. They simply are unconcerned and follow the course of least resistance, or seek ways by which they can seem intelligent and appreciative to incur popular favor. If the assumption that inherent sociality is desirable requires such conformity, it is a vicious doctrine, to say the least.

The assumption that it is necessary to refuse to take a position on important issues in order to avoid indoctrination is apparently without foundation in fact. The leaders in church, state, business and industry, labor, and education are not required to keep their minds to themselves so that other people can have minds of their own. In fact, one of the best ways to get people to think is to state propositions with which they agree or disagree about matters which are important to them. The more propositions about important social issues the better, provided that people are encouraged to analyze and appraise them without being obliged to take sides before having time to make up their minds. The great danger does not lie in having too many such propositions; it lies rather in having too few of them.

The same is true in the learning-teaching situation under school conditions. There is no reason whatever for the teacher to fear that stating properly his own position may result in indoctrination. In terms of education indoctrination means that the ideas, beliefs, and ways of behavior are prescribed in advance. At least, this is what it means in the minds of those who consider it objectionable. For a teacher to state his own conclusion to be used along with others is not indoctrination except under circumstances where pupils take the teacher's sayings as laws and his actions as models. When such a situation exists it is a result of something much more dominating than the teacher's exercise of his prerogative as a leader of the group. A remedy must be found in a more profound treatment than comes from the evasion of a statement of position or conviction on important issues.

The convictions of parents, friends, authors of textbooks, editors of papers, preachers, and speakers over the radio students may digest without any hindrance. If the teacher must refrain from taking a stand merely because his pupils may endorse it, then these other leaders should do likewise. But to bring about such a neutral attitude in the world of affairs is practically impossible. Any effort to remain neutral and without bias in writing textbooks — even textbooks on the philosophy of education — may for real, live men and women contribute more to indoctrination than would taking a public stand. One may produce an unjustifiable bias by unconsciously overweighting certain factors, neglecting others, and making suggestions without stating a position openly and above board. People in general and pupils in particular can deal with clear-cut propositions much more effectively than they can with relative emphases and concealed suggestions.

There is no foundation for the belief that the inherent social qualities of experience are immediately desirable. The theory of inherent sociality is one principle of the more inclusive point of view, which we have designated as educational laissez faire, that education is a process of development from within the individual. But, as we already have pointed out, such a conception represents a reaction to social conditions which are imposed from without. The native traits, whatever they may be, whether social or antisocial, do not constitute constructive standards of morals, education, and social policy in any field of human experience. When the theory of inherent sociality is assumed, it may easily slide to the left into irresponsibility and sentimentalism or to the right into the very indoctrination that it seeks to avoid, and thus become all the more vicious because it is often too subtle to be detected and therefore cannot easily be exposed.

THEORY OF WIDENING SOCIALITY
(EDUCATIONAL EXPERIMENTALISM)

In educational experimentalism, which is the philosophy of education the experimentalists themselves are developing, a third theory of sociality as a feature of experience is adopted. For convenience of reference, this attitude may be designated as *widening sociality*. It not only recognizes but emphasizes the difference between socialization as a psychological fact and desirable socialization. The social in a psychological sense is perhaps best illustrated by the different kinds of interaction that the experimentalists recognize.

Only interactions on certain levels may properly be called experiences. The levels of interaction that are most widely recognized are the physical, the vital, the mental, and the social. At just what level interactions become experience is unknown. Perhaps there are some aspects of experience present on the vital level, others on the mental level, and still others on the social level. These different levels are not separate; they are continuous, for one shades into the other somewhat in the same way that colors shade into one another when sunlight is analyzed by passing it through a prism. There may even be several sublevels in each general level. The social level may, for instance, include the slightly social, consisting of mere sensitivity to the presence of others, of the social in the ordinary sense with which we are all familiar, and even of the spiritual, in which one enters into communion with God. Nevertheless, there seems considerable reason to believe that the value of experience depends upon the number, variety, and complexity of associations and connections it involves. The decision that we have to make, then, is which level of experience involves the largest number, the widest variety, and the greatest complexity of associations and connections.

Perhaps the best way to render concrete the conception of the relationship of the different levels of experience is to define them in terms of a triangle. In the isosceles triangle below, certain allotments of space represent, respectively, the physical, the vital, the mental, and the social. Which allotment is most inclusive? The physical includes more space than the vital, the vital includes more space than the mental, and the mental includes more space than the social. In a quantitative sense, then, the social is the least inclusive of all levels of experience.

But in a qualitative sense the relative inclusiveness of the four levels of experience is reversed, the physical being the least inclusive and the

social the most inclusive. For instance, if we draw perpendiculars from the top of the sections of the triangle representing the four levels of interaction, it is clear that the one drawn from the top of the social to the base of the triangle is longer than any of the others, and in fact includes them all. An interaction, then, that includes activities that have physical, vital, and mental qualities as well as social, is, with respect to the number, variety, and complexity of associations and connections, of more value than those in which any one of the levels is excluded. The social includes the mental, but the mental does not include the social; the mental includes the vital, but the vital does not include the mental; the vital includes the physical, but the physical does not include the vital. From the standpoint of this analysis, the social is qualitatively the most inclusive level of experience, just as the physical is quantitatively the most inclusive level. However, we are here interested in the quality of experience which, when considered, will include a consideration of the other features.

A conception assumed in some quarters is that the physical is the most important level or category of experience. This physical and mechanical position, in so far as it is a reasoned theory, is based upon two considerations: one with respect to scope or inclusiveness, and the other with respect to the nature of cause and effect. According to the first considerations, the physical is more inclusive than the vital, the mental, or the social. There are more physical interactions than there are vital, mental, and social interactions combined. As we have already demonstrated, this much certainly must be admitted, for the physical is present not only at all levels of experience, but also in a wide realm of nature below the level of interactions that can properly be called experience. If we are thinking in quantitative terms and merely of the number of activities, each lower level includes the activities of each higher level. But from the standpoint of education we are not interested in mere quantity. We are not interested here in all kinds of interactions; we are interested only in experiences, and more particularly in those experiences which contain within themselves the most educative possibilities. There is a vast difference between the number and size of things and their quality. Social experiences from the standpoint of the number, variety, and complexity of associations and interactions are vastly more important than interactions or experiences in which the social is absent.[8]

According to the second consideration — the nature of cause and effect — the earlier event in any sequence of events is the cause of the event immediately following. And events must have some final and ultimate cause. From this point of view, the mental is more important than the social because it precedes it in the experience of the human race and also in the experience of the individual; the vital is more important than the mental because life precedes mind, biology precedes psychology, in the development of living things; finally, the physical is more important than the vital, which is supposed to have developed out of the physical at some distant time in some way yet unknown.

Although this position seems reasonable from the standpoint of causality as it is often understood, it is confronted with serious objections. In the first place, it seems to be in conflict with modern science. The scientist is primarily interested in determining the conditions under which certain events occur rather than in the problem of final causes. There is no first cause which does not require, in thought at least, some earlier cause, and this regression is endless. Furthermore, if the vital did emerge from the physical, it has nevertheless a quality of its own that is fundamentally different from the purely physical. The mental is likewise different in quality from the purely vital or from the purely physical; and the social, too, has its own distinctive quality. Each later level is qualitatively different from any preceding level and thus functions in a way that cannot be fully determined by any earlier stage of existence from which it may have

[8] John Dewey, *Philosophy and Civilization*. Minton Balch and Company, New York, 1942. Pp. 77–93.

emerged. Moreover, the conception of emergence is itself a theory and should not be taken as final. The assumption that the mental is derived from the vital or the physical signifies either that these later qualities are important on their own account, or that even the physical must have been in some sense more than physical. In other words, the quality of mentality must be different from the physical from which it is supposed to have emerged, either originally or since it emerged. If there is no difference between the functioning of the mental and the physical, there is no such thing as mentality. However, as we know, the mental is one factor of experience whose existence cannot be consistently denied, for such a denial is itself a mental fact. The distinctive quality on any level of existence, interaction, or experience is just as real as the distinctive quality on any other level. The social is just as real as the physical, and it is, from the standpoint of those interested in the quality of experience, much more important and significant.

Any objection to this recognition of the reality of distinctive qualities of existence and the attachment of importance to later levels as compared to earlier levels, on the ground that it represents an obsolete teleological conception, does not seem to hold. We are not insisting that earlier events are always caused by later ones, as have Aristotle, some scholastics, and certain exponents of objective idealism. Such a teleological conception, whether true or false, is irrelevant. Things may have final causes in the past or in the future, but to be things at all they must have their own qualities. We are merely contending that the later emergent does have its own peculiar function after it arises, no matter what the ultimate reality out of which it emerges. In being the latest and most inclusive emergent, the social represents a qualitative transformation of earlier and less inclusive factors, and activities embodying the quality of sociality involve more interactions and more complex connections and associations than do activities at any other level of existence.

Likewise, any objection to the inclusiveness of the quality of sociality on the ground that the spiritual is neglected also seems to lose its force when we realize that the spiritual itself is social. As we have already pointed out, the distinction of the physical, the vital, the mental, and the social levels of existence, interactions, and experience is only schematic. There are perhaps many gradations on each of these levels. For instance, there is no definite break between the physical and the vital, the vital and the mental, or the mental and the social. In other words, at some stage the physical is more like the typically vital, the vital more like the typically mental, the mental more like the typically social. Such a continuity of existence, which seems in accord with current thought in the biological and psychological sciences, suggests that from the social a higher level of reality is gradually emerging. In a word, the highest stage of the social may be even more than the social — namely, the spiritual. From the standpoint of education, we are interested in the social, but we are also interested in the spiritual, which, it seems to us, is also social whatever else it may be. From the standpoint of education, there are many important experiences that cannot be considered spiritual in any narrow sense of the current meaning of spiritual. We are interested in these experiences, but we are also interested in those that are spiritual, for they are also social.[9]

Psychologically, the presence and importance of the social aspects of experience are widely recognized. The individual is always, in some respects, dependent upon other people. In social relationships he emerges, develops, and dies. He owes his existence to his parents, and his nurture and his education to the love, protection, and guidance of others. He shares both directly and indirectly the life of social groups from his birth until his death.

Genetically, the consciousness of others precedes, or at least appears simultaneously with, the consciousness of one's self. Without the awareness of others there is no awareness of the self. It may be possible to experience other things without at the moment being aware of other persons. Nevertheless, other persons enter so much into one's dealing with things that the social may be considered an aspect of almost any significant experience. Our thinking, feeling, and voluntary activities almost always involve other people. Even in our dreams people play important roles. The separation of individuals from their fellows is one of the most severe types of punishment. The punishment is all the greater because of personal associations arising in memory and imagination that stone walls and prison bars cannot exclude. Personal immortality, which is almost a universal desire of the human heart, is explainable, at least in part, from the longing to be with friends and loved ones who have passed into the Great Beyond.

Language, which is peculiar to the human race as contrasted with other forms of existence, involves physical and physiological factors, but it is fundamentally social. The difficulty with the interpretation of thought in terms of language is not that thinking does not involve

[9] William James, *Principles of Psychology*. Henry Holt and Company, New York, 1890. Vol. I. Pp. 400–401.

language. Language is communication and communication is always social. When people begin to respond to things as signs of other things language emerges. Such responses always involve people in communication. They may consist in a form of overt activity such as waving or, on the other hand, they may involve such signs and symbols as are used in talking, reading, and telegraphy. Language is social through and through, any experience involving language is social, and educative experiences typically involve language.

In educational theory as well as practice, the importance of the social has long been recognized. Even when individualized instruction is distinguished from socialized instruction, reference is to the techniques involved rather than to the psychological character of the experience of the individuals. The activities of pupils working individually may be psychologically as social as when they are working together. Experiences that involve other people, or even language, in any form, are always social. Almost all school work is social in a psychological sense. The problem of social education is not that some education is social as contrasted with physical education, vocational education, and intellectual education. All education controlled by the schools is social, both psychologically and sociologically, in both process and effect. Social factors play an important part in the actual experiences of pupils everywhere and under all school conditions. The outcomes of the experiences of pupils are social in effect not only on the pupils themselves, but also on the social order.

Any objection, on the ground that current efforts to socialize education are illogical and without foundation if education is already social in the very nature of things, misses the point we are trying to make. The efforts at socialization are not to make education social psychologically; they are to make it social in an ethical and constructive sense. For instance, those who wish to substitute a socialized for an individualistic classroom procedure must assume that the most individualistic procedure is psychologically social. Competition involves people and is therefore practically, psychologically, and existentially just as social as is co-operation. Neither co-operation nor competition of just any kind deserves approval without qualification. But in a sense the one is no more social than the other. The emphasis on the social in the socialized recitation, the project method, and the unit method does not indicate that the individual is not social and needs to be made social. It signifies rather that he is social but that the quality of his sociality is not satisfactory. Even the individualized methods of instruction, such as supervised study, the Dalton plan, and the Winnetka system, do not assume that the individual is lacking in sociality or that sociality is undesirable. Men who advocate these procedures are seeking to improve the sociality that exists even when they emphasize methods of individual study. The emphasis on the social in current curriculum programs does not signify that the individual is lacking in sociality. It signifies rather that his activities are social in terms of his own experience and also in their effect upon society. The fact that education is social is the basis that must be assumed in any effort to improve its social quality.

As we have already pointed out, some people identify desirable sociality with psychological sociality. They merely seek to increase the social quality that exists without inquiring into its desirability. They are not only admitting the psychological quality of sociality; they are eager to foster its development whatever it may be. But we are not here approving their position; we are merely pointing out that the social is a quality of experience that must be taken into account in educational policies or programs. Such a position has been assumed, if not definitely expressed, by philosophers and psychologists for hundreds of years. Even Plato and Aristotle considered the nature of man incurably social. There is no problem of making education social in a psychological sense. It is social in origin, in process, and in results. Even the antisocial is psychologically social. The problem of so-called social education should be one of providing educative experiences in which the social qualities are positively desirable.

The theory of widening sociality agrees with the theory of inherent sociality in recognizing the fact that educative experience is incurably social. On the other hand, it agrees with the theory of doctrinaire sociality that this incurably social element of experience is an inadequate criterion of desirable sociality. Something more is required than to leave original nature to itself even if it should include social impulses. Still it is in sharp disagreement with the assumption of the authoritarian approach to the problem of desirable socialization. The existing quality, which in the principle of inherent sociality is assumed to be desirable, must be transformed and be reconstructed, but not through the process of indoctrination.

The theory of widening sociality is designed to provide a criterion of social direction which such formal conceptions as growth, reconstruction, and progressive adjustment do not supply, at least in the minds of many authoritarians. As a matter of fact, some of those who have endorsed the experimentalists' conception of education as growth, reconstruction, and progressive adjustment, have proceeded to define fixed aims as a means of supplying the direction which seems to them essential, but in doing so they have assumed consciously or unconsciously the authoritarian theory of doctrinaire sociality. Dewey, Kilpatrick, and Bode, however much they may disagree on terminology and on particular points of emphasis, have sought to provide the social direction required in some other way. In fact, as pointed out in the second chapter, they have always qualified the existential and psychological conception of growth, reconstruction, and the remaking of life to include the quality of growth, reconstruction, and life that is deemed desirable. The qualities considered desirable are suggested in various connections in the writings of the experimentalists rather than explicitly embodied in definitions and formal statements. They seem to represent interpretations of certain features of experience with regard to which other schools of thought also assume positions.

The quality of widening sociality as the proper interpretation of the feature of sociality in Bode's formula, is designated as "Continuous widening of the area of common interests and concerns." [10] Widening sociality is intended to indicate the spirit of the social philosophy that the experimentalists call the democratic way of life. It is intended to supply us with key words to which we can refer such conceptions as "sharing," "participation," and "respect for personality," with which educational literature is, thanks to the experimentalists, replete. It is conceived not solely as a recognition of the fact that experience is incurably social. Such a pervasive quality is assumed, but the theory of widening sociality signifies a positive, ethical, and constructive translation of this psychological and existential social quality into a quality that conforms not only to the heart's desire but also to intellectual approval. It is not merely a quality of experience to which they give their consent and approval, but an ideal quality toward which they should strive. It is not merely a principle of method, but it is also an aim of all those who are intent on improving the quality of their own experiences and the experiences of others. The quality of widening sociality involves many important factors of which (1) appreciation, (2) sympathy, (3) impartiality, and (4) sincerity are especially suggestive and significant.

1. Social *appreciation* is an essential aspect of widening sociality, for

[10] Boyd H. Bode, *Progressive Education at the Crossroads.* Newson and Company, New York, 1938. P. 109.

it involves both understanding and concern for others. It signifies meanings derived from understanding and interests, which are, in turn, derived from feeling. Appreciation of this kind is not limited to emotion and sentiment. It embodies feeling, but it is not mere affection. It is affection that is intellectualized. It is not just an original psychological quality of sensitivity to the presence of activities and interests of others. It is derived from participation in common undertakings.

By engaging in common pursuits, the individual learns the meaning of things, ideas, and procedures that can be secured in no other way. He learns the meaning of the ordinary things of the home, such as chairs, tables, and knives and forks, and the ordinary things of the school, such as desks, blackboards, and books, only through activities in which others also are engaged. He learns the meaning of general rules and principles in the same way that he learns the meaning of common, everyday objects. He learns them from their use in social intercourse and shared undertakings. He observes principles and rules that others observe in the home, in the school, and in other social institutions, and attaches to them the same meanings that others attach to them. He engages in the activities in which others engage and uses procedures that they use. Thus, he attaches the same meanings to the ways of doing things that others attach to them.

The individual thus builds up a body of social appreciations through his direct participation in common enterprises. Such social participation, then, is an essential aspect of widening sociality. The more conjoint activities engaged in by the individual, other things being equal, the better. Through participation with others in common undertakings new appreciations are deepened, extended, and enriched. Those who are interested in education, interested in providing conditions under which desirable experiences occur, should seek to develop sound appreciations. One way, perhaps the most important way, of securing, deepening, extending, and enriching appreciations is by social participation.

Although direct participation is essential in the development of those appreciations that involve both affection and understanding, indirect participation is also desirable. From appreciations already developed, other meanings may be derived through intellectual operations. For instance, those who appreciate the meaning of "buggies," "automobiles," "trains," and "kites" can have some appreciation of the meaning of "aeroplane" without actually riding in one. They are able to "put two and two together," so to speak. In this way the individual deepens and extends his appreciation not only of the culture of his own group, but also of the culture of other groups and peoples throughout the world. He may expand the appreciations gained in the home through reading, listening, and discussing in the school, the church, and the various organizations to which he may belong, as well as in the activities of everyday life. Through intellectual operation, or indirect participation, as well as through direct participation, the individual deepens and expands his earlier appreciations as well as develops new appreciations of the culture of other groups and of other peoples.

2. In the reference to culture, *sympathy* is suggested as the second factor of widening sociality. When culture is conceived as it is here — in terms of interests, values, conceptions, and ways of men rather than in terms of what particular men, particular classes, or particular races, approve, endorse, and prize — sympathy and appreciation can be secured through participation and intellectual operations. The individual who develops an appreciation of the culture of other peoples through intellectual operations and direct participation may find it acceptable, pleasing, and appealing, or repellent, annoying, and disgusting. He appreciates a culture in the sense that it has for him a meaning that is suffused with feeling. But this feeling may be negative rather than positive. Widening sociality requires that appreciations of the cultures of others be pervaded with sympathy.

Culture in its broadest sense — culture in the sense here under consideration — is a neutral conception. Conceived in this way, the interests, values, conceptions, and ways of different individuals, groups, and nations are not objects to be approved or disapproved. They are not objects merely to be clothed with meaning and significance derived from one's own experience, colored as it is with some particular culture, as that of the farmer, laborer, capitalist, or religionist; American, Englishman, or German; the white race, the yellow race, or the Negro race; Christian or pagan; Jew or Gentile; sorority or non-sorority; fraternity or non-fraternity; old or young; man or woman; rich or poor. Sympathy involves placing one's self in the position of other people. One may not be able to sit "where they sat," as did the Hebrew prophet in referring to the plight of his countrymen, but nevertheless he can do so in imagination. Although we may not be able to see ourselves as others see us, we can, if we will, see others to some extent as they see themselves. Through sympathy we are able to project ourselves in imagination into the position of others.

An old policeman friend of mine who had spent a long life dealing with lawbreakers and criminals said near the end of his career that he had changed his mind about those who fall into the hands of the law. He said he had once thought that such people were just bad and deserved to be punished. But after dealing with them for many years, imagining himself in their positions, in most cases he did not blame them much. Anyone who could see and appreciate the conditions under which these people live and the obstacles that confront them in many complex situations would be convinced that under the same circumstances he might not have done any better than many of them had done. Such an attitude on the part of an experienced officer of the law was the result of sympathy and imagination.

It goes without saying that if we are ever to understand and appreciate the past sympathetically, we must have an "eye for history," to use an expression of Professor W. T. Laprade of Duke University. It is not enough to know that men did certain things at distant times and places. To appraise them we must see their problems from their own standpoint; we must imaginatively place ourselves in their positions. It is necessary to study the cultures of other groups and peoples, of other times and places, if we are to widen continually the area of common interests and concerns; but such study must be pervaded with sympathy. We must think of the culture of others from their standpoint rather than from ours. Such sympathy leads to an appreciative understanding of the interests, values, conceptions, and ways of others that is possible in no other way. But it does more. It provides a basis for a fuller and deeper appreciation of our own culture. Through the sympathetic understanding of the culture of others, we are thus able to become more modest and reasonable in the appraisal of our own interests, values, conceptions, and ways. One who constantly enters constructively into the lives and experiences of others through the exercise of sympathetic imagination makes a better friend and neighbor, thus extending, expanding, and deepening the meaning and significance of social experience, which the theory of widening sociality is intended to emphasize.

3. *Impartiality*, the third factor of widening sociality to be considered, is closely related to sympathy. A sympathetic appreciation of the interests, values, conceptions, and ways of one's own group and people and the interests, values, conceptions, and ways of other groups and of other peoples supplies the foundation for impartiality. But social impartiality includes additional factors. Appreciation is intellectual

and affectionate; sympathy is social and positively emotional; impartiality is purposeful and ethical.

It is probably impossible to deal with important social issues and practical problems without at least some bias; but the individual who has an appreciative understanding of the cultural objects of the situation and who sympathetically realizes the just claims of all parties affected is in a position of moral responsibility. Widening sociality involves just this very effort to do justice to all those directly or indirectly involved in moral situations, including one's own inclinations, impulses, propensities, and limitations of judgment. Complete justice perceived in terms of results is doubtless impossible. It is important to recall, however, that we are considering sociality as a quality of experience. Under particular conditions the results may be very partial while the quality of experience is very impartial; under other conditions the results may be very impartial while the quality of experience is very partial. On the whole, impartiality as an aspect of widening sociality signifies an extension of justice beyond anything that could be possible when attention is focused upon mere results. If the quality of experience is impartial, results in the long run and on the whole should gradually improve the social order.

4. *Sincerity*, the fourth and final factor of widening sociality to be considered, has been implicit in the foregoing considerations of the other aspects of this principle. Sincerity signifies truthfulness as contrasted with deceitfulness. Truthfulness includes all forms of truth-telling, honesty, and straightforwardness. Deceitfulness includes all forms of lying, dishonesty, and hypocrisy. Sincerity includes also the positive wish to be faithful to facts and responsibility in observing, recording, and reporting evidence. It signifies keeping one's promises, doing what is expected, and playing fair.

Only when sincerity is a quality of experience can the other aspects of the quality of widening sociality prevail. Expanding appreciation of things, ideas, and procedures signifies honesty, truthfulness, and faithfulness to the facts and conditions of associated living. Without such responsibility intellectual understanding, an essential ingredient of appreciation, is incomplete, unreliable, and therefore inadequate. Without it, sympathy is misplaced and misguided, and important factors are neglected. When appreciations are inadequate and important factors are neglected, impartiality is impossible.

The implications of the quality of widening sociality, involving appreciation, sympathy, impartiality, and sincerity, are far-reaching.

Its acceptance requires the continuous development of a sympathetic understanding and appreciation of the interests, values, conceptions, and ways of one's associates, of one's own people, and of the peoples of distant times and places. It requires an honest effort to see others from their own standpoint, and impartiality in adjusting the claims of all parties involved in moral situations. It requires sincerity in dealing with one's self and others in all the relationships of life.

When emphasis is placed upon this quality of sociality, there is no place for indoctrination as a desirable aspect of educative experience. It may be admitted only as a factor involved in training when time and opportunity are not sufficient for education. But indoctrination thus permitted will be tempered by the conviction that people should not be deprived of their freedom for once and for all in consequence of loyalty to fixed and external conceptions, beliefs, and practices, although they may be deprived of as much freedom, for the time being, as is necessary for their protection, as in early childhood and in time of war.

When emphasis is placed upon the quality of inherent sociality, social direction is inadequate. The pervasive psychological quality of sociality that is all but universally recognized is assumed. The qualities of social appreciation, sympathy, impartiality, and sincerity are possible rather than inherent traits of human nature. To provide the conditions under which they may prevail requires much more than letting things take their course. Such qualities do not regularly and consistently prevail in social life, and those who adopt this principle have assumed an important responsibility in directing their own activities as well as the activities of others whom they control, direct, or influence.

It is easy to understand the attitude of the reader who feels that the foregoing elaboration is still too general and abstract. Most people want to know just what ideas, ideals, and beliefs one should adopt for one's self and inculcate in others. Such information is just what many parents, teachers, and religious, political, and social leaders, as well as the average individual, would most like to know. To supply such specific information apart from practical situations is just the obligation which the authoritarian, in accord with his theory of socialization, assumes, and it is exactly the possibility of supplying such information that the educational experimentalist, in accord with his theory of widening sociality, denies. The educational experimentalist does not deny that in practical life one should learn specific things and lead others to learn specific things. What he denies is that anyone outside specific situations can predict with certainty just what ends should be sought and just what procedures should be used in such situations. Everyone should be to some extent responsible for his own actions.

From the standpoint of the theory of widening sociality, the social values one learns and the activities included in learning them should involve social appreciation, sympathy, impartiality, and sincerity. Such principles as these contain no prescription as to what specific ends individuals should seek nor what specific means they should use. All depends upon the implications for specific situations of the theory of desirable experience, of which the theory of widening sociality constitutes one general aspect. One person may widen the areas of his common interests and concerns in one way and someone else in other ways. To some it means travel; to others it means reading; to others it means engaging in the activities of a social organization; to still others it means taking formal courses in school. To some pupils it means studying Latin, French, Spanish, or German; to others it means studying history. To those who are taking a subject such as history, it means emphasis on one topic; and to others, emphasis on other topics. To some it means overcoming a particular prejudice; to others it means securing specific information; and to still others it means developing a particular skill. What should be the emphasis at any place and time depends upon the implication of the principle or the theory of widening sociality as applied under the conditions prevailing in the individual and the social situation. But even the theory of widening sociality is only one among a number of principles constituting the philosophy of educational experimentalism, and these other principles should be considered also in all the varying situations of life. In some situations there may be considerable uniformity, but whatever uniformity or variety there should be must be determined by those in the situation itself and not by others unfamiliar with its requirements, however capable, wise, and powerful they may be considered.

CHAPTER 5

Motivation of Experience

ACCORDING TO SOME recognized authorities, interest is the most important conception in educational literature. Even those who do not give it such priority and pre-eminence still recognize its significance. Its value varies somewhat in consequence of the meaning attached to it. When they use the word, some people have in mind an established emotionalized structure, whether derived from experience or from some other source. Others have in mind, as we do here, some quality of present experience. Some think of this quality as either positive or negative. In other words, we may be interested in the disagreeable as well as in the agreeable. Doubtless, everyone admits that all our experiences result from either positive or negative interest. Therefore, the term *interest* may be used to include both the acceptable and the repellent. Most people, however, identify the interesting with the acceptable and the uninteresting with the repellent. Furthermore, they prefer, other things being equal, interesting to uninteresting motivation — that is, the acceptable to the repellent. It seems quite appropriate, therefore, to use the term *interest* unqualified to signify positive interest. That is the way the term is used here, and the different theories of motivation, or the cause of experience to which the adherents of the three philosophies of education here under consideration subscribe, are designated as theories of interest.

THEORY OF PROVISIONAL INTEREST
(EDUCATIONAL AUTHORITARIANISM)

In educational authoritarianism, interest is often conceived of as either positive or negative and as intrinsic or extrinsic. To most authoritarians any of these types of interest constitute legitimate initiating and sustaining conditions of educative experience. To some, even effort, in the sense of a conscious strain involved in attending to the uninteresting, is permissible. Positive interest, interest in the sense here under consideration, is only one way of motivating educational activities, according to the authoritarians. However, the conception of interest in the broad, positive sense recognized as indispensable by the experimentalists has only a limited, conditional, or provisional motivating function in the theory and practice of authoritarians. It is the authoritarian attitude toward interest in this broad positive sense which is here under consideration. Inasmuch as the authoritarians consider it desirable as a means to indispensable ends but do not consider it an indispensable end itself, it is always provisional. To the authoritarians, interest is desirable provided it serves effectively as a means. In other words, interest is always a provisional end, never a necessary end; it is provisional or secondary to some other ends considered primary and absolute. For this reason, the term *interest* as conceived by educational authoritarians is here designated as *provisional interest*.

As already indicated, some authoritarians distinguish between positive and negative interest. Positive interest in the sense in which the experimentalists use the term signifies satisfaction or "acceptance." In the words of Dewey, an educative experience should not be "repellent." Negative interest signifies annoyance indicated in reactions of withdrawal or avoidance. The authoritarians want the individual to do what is required of him without causing any trouble. They hope to initiate activities in such a way that they will be satisfying, acceptable, or even pleasing. But they do not hesitate to use negative interests if necessary. They may use penalties of various kinds. Those for whom educational work is distasteful may engage in it to avoid punishment. They will study rather than do worse, so to speak. They are interested in penalties in the negative sense of wishing to avoid them; but they do not have any positive interest in the work for its own sake.

The emphasis given to these two forms of interest depends somewhat on the personal qualities of the leader. Some people are so sensitive to the interests and needs of others that they seldom have to resort to punishment. They are able to imagine themselves in the places of those whom they guide and direct so that otherwise disagreeable tasks can at least be tolerated. In other words, their theories do not interfere very much with their practices. The authoritarian parent may be so sympathetic with his children that they will do willingly almost anything he wishes them to do. An occasional authoritarian leader in any field may, through the influence of superior personality, get his followers to do things just to please him. The authoritarian teacher may control his pupils in the same way. He does not have to use the "big stick," although he does not have any theoretical objection to using it if necessary to get the things done that he has prescribed. All of us are doubtless familiar with leaders in other fields who are thus able to command the services of others not because of their interest in what is required, but because of a desire to please.

On the other hand, there are some authoritarians who find it necessary to resort to punishment quite often. They do not have the social sensitivity and imagination that will get people to do easily what they require. They may not even worry much about positive interest. They may be satisfied to get things done without any regard for the feelings of those who do them. All of us are acquainted with people in positions of leadership who simply force their will in one way or another upon those who are under their direction. We see them in the home, in the school, in the church, and in social organizations of every kind. Educational authoritarians often thus exert their authority over those who are responsible to them. Teachers simply force pupils to do what is required. Even children in the home, pupils in the schools, and students in our colleges find ways to force others to do what they want done. Those who adopt this authoritarian attitude toward positive and negative interest are satisfied if they get things done and they do not worry, at least not very much, over the annoyance of those who have to do the work.

Some authoritarians recognize the distinction between intrinsic and extrinsic interest. Some things are appealing, attractive, and challenging to us in and of themselves without reference to other things. We engage in some activities just because we like to do so. The experiences involved in dealing with such things and engaging in such activities are satisfying, acceptable, and enjoyable. They contain their own ends without reference to other ends to the realization of which they contribute. The interest which initiates and sustains these experiences is intrinsic.

On the other hand, there are many things which have no direct appeal for us. We deal with some things and engage in some activities not because they seem good to us, but because they are seen as means of securing other things and of engaging in other activities which are intrinsically interesting. The interest that serves merely as means to external ends is said to be extrinsic; that is to say, it lies outside the experience itself. For instance, the laborer may perform his daily tasks not because he likes to do so but because this work enables him to feed, clothe, and house himself and his family. The student may tolerate, accept, and even seem to enjoy certain courses in which he receives high marks. Children seem to take much pleasure in some activities for which they secure pay in the form of money, stars, and distinction, or even praise and approval.

The authoritarians who emphasize the distinction between intrinsic and extrinsic interest insist that both are essential in life and education. They may insist that rewards are more effective than punishment — even refuse to employ punishment at all — but they contend that artificial means must be used to inspire people to engage in activities that are in themselves unimportant, perhaps even disagreeable. At times they themselves have to do the uninteresting for the sake of a particular goal. Consequently, authoritarians consider the use of external rewards not only a desirable, but an indispensable means. Extrinsic interest in many forms is employed by both parents and teachers to get children to do what they consider good for them. The politicians who are dependent upon the good will of others to realize the ends they seek hold out personal rewards to those who can help them. Most people engage in uninteresting activities as a means to desired ends. Therefore, important and necessary but uninteresting activity should be made as interesting as possible, and punishment for failure to do a particular assignment should be used only as a last resort. Positive interest is preferable to negative interest, but positive interest may be extrinsic as well as intrinsic.

Some authoritarians emphasize the distinction between interest and effort. They prefer interest, even positive interest, as a means to an end, but they are convinced that interest in and of itself is insufficient as an occasioning and sustaining condition of all educative experiences. They insist that many desirable experiences in which all of us must engage require mental effort in the sense of keeping the attention fixed on an object which in and of itself has no appeal for us.

From this point of view, all the home, the school, the church, or any other educational agency can do is to indicate to those whom they seek to guide and direct what should be done. If the activities suggested are interesting, all is well, but if they are not interesting, they should be performed anyway. Somehow or other, everyone is capable, so it is contended, through insight or intuition, of understanding what his duty is in every situation. If those responsible for educational activities have indicated what should be done, they have done all that is expected of them. "We can lead a horse to water, but we cannot make him drink." Every individual is, in the last analysis, responsible for his own education. On many occasions he cannot rely on interest, and will have to heed the call of duty or the still small voice of conscience and intuition. If he fails to exert the necessary effort that duty demands, he has no one to blame for his failures but himself.

In times past, some authoritarians have preferred indifference, even annoyance, to positive interest and satisfaction. A few have gone so far as to attach special educational significance to the performance of disagreeable tasks. If the same ends could be secured, motivated either by satisfaction or by dissatisfaction, they considered dissatisfaction the more desirable force. Some have even attributed superior influence to pain as a motivating factor. But those who have preferred the disagreeable to the agreeable as a motivating stimulus have had some special factor in mind. They believed that the most desirable activities, from the standpoint of education, involved experiences that were disagreeable because they were difficult to perform. These people adopted the principle that was known as unmotivated action. Doing things merely from a sense of duty or doing something in particular because it was thought to be proper and right, although done against one's inclinations, was thought to be especially good for the will. Performing a disagreeable task against one's inclinations was supposed to strengthen will power. Very few people now responsible for educational policies and programs consider disagreeableness a quality of desirable experience. Probably no one today would endorse the slogan that the satirist directed at these old timers when he said, "It makes no difference what a boy studies, so long as he doesn't like it."

All recognized students of education *may* consider positive interest essential but none of them considers disagreeable activities preferable to agreeable ones merely because they are disagreeable. If they do not endorse interest as an essential quality of desirable experience, neither do they endorse pain or annoyance as a desirable quality. The educational authoritarians today usually are not so interested in the qualities of experiences involved in study as they are in what is studied. Some of them may be tempted to believe that it makes little difference how the individual feels about his study so long as he studies the right things. But certainly, if they do not believe that positive interest is always possible, they do not endorse the lack of such interest as desirable. Most authoritarians would use interest as a means to make the pupil study what they think he ought to study. But if interest fails, some other more effective measures should be used without hesitation.

The educational authoritarian today does not include activities in the educational program just because they are uninteresting. On the other hand, he does not exclude them just because they are interesting. The notion of including activities merely because they are interesting is to him, of course, preposterous. But to leave them out because they are uninteresting may be considered just as unreasonable.

Many authoritarians go much further. They not only reject annoyance as a desirable quality of experience; they prefer interest to lack of interest, satisfaction to annoyance. Other things being equal, they always prefer interest to any other form of motivation as the means of getting the right things done and the right things learned. Although they prefer interest to any other means, however, they have in mind certain ends that must be attained even if interest cannot be secured. Interest is therefore considered provisional. Interest is desirable only if the right things are done and only if the right things are learned.

This theory of provisional interest thus assumes the theories of objective contingency and doctrinaire sociality. The things to be learned are fixed. They may be determined by tradition, the authority of the church, the authority of the state, the authority of scholarship, or the authority of science; but however they are determined and whatever they may be, they are the indispensable ends of education. Whether determined by authoritative students of education, by school officials, by the faculty of the school, or even by the teacher, they are considered essential. If interest stimulates learning, all well and good; but if the studies are uninteresting, they must be learned nevertheless.

The ends of education are to be determined outside the educational situation. It therefore becomes the obligation of those in charge of practical educational operations to see that these ends are embodied in the personality as expeditiously and economically as possible. The process of learning should be as interesting as possible. If the ends — the results of education — cannot be achieved by activities that are interesting, however, then they must be secured by activities that are lacking in interest, or even by activities that on the whole are disagreeable.

According to another form of provisional interest, any desirable educative experience of considerable length must be interesting. Sustaining interest in activities is the only means, so it is thought, of getting essentials learned. Effort, however, is also a requirement. There are times when the individual simply has to force himself to hold his attention on matters that are absolutely uninteresting. From this point of view, both his interest and his effort are indispensable qualities of experience. Some desirable experiences are pervaded throughout with interest, but others require effort.[1]

Effort as an indispensable quality of desirable experience has a technical meaning. It does not signify merely the expenditure of energy in eventually overcoming obstacles to the progress of activities in which one is interested. It refers to what is known as a strain on consciousness. The individual is somehow aware of just what task should be performed; however, he is not inclined to do what he knows he ought to do. His attention simply turns to other things. He knows his duty, but he is naturally weak. Under such conditions he has to rely on deeper resources to hold his mind for a few moments on the job to be done. If he forces his attention by the sheer *fiat* of will, the activity will gradually become more appealing. After a conscientious struggle, interest will continue to grow until the individual can work with pleasure and joy on what was erstwhile psychologically an impossible task.

The interesting thing about this theory is that although interest is an indispensable means, it is a necessary quality of any experience that is carried through to completion. Still it does not make the experience desirable so much as it makes it possible. Effort not only makes certain experiences possible, but it makes them desirable. According to this theory, the most educative experiences require mental strain.

From this point of view, it is not necessary to select educational activities that require the mental strain called effort. If one does what he ought to do, enough effort will be required. The requirements of a desirable life and a desirable education cannot all be positively interesting through and through. Many activities not only will be uninteresting at certain points but will require effort. Without effort the necessary work in life and education cannot be performed. We can give the individual the opportunity to engage in the right educational activities, but we cannot make him pursue them. We cannot make all educational activities interesting, but they may be interesting or uninteresting and still be satisfactory. Yet we can, if we will, make them interesting by exerting effort. When a person heeds the call to duty of the still small voice of conscience, he can put forth effort. If he does exert his will, what was once annoying will

---

[1] Herman Harrell Horne, *The Philosophy of Education.* The Macmillan Company, New York, 1904. Pp. 103–106.

become increasingly acceptable and satisfying. Effort stimulates interest as inevitably as interest stimulates effort. It is the obligation of those in charge of educational programs and activities to see to it, in so far as possible, that pupils exert effort when effort is required in the performance of tasks that are known to be educationally important If the subject matter to be learned has been selected on the basis of the principles of objective contingency and doctrinaire sociality, it is desirable. If it requires effort to be mastered, it is not any the less desirable, but may even be more desirable.

Perhaps the most widely accepted form of the theory of provisional interest today is reflected in the conception of need as the cause of experience and the justification of activity. But need, like interest and effort, has different interpretations. Some educational authoritarians adopt the theory of need as the cause of experience or, perhaps more accurately speaking, as the justification of educational activities. They do not accept positive and constructive interest as the only indispensable and desirable quality of experience arising from need, but they are willing to adopt the theory that need is the sufficient cause and justification of any experience, if their own conception of need is accepted.

Authoritarians adopt two conceptions of the nature and function of need. Some mean by need anything they consider good *for* the individual in the future, without regard to whether or not it is good *to* him in the present. Others consider need to be the invariable cause of experience, whether or not it is good *to* the individual in the present or good *for* him in the future. Authoritarians who adopt the first conception justify their requirements on the basis of the probable future needs of those whom they guide and direct. Those who adopt the second conception contend that need is the cause of all activities, and that those needs are desirable which cause individuals to engage in educative activities that will benefit them in the future.

An analysis of these two authoritarian conceptions of need as the justification for the selection of educative activities and experiences is perhaps the best way to illustrate the theory of provisional interest that now seems most congenial to some educational authoritarians. Need in these two senses embodies the essential elements of interest as mere means, interest as a preferable means, and interest as an indispensable means; but like these other conceptions, provisional interest is still a means and not a quality of experience desirable for its own sake.

Need as thus conceived does not commit one to the acceptance of positive interest as the single indispensable quality that initiates and sustains all desirable experiences. Need in this sense has no reference to interest of any kind. It may be conceived as another way of stating the requirements of the principles of objective contingency and doctrinaire sociality that already have been considered as principles of educational authoritarianism. Need does not require any all-inclusive occasioning and sustaining quality of desirable experience. It has no reference to what the individual desires, wishes, wants, or feels that he needs. It refers solely to what those responsible for his education consider good for him. They may, of course, give some attention to his present interest or his felt needs in deciding what is good for him or in deciding what he needs. But such consideration of present inclinations is intended not so much to discover needs as to discover means of causing him to engage in activities through which he may learn the things he is expected to need some time in the future.

In other words, need in this sense is noncommittal with respect to interest. Those who accept this theory may adopt any of the attitudes toward interest as a means that have so far been considered. Interest may be conceived as merely one means, or as the best means, or even as an indispensable means of satisfying needs, but this conception does not signify that interest is a desirable quality of experience. The needs of the student, for instance, are what educational authorities consider to be for the student's future good, and interest, at best, is a means of getting the student to satisfy the demands of anticipated needs.

Those authoritarians who consider need as the invariable cause of educative experiences have taken a step in the right direction in adopting a single all-inclusive principle as the initiating and sustaining cause of experience; but they have not yet committed themselves to acceptance of positive interest as the single indispensable quality of desirable experience arising from need as the efficient and occasioning condition of any experience. They have learned from developments in biology and psychology that there is no such thing as unmotivated activity; that any change in activity is due to lack of adjustment; and that lack of adjustment is so great on some occasions that experiences are needed for education or adjustment. They see that all experience arises from that lack of adjustment which is known as need — need of experience without which adjustment is impossible. They recognize the fact that the experiences which meet such needs may be agreeable or disagreeable.

Still, in adopting the theory that need is the cause of experience, authoritarians are not committed to anything like agreeableness, acceptability, satisfaction, or positive interest as the indispensable quality characterizing all desirable experiences. Suppose, for instance, one has the choice between doing two things, either of which he can never like to do. Regardless of which he does and of what experiences he has in doing it, his choice is initiated and sustained by a lack of adjustment that may properly be called a need. But the experience itself may be either agreeable or disagreeable. Thus, we are back exactly where we were at the beginning of our discussion of interest. True, the authoritarian recognizes need as the fundamental initiating and sustaining cause of experience. But according to him, desirable experiences themselves may be interesting or uninteresting. Therefore, interest is still only a means. If those whom we guide and direct engage in interesting activities which meet their immediate needs, well and good. But they are required to engage in the activities necessary to meet their needs even if the activities are disagreeable. Meeting an immediate need may, contrary to the belief of some, be very uninteresting, annoying, and unacceptable.

In fact, according to this theory, those in charge of educational programs and activities may provoke the immediate needs that cause those under their guidance to do what authorities consider good for them in the future. The resulting experiences may be positively and directly interesting, even preferably so; but, according to this theory, interest still is not an essential element of desirable and constructive educative experience. The educational authoritarian accepts interest as a means only. He does not ever quite accept interest as a necessary means, and he never commits himself to any principle which requires satisfaction, acceptability, or positive interest. Interest in the development of any authoritarian educational program functions as a means of securing the external ends which those in power prescribe for those under their control. To authoritarians the acceptability of the experiences required to realize these ends is at most a secondary consideration.

The theory of provisional interest in any form seems to be an aspect of a more inclusive philosophical theory of the relationship of means and ends. According to this theory, means and ends are separate and independent. The ends consist of values that are determined without reference to how they are to be achieved. These ends are good in the abstract without reference to the means by which they are to be realized.

Such values are conceived in many ways. They may consist of features of reality lying outside and beyond experience, such as the universals, forms, or ideas of a supersensible world as conceived by Plato, to be discovered through contemplation, through the voice of conscience, through reading the great literary classics, or in some other way. They may consist of spiritual ideals of God, the Father of mankind, embodied in the dogmas of the church, or of aspects of the divine Reason which is unfolding in the process of actualizing some all-inclusive, distant goal unknown to man. They may consist of the ideals which philosophers, scientists, and students of education, from whatever source they derive them, propose from time to time. They may consist of anything those in authority consider, on whatever grounds, to be socially useful at some given time and place. But whatever they are, these values have no reference to the means by which they are to be realized in concrete situations.

Since such values are good in themselves, they are determined in advance of practical situations. Those directly responsible for practical programs must realize prescribed aims by any means that may be available. The ends always justify the means. If the end is good, it should be sought at any and all costs. Its value and significance are independent of the way it is obtained.

Some such conception of the relationship of means and ends seems to be implicit in all forms of the theory of provisional interest. Interest at best is a provisional good. As a mere means it may not be any better than any other means. As a preferable means it signifies only that it is more often effective than other means, say unmotivated effort or punishment. As an indispensable means it is still not an end in and of itself. It gets its meaning and significance from its use in securing other ends which are good within themselves. Even when it appears to be an immediate end of the parent or teacher, it is still only a means. It is sought as an immediate incentive to get learned those things that are thought to be good in themselves.

From the authoritarian viewpoint, those in charge of practical school programs should make subject matter interesting, because its use is essential to the achievement of fixed, authoritative values. It may be interesting or uninteresting. When subject matter fails to command attention because it lacks immediate appeal, it must be made to do so if possible. It must be made appealing, however, in order to facilitate learning. If the subject matter to be learned cannot be made appealing to the pupil, then other means must be used to effect learning. The ends are fixed and cannot be varied; only the means are subject to change. One means may be conceived as better than another, but the ends, which are primary and fundamental in the last analysis, may be used to justify any means that effects their realization.

From the standpoint of the philosophy of experimentalism, the theory that interest is an indispensable means is the most satisfactory form of the theory of provisional interest. Its acceptance implies the admission that unmotivated effort in and of itself is insufficient. Still it does not signify that interest as a quality of experience is desirable for its own sake, a principle which to the experimentalists is fundamental. According to them, an experience that is in no sense satisfying or good to one is not as good as it might be. Those in charge of educational programs may consider a thing good for us in the future; but if we never see it as good to us and if the future turns out contrary to the anticipation of those in authority, the predetermined so-called good certainly is bad. If the future is not what it is expected to be, the authoritarians' predicted good cannot be good except by accident. According to the theory of provisional interest, satisfaction, or the fulfillment of desire, other things being equal, is superior as an initiating and sustaining cause of experience to a sense of compulsion, from whatever source it may come.

However, other things are not always equal. Some values are thought to be so desirable that they must be sought by whatever means are available; some things must be done whether we want to do them or not. Interest may be a means, even a preferred means, but it is not conceived as an all-pervasive quality of desirable experience. Now, according to experimentalists, interest, satisfaction, or agreeableness constitutes a quality without which life would not be worth living. Any experience, then, which is lacking in this essential quality is not as desirable as it might be, however desirable it may seem in other respects. This much the theory of provisional interest as conceived by most educational authorities seems to assume. This theory suggests, however, that other means as the motivating and sustaining cause of experience may on occasion be superior to interest or to satisfaction. But as a matter of fact, according to experimentalists, without some satisfaction experiences are not good at all. In truth, present good consists in interest or in satisfaction. When this quality is lacking, the experience is not good, it matters not what other desirable qualities may characterize it.

The theory of provisional interest seems to adopt the theory that life is a process of preparation. The present is thought to be good or bad, desirable or undesirable, in consequence of its relationship to the future. The significance of childhood is determined by the contribution it is expected to make to adulthood, and life in this world is significant in consequence of the contribution it is expected to make to life in the next world. The experiences in the elementary school are significant in consequence of the contribution they are expected to make to experiences in the high school; experiences in the high school are significant in consequence of the contribution they are expected to make to experiences in college and the professions, and the experiences in the colleges and technical schools are significant in consequence of the contribution they are expected to make to the experiences of later life. Of course, it must be admitted that experiences are continuous, and experiences at one time affect experiences at later times. But many people today are convinced that only experiences that are good in the present are good in their effect. According to experimentalists, on the whole experiences which are good in the present are most effective in preparing people for the future in this world or in the world to come. Everything that is good to us in the present is not necessarily good for us, but unless things are at least good to us in the present, there is little assurance that they will ever be experienced as good at all.

Another argument, often used not so much to support this theory of provisional interest as to support its failure to consider interest other than provisional — that is, failure to consider it an essential quality of any desirable experience — is that in this world we have to endure some uninteresting things, anyway. As a matter of fact, people do have experiences which are not satisfying, acceptable, or interesting in any positive and constructive sense. On the basis of this premise the conclusion is that people must, therefore, have disagreeable experiences in order to prepare themselves properly for later disagreeable experiences, which they are sure to have. Even most authoritarians, as already suggested, would hesitate to search for disagreeable undertakings for those under their direction. Nevertheless, they usually insist that some uninteresting experiences are so important that they must be endured. Only thus, they seem to think, is it possible for the young to learn and do what in their opinion will prepare them for getting along in the world where they will have to "take it," so to speak.

From this standpoint, experiences are not good because they are bad — bad to us; they are good in spite of the fact that they are bad — bad to us. They are good because they prepare us to live in a bad world. If we have to live in a bad world, we might as well get used to it as soon as possible. Of course, we should not try to make the present bad, but we should not try very hard to keep the bad out of it. Certain things should be learned whether the activities required are agreeable or disagreeable. Learning these things may seem unnecessary; however, not only will they benefit us in the future, but the very fact that the process of learning was disagreeable will enable us to endure unpleasant experiences in the days to come.

Such a conception, from the standpoint of the philosophy of experimentalism, is confronted with serious objections. The actual world of experience is subject to continuous cumulative and undetermined change. It is continuously moving in directions that cannot be determined in advance, it is changing all the time, and the rate of change is becoming faster and faster. It is impossible to tell what the nature of the world eventually will be. Any so-called blueprint of a future order to which the younger generation is made to conform will not be the kind of world they will find in later years. Why, then, should young people be subjected to disagreeable experiences in the present to learn the things they are expected to need in a world that cannot be known in advance? If those in control of the educational influences of the home, of the school, and of other social institutions cannot know the kind of world into which young people are to enter, they should not subject them to disagreeable activities to prepare them for the fictional world of their own imagination.

Also, the experimentalists may insist that although the world is bad in many respects this fact is no reason why it might not be better in some respects. To prepare young people to fit into the world as it exists does not seem to the experimentalists to be the primary function of education. The primary function of education in the home, school, church, and everywhere else, is to make the world better. The world can be improved only as it is pervaded with experiences that are good. Young people should really have interesting, satisfying, and agreeable experiences because only experiences pervaded with such qualities are good either in the present or in the future. They should become interested in causing other people to have interesting and satisfying experiences. Perhaps sophomores should make freshmen happy rather than unhappy. The current methods of control used by these last year's freshmen emphasize the same qualities that are developed in primitive tribes and in some totalitarian states. The older, the more powerful, the more favored subject the younger, the weaker, and the less favored to disagreeable experiences to prepare them for the future. Although such practices exist, are even characteristic of the world, this fact does not make the experiences they produce desirable.

If we wish desirable experiences, and this is another way of saying we wish a better world, the barbaric custom of trying to make life unbearable for freshmen might be outlawed. For instance, the sophomores might convert Rat Week into a period in which they so direct the activities of freshmen that their experiences will be pleasant. Thus, instead of trying to "torture" the new freshmen as they themselves were tortured the year before, sophomores might work to make the freshmen's lot more agreeable. In other words, in this respect sophomores then would be tending to make a better world. The same applies to people everywhere who are working for a better world instead of merely adapting themselves to existing conditions.

The main objection of the experimentalists to the theory of provisional interest is, however, that it paves the way for the imposition of authoritarian standards on people, even in the name of democracy. Democracy, as the experimentalists interpret it, does not mean merely a political organization or system of government. It means that state of affairs in which certain privileges, opportunities, and rights, as well as responsibilities, of individuals are prized and esteemed. This conception of democracy recognizes the fact that men are not infallible — that they are not able to shape things to meet the heart's desire in all respects — but it also embodies the belief that it is possible to develop a state of affairs among men in which the interests of each human being can become increasingly the concern of all. Our forefathers had some such conviction in mind when they projected the principles of liberty, freedom, and equality as inalienable rights of man that should be practiced, extended, and preserved at all times.

Educational reformers have generally realized that if the rights of men as individuals must be respected, the rights of childhood and youth must also be respected. They have thus sought to develop some principle that would assure this respect in theory and extend it in practice. They have gradually come to see that such a principle, however it is to be stated, must have reference to the value and significance of present experience. They have called it interest, satisfaction, happiness, and other things. But however they have defined it, they have meant that our educational programs and activities should provide acceptable experiences.

The experimentalist is willing to admit that circumstances are such

at times that other things are more important than education conceived as desirable experience. During wars, epidemics, and depressions we must frequently engage in activities without regard to the
immediate satisfaction which they yield. But those who emphasize
acceptability as an essential quality of desirable experience would not
call such activities positively desirable or educative. Such experiences
are necessary in some forms of productive work and in some forms of
training, such as military drill in time of war. All experiences may
have some educative effect, but they are positively and constructively
educative only to the degree that they are interesting or acceptable to
those who have them. Unless we have some such conception as interest
or acceptability as a criterion of desirable or educative experience, the
way is left open in theory for the strong to impose disagreeable tasks
on the weak, especially the young — tasks that are immediately disagreeable and ultimately enslaving.

Unless there is some such safeguarding principle as this, the young
may be required to do almost anything in the name of education,
good citizenship, and religion. Any social group which happens to be
in power in the community may impose its ideas and beliefs on the
individual in the name of education and the good of society. It can
require the individual to do and to become what it wishes. The teacher
who adopts the theory of provisional interest may prefer satisfaction
to dissatisfaction as a quality of experience, but he must not on this
account hesitate to have pupils learn what he thinks they should learn,
even if they have to suffer tortures in the process. He may even strive
in every way possible to secure interest, as most good teachers do,
although he does not feel that interest is an essential quality of desirable experience. There are at least some teachers who do not worry
much about interest. They have pupils do what they consider to be of
future good. If the pupils are not interested in some nebulous future
good, the teacher is not very much concerned about the fact. He uses
whatever means are available to get done what he deems important,
without regard to whether the experiences involved seem good to the
pupil or not. He does not feel that there is any quality of experience
involving the attitude of the pupils which he must at all times consider inviolable in educational activities. Thus, in the absence of some
such principle as interest or acceptability of experience, pupils may
be immediately tortured and ultimately enslaved in the name of education and the good life.[2]

---

[2] William H. Burton, *The Guidance of Learning Activities*. D. Appleton-Century
Company, New York, 1944. Pp. 105–120.

Finally, the underlying theory of the separation of means and ends which this authoritarian attitude toward interest assumes is logically difficult to defend. An aim that does not take into account the means by which it is to be achieved is defective even as an aim. Unless an end is also an end in view, it is difficult to see how it could be an adequate aim. An end in view must take into account the practical means of its achievement, and a satisfactory aim is not separated from these means but emerges out of the considerations involved in dealing with them. An aim is a program of action arising in a practical situation and serving as a means of control and direction. It is not some value lying outside practical situations to which they must conform. In other words, adequate ends take into account the means by which they are to be realized. Adequate ends are always purposes or aims that reflect the demands of concrete situations.

The suggestion may occur to some readers that the continuity of means and the conception of interest as an aim are contradictory. In other words, so it may be asserted, interest as an end does not take into account the means by which it is to be secured and so is external, fixed, and irrelevant to practical situations just as are the other ends to which objection has been raised. Such an objection, at first sight, seems unanswerable. Nevertheless, a little reflection is sufficient to bring one to the realization that interest does not represent the obligation to learn any particular thing. It has no reference to any fixed structure to be embodied in the experience of those engaged in educational activities. It is a quality of experience that is desirable at all times, it matters not what particular thing one is doing. The things may be desirable or undesirable for other reasons. But they cannot be educative unless the experiences involved in learning them are at least acceptable. That interest is no fixed value is indicated by the fact that what is interesting to one person may not be interesting to another, and what is interesting to the same person at one time may not be interesting to him at another. The content, substance, or meaning of interest varies with concrete situations and is not, therefore, an absolute.

According to experimentalists, things which those in charge of educational programs and activities consider as ends or aims should be modified in the process of realizing them. A thing learned without interest is not the same as when it is learned with interest. Unless learned with interest, not only is it not learned effectively, but it is not learned as a good. At best, it seems unimportant; at worst, it seems an evil to be avoided. Desirable things are learned only through experiences that are desirable, and indifferent and uninteresting experiences are undesirable, it matters not how effective they may be as means of incorporating fixed values in mind, heart, or muscle.

THEORY OF IMMEDIATE INTEREST
(EDUCATIONAL LAISSEZ FAIRE)

In educational laissez faire, interest is not merely an indispensable means: it is a quality of all desirable experience. The difference between the satisfying and the annoying, the acceptable and the unacceptable, which some of the authoritarians designate as positive interest and negative interest, is recognized, but the term *interest* is reserved for what the authoritarians call positive interest. However, interest is not merely positive; it is immediate, direct, and continuous. Those who adopt the laissez-faire attitude toward interest as the occasioning and sustaining condition of experience may or may not refer to immediate interest, but the term is often used in referring to their theory of interest, especially by those authoritarians and middle-of-the-road groups who insist on attributing the conception even to the educational experimentalists.

In the minds of those who adopt or condemn the principle of immediate interest, the word "interest" signifies conscious pleasure, joy, or satisfaction. The individual interested in any object, idea, or activity likes it and knows that he likes it. He gives it his attention and enjoys doing so. In *immediate interest*, he gives his eager attention spontaneously and directly from start to finish. A clear understanding of this principle, therefore, requires us to consider various factors which it embodies, such as (1) attention, (2) spontaneity, and (3) continuity of pleasure or satisfaction.

1. *Attention* signifies that the individual keeps his mind on what he is doing. He does not let his mind wander to irrelevant things. He examines what interests him in its various aspects, and when he gives thought to other things, it is because they are related to the matter at hand. He is searching not for a way to escape from the situation but for data with which to deal with it more effectively. He has something to do that is worth while to him. The interested individual is attentive, mindful of his business, and intellectually alert. He is not merely unconsciously adjusting himself without thought. He is fully aware of what he is doing.

2. *Spontaneity* signifies that interest arises independently in response

to actual situations without the aid or help of others. Its emergence, development, and culmination do not depend upon outside factors, whether positive or negative. Rewards are external and hinder spontaneity. Punishment not only distracts attention, but deprives one of the pleasure and satisfaction inherent in spontaneous interest.

From the standpoint of this principle, spontaneous interest is initiated and directed from within the individual. It requires no force or inducement from others. It is its own excuse for being, and is inherently good in and of itself without regard to external conditions either in the present or in the future. It is always intrinsic, never extrinsic.

3. *Continuity* of pleasure or satisfaction signifies that interest is direct and immediate from the beginning of the experience until the end. It causes the experience and is always present as long as the experience lasts. It is not only present from first to last; but it is completely present. Thought, feeling, and action are all there all the time, not merely by implication, but in full force. They do not represent stages in a developing experience from unconscious impulse to purposeful activity, from vague feeling or satisfaction to pleasure, joy, and enthusiasm. The immediate interest includes all these phases on its first appearance and continues to include them until the end.

Feeling, suggested in such terms as satisfaction, joy, pleasure, happiness, and enthusiasm frequently used by those who adopt the principle of immediate interest, represents no state of indifference, toleration, acceptance, or calm satisfaction. It typically signifies strong emotion, or at least intense feeling. Such feeling is never annoying, unpleasant, disagreeable, or painful. It is always positive, never negative.

Like all analyses of theories and principles, such a conception as we have here elaborated represents a general tendency that is clearly observable in both theory and practice. Whether they realize it or not, the importance of continuous pleasure is suggested in the statements of some students of education who formulate the principles by which practical workers justify their policies, programs, and activities. Continuous, direct, and immediate interest is a typical principle which many other students of education representing opposing points of view tend to criticize, ridicule, and condemn. Such a principle seems implicit in some current practice in the field of teaching and curriculum-making, and even in the fields of school supervision and administration.

Perhaps the meaning of the theory of immediate interest may be clarified still more by comparing it with the theory of provisional interest. According to the former theory, interest is itself an end; according to the latter theory, it is a means to an end. According to the former, only interesting experiences are desirable; according to the latter, interesting experiences may be more desirable than uninteresting ones. According to the former, interest is an essential quality of any experience that is desirable; according to the latter, interest at its best is a desirable quality of desirable experience. According to the former, any uninteresting experience is undesirable; according to the latter, experiences lacking in interest may be desirable.

In contrasting the two theories, we do not intend, however, to say that the principle of immediate interest is to be approved in all respects. It is seldom true that, when principles can be so easily contrasted, as in this instance, one of them is sound and the other unsound. One principle may be weak where the other is strong and strong where the other is weak. These two interpretations of interest seem to neutralize each other. Those who adopt the theory of provisional interest can never agree that all desirable experiences are intensely and continuously interesting from beginning to end.

As we have already pointed out, such an assumption is contrary to ordinary experience and common sense. On the other hand, the theory of immediate interest does signify that the present living of the individual here and now is safeguarded. Interest is no longer to be used or not used as we see fit in the light of some recondite or hidden principle that is assumed rather than expressed. The importance of a universal quality derived from an interpretation of the cause or need of experience is clearly recognized in the principle of immediate interest. Any objection that may be raised to the theory of immediate interest lies in the nature of the quality of experience it emphasizes and the practical applications it suggests. Consequently, in appraising this principle of interest these are the two factors we shall keep in mind.

In the first place, from the standpoint of the philosophy of experimentalism, the assumption that individuals are consciously interested in all desirable activities from beginning to end is contrary to fact. Conscious interest is seldom, if ever, initial, and is typically eventual. It often arises out of a state of vague dissatisfaction that in its inception may not be conscious at all. It becomes increasingly conscious, involving concentrated attention when effort at adjustment meets with obstruction. It becomes more and more satisfying as the difficulty is progressively overcome.

In the second place, the conception of spontaneity typically assumed in the principle of immediate interest is open to serious objection. Spontaneity in the sense of curiosity, wonder, initiative, and responsibility in offering pertinent suggestions and making practical proposals, is always to be welcomed. But spontaneity in the minds of some who adopt the principle of immediate interest signifies something quite different. It seems to signify a kind of spontaneous combustion going on in the individual's mind. It has long been recognized in the field of psychology that experience involves an object as well as a subject, and activity involves stimuli as well as responses. The individual does not generate ideas, suggestions, proposals, and propositions by spontaneous combustion; that is, without receiving suggestions from other persons or things in his environment. The assumption that the responses of the individual are thus spontaneous implies that those responsible for guidance and direction expect all suggestions to come from those whom they undertake to guide and direct. They thus relieve themselves of the responsibility of making definite proposals on the ground that the spontaneous proposals of the individuals whom they are directing are preferable. They do not realize that so-called spontaneous proposals are really suggested by factors in the environment. As a matter of fact, whatever is proposed by anybody is suggested by something or somebody. Those in control of educational activities should not hesitate to consider themselves at least as well qualified as any one else to make suggestions and proposals. For instance, the pupil's suggestion that his grade construct a post office or have a Valentine party is prompted by somebody or something. It certainly could not be any worse — and it might be better — if such an undertaking were proposed by a good teacher who knew the pupils and the practical situation.

In the third place, the importance of the intensity of the feelings often emphasized by those who adopt the theory of immediate interest is also questionable. As we have already suggested, there is no evidence that a strong emotion, either positive or negative, is required for efficiency in learning. It appears unreasonable to believe that intensity of feeling which does not facilitate learning should be a quality of experience that is good within itself. Certainly when immediate interest is conceived in terms of strong feeling — as is often indicated in current descriptions of school practice — and then considered as the only criterion of a desirable experience, we are on dangerous ground.

The practical implications contained in these aspects of the principle of immediate interest, to which the foregoing objections are raised, are often put into effect. Those who assume responsibility for guidance and direction of others use the logical suggestions implicit in these conceptions of immediate interest to justify educational policies, programs, and activities that contradict the common sense of the public, subject themselves to ridicule, and reflect discredit on the whole movement of progressive education with which they are usually identified. The practical implications are the same in quality for all social institutions and for all phases of school practice.

Reference to their effect on the attitude of the teacher in dealing with pupils in the school should be sufficient to indicate their effect on other educational and social leaders. The teacher who assumes that individuals must be consciously interested in whatever they do from beginning to end, who believes that the ideas, suggestions, and proposals of pupils are the result of spontaneous generation in the mind without reference to the influence of the environment, and who considers strong emotion an essential quality of desirable experience, reflects these conceptions in his practices, in his descriptions of them, and in the slogans he uses to justify them.

The teacher who accepts the theory of immediate interest expresses himself in various ways, but the spirit of his position is always the same. Sometimes he insists that his pupils always propose their undertakings, and not be dominated by the suggestions and proposals of the teacher. He intervenes only as a last resort after the pupils have had ample time and opportunity to make their own proposals. He sometimes admits setting the stage by placing on display maps, pictures, and other things, but he does not tell pupils what to do; they tell him what they want to do. He more often points with pride to the fact that some pupil suggested the project, problem, enterprise, or unit which all accepted with enthusiasm. At times he assumes that his pupils are happy and enthusiastic about their work from beginning to end.

As we have already suggested, there is no reason to believe that pupils generally are consciously interested in desirable educational undertakings at the outset, that desirable proposals are generated by spontaneous combustion, or that strong emotion is typically a desirable quality of experience. The practices which these conceptions suggest do not meet the approval of practical common sense in the learning-teaching situation or anywhere else. Such practices and the conceptions by which they are justified are usually identified with progressive education, and therefore reflect discredit on the effort of others who conceive interest in quite a different way and who do not endorse the theory of immediate interest and its implications. We must therefore conclude our appraisal of this attitude toward motivation or interest as a feature of educative experience with the conviction that, although it is commendable in recognizing the importance of a criterion of the present worth of life in the here and now, it is still far from adequate. The need for such a *standard* still persists and thus warrants the effort which others are making to develop an interpretation of this feature that is different in important respects from either provisional interest or immediate interest.

THEORY OF PERVASIVE INTEREST
(EDUCATIONAL EXPERIMENTALISM)

The educational experimentalists recognize the failure of the authoritarian principle of provisional interest to safeguard in theory the individual against exploitation, but they refuse to acknowledge responsibility for the laissez-faire principle of immediate interest, which is often attributed to them by both progressives and reactionaries. For convenience of reference, their attitude toward motivation as a feature of experience may be designated as the theory of *pervasive interest*. It represents an effort to do justice to the points of emphasis contained in the other two theories without accepting the validity of certain assumptions which seem to be inherent in them. It recognizes as valid the conviction embodied in provisional interest that people cannot do what they ought to do on many occasions and be immediately, consciously, and directly enthusiastic in the pursuit of all their activities. It recognizes also the importance of the conviction embodied in immediate interest that desirable experiences must be acceptable. The theory of pervasive interest means that every desirable experience is, as a whole, at least, acceptable to the individual who has it.

As a basis of their attitude toward desirable motivation and interest, the educational experimentalists assume the principle that experience need is the initiating and sustaining condition of all experience. From this point of view, the typical educative experience, which involves the interaction of the individual with his environment and which occurs on the social level of existence, like all other interactions, must be caused, occasioned, initiated, sustained, and maintained by some state of affairs. Particular factors of such initiating and sustaining causes vary, but they always embody some qualitative factor that pervades all educative experiences. Otherwise, there would be no difference between an experience and any other interaction, educative experience and any other activity. The initiating and sustaining cause of interactions on the physical level, on the vital level, and on the human level differ somewhat. In other words, the cause of an educative experience is different from that of a mere physical activity on the one hand, and from that of a mere animal response on the other. The nature of such a psychological, practical, and existential cause of experience which must be present affects the quality of experiences that are desirable. The position here assumed is that the initiating and sustaining cause of experience is that state of affairs which may be properly designated as experience need. If experience need is found to be the initiating and sustaining cause of experience, it must, therefore, be considered an essential feature of educative experience. The motivation of experience becomes, for the experimentalist, need of experience. His theory of interest is an interpretation of this feature into a positive and constructive quality of any desirable experience.[3]

Perhaps the best approach to an understanding of need as a possible cause of educative experience is to consider the cause of other interactions among physical things, such as the movement of sands on the seashore or the falling of objects to the ground from tables and high buildings, and chemical reactions such as are involved in the interactions of sodium and hydrochloric acid, or in the oxidation of iron when exposed to air or water. These interactions do not occur without some initiating and sustaining condition. The common qualitative element in all such physical and chemical changes is known in the physical sciences as loss of equilibrium. Physical objects move as long as they are unbalanced and come to rest as soon as their balance is established. Just as a disturbance of the normal relation of physical objects causes interaction among them, so does a disturbance of the normal relations of chemical elements cause interaction among them. Now, it is just this disturbance of relations in the physical world that is known as loss of equilibrium.

On the vital or biological level, an animal is in constant interaction with the physical and biological world, even as are physical objects and chemical elements. In his own physiological structure and the relationship which the organs of the body bear to one another, he includes many physical and chemical interactions. But the interactions of the whole animal with his environment is more inclusive

---

[3] L. Thomas Hopkins, *Interaction: The Democratic Process.* D. C. Heath and Company, New York, 1941. Pp. 136–141.

than the interactions of merely physical and chemical things. Living things as contrasted with inorganic things tend to maintain a dynamic organization of energies. In his interactions with his environment, the organism learns something, whereas inanimate and inorganic things do not learn anything. Living organisms are not merely passive recipients of external influences. The most inactive of them, such as the oyster, does not merely take what comes. They all without exception rise to the occasion and meet the factors that impinge upon them. Life is a process of adjustment in which the animal on all levels tends to maintain his normal balance with the world. The initiating and sustaining cause of physiological interactions is known in biology and psychology as lack of adjustment. Life is a process of losing balance in one respect and regaining it in others. The cause of the interactions is still a loss of equilibrium, but the equilibrium that is lost is different in important respects from the loss of equilibrium on the physical level. It is just this difference that the lack of adjustment is designed to indicate.

Just as the loss of equilibrium is the cause of reactions on the physical level, and lack of adjustment is the cause of response on the biological level, so need is the cause of experience on the human level. The establishment of an equilibrium on the physical level can be secured without what is known in biology and psychology as adjustment, involving an integration of physical and chemical factors which must occur in activities on the higher levels. The activities required in ordinary adjustment do not necessitate that qualitative adjustment known as experience. But the establishment of equilibrium or adjustment on the highest human level involves a special sort of movement or response, that is properly called experience. Parts and factors of the individual are always engaged in the restoration of a physical equilibrium and other parts and factors are involved in the process of biological adjustment. But there are times when the individual not only acts as a whole but has experiences. Stated somewhat differently, some activities are at the same time experiences. Certain situations cannot be settled satisfactorily without experiences. It is just this state of affairs that we have designated as the need of experience. Need of experience is the initiating and sustaining cause of experience that is continuous with mere lack of adjustment on the biological level and loss of equilibrium on the physical level. Without need, which includes the loss of equilibrium and lack of adjustment, there would be no experience on the social level of existence.

Perhaps the conception of need as the initiating and sustaining cause of experience supplies a basis on which all parties may agree. It seems to be a fact of experience itself that we do have to engage in uninteresting as well as in interesting activities. Everything cannot be interesting in the ordinary sense of interesting. But need of experience is different from interest. An activity initiated and sustained by a need may be pleasant, but it may also be unpleasant, even painful. Since experience need is simply a tension, strain, or stress that necessitates a certain kind of activity, this kind of activity continues as long as the tension, strain, or stress persists. It is designated as experience need not because of the consciousness of need, but rather because the need can be overcome only by an activity that is also a conscious experience.

The need of experience is neither desirable nor undesirable. It is simply the state of affairs that causes an experiential activity. Such activity is interesting in the sense that the individual seeks to do those things that will resolve his problem. Also he puts forth effort to overcome obstacles to his endeavors to satisfy his experience need. Some of his activities are thus interesting, and some are uninteresting. We therefore have a principle that explains the initiating and sustaining cause of experience, a principle to which all parties may agree. Still we do not have a theory of a quality that makes life, experience, and education worth while for itself in the here and now.

The significance of the living present for its own sake has been an important point of emphasis in educational theory during modern times. Interest, pleasure, or satisfaction has been recognized as an influence on learning for thousands of years. But only within the last two centuries have we developed the notion that the initiating and sustaining cause of experience must be such that every experience is a good in and of itself. From this point of view, life at one stage is no more valuable than at any other stage. Every period in life has its own meaning and worth and does not owe its value to the reflection of some unperceived future life in this world or the next. It may be necessary to have experiences that are not in all respects interesting or pleasant, as some people contend. Nevertheless, from the standpoint of some educational reformers for more than a century, every experience must be somehow good in itself. Experience need seems to be the initiating and sustaining cause of any and every experience. The experiences that are required to meet needs are not always satisfying or desirable for their own sake, but, according to the theory of pervasive interest, they should be at least acceptable.

According to this theory of motivation, every experience as a whole should be interesting, or, perhaps better, it should not be repellent. It may become increasingly acceptable. The individual may become increasingly glad that he is having it. At least, he does not regret having had it by the time it draws to a close. This kind of interest is present in situations which the individual seeks or at least does not try to change. It is not necessarily, although on occasion it may be, conscious, involving concentrated attention. Such interest may involve heightened feeling and even emotion, but it does not require them. This conception of interest signifies rather a calm tone of satisfaction, and even this is not typically continuous from the beginning to the end of desirable experiences. But according to this theory, no experience is desirable in which acceptability is not present at one time or another. Acceptability is an essential quality of desirable experience, and must, therefore, be recognized as a fundamental criterion in any effort to influence the experiences of people positively and constructively for their own good.

The quality of acceptability or pervasive interest may be thus contrasted with the theories of provisional interest and immediate interest. In both these theories, interest seems to mean a conscious and continuous satisfaction of the individual with the activities in which he engages. According to the theory of pervasive interest, such consciousness is not necessarily always objectionable. The point we are making is that the presence of conscious interest throughout an experience is not essential to its desirability. Typically, experiences, even the most desirable, are not satisfying or agreeable at all times. The individuals whom we seek to influence in such a way as to improve them do not usually know what they should do, and they are not consciously interested in advancing in the activities in which they should engage. If they knew their interests and the activities through which they would be fulfilled, they would require little or none of our help. In many cases people become consciously interested, if at all, after their undertakings are already under way. The proponents of provisional interest are constantly insisting that immediate and direct interest cannot always be secured, as the exponents of immediate interest seem so often to assume. If immediate interest is conceived as conscious and continuous, so far from being wrong, the former have both psychology and common sense on their side.

The annoying, the unpleasant, the disagreeable, and even the painful are unavoidable factors in many of the most acceptable experiences.

Making mistakes or entering blind alleys from time to time, whether in overt activity or in imagination, is not agreeable. But it is in situations that involve false moves, retracing one's steps, coming out wrong and beginning again, that learning is best and experiences are most acceptable. But in case the reader concludes that we must be insane, or at least abnormal, in not being able to distinguish between pleasure and pain, the agreeable and the disagreeable, we hasten to say that experiences must be considered as wholes. The important thing is not that one shall be happy and joyous at every moment. It is quite sufficient if the experience as a whole is even mildly satisfying. If it becomes satisfying and seems good by the time it comes to a close, it is an acceptable experience. Interest is pervasive since all that has gone before has been transformed by the quality of satisfaction that now pervades it.

It is too much to expect everything to be satisfying, pleasant, and agreeable continuously in this human world here below. The emphasis on the worth and significance of life for its own sake in the present does not signify perennial bliss. The present experience does not correspond to moments or units of what is known in psychology as "short time." The duration of these short-time units is about equal to the time required to utter such a word as "now." A present experience, in order for its true character to be developed and revealed, corresponds to "long time" in psychology. It involves at least minutes, more often hours, or even days and weeks. It is therefore possible for an experience which involves many disagreeable moments still to seem, on the whole, very acceptable and positively valuable. In fact, the most desirable experiences include clouds as well as sunshine, pain and suffering as well as happiness and joy.

The theory of pervasive interest signifies that the good life should be good to us in the present, but any particular present is conceived as some particular one of the experiences that go to make up the life of the individual and not just as some momentary conscious response. If everything were immediately good, there would be nothing for us to do but to bask in the sunshine of our own souls and contemplate the true, the beautiful, and the good. The theory of pervasive interest does not justify the effort to deprive man of living by the sweat of his brow and of the satisfaction that comes from a disagreeable task well done. It leaves a place for drill, routine, and even drudgery when these things are required in experiences that are on the whole found to be good. It signifies caring for details, keeping things straight, following directions, keeping order, being punctual and accurate, not because the effort involved is good within itself but because it contributes to the satisfaction and joy of experiences which are more inclusive.

The theory of pervasive interest does not require that activities designed for education or improvement of the experiences of those who engage in them be made easy. It does require that things be within the range of the ability of those who are expected to do them. The psychologist has shown that almost any individual feels satisfaction in almost any useful work that he can do well.[4] But things must not be so easy that they fail to challenge one to put forth effort. Mere routine is not acceptable to the normal individual, to the individual who has not become routinized. Least of all does the theory of pervasive interest require that all the rough spots be ironed out of activities. They are a part of life and a part of education, and dealing with them successfully is a source of interest, pleasure, and joy.

The theory of pervasive interest recognizes the importance of intellectual alertness, curiosity, and wonder usually embodied in spontaneity, but it does not demand that all desirable experiences be initiated by the immature and inexperienced without help from others. From the standpoint of this theory, the only requirement is that the experience as a whole be acceptable. What particular thing or person suggests any given activity, undertaking, or experience is an irrelevant matter. As Dewey has so well shown, every activity or experience is suggested by some factor in the environment.[5] The leader in any educational situation in the home, in the school, in the church, in the business concern, in the state, or in the social organization is as much a part of the environment as anything else. If he is responsible for getting things done, he should take the lead in making suggestions and proposals. No perverted notion in regard to spontaneity as an aspect of interest should justify him in failing to assume responsibility in the matter of suggesting policies, programs, and activities. It is the quality of experience that is to be considered. Sometimes the desirable quality can be secured in one way and sometimes it can be secured in another. What procedure should be used must be left to the judgment of those in charge.

---

[4] E. L. Thorndike, *Human Nature and the Social Order*. The Macmillan Company, New York, 1940. Pp. 55–56.

[5] John Dewey, Individuality and Freedom, *Journal of the Barnes Foundation*, 2: 1–16, January, 1926. Also available in Ratner, Joseph (Editor), *Intelligence and the Modern World: John Dewey's Philosophy*. The Modern Library, New York, 1939. Pp. 619–627.

The theory of pervasive interest embodies the essential demands of both the authoritarian and the laissez-faire theories of interest without involving the logical difficulties and undesirable practical implications seemingly inherent in them. It recognizes the necessity of experiences involving hard work and disagreeable factors. It establishes a universal principle safeguarding present living. It avoids continuous conscious interest, intense feeling, and subjective spontaneity with all their objectionable psychological and practical results. In this theory, the need of experience is assumed to be the cause of experience, but experience need is the initiating and sustaining cause of all experiences, the good and bad alike. The opportunity to have only experiences which are disagreeable through and through cannot be justified on the basis of the quality of pervasive interest. *Only those experiences are educative or desirable which are, on the whole, acceptable to the individual.*

CHAPTER 6

Creativity of Experience

THAT THE NATURE OF LEARNING is an important educational consideration is widely recognized. Learning is indispensable for the survival of the individual and the maintenance of the social group. Culture, civilization, and even human survival depend upon it. Our conception of the way people learn influences the ways we direct, control, guide, and teach them; that is, educate them. Parents and teachers, and everybody else who assumes any responsibility for his own education or that of others in the school or anywhere else, are under obligation to study the nature of learning. In general, it functions in two ways. It is both conservative and progressive. As conservative, it reaffirms, substantiates, and fixes the structure that has already been produced, learned, or created. As progressive, it produces a new structure in some individual. An experience that is educative involves the production of a new structure. The production of the new structure is creative in the sense that the individual now has something in his mind, heart, or muscles that he has never had before. Experience is thus creative in the broad sense that it involves the learning of things new to the individual. From the standpoint of educational authoritarianism, this creativity of experience involves the embodiment in the individual of patterns of thought, feeling, and action that already exist in the minds of others or in the objective world. From the standpoint of educational laissez faire, it involves the elaboration of patterns already existing and vaguely implicit in the structure of the self, of the individual. From the standpoint of educational experimentalism, it consists in the reconstruction of factors existing in both the individual and his environment, which signifies creative originality as a quality of experience.

THEORY OF CREATIVE EMBODIMENT
(EDUCATIONAL AUTHORITARIANISM)

Creative embodiment has reference only to the production of patterns in the individual that already exist in his environment. Experience does not produce anything new; it merely distributes wares that are old and established. What has long been a part of the world and a part of the mind of others becomes a part of the mind of the individual. New structures are created in the individual but they are not created in the world in which they are already embodied.

Just exactly how existing patterns of the objective world can also become patterns of any individual through experience is conceived in different ways. According to some authoritarians, the individual is relatively passive and waits for these patterns to be passed to him by some more active agent, such as parent, teacher, textbook, or other recognized authority. Creativity is thus a process of absorption. According to other authoritarians, the individual is relatively active and operates on the environment so as to extract from it the proper patterns. Creativity is thus a process of appropriation. But whether the new structures are absorbed or appropriated, they are embodiments of antecedent patterns already established in the physical, spiritual, or social world.

Other authoritarians differ as to the nature of the content of the patterns thus embodied. According to some, the individual incorporates structural factors directly just as they exist in the physical world, in social institutions, or in the minds of others. For instance, his mind absorbs the ideas of his parents, teacher, pastor, author, or some other authority. According to others, the structures are incorporated into his mind or nervous system only indirectly. For instance, since no idea is original, according to this theory, an idea incorporated in the mind of an individual through experience merely represents or corresponds to the same idea in the mind of the parent, teacher, or author.

Philosophers and students of education in times past have made much of the foregoing distinctions. They have shown that the individual is active and not passive and, on the basis of this psychological principle, have condemned passivity and advocated activity on the part of pupils. They have often rejected the naïve conception that we know the world just as it is and have contended that at best our ideas merely copy or represent the realities of the objective world. In other words, whatever the individual learns is at best only an approximation to reality. But regardless of whether the mind is active or passive, and regardless of whether the patterns formed in the individual consist of structures just as they are in the world or whether they merely in some way approximate such structures, these patterns are nevertheless embodied in the individual. Experience is creative in the sense that the individual becomes different because something new to him has merged into his being but not in the sense that anything new has been produced in the world.

Educational authoritarians also differ as to the psychological character of the individual, and therefore differ about the nature of the structure in which these fixed patterns are embodied within the self. The mind or self may be conceived in terms of substance that is purely mental as contrasted with the purely physical. When psychological structure is so conceived, the patterns are mental in character. On the other hand, when the structure of the self is conceived as physical, the structure of the patterns produced in the individual are also physical. For instance, the content of the things we learn is then conceived as mechanical habits rather than as ideas or as combinations of ideas. From the standpoint of the theory of creative embodiment, such psychological distinctions are actually irrelevant. The main thing is that the patterns learned or embodied in the individual, whether they are absorbed or appropriated, whether they are identical in structure or different in structure from the pattern of the objective world, or whether they are physical or spiritual, are nothing fundamentally new. The new structures in the individual are adequate to the degree that they approach the forms of the old structures already established in the world.

In the theory of creative embodiment the existence of established content of some kind is accepted as fundamental. No matter whether such subject matter is physical, social, or spiritual, it is the very stuff that passes in and out of conscious experience. It is the very stuff that is incorporated into the mind, heart, or nervous system. The consciousness of one content is different from the consciousness of another content. The individual who incorporates in himself one kind of subject matter builds in himself one kind of structure, and the individual who incorporates in himself another kind of subject matter builds in himself another kind of structure. They both build structures in themselves, one of one kind and one of another. The subject matter passes in and out of consciousness without undergoing change; it is built into the structure of the individual to abide for a time, but it tends to remain the same. The nearer it approximates reality the longer it will endure, for ultimate reality is now as it was in the beginning and ever will be.

The content represents a reality that has never been created, remains the same from first to last, and is the very material to which the structure of experience corresponds. The teacher, the school, or the books are mere instruments through which the facts, principles, or values, whatever their nature, are brought within reach of the individual. The sense organs and the muscles and the mind and the nervous system are the means by which individuals lay hold of such facts, principles, and values as may be within their reach. Those responsible for education and the improvement of experience are the authorities on whom pupils rely to discover these important elements which are used in the construction of the structure of experience; but no one modifies or changes them in the process of making them available. The individual who incorporates them in his structural system does not change them. The process of building a new structure in any individual involves two stages — discovery and incorporation. In school practice, for instance, the authorities are responsible for making the proper discoveries, and practitioners are responsible for making them available for incorporation.

This authoritarian principle is assumed in all those practices in which facts, skills, principles, or values, however defined, are conceived as ends in themselves without reference to their acceptability to the individual or to their usefulness to society. It dominates the minds of those who want things learned just because they are conceived as true, right, or good in themselves. From this point of view ultimate truth, ultimate justice, and ultimate goodness can never be firmly grasped, but they can be approached. The best that man can do here in this life is to incorporate into his mind and heart those factors which contribute to these ends.

This authoritarian principle is also assumed by all those institutions which seek to incorporate certain fixed ideals, skills, or knowledge in the minds and hearts of their members. Even if these values are conceived as the outcome of research in the field of value or as the outcome of scientific investigation, they are fixed and changeless until they are modified through future studies. They are conceived as approximations to the true, the beautiful, the good, and the effective, and therefore cannot be modified in the process of transmission. They are fixed, at least for the time being, and must remain fixed until those who somehow have special access to reality see fit to change them. The values discovered by those especially qualified to discover the secrets of nature and society are conceived as the nearest approach to the real that has been discovered up to date. These values must remain the ends of all practical workers until they are revised by such authorities as first discovered and defined them; they should be embodied just as they are in the minds and hearts of the rank and file of the people.

The personality or experience of the individual is produced in the sense that it represents accumulation of structure through a process of absorbing or appropriating values that already exist in the nature of things, or of approximating such values as those in authority are able to discover. But no human being is creative in the sense of being able to produce new elements of reality through experience. Such a power is beyond the capacity of the most wise and the most powerful. From a limited point of view, new approximations to the true, the beautiful, and the good may be discovered by the wise, the good, and the powerful. Only the chosen few are able to approach reality closer than others have approached it in the past.

The price any individual has to pay for such a capacity is the mastery of what the specially qualified who have gone before him have produced. When these factors are incorporated or embodied into his experience, he may make some advance toward reality if he has the opportunity, the genius, the time, the energy, and the perseverance. It is the business of the rank and file to build the structure of their personalities out of the material that the elect and elite provide. To discover such material is a special service of special individuals. The performance of such a recognized social service is a source of great satisfaction, but such achievement and the kind of joy that attends it are possible, even in the smallest measure, for only a few of the most capable, the most favorably situated, and the most persevering.

In the theory of creative embodiment, the creative quality of the experience involved in the process of incorporating ready-made patterns in the heart, soul, mind, or body of the individual is not considered. It is the product rather than the quality of experience that is important. The nature of the product is conceived as the reality or the approximations to the reality which it embodies. The quality of the experience involved in such dependence on authority in autocratic societies is usually idealized; but in democratic societies its presence is seldom realized. The structure that is embodied, whatever it may be, is satisfactory to the degree that it incorporates reality or its authoritative approximations. In the process of embodying such content, the problem of method is confined to questions of economy and efficiency of learning without reference to the quality of thought, feeling, or attitude of the learner.

The practical implication of this conception has already been suggested. It signifies that there are certain values which, whether for eternity or for a relatively short period of time, are fundamental aspects of reality. It is the business of all those in a position to do so to aid in incorporating these fixed and inflexible values in the structure of the personalities of the rank and file to the extent of their capacities. Such a conception signifies that those who are responsible for the immediate process of instruction, propaganda, or indoctrination have little or nothing to do with the content of these values. Their function is to serve the ends or purposes of others. The individuals to be educated have nothing to do with selecting the content of the structures that they are to appropriate or absorb.

With respect to methods and materials, the situation must be the same. Only the elite are able to discover the best ways to do things. Those who actually do them should use the methods that have been found to be best by those who have the capacity and responsibility to discover the measures reality prescribes. The materials to be used are either prescribed or are implicit in the values to be incorporated.

From the standpoint of the philosophy of experimentalism, the authoritarian theory of creativity is very unsatisfactory. If those who accept their purposes ready-made from others are slaves, certainly those who incorporate ready-made values in the minds and hearts of others are making slaves of them. Authoritarian methods and materials — the results of authoritative decisions and recommendations — cannot be revised to meet changing conditions. The rank and file gradually become tools to be moved like men on a chess board. They are thought to be incapable by nature of discovering the values that constitute or represent features of reality. By accepting the values that others have decreed, by following the ways others have prescribed, they actually do become incapable of making their own decisions. By systematic treatment they are rendered helpless and their helplessness is then used as a justification for the continuation of the same treatment.

In other words, when the quality of experience is neglected in learning or in the process of creating new structures, some quality nevertheless is invariably present. If it is not deliberately considered, it will less often perhaps be a quality that experience itself will find desirable. The quality that often pervades the experience of the rank and file may be something like the quality of silent obedience which Adolph Hitler prized above all other qualities. Conformity to requirements and faith in myths, such as the program of national socialism developed in Nazi Germany, may result from neglect as well as from deliberate effort. Of course, such a quality is not always, or even usually, consciously sought in democratic countries, but it is the logical outcome of the principle of creative embodiment wherever it is systematically applied, even as it is in totalitarian states where it is deliberately sought.

The implications that may be logically inferred from this interpretation of the feature of creativity may be easily illustrated by reference to certain school practices typical of those that may be found elsewhere. Teachers who accept everything stated in a textbook as literally true and try to incorporate its contents into the minds of the pupils in the form and order given accept the spirit of the principle of creative embodiment. Likewise, those who take their aims, subject matter, and procedures ready-made from official curriculum-makers and seek to incorporate them directly in the personality of immature childhood and youth are endorsing this principle. Also endorsing it are those who classify individuals into two groups — the leaders and the followers — and devote their efforts largely to the education of the leaders. From this point of view the leaders are to be "educated" and the followers are to be "trained," [1] in that the qualities of experience emphasized in the activities of the two groups are different.

From the standpoint of the philosophy of experimentalism, it is important that followers as well as leaders be educated. In fact, leaders and followers cannot be sharply differentiated into two distinct groups. Almost any normal person may lead in some things, and almost anybody should be a follower in some things. There are too many occupations and activities in the modern world for anyone to be a leader in everything. Moreover, to be a good leader one must also be a good follower. Furthermore, if leadership is to be really appreciated by followers, followers must themselves be leaders in some things. It may very well be that some people, the so-called followers, cannot

---

[1] Ross L. Finney, *A Sociological Philosophy of Education*. The Macmillan Company, New York, 1928. Pp. 385–398.

148   CREATIVITY OF EXPERIENCE

learn and do. But this fact does not mean that the quality of creativity is any less desirable for the rank and file than for the elect.[2]

Even many authoritarians who recognize the importance of creative education have in mind the absorption or appropriation of some particular kind of subject matter, such as music, poetry, drawing, sculpture, and other fine arts. In accordance with the theory of objective contingency there are as many different kinds of education as there are different kinds of subject matter. Creative education, then, according to the theory of creative embodiment, consists in incorporating into the structure of the personality the subject matter of the so-called creative subjects. Exponents of this conception of creativity have in mind again no special quality of experience, but merely certain specific kinds of subject matter to be learned. They are quite convinced that such subject matter should be learned, though perhaps they may not consider it so important as other subject matter. Usually, however, they consider the so-called fine arts fads and frills that may be neglected, except for the benefit of the gifted few. But whatever the attitude of the proponents of this theory may be with respect to the relative importance of the subjects, they are still interested in having people acquire certain patterns rather than in their having the creative quality of experience in the acquisition of any patterns.

This theory of creative embodiment is exemplified in the attitude of people everywhere who think of learning as incorporating in the mind or self antecedent subject matter without changing it in the process. When individuals deal with the same materials, in so far as the learning is satisfactory they achieve identical results. Many authoritarians who recognize and even emphasize the importance of different subject matters insist on uniformity of procedure. The same things are learned in the same way, in so far as they are learned properly. Proponents of educational authoritarianism and the theory of creative embodiment thus frown upon individual methods. Everyone is expected to use the recognized authoritative procedures. The only choice possible is a choice among materials, and even here the things to which attention should be devoted depend upon the implications of the principle of objective contingency and doctrinaire sociality rather than upon the disposition of the individual. Any difference in outcome is due either to difference in subject matter, which is to be expected, or to a deficiency in procedure — variation in method — which is to be rejected.

[2] L. Thomas Hopkins, *Interaction: The Democratic Process*. D. C. Heath and Company, New York, 1941. Pp. 167–171.

From the standpoint of the philosophy of experimentalism, the fine arts constitute a subject matter that should not be neglected. They constitute an important phase of experience, as does also the subject matter in other fields. In fact, everyone should have some access to the fine arts. But from this point of view, the creative quality of experience is the primary consideration, and it is not the function of any particular kind of subject matter. The quality of experience through which various patterns of conduct are built into the structure of the self is the important thing. For some one kind of subject matter is more useful, and for others other kinds are more useful. There is no particular kind of subject matter or particular piece of art that can serve as an adequate substitute for the creative quality which should be a quality of all desirable experience. The creative quality of experience is important for all in all fields and not merely for the few in some fields, or even for the many in any field.

Those who recognize the importance of the joy and pride that comes from planning and achieving personal ends, from trying out new procedures, and from straying from the beaten path or the prescribed rule, can never accept the embodiment theory that neglects the creative quality of experience. If the quality of creativity is good for one, it is good for all. If the qualities of silent obedience, mechanical conformity, and faith in myths are implicit in the application of the embodiment theory, it is unacceptable, no matter what the tangible results may be in terms of objective things or psychological products. From this point of view, how things are learned is as important as what is learned. An experience that is educationally desirable must be pervaded by the quality of creativity involving wonder and adventure as it never can be when attention is centered upon mere products, structures, or tangible outcomes. *The values of life pervade the process of learning and determine the value of the outcomes themselves.* The quality of creativity is one of these values, and in the embodiment theory it is not only neglected but often deliberately rejected.

Theory of Creative Self-Expression [3]
(Educational Laissez Faire)

In educational laissez faire the disposition of the individual determines what patterns should be learned. For many proponents of this

---

[3] The term *creative self-expression* is here used in the technical sense of direct self-expression.

philosophy of education, the principles, conceptions, techniques, and the like to be learned are implicit in patterns included in the self prior to experience. Such a conception thus seems to be consistent with the theory of subjective contingency, inherent sociality, and immediate interest, the other aspects of the philosophy of educational laissez faire already considered. It signifies that desirable experience, educative experience, consists primarily in the elaboration, expression, or development of factors which are already present within the individual himself, apart from experience. It thus contrasts sharply with the creative embodiment theory, according to which the products learned through experience are factors incorporated into the individual from the objective world.

Nevertheless, to discover an adequate term with which to designate the theory of creativity is not easy. Although it may be considered the direct opposite of creative embodiment, to call it creative unfoldment might be misunderstood because there are certain conceptions of unfoldment which signify in practice the authoritarian theory of direct embodiment instead of direct expression. On the other hand, to call it creative self-expression might cause some to confuse it with the theory of self-expression to which experimentalists subscribe. In other words, there are two clearly defined theories of creative self-expression — the theory which the experimentalists condemn and the theory which they endorse. The laissez-faire theory, which they condemn, might be designated as *direct self-expression*, and the one which they endorse might be designated as *critical self-expression*. Since constant reference to two forms of self-expression may be confusing, we have decided to designate the direct, uncritical self-expression, which proponents of educational laissez faire endorse, as *creative self-expression*, and the theory of critical self-expression, which educational experimentalists endorse, as *creative originality*.

The meaning and significance of this direct self-expression theory of creativity as an aspect of educational laissez faire may be clarified somewhat through reference to the conceptions of the world and man already noted in the consideration of the laissez-faire theories of relativity, sociality, and motivation of experience. From the point of view of this theoretical background of educational laissez faire, the principle of direct self-expression is the logical implication of the belief that nature is good and right within itself.

From this point of view, man is continuous with the rest of nature and embodies it in himself. Since nature is good, man apart from experience embodies within himself not only the means but also the ends of the good life. The problem that thus confronts the student of education in the broader sense, including morals, economics, and politics, is to elaborate this conception of life and education; and the problem of practical workers everywhere who are responsible for constructively influencing people, young or old, consists in providing the conditions under which human nature as it exists may best realize itself. The building of new structures in the individual is conceived as a process of expressing patterns already inherent in him.

According to this theory, inherent in the nature of the individual apart from experience are certain propensities or dispositions whose direct and immediate expression is essential to the welfare of the individual and the race. The development of these tendencies, however, will be restrained, inhibited, and repressed by the artificialities of civilization unless pains are taken to nurture them and expand them into the structural constitution of the individual. The activities through which they are realized are the mere expressions of tendencies inherent in nature. Activities are to be appraised not on the basis of their consequences but on the basis of their origin. If the impulse expressed is natural, it is good, it matters not what the consequences may be, for the consequences would invariably be good, were it not for the artificial standards of civilization on the basis of which they are judged. The only way, therefore, by which the creative factors of nature may find their way into experience and civilization is through direct self-expression. Experience is creative not because it conforms to an ideal pattern of the state, the church, or of any other social institution. It is creative not because it conforms to the accepted standards of science, morals, or art. It is creative because it expresses patterns that are new to the individual since for him they have never before taken on form. Patterns which have never before taken on form anywhere are new also to civilization itself.

Education and the good life thus involve the expression of the inherent dispositions of the individual to actualize themselves through experience. Direct self-expression is psychologically creative because it involves building into the individual structures that were never built into him before — structures that are constructively creative because they are desirable, and they are desirable merely because they are manifestations of factors in nature. These factors are sociologically creative because their manifestation and actualization affect existing conditions; they are constructively creative for civilization because whatever they are, they do not conform to those that already objectively exist.

As contrasted with the authoritarian principle of direct embodiment which assumes that reality is to be found in the external world of nature and society rather than in the individual, the principle of direct self-expression assumes that reality is to be found in the individual himself. According to the authoritarian principle, the patterns to be incorporated in the structure of the individual are to be discovered through investigation by competent students, or by others especially qualified to determine the proper objective values to be sought. According to the laissez-faire principle, the patterns to be developed are to be discovered through direct inspection of the individual himself. If it were not for obstructions which the artificialities of social life have imposed upon the individual, he might actualize himself without aid and help from others, but under the practical conditions that prevent free expression, the help of others is essential. Their duty consists largely in determining through observation the nature of the impulses that manifest themselves in the individual and in removing obstructions to their development.

This laissez-faire theory of creativity is held in the field of morals, and so men identify wants, desires, and wishes with the desirable; in art any form, figure, or shape is freely expressed without regard to tradition, authoritative standards, or the condemnation of the sophisticated; in politics the best government is conceived as one which governs least; in religion God is identified with change; and in the schools both aims and methods are derived from the impulses that manifest themselves in childhood and youth. In practical life many people adopt the principle of creative self-expression, in one or more fields. In fact, every one who freely does what his wishes, desires, and wants suggest, insofar as conditions permit, is actually adopting this laissez-faire principle. Doubtless, many of us exemplify it in our daily lives more often than we realize or than we are willing to admit.

There is a difference, however, between unconsciously adopting and exemplifying a principle in one's actions — or even in justifying it — and consciously striving to extend the application and influence of a principle. So far, we have sought to render the meaning and significance of this conception intelligible without undertaking to condemn or approve it. Those who deliberately adopt the principle of direct self-expression, as in the case of other principles, are disposed, in the analysis of their activities and the activities of others, to note the qualities that exemplify the principle of direct self-expression and consciously seek to develop and extend these qualities. Proponents of direct self-expression tend to use this principle as one criterion among others in appraising activities, programs, and policies whose educational significance is important. Perhaps many more people exemplify the theory of direct self-expression in their activities in dealing with themselves and others than deliberately advocate and promote its application. Its practical application has often been attributed to the progressive schools, and its intellectual justification has often been attributed to John Dewey and other experimentalists. It seems important, therefore, to indicate the attitude of the experimentalists toward this theory.

From the standpoint of the philosophy of experimentalism, there are many objections to the theoretical assumptions underlying this conception of creativity and the more inclusive philosophy which it represents. As we have already pointed out, the general theory typically represents a protest against conditions that directly constrain, inhibit, and suppress normal human impulses. Human impulses cannot be directly and immediately suppressed. They live in the form of complexes that have been variously classified and described in the psychology of the unconscious and the psychology of behaviorism, as well as in fable and story. They still live on in some form, however they may be defined, and repeatedly disturb the equilibrium of the individual and the social order. Although they operate in secret and behind closed doors, they influence what takes place in the open and in public view. They are ever seeking some avenue of return and take advantage of every opportunity. If they cannot express themselves normally, then they will do so abnormally. The direct repression of normal impulses causes complexes and other abnormalities, and sooner or later some sensitive individual rebels at the conditions that enforce such restraint and formulates the theory that the great need of everyone is direct self-expression.

Regardless of the justification of this theory of direct self-expression on the basis of the hypothetical goodness of nature, it is a doctrine of protest that arises time and again. It justifies the direct expression of pent-up energies that are seeking release; and it therefore seems acceptable to many who suffer from long restraint and repression. Nevertheless, the conclusion that self-expression is the remedy for self-repression does not logically follow. If direct self-repression is bad, direct self-expression may likewise be bad, and any principle which justifies it may be bad also.

That direct expression of impulse involves the production of structures in the individual definable psychologically in terms of skill, knowledge, appreciation, and attitude may well be granted. It may be granted further that the products resulting from such expression are new to the individual and, also, even to the community. It must be admitted, however, that the quality of the experiences involved in direct self-expression enters into the products resulting from it. If these qualities are not desirable, the experiences are not desirable and the products are not desirable, it matters not how new and original they may be.

An individual who is aided in every way possible to do whatever he is inclined to do without thought of consequences to himself or to others is not qualifying himself for living in the world as it is. The actual world of experience outside the home and the school displays little sentimental regard for those who thoughtlessly do what their inclinations dictate. Childhood and youth should not be relieved of difficulties and hard work. It may be admitted that things should not be made difficult, but such admission does not signify that things should be made easy.

If the qualities of immediate experiences are continuous in terms of their effect, they are qualities of subsequent experiences. It appears that experiences which consist in direct and immediate response are undesirable when positively and constructively considered. When a person does whatever he is immediately inclined to do in response to stimuli in his present environment, he is strengthening the disposition to respond immediately and directly to other stimuli that appear later. He may develop new structures in himself and possibly in the community, but he is becoming more and more dependent upon conditions that are external to him. When things appeal to him, he seeks them; when they annoy him, he avoids them. This kind of reaction may be perfectly natural. Nevertheless, one who does only what he is directly and immediately inclined to do becomes increasingly dependent upon factors over which he has no control, but which he might have been able to control had he not constantly yielded to mere impulse. *It is possible to become a slave to self-suppression; but it is also possible to become a slave to self-expression.* The quality of experience involved in restraining and suppressing one's impulses and desires is enslaving, but the quality of directly expressing them is also enslaving. Dependence and slavery, however they may be caused, are not desirable, it matters not how novel the resulting structures may be. Immediate expression without regard for consequences is bad for the individual, and it may be bad for the community as well. But as everyone knows, what seems immediately bad in the present may not seem bad when viewed in terms of probable consequences, just as what seems immediately good may not seem good when considered in the light of prospective results. The quality of experience involved in immediate and direct self-expression renders the individual more and more helpless and undermines the stability of the community. Those who are seeking in the home, in the school, and in the state the means to create a new world through direct self-expression may destroy the kind of world we now have without giving us anything better with which to replace it. The quality of experience which direct self-expression generates is not good for individuals nor for the society to which they belong.

It may be assumed by some that the patterns of the self manifested as impulse are new. As a matter of fact, many propensities and tendencies are habits acquired through custom and tradition. As such, they do not necessarily constitute desirable ends which nature or Providence reveals in the impulses of the immature, the primitive, or the romantic. In other words, the theory that new structures consisting of new ways of thinking, feeling, and acting are the manifestation of some vital, mental, or spiritual force pervading nature is unsatisfactory. Such projected ends in the name of progress may be old ends which reveal themselves in a new form. The way to overcome the absolutes which the authoritarians often idealize is not to produce other absolutes which the adherents of the laissez-faire philosophy of education idealize. The patterns to be sought through educative experiences do not correspond to patterns to be found within either the objective world or the individual. No new world can be produced merely through expanding, elaborating, or developing the forms of a world that already exists, whether they are imputed to the individual or to the social order.

THEORY OF CREATIVE ORIGINALITY
(EDUCATIONAL EXPERIMENTALISM)

The theory of self-expression which experimentalists endorse is here designated as *creative originality* or *critical self-expression* to distinguish it from the theory of direct or uncritical self-expression to which proponents of educational laissez faire subscribe. The difference between the two theories lies in the conceptions of the self. According to the laissez-faire theory, the mind or self exists prior to experience and expresses itself through experience; while according to the experimentalist theory, the mind or self is a product of experience on the distinctly human level of existence. According to the laissez-faire theory, self-expression requires the adaptation of experience to the demands of an antecedent self; according to the experimentalist theory, self-expression requires a reconstruction, a re-creation, of the self as well as of the environment. The experimentalist conception of self-expression is so different from the laissez-faire conception that it should have a new name, such as *creative originality*, although there is no objection, if one prefers, to calling it *critical self-expression*.

According to the theory of creative originality as a principle of educational experimentalism, the structures built in the self are actually reconstructions. They have never existed before as patterns immanent in the environment or in the individual. Any pattern that is nothing more than a transplanting or an elaboration of what already exists cannot produce a new world, and the production of a new world is just what the experimentalists are advocating in theory and working for in practice. The patterns to be sought, therefore, consist of unique structures that can be found neither in the objective world of nature and society nor in the inner world of the individual. They are constructions derived through experiences that involve the reconstruction, transformation, and remaking of factors derived from both sources. Dewey, who is considered the outstanding philosopher and student of education among the experimentalists, says, "Immature, undeveloped activity has succeeded in modifying adult organized society accidentally and surreptitiously. But with the dawn of the idea of progressive betterment and an interest in new uses of impulses, there has grown up some consciousness of the extent to which a future new society of changed purposes and desires can be created by a deliberate treatment of the impulses of youth. This is the meaning of education." [4]

Like both the authoritarian theory of creative embodiment and the laissez-faire theory of creative self-expression, the experimentalist theory of creative originality assumes creativity in the sense that the

[4] John Dewey, *Human Nature and Conduct*. Henry Holt and Company, New York, 1922. (Modern Library Edition.) P. 96.

individual creates or builds through learning mental or neural structures that are new for him. But it also emphasizes the importance of the quality of creativity involved in thinking, acting, and feeling in unusual, unique, and original ways. The proponents of all three theories consciously or unconsciously emphasize certain qualities of experience. The educational authoritarians emphasize the quality of conformity, adherents of educational laissez faire emphasize the quality of capricious spontaneity, and the educational experimentalists emphasize creative originality. In practice both the authoritarian and the laissez-faire principles lead to dependence, the former to dependence upon routine or prescribed directions, and the latter to dependence upon blind impulse or inclination. But the critical reconstruction of experience emphasized in the experimentalist principle of creative originality provides for a degree of independence on the part of the individual from external control or the caprice of immediate inclination.

According to this principle, both the structures and the process by which they are produced are new in important respects. They are new to the individual and may also be new to the world. The structures are new to the individual to the degree that they transform, remake, or reconstruct the existing personality, conduct, or self consisting of established structures. The building of a structure makes the individual new to some degree, it matters not how slight the change may be. In some instances, it may be very slight; in fact, so slight that it cannot be determined through the observation of behavior. In other instances, one's whole life may be transformed, as in the case of certain religious conversions. But a new individual also means a new society to some degree, however slight. If the changes in the individual correspond closely to the structures that exist in others, the changes in the world are not perceptible. If the changes are widely at variance with structures that exist in others, the environment itself is subject to important reconstruction, depending upon the opportunities and circumstances surrounding the individual. If the changes are very great and circumstances are very favorable, the future course of civilization may be modified, as in the case of Columbus, Martin Luther, and John Wesley. In other cases where changes are very slight, as in distinguishing green from red, and people in general are able to make a corresponding distinction, the changes in the social order are very slight. But even here the quality of the character of one individual differs somewhat from the quality of the character of other individuals, and probably under certain circumstances adds something significant to the world.

But more important from the standpoint of the desirable quality of experience is the process through which the structures are built. A process of merely incorporating in the mind what already exists is not qualitatively creative. It is merely a means to an end. But the process of reconstructing what already exists is not merely a means to an end; it is a phase of the end itself. From the standpoint of both the theory of direct creative embodiment and the theory of direct creative self-expression, the patterns that enter experience are already existing outside of experience. In the one case, they exist in the environment; in the other, they exist in the individual. From the standpoint of the theory of creative originality, the structures do not exist anywhere prior to experience in either the environment or the individual. They are made on the spot so to speak. Experience is no mere highway on which products are transferred. It is more like a manufacturing plant in which materials are received from both the individual and the environment and combined into new products. Experience is thus qualitatively a creative process.

Everything really learned is pervaded by this quality of creativity. The individual does not learn what others say and do. He learns only what he himself says and does. He learns his own responses and only his own responses; and he learns them in the way he experiences them. His responses are always unique in some respects because he, as well as the situation, is unique. The things he learns are new to him, it matters not how old they are to others. But they are somewhat different to him from what they are to others. Each individual is different from every other individual, and each situation which confronts an individual is different from every other situation. Experiences are never identical; each is somewhat different from every other. As William James has pointed out, men are not very different, but what little difference there is is the most important thing in all the world. It is this individuality that the theory of creative originality emphasizes. Inventions and discoveries, as they are usually conceived, are important. The course of civilization turns on them; and it is creativeness that produces them. Consequently the more recognition is given the manifestation of this quality of experience the more inventions and discoveries there will be.

The scope and content of the experiences through which great discoveries and inventions are achieved are, of course, different from the scope and content of ordinary experiences. But what we are trying to show is that the quality of originality may be the same. For instance, the way a very young child handles his blocks in the kindergarten may be quite original and unusual, or the way an older child manipulates number combinations may be quite original. If the great discoveries and inventions of the few are to be accepted and applied, the quality of originality of the many must be preserved and extended. The natural tendency to accept, endorse, and approve the usual and the customary as right and good must, where education is considered important, be modified somewhat, and the peculiar, the unusual, and the new should at least be tolerated and be given opportunity to prove themselves.

The emphasis on the new, however, does not signify, as in the case of the theory of direct self-expression, that everyone shall be permitted to express directly his every impulse. Neither does it mean that he shall so express all those that are new. It means rather that ideas, impulses, and proposals that emerge shall be entertained as suggestions. All of us know that new ideas or new ways of doing things are often rejected without being given a chance. The implication of the principle of creative originality is that new ideas and new ways of doing things should be welcomed as suggestions and tried out in imagination or in objective experiment before they are rejected. They are not to be taken as adequate beliefs and effective methods, and endorsed for general application just because someone proposes them. Things are not true, good, and right merely because they are suggested. Proposals in their incipiency are only suggestions; they are not things that must be done or that must be believed. Adequate consideration might justify their adoption, but they are not to be accepted in their original form. They must be subjected to trial and experiment. The principle of creative reconstruction does not require the endorsement of direct and immediate expression of impulse. It requires that immediate impulse be given an opportunity to prove itself. Only after criticism and appraisal are suggestions and proposals to be accepted as valid or to be rejected as invalid. New suggestions and proposals should have a hearing at the bar of criticism before their rejection.

The nature of creative originality as a desirable quality of experience thus indicated suggests certain factors which condition it. Among the more important of these are: (1) expansion, (2) toleration, and (3) criticism. Experience must be increasingly expanded so that new responses, suggestions, and proposals constantly and regularly can emerge. These must be sympathetically received, or at least tolerated, if they are to amount to anything, or if they are to manifest themselves in subsequent experience. Suggestions must be subjected to criticism or appraisal before being accepted either as means or as ends, as worthy goals or as efficient methods by which such values may be achieved. Since these three factors conditioning the quality of originality are important, we shall elaborate each of them in some further detail.

1. *Creative originality requires the expansion of experience.* It seems apparent that when learning is conceived as a process of creative reconstruction rather than as a process of formation from without or development from within, the wider, richer, and more varied the environment, the wider, richer, and more varied the experiences. The individual is continuously responding to something. Activities always involve the interaction of the individual with his environment. Any change in the one requires a change in the other. The environment is the factor with which the educator in the home, in the school, or anywhere else, must work. The more he enriches the environment of those under his guidance, the more new stimuli will appear to them and the more they will make new responses.

Expansion of one's environment involves interactions with more things, more people, and more ideas. But mere numbers and quantities are insufficient. There must be a variety of associations. Within limits, the wider the variety, the better. But traveling long distances, visiting many places, reading many books and many authors, engaging in many occupations, and meeting many people are not alone sufficient. Some individuals will see more on a short trip than others will see on a long trip, some will see more in one place than others will see in many places. Some will learn more in reading a few books and a few authors than others will learn in extensive reading of many books and many authors. Some will learn more in one occupation than others will learn in several occupations; some will learn more from associating with one person than others will learn from associating with many people. The expansion of the environment is not merely a question of increasing the quantity and number of external things. Nevertheless, quantity is one factor to be considered. Without some variety, which quantity and number provide, the opportunity for new responses is limited. Still, the quality of creativity that we seek is an attitude rather than a product. It is a quality of desirable experience that suffuses the desirable products of experience.

Even the actual environment can be expanded by taking advantage of the limited opportunities available to most people. For instance, a person going to some distant place to which he has been before may follow a different route. If he is primarily interested in the quality of originality, he should by all means do so. There are many ways of doing things that we have to do. Where the cost is not prohibitive, we should try out the new ways. We may call a person on the telephone, go to see him, or write to him. Perhaps any method is sufficient for the immediate end we seek. But from the standpoint of creative originality, we may prefer one method to another. Perhaps we are not so sure of how to find the numbers, manipulate the dial, or do some other thing necessary in using the telephone and therefore hesitate to use it. One who is thus inclined should use the telephone the first opportunity he has. Those who are responsible for the education of óthers should discover such common deficiencies and aid in their removal as rapidly as possible. When such obstructions are overcome, creativity is extended in small things and serves as a gateway to originality in big things.

In terms of the school, the quality of creative originality is not limited to particular kinds of subject matter, such as the fine arts. All learning is creative; usually, the greater the number of courses and the more extensive the subject matter in all courses, the better. Both vicarious experience and environmental materials, including the humanities, the natural sciences and mathematics, the social sciences, and the practical arts, should be given attention. When there is a gap of any kind, it should be filled. No type of material should be stigmatized as fads and frills. Basic and necessary skills and techniques should be mastered so that the mind is free to concentrate on the more important and more complex things that stimulate creative and intellectual inventiveness. But skills and techniques should be learned in such manner that the other qualities of desirable experience penetrate and color them.

2. *Creative originality requires sympathetic toleration.* The expansion of experience increases an individual's capacity for making suggestions. But, in a sense, the more we learn, the less capable we are of learning new things, for we are inclined to accept what we have already learned as standards in dealing with new things. In other words, we accept whatever seems to agree with our established patterns of thought, feeling and action; we reject what does not agree with them. In the last analysis, all learning is habit-forming, and whatever is learned insofar as it is really learned is a habit. Habit is both active and passive. It is active in the sense that the individual is ready and prepared to act whenever he can secure an adequate stimulus. But an adequate stimu-

lus is similar to the stimulus with respect to which the habit was formed as an acceptable way of behaving. We are always ready and willing to think and act but only in ways that conform to the ways we have thought and acted in the past.

In other words, the richer the background of experience, the more and more varied are the suggestions that occur to us in new situations. But the presence of a large number of different suggestions is not in itself sufficient to cause us to think and act in new ways. Suggestions of new ways may be rejected because they are inconsistent with old ways, and constitute a threat to established habits. It is much easier to stay in the same old rut than it is to reconstruct old habits to meet new needs, and so new ways are often rejected without a chance to prove their worth.

The individual, then, who wishes his experiences to be pervaded with the quality of creative originality must tolerate suggestions of new ways. He must not condemn them at first sight, as some people do strangers. Every stranger is not dangerous just because he looks different and acts differently from the way we look and act. Every suggestion that is inconsistent with our established habits is not dangerous. Just as the stranger should not be condemned at sight, so the suggestion of new ways should not be condemned at the moment it occurs. The stranger may have a contribution to make to the activities of the group. Likewise the suggestion of new ways may be a contribution to the life of the individual. The presence of a stranger within our gates does not require that he be either accepted or rejected. He may be entertained, and be put under observation, until he proves himself. Likewise a new suggestion may be entertained and put under observation until it proves itself. Toleration of the ideas, beliefs, and ways of others does not mean that we must change our own ideas, beliefs, and ways. It means only that we should give the new ones time to prove themselves. Toleration of the suggestion of new patterns of thought, feeling, and action that occur to us does not mean that they are to be accepted. It means only that they should be given time to show their worth.

Likewise educational leaders in the home, the school, the church, the state, business and industry, and everywhere else who wish those under their guidance and direction to have experiences that are pervaded with the quality of creative originality, should not only provide the conditions conducive to the expansion and enrichment of experience, but should also tolerate the suggestion of new ideas and new ways of doing things. It goes without saying that the experiences of individuals who occupy positions of leadership vary in quality of creative originality. Those who are least capable of originality imitate standard models, observe recognized procedures, and vary little from the beaten path themselves; and they are the people who usually refuse to tolerate even the suggestions of others concerning new ideas and new methods. But even the most original leaders may fail to stimulate originality on the part of their followers. It is well known that great thinkers have often taught their disciples conformity rather than originality. They have asked all the questions and supplied all the answers. Consequently, there is little left for the followers to do except to expound the theories of the masters.

The theory of creative originality calls for something beyond mere observance of models and standards. It signifies that people should produce their own models and standards. To this end, the leader must be sensitive to, and tolerant of, new suggestions that occur not only to him, but also to those under his direction. They may not produce much that is new in the world, but they can produce things that are new to themselves. Furthermore, it is not the products that are of primary interest, from the standpoint of the theory of creative originality. The primary consideration is the quality of originality that pervades experience, whatever the products may be. *It is surprising how many peculiar and strange ideas and procedures will be suggested by even ordinary people if the conditions are adequate.*

Tolerance of suggestions is one of the indispensable conditions. People who are held down to prescribed rules, forms, standards, and procedures may produce more, do more, and learn more than when suggestions of different possibilities are encouraged and tolerated, but we are thinking here in terms of quality rather than quantity. Only individuals whose suggestions are given attention, welcomed, or at least tolerated, can have experiences suffused with the quality of creativeness. It matters not how strange and peculiar the suggestions may be, they should at least be tolerated. They are not to be accepted as standards to be observed. They are to be accepted only as possibilities to be considered. New products are impossible without new experiences, and new experiences are impossible without entertaining suggestions and new ideas. From the standpoint of the theory of creative originality, we should tolerate suggestions not only from ourselves but also from others for whose guidance we are in any way responsible. Creativeness is impossible without intellectual curiosity and wonder, and these thrive only under conditions that encourage thinking that is independent of accepted forms, standards, and procedures.

3. *Creative originality requires criticism.* The expansion of experience makes possible suggestions of new forms, standards, and procedures. Toleration encourages them. But it takes criticism to test their worth and select the good from the bad, the useful from the useless. Often criticism may be confined to trying out in imagination alternative courses of action that suggest themselves, but it may be necessary at times to try these courses out in overt behavior — that is, experiment with them. Experimental criticism is an indispensable element in the quality of creative originality, and we should require it of ourselves as well as of those for whose education we may be responsible.

Expansion, toleration, and criticism, as conducive to the operation of the principle of creative originality, seem so important and significant that they should be emphasized in bringing this section to a close. The theory of creative originality has far-reaching practical implications for all of us in our relations with each other and with those for whose education we are responsible. People who accept this principle hesitate to work at the same job exclusively, to narrow their friendships, or to follow the same routine too regularly. They resist the ever-present human propensity to oppose without reflective consideration the new, the strange, and the untried. They look for evidence that contradicts as well as evidence that supports their own theories and ideas. They encourage their wonder and intellectual curiosity by examining things that challenge their interest and attention.

In exercising their responsibility for the guidance and direction of others, experimentalists are sensitive not only to products, whether conceived in terms of objective things or in terms of learning, but also to the qualities of the experiences involved in the process. As a matter of fact, many business organizations are following this policy. They recognize the fact that quantitative production in the field of business and industry is usually facilitated by division of labor and routine performance, but they also realize that mechanical operations are lacking in the quality of originality. Hence, when practical conditions permit, they seek to provide workers with general information about the business, have them work at many different jobs, and encourage them to suggest methods of improvement. Parents and teachers who adopt this principle resist the tendency to discourage the constant questioning of children. They encourage suggestions and proposals and give recognition to those who do things in new ways. They provide a variety of activities and experiences and resist the tendency to fall into the rut of a daily repetitive routine in their guidance and teaching. Teachers everywhere should realize that the efficiency of mechanical performance, however desirable for the achievement of immediate results, is less desirable from the standpoint of ultimate results than activities in which variety, curiosity, and wonder have an opportunity to operate. *The quality of creative originality not only is desirable for its own sake, but becomes embodied in the quality of the products of experience, whether conceived in terms of changes in behavior and character or in terms of objective things.*

CHAPTER 7

Selectivity of Experience

FREEDOM IS ONE of the widely recognized values of human life. For it men work, fight, and even die. Its nature, scope, and function are no less permanent issues in education than in the fields of religion, government, and business and industry. In fact, those interested in education, whether in the school, the home, or the community, are always faced with the problem of freedom. From the standpoint of the philosophy of experimentalism, the problem of freedom is, in the last analysis, a problem which may best be defined in terms of the selective character of experience. The selectivity of experience necessitates choice. Different attitudes toward the kind of choice considered desirable may be conceived as different theories of freedom. In educational authoritarianism the importance of selective or limited choice is emphasized; in educational laissez faire the importance of unlimited or free choice is emphasized; and in educational experimentalism the importance of intelligent or reflective choice is emphasized.

THEORY OF SELECTIVE CHOICE
(EDUCATIONAL AUTHORITARIANISM)

Authoritarian proponents of selective choice assume (1) that freedom consists in freedom of movement; (2) that freedom of movement must be limited; and (3) that the extent of freedom of movement desirable varies with practical conditions. An understanding of the meaning and significance of the theory of selective choice thus requires a consideration of the foregoing conceptions.

1. That *freedom consists in freedom of movement* most people usually take for granted. Doubtless this conception of freedom emerged in human thought to designate the desire of men for relief from some power, force, or condition that prevented them from doing what they wished to do. Relief from all external restraint, inhibition, or control of one's activities is thus identified with freedom and is its whole meaning in

the minds of many people. From this point of view the individual is completely free who has the right and privilege of doing and saying whatever he wishes. Psychologically, freedom thus conceived is one of the primary values that everyone wishes, desires, and wants. Ethically, it is a value which one should seek not only for himself but for others as well.

Freedom, conceived in terms of activity, is usually considered one of the most precious of human values. It represents an achievement of the brave, the strong, and the persevering against tyranny, persecution, and prejudice in the long battle of the ages. But the battle is never ended. Freedom is never complete. It may be approached but it is never fully realized. When freedom is once achieved in any field, without eternal vigilance it may be lost. But there are many kinds of freedom. The achievement of political freedom is only the beginning. Religious freedom and economic freedom are also to be sought. Freedom is an enduring good, and everyone should work to preserve and extend it. But the very fact that there is something which exists in spots and in varying quantities suggests that its actualization or realization will never be completely achieved.

2. That *freedom of movement should be limited* seems perfectly obvious to most people. Freedom, conceived in terms of freedom of action as assumed in the principle of selective choice, can never be absolute in this world. So far is this from being false that we need only look around us for the evidence. We cannot do anything and everything we wish to do. Frequently, we are hemmed in and hedged in by conditions over which we have no control. We may lack the physical means of doing what we wish to do. We may lack the knowledge, the courage, or the perseverance. What we wish to do may, and often does, conflict with what others wish to do. So there cannot be any such thing as complete freedom in this world for the individual, the group, or the nation.

Such reasoning certainly seems to square with the facts as we see them every day all around us. They square with our own experience in the effort to realize our own ends. Some limitation certainly must be placed upon freedom under practical conditions. No one can or should do whatever he wishes to do without regard to circumstances and conditions. We are thus faced with the problem of determining a standard on the basis of which we can decide in practical situations the degree of freedom that is most desirable.

3. That *the extent of freedom of movement desirable varies with practical conditions* seems certain. According to this conception, the extent of

freedom should be whatever the occasion demands. Such a rule takes two forms, depending upon whether the individual is assuming responsibility for his own direction or for the direction of others. From the standpoint of the individual who assumes responsibility for his own conduct, the ethical rule that is most often suggested is that he should do whatever he wishes to do to the extent that his so doing does not prevent others from having the same privilege.

There are, of course, obvious objections to such a practical rule. In fact, it does not seem to be practical at all. We do not always know what others wish to do and, therefore, cannot know whether or not our activities are in conflict with theirs. If they follow the same rule, they do not know whether or not their activities are in conflict with ours. Furthermore, even if two people acting on the basis of this rule should realize that their activities were in conflict, what should they do then? Should either give way to the other? Should both undertakings be given up? Clearly the so-called rule of doing what the occasion requires is impractical when there is no way of telling what the occasion requires. The difficulty of using such a rule in directing one's own educational activities seems evident.

According to the second form of this conception — and this is the form in which we are chiefly interested — the educator should assume responsibility for determining the scope of freedom to be permitted those whose activities he guides and directs. He must, of course, provide them with such freedom as the occasion demands. But he is not given any standard by which he may decide what the occasion demands. He is left with the problem of supplying enough freedom but not too much. He has no way of knowing what is too much and what is too little. If he "passes the buck" to the individuals and places them on their own, they have no standard. Even if he has them follow the rule of doing whatever they wish to do to the extent that everyone else has the same privilege, such a rule is meaningless in actual situations, as we have already pointed out. There is no logical way out. He must determine arbitrarily what his charges may do and may not do.

Freedom, from the standpoint of selective choice, logically must be subject to routine and caprice. It must vary according to the customs and traditions of the community on the one hand and the inclinations of the educator on the other. The teacher, the priest, the employer, or any other individual responsible for educational activities may give as much or as little freedom as he sees fit. What will seem too much liberty to one person will seem too little to another. What will seem practical in one situation will not seem practical in another. What will seem desirable to an individual when he is feeling well will be different from what will seem desirable to him when he is feeling badly. Since it is the chief function of any principle to overcome such routine and caprice, the principle or theory of selective choice does not seem satisfactory.

Such logical implications of the principle of selective choice are exemplified in current practice. Perhaps the best illustrations are to be found in the school, which after all is the primary educational institution. There are many teachers, supervisors, and administrators who do not hesitate to assert their devotion to democracy, liberty, and freedom; who insist that freedom must always be limited; and who contend that the school is responsible for determining the scope of freedom which the occasion demands. The work of these recognized educators is available for the examination of all. In some instances, pupils and teachers are told exactly what they may do and exactly what they may not do. Sometimes everyone is permitted to do virtually anything that he desires to do and can do. In the survey of ninety-one high schools, sponsored by the Educational Policies Commission and published in 1940, six types of education are described which the pupils, teachers, principals, and patrons all consider democratic. Most of them clearly assume the principle of selective choice. They recognize freedom as a good thing, but they assume without question that it must vary with what the occasion demands. Still the six different types of practice they idealize vary widely, depending upon the customs and traditions of the community and the habits and inclinations of the principals and their faculties.[1]

The same situation may be seen also in the same school. There may be one teacher who lets pupils do and say whatever occurs to them with little or no direction, while on the other side of the hall one can almost hear a pin drop. In one room pupils always move about freely and talk to anyone they wish; in another room they ask permission from the teacher to do every little thing. There are all kinds of variations between these extremes. Yet virtually everyone accepts political, religious, and economic freedom as desirable. Virtually everybody also admits that freedom is limited and must vary according to the demands of the occasion. But in practice the demands of the occasion vary all the way from despotism to anarchy. What the occasion demands in the

---

[1] Educational Policies Commission, *Learning the Ways of Democracy*. National Education Association, Washington, D. C., 1940. Pp. 2–14.

minds of some teachers differs widely from what it demands in the minds of other teachers. What it demands in the mind of the same teacher often varies according to his health and his moods. What is true of teachers is also true of pupils, principals, and citizens of the community, as indicated in the survey of the high-school theories and practices to which we have referred.

Of course, every individual or group responsible for educational activities and programs does not assume the principle of selective choice as we have defined it. Many of them, however, perhaps the majority of them, do assume it. Some of the practices and justifications used in their support represent other attitudes toward the feature of selectivity. But the practices of those who adopt the theory of selective choice vary as widely with respect to the scope of freedom as do the practices of those who adopt different principles. When everyone has the conviction that the extent of freedom should vary with the demands of the occasion, there is actually no standard of freedom available, except the arbitrary inclinations of those in authority, whose dispositions vary all the way from conformity to custom and tradition to yielding uncritically to impulses and desires. Thus there is no criterion as to the quality of desirable selectivity on the part of those to be educated. Selective choice, determined by those in authority, signifies whatever freedom of action seems to be practical in varying situations. The selectivity that pervades experience varies from place to place and from time to time.

From the standpoint of the philosophy of experimentalism, selective choice as a theory of freedom is very unsatisfactory. It has no reference to any desirable quality of experience to be sought through education. In other words, limited choice, like the authoritarian theory of provisional interest, is conceived as a means rather than as an end. From the standpoint of the authoritarian, the individual must be allowed to choose only when he chooses what he should choose and when he can succeed. He must not be permitted to do wrong and take chances. He should be permitted to choose when he cannot do any harm, but not when he may make the wrong choice. The qualities of experience in their cumulative effect implied in the application of such a principle are obedience, contentment, and dependence on authority. They do not constitute desirable freedom as a quality of experience. *Those who may decide only in matters in which they are allowed to decide and must follow directions in everything else are not free.* They are not even free to determine when they must decide things for themselves and when they must seek the advice of others. Such a quality of subservience and dependence is not desirable, even when advocated in the name of freedom.

THEORY OF FREE CHOICE
(EDUCATIONAL LAISSEZ FAIRE)

Adherents of educational laissez faire, like educational authoritarians, approach the problem of freedom from the standpoint of action rather than from the standpoint of the selectivity of experience. Nevertheless, they assume a different attitude toward what constitutes desirable freedom. While the authoritarians by implication advocate selective or limited choice, the adherents of educational laissez faire advocate free or unlimited choice, which they often call freedom. In both theories selectivity and freedom are conceived in terms of activity. The extent of freedom depends upon the range of activities among which the individual may choose. One who engages in whatever he wishes to engage in, in so far as general physical and social conditions permit, is free. Those who are in any way prevented from thus expressing themselves are to that extent limited in their freedom. So far both interpretations are in accord with one another. But here the agreement ends.

According to the theory of selective choice, the scope of freedom should always be limited, while according to the theory of free choice there should be no limitation beyond that which nature itself imposes. From the standpoint of the first principle, we are faced with the problem of deciding upon the rule or criterion by which the proper limitations can be judged; according to the second, the problem is merely a matter of removing all artificial obstructions to complete self-expression. The principle of selective choice is consistent with the principles of objective contingency, doctrinaire sociality, provisional interest, and creative embodiment; and the principle of free choice is consistent with the principles of subjective contingency, inherent sociality, immediate interest, and direct creative self-expression. From the standpoint of the first set of principles, education is a process by which the individual gradually learns to conform to the conditions of the environment through the proper guidance of those who know them. From the standpoint of the second set of principles, education is a process by which the individual transforms the world through expressing himself in it and through it. As the principle of selective choice is one aspect of a more inclusive conception, so the principle of free choice is one aspect of another more inclusive conception.

The theory of free choice signifies that freedom is an absolute good. In this respect, it is in agreement with the principle of selective choice. Both assume that as much freedom as possible is desirable. But they disagree as to what is possible. When the standard of reality is thought to lie outside the individual he must conform to it. His choice must always be selective. Only those who know such a standard should assume responsibility for determining the scope of freedom. But when the standard is thought to be within the individual, the external environment, so it is assumed, should be shaped, certainly insofar as it has been developed by custom, tradition, and education, so as to make it conform to this inner nature of the individual. His own inherent nature becomes the standard for his guidance and direction. Those responsible for his education center their attention upon him. What can he do? What does he wish? What does he desire? What are the conditions that prevent the realization, expression, and actualization of his desires? How may these conditions be so modified as to enable him to realize the ends implicit within him?

It is true that environmental conditions often prevent the individual from doing what he is inclined to do. In so far as they are inherent in nature and cannot be removed they are themselves educative. They are a part of the very nature of which the individual himself is the highest manifestation. They are means to his realization and development and are a limiting factor only when he goes wrong, contrary to nature. But there are many obstructions that are not natural. These are the ones that must be removed.

According to this theory, the obstructions and hindrances produced by civilization, as contrasted with nature, are artificial. Many habits, customs, and mores reflect the impositions of the strong on the weak, and the privileged on the unfortunate. Only by means of habit is the natural man subjected to the purposes of the ruling class. There is no way by which the conditions that enslave the common people can be changed except through the expression, realization, and actualization of the natural impulses of the individual. Many so-called moral patterns, virtues, and ideals are nothing more than means by which one group controls others. Many forms of courtesy and good manners, as well as styles in dress, serve to enslave rather than liberate human nature. According to this theory, freedom is the absence of restraint imposed by habit, custom, tradition, or external standards of any kind.

In accord with this theory it is the function of those who assume educational responsibility to break down these artificial barriers to freedom. Such artificialities are limiting factors actually imposed on the individual in all walks of life in civilized countries. The only hope of freedom is a new social order consistent with the demands of nature. The demands of nature are to be found directly in the impulses, desires, wishes, and wants of the individual, particularly the young. There is sufficient dynamic energy dammed up in the minds and hearts of the people to convert even a static society into a progressive society if only they are given a chance to release it. It is the function of the educator to give the natural propensities of the individual the opportunity to express themselves so that they may contribute most to human betterment.

For both the ends and the means of education, the educator must take his cues from the activities of those to be educated. He should not only observe individuals in order to discover their impulses, wishes, desires, and interests, but he should use all available resources to remove whatever obstruction prevents their direct expansion and development.

According to this theory, the individual should be left free to choose and select everything that he sees fit, unless perhaps because of his immaturity he might do something that would maim or crush him. Nothing in the way of form, custom, or style should stand in his way. The standards of right and wrong he carries within his own breast. He is not expected to conform to the environment; he must cause the environment to conform to him. He has wishes and desires, which he would not have if they were not good, and, thus, they should be realized. If they come in conflict with the standards of society and civilization, it is the latter that must be wrong.

Only if the young are brought up to express their desires and wishes will they be able to break through the artificialities of civilization and fashion things more in accord with the impulses and desires of the generations to come. Practical considerations, of course, must guide the educator. He will have to restrain the impulses of those whom he guides and directs from time to time. But such restraint is to him a necessary evil. It must be suffered and endured for the moment, to provide fuller expression later.

Thought and judgment on the part of the individual must be encouraged. But he is never expected to choose among desires. The desires are all good, merely because they exist. The individual is free to choose his activities. But his desires determine always the general course of action to be followed. Thought, reflection, and judgment play their part in discovering means by which such courses of action may be pursued. The individual must be left free to choose which course of action he will pursue and the means by which he will pursue it; but he is only truly free to the extent that he can express his desires without restraint, control, and obstruction from others and without the standards that others have developed.

Obviously, the logical implications of this theory or principle of free choice are far reaching. If the individual is to be free to act in accordance with his desires, he must be free from imposition. Those in authority should relax their control in every possible way. Their own aims and desires must be surrendered when they conflict with the aims and desires of the individual for whose activities they are responsible. Rules and regulations of all sorts must be abandoned, and so the only standards that have any justification are the individual's wants and desires. Parents must follow the lead of their children, employers must follow the lead of their employees; political leaders must follow the lead of their constituents; teachers must follow the lead of their pupils; and school administrators must follow the lead of the pupils, teachers, and parents.

The practical applications of such a principle have long been in evidence in many quarters. Many parents exert every effort to enable their children to do whatever they wish to do. There are political leaders who always watch their constituents not merely to see what is practical at the moment but to see what is desirable. Employers usually do not base their programs on the wishes and desires of their employees, but the tendency is now observable among employees in many quarters to demand such programs on the part of business and industry.

The logical implications of the principle of free choice and of other principles of educational laissez faire have been reduced to actual practice in many schools. There are some teachers who refrain from planning in advance for fear that they will impose their own conceptions upon pupils, who neglect to correct pupils' discourtesy and bad manners for fear they will cramp natural impulses, who refrain from making definite assignments to avoid confining pupils to fixed tasks, and who invariably urge pupils to suggest at the outset the undertakings in which they wish to engage. There are administrators and supervisors who limit their policies and programs very largely to aiding teachers and pupils in the realization of their wishes and desires. All of us are acquainted with leaders in all walks of life who seek primarily to please everybody without giving much thought to the question of whether or not everybody ought to be pleased. In other words much current practice in many fields conforms to the logical implications of the theory of free choice.

From the standpoint of the philosophy of experimentalism, the policies, programs and activities which may have their justification in this interpretation of the feature of selectivity are not very satisfactory. As a matter of fact, all people have desires, wishes, and impulses, but it is difficult for any practical person who is interested in the advancement of the general welfare to admit that such tendencies to action are legitimate goals of social policy in any field. Should parents merely limit their educational programs to the direct satisfaction of every desire of their children? Should teachers always wait for pupils to indicate what they wish to do before they put them to work? Even to ask such questions seems silly on the basis of actual experience. In the first place, such a program must result in delay, hesitation, lost motion, and fooling around. In the second place, the activities in which those to be educated engage may or may not be socially desirable. There is no common-sense basis anywhere for the belief that whatever is good for an individual is necessarily good for his neighbors or that whatever is good for the young will invariably be good for the old. The young who are allowed to have their own way in everything will demand to have their way as they grow older. If pupils are said to be free when they do whatever they wish to do, those who are responsible for their education are slaves. Now if free choice is good for the child, pupil, or any other individual whose education is desired, it should be good for the parent, teacher, or any other educational leader. But if the wishes of a leader must be subservient to the wishes of the followers, the importance of his freedom is entirely neglected. *If a quality of experience is good, it must be good for the individual in the future as well as good to him in the present; if it is good for the follower, it must be good for the leader.* The principle of free choice does not seem to meet these demands and must, therefore, be rejected.

Theory of Intelligent Choice
(Educational Experimentalism)

In support of the theory of intelligent choice as the solution to the problem of freedom, educational experimentalists take selectivity as their point of departure. From this point of view selectivity is directly noticeable or clearly implicit in experience, however it may be conceived. Even when experience is reduced to behavior it is always selective in character. We are always doing some things rather than others. As a matter of fact, we are so constructed that we cannot do some things. Among the things which we can do, some we do and others we leave undone. If we think of experience in terms of learning, the very word "learning" signifies selectivity. Some things can be learned and others cannot. Among the things which we are capable of learning, some we learn and others we leave unlearned. Some we learn in some ways and others we learn in other ways. If we think of experience in terms of consciousness, some things are emphasized, others relegated to the background, and others neglected altogether. In fact, attention may be considered as a name for this selective character of conscious experience. As already indicated, behavior, learning, and consciousness, which may be conceived as stages, levels, or aspects of experiences, are selective in character. No matter how behavior is conceived it involves selectivity. In the words of Dewey, "Preferential action in the sense of selective behavior is a universal trait of all things, atoms, and molecules, as well as plants, animals, and man. Existences, universally so far as we can tell, are cold and indifferent in the presence of some things and react energetically in either a positive or negative way to other things. Selective behavior is the evidence of at least a rudimentary individuality or uniqueness in things." [2]

One of the facts most obvious to the student of the physical sciences is the partiality of physical things. Certain things simply will not respond to other substances that surround them. They behave as if those other things did not exist at all. There are substances with which they simply will not keep company. They avoid them as though they were poison, so to speak. On the other hand, there are other substances that they will embrace as long lost friends from which they can be separated only by great force. The science of chemistry is very largely a study of the selective behavior of atoms and molecules and methods of controlling it in the interest of human purposes. The science of physics, too, certainly in its practical applications, consists in no small part in utilizing the selective character of things as a means of managing them. If we may take electricity as one of the outstanding topics of physics, one may readily see how impossible it would be to control without the use of carbon, copper, rubber, asbestos, and similar substances.

[2] John Dewey, *Philosophy and Civilization*. Minton, Balch and Co., New York, 1931. Pp. 274–275.

Not only is the behavior of electricity unique, but so are other things that are used to control it.

Ordinary observations that plants and animals respond in different ways to physical conditions are substantiated in geography and biology. They prosper and thrive under certain conditions and wither and die under certain other conditions. Even as men and women, they have both friends and enemies. Their enemies they avoid in so far as possible and to their friends they forever cling with a tenacity and faithfulness that, when revealed in the human world, are expressed in song and story. And too, there are many things to which they, like us, are indifferent. They treat some things as though they did not exist. They are incurably partial, biased, and selective. If we are to deal with them effectively, either in promoting their own welfare or the welfare of others, we must take into account their selective behavior.

The behavior of the human being is still more selective. He typically avoids some things, approaches others, and neglects others. Like the plants and the lower animals, he seems to be so constructed that he is entirely indifferent and insensitive to a large part of what goes on in the external world. The organs of the five senses are so constructed that only certain stimuli affect them. Seeing, hearing, smelling, tasting, and feeling occur under certain conditions. Perhaps the larger part of the events or happenings in the physical world are beyond the reach of our senses. Nature itself places upon us certain limitations that we can never overcome. Even within these broad limits, however, individuals vary. Some are sensitive to things that are beyond the reach of others. The realm within which we may choose has been selected for us collectively and individually.

Within the limits imposed by nature we are selective. It is not difficult to tell what an inanimate object, an atom, or a molecule will do under specific conditions. It is selective, but it always chooses in a certain way. Once a friend, always a friend; once an enemy, always an enemy; once a stranger, always a stranger. As we move up the ladder of existence from the physical to the social world, it is more and more difficult to determine in advance what specific things an organism will do under specific conditions. On the biological level, the variability of behavior is directly proportional to the complexity of the nervous system. On the psychological level, this variability becomes wider and more complex in consequence of learning through experience. Nature sets wide limits on human behavior, but the individual is con-stantly making himself over through experience. In any situation he does some things when, so far as we can see, he might as well do something else. We may determine statistically what individuals in general will do when confronted with a specified situation, but it is frequently impossible to predict what particular individuals will do in a particular situation. In consequence of experience and past behavior, as well as of original structure, the human being is so flexible that his activities represent selections from among a variety of possibilities.

Selection is an important feature of all learning. In the so-called trial-and-error method of learning, the individual does first one thing and then another until he makes the right choice; however, he not only learns the right thing as right, but he learns many other things as wrong. He selects the responses that he will positively adopt as good and rejects the others. The same is true on the level of imagination and thought. The individual tries out in his mind different possibilities and selects the one which seems to fit the situation. The feature of selection is so pervasive in learning that psychologists investigating the problems of learning devote considerable attention to it. They undertake to determine not only the basis of an individual's responses, but the basis of his selection of those responses he acts upon. Psychologists vary widely in their explanation of this feature of learning, but all of them without exception consider it an important problem.

Perhaps the most striking characteristic of consciousness is its selectivity. The fact that our minds are continually running from one thing to another and from one aspect of the same thing to another is familiar to us all. Consciousness selects some things to emphasize, consider, and analyze. At the same time it neglects others and relegates them to the background. Introspective psychologists have always recognized this selective aspect of consciousness as one of its fundamental and pervasive characteristics. In the words of William James, "Consciousness is at all times primarily a *selecting agency*. Whether we take it in the lowest sphere of sense, or in the highest of intellection, we find it always doing one thing, choosing one out of several of the materials so presented to its notice, emphasizing and accentuating that and suppressing as far as possible all the rest. The item emphasized is always in close communication with some *interest* felt by consciousness to be paramount at the time." [3]

Psychologists usually define attention, which is certainly a phenomenon of conscious activity, in terms of selectivity. To some, attention

[3] William James, *Principles of Psychology*, Vol. I. Henry Holt and Company, New York, 1890. P. 139.

merely means the fact that consciousness is selective. From this point of view, it is no particular state of consciousness; it is a feature of all consciousness — in daydreaming as well as in concentrating. We are continually choosing the things and the aspects of things to which we devote our attention. The degree of concentration varies from one individual to another and from one situation to another, but consciousness is a continuous process of selecting and choosing; it is attentive.

Some psychologists, like William James, distinguish between those states of consciousness which are passive and those which are active. They designate only the active states as states of attention. "Everyone," says James, "knows what attention is. It is the taking possession by the mind, in clear and vivid form, of one out of what seems several simultaneously possible objects or trains of thought. Focalization, concentration, of consciousness are of its essence. It implies withdrawal from some things in order to deal effectively with others, and is a condition which has a real opposite in the confused, dazed, and scatterbrained state which in French is called *distraction*, and *zerstreutheit* in German." [4] However, these more active states of attention are much more important than are the states of distraction and mind-wandering. Only during attention does the individual control and direct himself. Only through gaining his attention can the educator directly influence him.

It appears that experience is selective beyond question. If we consider it in terms of physical and bodily movements, it seems to be always a process of neglecting, avoiding, and choosing. If we think of it in terms of learning, then some responses rather than others are made, but of those that are made some are chosen to act upon while others are rejected. If we think of it from the inside and in terms of consciousness, it is a process of accentuation and suppression.

The educator in the broad sense has long been interested in the problem of freedom. The very conception of freedom must assume this selective factor of experience. Were this phenomenon of selecting and choosing absent from experience, one thing would be as good as another, and there would be no problem of freedom. The position which one assumes toward the problem of freedom is, in the last analysis, the position which he assumes toward the feature of selectivity.

Human freedom is a problem of long standing in the field of general philosophy which usually contains implications for educational theory

[4] William James, *Principles of Psychology*, Vol. I. Henry Holt and Company, New York, 1890. Pp. 403–404.

and practice. To some, the destiny of man is in the lap of the gods or in the hands of the fates; neither the race nor the individual is able to play a controlling part in the direction of human affairs. As Epictetus said, "Remember that you are an actor in a drama, of such a kind as the author pleases to make it. If short, of a short one; if long, of a long one. If it be his pleasure, you should act a poor man, a cripple, a governor, or a private person, see that you act it naturally. For this is your business to act well the character assigned you; to choose it is another's." [5] To others, the individual can do whatever he wills regardless of circumstances and conditions; he may not be able to control the world, but he can control his own mind and heart. The human will, according to this point of view, is independent and self-determining regardless of what the circumstances may be. The human being is the master of his fate, the captain of his soul.

The problem of freedom arises from a conflict of desire and thought. As a matter of fact, the estate of man has never been free from trials and tribulations. Nevertheless, it has always been a characteristic human conviction that the individual has the power to mitigate the evils that beset him and thus improve his lot. One essential feature of magic developed among primitive peoples is that in the precarious world of chance, accident, and misfortune, there are human means of somehow mastering all the evils which superstition suggests. The methods of magic have no cause-and-effect relation. Particular superstitions, as well as the particular methods of magic, may be entirely without foundation in fact. Nevertheless, the belief and practice are sufficient evidence of the tenacity of the human conviction that man has some control over his estate.

Science itself is probably the result of the desire to control those factors that influence human life. It differs from magic in the kinds of connections assumed to exist among events rather than in the urgent need which brings it into existence. Both have their motivation in the propensity of man to try to improve his lot.

Any development which challenges not merely the methods employed in the effort to control affairs in the interest of human welfare but even the possibility of such control occasions a serious intellectual conflict among more reflective individuals. It is difficult for the human being to surrender deep-seated beliefs, even when he is faced with evidence that refutes his beliefs. The threatening tragedy seems all the greater

---

[5] *The Enchiridion of Epictetus*, Section XVII, in *Discourse of Epictetus*, Carter translation, Everyman's Library, P. 260.

because the very science that is the chief instrument of control is thought to be responsible for the theory that all effort at control is futile. According to the mechanistic interpretation of science, this enduring aspiration of man for the control of his own destiny is all in vain. The whole story is told in a single word — determinism. The individual is not responsible for his existence or anything that he may feel, think, or do. His every thought, feeling, and act is determined by factors beyond his control. Any event is the mechanical result of still earlier events in an unending regression. From the standpoint of the mechanist, this seems to be the law of science.

Nevertheless, human aspirations will not down. Those who still maintain the primitive faith point out that some things have not been explained in terms of cause and effect. Furthermore, it seems at least possible to think that in those fields the causal relationship may be reversed. As can be easily seen after an event has occurred, the events out of which it developed may be taken as preparatory to it. From this standpoint, the present occurrence is not the result of the past, but it is rather the goal for which the past was merely preparatory. The human individual and the world of nature, so it seems, are teleological or purposive through and through. Some purpose runs through all things and the principle of cause and effect is only a working hypothesis in the field of science, and has nothing to do with the ultimate nature of the world and the spiritual nature of man. According to this conception, the purposes of man, typical of the purposive character of the world, are the determining agencies that arrange the matter of cause and effect so as to realize themselves. Man can thus control his own destiny, although it appears that he is still somehow under the general control of the world order. In some such way the standing conflict has developed between the mechanists and the vitalists, the materialists and the teleologists, the determinists and the indeterminists, — representing the different ways of stating the opposed positions with respect to this age-old problem of human experience.

The arguments of the two schools of thought with respect to freedom seem to neutralize each other. Those who deny the possibility of freedom cannot answer the objections of those who are convinced of its reality. Those who sponsor the cause of freedom cannot answer the objections of the determinists, who, beyond all things, wish to be scientific. But the fact that the problem of freedom exists at all supports the conclusion that selectivity is an important feature of educative experience, for without selectivity there can be no problem of freedom.

Furthermore, interest in freedom is not limited to psychology and philosophy. Religious freedom, political freedom, and economic freedom have all challenged the loyalties of men. It is for freedom of one kind or another that our fathers have fought and died for hundreds of years, and it is for these freedoms that men are fighting and dying today. The interest in freedom is increasing rather than decreasing.

Even the totalitarian groups, which openly attack individual freedom and liberty as we have known it, contend that they are working to extend freedom and liberty. Freedom and liberty are words that to people throughout the world, even in autocratic countries, signify rights, privileges, and responsibilities which even the despot in time of war cannot afford to despise for long. In democratic countries freedom, so long taken for granted, has at long last become again the watchword. The four freedoms defined by Winston Churchill and the late Franklin D. Roosevelt in the Atlantic Charter represent only one of the most notable among the many efforts to define the aims of democratic peoples in the recent world-wide conflict.

In education, the problem of freedom and control is ever with us. Usually those who consider themselves conservatives emphasize control while those who consider themselves progressives emphasize freedom. Students of education and field workers alike consider the question of pupil freedom a permanent issue. Some wish to extend freedom and others wish to restrict it. They may differ as to what they mean by freedom as well as what should be done about it. Everyone admits, however, that the problem is important and that something should be done about it.

From the standpoint of the philosophy of experimentalism, the problem of freedom in philosophy and education is clearly related to selectivity as a feature of experience. If the individual has any freedom, he must be free to choose or to select his own courses of action. Actually the problem of freedom is not whether the individual chooses and selects; the problem is rather what kind of choosing and selecting is preferable or desirable. The authoritarians, as well as the exponents of laissez faire, as we have already pointed out, in taking freedom of action as their point of departure have been compelled to assume positions with respect to selectivity that are theoretically unsound and practically dangerous. In dealing with the problem of freedom the educational experimentalist takes as his point of departure selectivity as a characteristic feature of all experience and concludes that all desirable freedom involves intelligent choice.

The theories of selective choice and free choice assume a quantitative attitude toward freedom, while the theory of intelligent choice assumes a qualitative attitude. The theory of selective choice assumes that freedom of action, although desirable, must be limited under practical conditions not only in the interest of the individual, but also in the interest of society. The theory of free choice assumes that freedom of action should be absolute in the interest of both the individual and society. According to both, freedom is an absolute good. But according to the conception of selective choice, freedom can be approached, but never attained. According to free choice, freedom is not only an absolute good, but a good that can be achieved in educational situations in the here and now. According to the theory of intelligent choice, freedom of action as such is neither good nor bad: it is the quality of the action that is good or bad. Some qualities are desirable and some undesirable. Such selectivity of action as is desirable is pervaded with intelligence, and the quality of intelligence thus becomes the criterion of selectivity that is desirable.

The principle of intelligent choice signifies the quality of experience rather than the results of activity, whether conceived in terms of objective products or quantitative achievement. This distinction is not always understood even in authoritative discussions of intelligence. Often — perhaps usually — people consider activities intelligent if they are successful. According to Thorndike, intellect or intelligence is "the power of good responses from the point of view of truth and fact." [6] In a sense, this is true. A person may be said to be intelligent if he does the right thing at the right time. We may estimate the intelligence of people upon this basis. If we are trying to determine who will be the most successful and efficient in terms of objective achievement, such a criterion may be adequate. But when we are trying to improve the quality of experience, we must keep our minds on the quality of experience rather than on the quantitative outcomes.

A person's activities may be intelligent when considered with respect to results and at the same time be unintelligent when considered with respect to the quality of the results. Some of the most successful performances are almost entirely lacking in critical intelligence. A person may be successful in a business venture, in a love affair, or in a battle without exercising critical intelligence. He may act on the basis of mere impulse and buy the right stock, court the right girl, and get

---

[6] E. L. Thorndike, *Intelligence and Its Measurement: A Symposium.* Journal of Educational Psychology, 12: 124, March, 1921.

into the right shell hole largely in consequence of custom, routine, or direction. Successful activity is qualitatively intelligent to the extent that the choice of activity — yielding to this impulse or that, following this rule or that, observing this order or that — is considered in relation to present conditions and probable consequences.

On the other hand, it is possible for a man to buy the wrong stock, court the wrong girl, and get into the wrong shell hole, and still act intelligently from the standpoint of the quality of his experiences. Stated in a somewhat different way, the quality of activities may be intelligent in the sense of doing the most logically appropriate thing and yet be unintelligent in the sense that the results practically fall short of expectations. The quality of experience that the principle of intelligent choice emphasizes places responsibility squarely on the shoulders of the individual. Whoever assumes such responsibility is always running a risk. He may do wrong as well as right. From the standpoint of intelligence conceived in terms of the right responses, he may be considered a moron or a genius. From the standpoint of objective achievement, doubtless many people might be more successful in certain situations if they were to follow orders and directions prescribed by others. There are times certainly when it would be best for most of us to do as we are told. But we are not here thinking in terms of success and achievement as the world usually understands these things. We are thinking in terms of the quality of living in the present whatever the consequences may be. From the standpoint of the theory of intelligent choice, it is better to take the chances of defeat than to win victories that belong entirely to others. It is better to consider various alternatives than to yield to immediate desire, even if we often waste time and miss our chance. There is still more time and there will still be more chances. If we merely follow routine, some day, under changed conditions, our rules will prove inadequate. If we act purely on impulse, some day we shall act too quickly.

If we follow customs, rules, or orders uncritically, we become slaves to routine. Customs, mores, or social habits represent ways of thinking, feeling, and acting that have seemed to meet the demands of the race. Perhaps at one time they have all served real needs. The conditions out of which the needs developed may no longer exist, but some people act, think, and feel as they did when these conditions existed. Rules are prescribed ways of acting to achieve certain definite results under known conditions. In a dynamic and changing social order any set of conditions does not remain forever fixed and static at all places and under all circumstances. Yet those who follow rules uncritically and unintelligently tend to follow them literally under varying conditions. Orders are prescribed performances issued by those in authority to those under their control. People who follow orders uncritically, regardless of circumstances, will increasingly tend to do as they are told regardless of the character and ability of those in authority. Strict conformity to custom, observation of rules, and obedience to orders often lead to system, order, and efficiency under known conditions, in certain places, for a limited time. But as conditions change, the routine that signifies order, system, and efficiency may cause suffering, defeat, and destruction.

If we follow our impulses and desires uncritically, we become slaves to our own inclinations. The world was not made for us alone. Sometimes we can get what we desire and need by just taking it. Sometimes we cannot. Sometimes our getting what we desire and need deprives others of getting what they desire and need. If we persist in seeking our own ends without considering practical conditions and the desires and needs of others, we shall forever remain children in a world and a society that have their own ways regardless of our wishes and desires. Our parents, teachers, and friends may allow us to have our own way, but society is not always activated by love and sentiment. The sooner the individual learns that some of his desires and wishes must be modified to meet the demands of reality, the better off he will be.

These implications of routine and caprice are usually recognized by those who adopt the principle of selective choice. Only the totalitarian despots in times of war would demand absolute and silent obedience of all under penalty of imprisonment and death. Not all authoritarians — not even those who love authority for its own sake — consider blind obedience desirable. Most educational leaders in all walks of life wish to give the individual as much liberty as conditions permit. From the standpoint of the principle of intelligent choice, so far so good. The difference in the two principles lies in the method by which the spheres of choice and conformity are to be decided. From the standpoint of the principle of selective choice, some things are to be done blindly according to customs, rules, or orders. From the standpoint of the principle of intelligent choice, some things are to be done according to customs, rules, and orders, but not blindly. From this point of view, order, system, and efficiency are always desirable, but they must not be purchased at the price of intelligence. The people who do things should at least know why they do them, and should have the privilege of doing them or not, when conditions permit. There is no place where intelligence should be ruled out entirely by authority of any kind. From this point of view, customs, rules, and orders should represent a consensus, as far as possible, of what is desirable, and should by all means be respected. But they should be questioned, modified, and adapted to the requirements of specific situations. Such adjustments should not be made merely by the powers that be; they should also be made by those who put regulations into effect. For instance, not only should school authorities make and remake the aims of education; teachers should also make and remake their own aims, even when they do not thus contribute to the aims provided by those in authoritative control. Intelligence should pervade the experiences of all.

Only to the degree that experiences are pervaded with critical intelligence can individuals readjust themselves continuously as conditions change. A person who does something without thinking is developing a habit of doing that thing without thinking. Routine habits developed without the operation of intelligence cannot be changed readily, even with thinking. In fact, thinking in this connection becomes almost impossible. Immediate efficiency that is purchased in any field at the price of intelligence is not efficiency in the long view, it matters not how successful the results seem to be at the time. When habits are formed, rules adopted, and orders observed because their meaning and significance are appreciated, the experiences of the individual are pervaded with intelligence. Those who have such experiences are not doing things merely because they must; they are doing them because they must, as they see it, if certain desirable ends are to be achieved. Even the ends should be intelligently desired. They are not merely the ends set up by authorities. They are the ends of all those who participate in the programs through which they are to be achieved. Even if some people do not agree upon the ends, they will be acting more intelligently if they know what the ends are.

From the standpoint of the theory of intelligent choice, freedom of action should not be arbitrarily confined to certain spheres. The only limitation that should be placed upon it is that which the continuous operation of intelligence requires. Normally individuals should not be permitted freedom of action where and when it endangers life and limb, or entails the needless waste of energy and the destruction of property. The extent of human suffering, destruction of property, and waste of energy that may be permitted must be decided by those in charge in specific situations, if they are themselves to act intelligently.

But wherever and whenever individuals may consider the various possibilities of handling a situation and choose among alternative ends and means, they should have the responsibility of doing so to the extent to which their doing so would not be so costly as to indicate lack of intelligent decision on the part of those in control. In the principle of intelligent choice, we thus have a criterion of the freedom of action that is desirable. This interpretation of the feature of selectivity emphasizes the importance of freedom of action assumed in the principle of free choice and the importance of the limitation of freedom of action assumed in the principle of selective choice. It is necessary to have freedom of action, not because it is good in and of itself, but because it is an indispensable condition for the operation of intelligence. Without the possibility of alternative courses of action, intelligence can do nothing. When the individual has to do the right thing or nothing at all, the outcome may appear successful but the quality of the performance, and therefore the quality of the effect on the individual, is not morally and educationally desirable. On the other hand, when the individual is placed in a situation where he can always do what he is inclined to do without regard to consequences, either to himself or others, the selective quality of his experiences and the effect upon him are likewise morally and educationally undesirable. This regard for the probable consequences of alternative courses of action is indispensable to intelligent action. When people do as they immediately desire, uncritically and without consideration of the consequences, they are not acting intelligently. If those who blindly follow directions are limiting their freedom, so also are those who blindly follow their impulses.

Consideration of what the occasion demands emphasized in the principle of selective choice is an indispensable factor in the principle of intelligent choice. But to determine what the occasion demands is the function of intelligence. Just where intelligence should be trusted in practice to determine what the conditions demand must be left to the intelligent choice of those in charge. However, it must be remembered that the quality of intelligence is not to be identified with successful achievement. The quality of intelligence may be present even when the results are unsatisfactory and may be absent when the results are satisfactory. The inexperienced and uneducated must often be permitted to do wrong as well as right from the standpoint of results if they are to make intelligent choices.

Impulse emphasized in the principle of free choice is an indispensable factor in intelligent choice. If impulse, desire, and wish were not important, there would be no problem of freedom. All selectivity would be mere bias. One thing would be as good as another. Experience is selective, certainly on the human level, in consequence of the presence of impulse and desire. The individual tends to respond immediately and directly. Impulse is blind. The function of intelligence is to criticize, appraise, or evaluate impulses. Desirable freedom does not consist in doing what one immediately desires to do, nor does it consist in doing what one does not desire to do. It is not a choice between the immediately good and the immediately bad. It is a choice among desires, all of which are immediately and directly good. Such choice requires critical intelligence. Regardless of whether the results are satisfactory or unsatisfactory, only through practice in criticizing, appraising, or evaluating impulse and desire is one exercising intelligent choice and becoming free in the only desirable sense of freedom.

The implications of the principle of intelligent choice are far reaching. It signifies first of all that the debate over the extent of freedom in a quantitative sense conceived solely in terms of action should be closed; that educational activities should involve sufficient freedom of action to provide for the operation of intelligence; and that people should come to wish to do what they do through the operation of intelligence rather than do what they immediately wish. It suggests that more inclusive undertakings and activities usually provide more opportunity for intelligence to operate than narrowly prescribed ones. It indicates that more rather than less preliminary planning and organization is desirable. It is more difficult to plan situations where intelligence may operate than it is to plan for routine performance. When the leaders fail to engage in preliminary planning and organization, the followers may express their impulses and desires without exercising intelligence. The freedom of intelligence is not a free gift of nature. It is an achievement that can be realized only through the exercise of intelligent choice. The conditions under which intelligent choice is to be secured are not inherent in the individual. They can be provided only through the constant attention and continuous effort of those who are responsible for educational activities, programs, and policies in the home, the school, the church, in business and industry, and in other institutions and organizations which influence the experiences of the people.

CHAPTER 8

Unity of Experience

IN THE MIDST OF DIVISION, conflict, and disunity, the human heart
hungers and thirsts for harmony and unity. The very variety which
the analysis of experience reveals emphasizes the significance of its
unity. For a description of the various aspects, phases, and processes
of experience we look to the analytical operations of the psychologists.
In both common sense and psychology, the typical experience on the
social level involves action, including both overt and implicit response;
feeling, including satisfying and annoying factors; and thinking, involving perception, memory, imagination, and reasoning. It is perfectly
clear to all that the factors of action, affection, and intellect are present
in any given conscious experience lasting for any considerable period,
such as an hour, a day, a week, or a year. It is also assumed among
competent observers that the general psychological processes involve
less inclusive ones. In thought or intellect these more specific processes
may be easily distinguished through observation and introspection.
For instance, perception involves seeing, hearing, testing, smelling, and
a sense of movement; memory involves such factors as retention, recall,
and recognition; imagination involves reproductive and constructive
operations; and reasoning involves perception and conception, analysis
and synthesis, induction and deduction, and the use of particulars and
universals, the specific and the general, the concrete and the abstract.
The logical implication of the presence of the various aspects of experience open to ordinary observation and introspection and of more
refined psychological analysis is that some positive and constructive
attitude must be assumed toward their relationship in dealing with
practical, moral, and educational issues. In other words, the inter-
relationship of the various aspects of experience that should be sought
constitutes a feature of experience with respect to which any philosophy
of education must assume some theoretical position.

189

SIGNIFICANCE OF UNITY

The development of a well-rounded, integrated, and balanced personality is an ideal that has long commanded the attention and respect of students of morals and education. The conception of the most desirable human individual as one who is well proportioned in all features and capacities was first developed among the ancient Greeks, and it has influenced educational and social theories from that day until this. It is expressed in different forms in accordance with changes in psychology, but the ideal itself tends to abide. Among modern educational and social reformers this conception has been defined as the harmonious development of all the powers of the human being, as the development of well-balanced and many-sided interests, as the maintenance of a sense of measure or proportion, and as the development of an integrated personality. Current educational literature is replete with such expressions as "the integrated personality," "the education of the whole child," and "the unity of experience."

The constant attention in social and moral theory given to this problem of balance, measure, integration, or unity seems to reflect the kind of world in which we must make our way. People everywhere and under all conditions are subject to the constant pull of many conflicting forces. Often the very integrity of one's personality is severely challenged. Everyone of us has experienced more than once what St. Paul expressed so well when he said, "What I would, that do I not; but what I hate, that do I." [1] Everyone of us knows what it is to be a house divided against itself. Existing abilities and resources are often inadequate to meet the demands of desire and aspiration. Many persons cannot stand the strain which the normal battle of life involves. Their personalities are divided, and they are beaten and broken in an unending struggle with forces over which they are unable to exercise adequate control. Under ordinary conditions, the conflict is severe enough for most of us and too much for many. Under some conditions it becomes almost unbearable for all. In time of war, economic depressions, and general intellectual and moral struggle it is particularly severe. It is not strange, therefore, that the problem of integration, which is a modern way of defining an age-long problem of personality, has become an important point of emphasis in the reflections of the serious-minded on the meaning and possibilities of life in our time.

---

[1] Rom. 7 : 15.

In recent years, wars, droughts, floods, depressions, and the conflicts of ideals have become especially prevalent. We have the conflicts between the "have and have-not" nations and the "have and have-not" individuals and groups in all nations. We have the conflict of capital and labor in a new form, and the conflict of the old and the young, not only with respect to standards and ideals but with respect to economic goods. The lack of economic security affects the intellectual integrity of both young and old throughout the world. The life-and-death struggle of the democracies with the Fascist states was only an outward manifestation of the seething impulses and emotions of the great masses of people in these countries.

The breakdown in traditional standards is disconcerting to the rank and file as well as to those who attempt to think their way through the prevailing confusion to new standards. According to some authorities the separation of morals, economics, and art in social life — that is, the acceptance of the ideals of the one as the standard without regard to the ideals of the other — helps maintain and even accentuates the conflicts that already exist. When moral principles, aesthetic principles, business principles, political principles, and educational principles are in constant conflict, the individual may feel constrained to adopt one of two alternatives. He may take the ideals of one department of life as primary — for instance, the economic — and crowd out other factors that under normal conditions require attention; or he may oscillate from one set of ideals to another as the exigencies of the changing conditions seem to demand. In either instance, the lack of unity and lack of integration continues. If he accepts the first alternative, he may suffer the pangs of conscience over compromises and exceptions which practical circumstances force upon him, or else he may gradually become insensitive to the inconsistencies which such compromises and exceptions involve. If he accepts the second alternative, he deliberately tries to crowd out through the front door the factors in life that invariably return through the back door and remain to threaten him from the rear. It is impossible to kill off important impulses by suppressive voluntary effort or neglect. They will play a part in one way or another. If they cannot do so in the open, they will do so under cover; if the intellect suppresses them, they will torment the conscience. Man is not by nature exclusively economic, political, religious, aesthetic, or moral. To treat his impulses as if they were of only one kind, such as the economic, does not eradicate them. All efforts to smother out impulses and desires by direct measures make conditions worse rather than better.

Specialization in all departments of life has tended to emphasize the separations, antagonisms, and conflicts of modern life. It has always been a feature of progress and civilization. During the Industrial Revolution it became a principle to be deliberately applied, and during the Power Age its application has been constantly extended. Today, the production of a single article, however small and simple, requires the work of many hands. On the whole, individual workmen are separated widely in time, in space, and in occupation. Different types of workmen know little about what other types of workmen are doing, and the interests of the consumer and the producer are seldom, if ever, seen in their proper relation. Moreover, such isolated jobs as tending machines can usually be performed without thought since routine habit is typically sufficient to meet all requirements. In work of this sort, intelligence is often a liability rather than an asset, and there is no place for emotion and affection. Work becomes labor and few take delight in what they are doing. The daily bread is often won in a daily grind without meaning and without significance to the individual. Most people, therefore, must have some release for emotions which find no expression in their regular occupations. Such compensation is commonly supplied by commercialized entertainment which often requires little or no executive skill or discriminating intelligence.

Specialization in the field of education proceeds at a corresponding pace. The accumulation and classification of subject matter continues with the advance of civilization. More types of schools, subjects, and courses emerge and take their place beside those that already exist. The mechanical schemes of measurement that have developed place a premium on routine skills and factual information that can be readily tested, graded, and scored, to the neglect of other phases of experience that are equally important. Since teachers and pupils learn that for which they are held responsible, school life often becomes as monotonous and as lacking in meaning and significance as routine labor in the mills and factories. Pupils and teachers too often feel the same impulse to seek compensation through commercial entertainment lacking in executive and intellectual demands, as do industrial laborers.

The demand for the purely sentimental in music, art, and literature continues, regardless of the preaching and complaining of the critics. The problem of mental health continues to increase, regardless of the accumulation of hospitals and improved methods of treatment. These are only the outward manifestation of the effect of conflict on individuals — of having their attention divided among a multiplicity of

forces pulling in every direction. No wonder educators are sensitive
to the situation and are seeking some means of securing more balance,
integration, and unity in the experiences of people, especially those
in school. They hope at least to render the present living of the young
sufficiently meaningful and significant to enable them to develop integrated personalities that can resolve inevitable conflict, and perhaps
assume responsibility for improving conditions under which integrated
personalities can eventually develop more easily than they do now.

Systematic effort and successful achievement over a wide front in
any undertaking require the development and application of some
guiding principle or theory. Such a guiding principle or theory in the
campaign for integration must be found in the nature of human experience as it actually occurs and develops. The kind of unity that is
desired must be based, in the last analysis, upon the kind of unity that
actually does or that could prevail. If experience itself is found to be
divided into separate compartments in which the whole is merely
equal to the sum of its parts, and thought, feeling, and action have no
inherent relation, provision for integration requires a decidedly different program from what it requires if some inherent functional relationship among all phases of experiences is already established. In the
one case, a balance must be artificially produced, and, in the other
case, it must be maintained and improved.

The importance of unity in the minds of students of morals and education thus seems to be a reflection of the conditions of life. Unity is
not important merely because educators emphasize it; they emphasize it
because it is important. In our effort to interpret this feature of experience we are considering a phenomenon of life that has long been given
attention and that now increasingly demands it. The attitude assumed
toward the feature of unity must thus emphasize a quality of experience
which, by implication at least, becomes an important aspect of any
philosophy of life and education. *Interpretations may vary, but as to the
meaning and significance of unity itself there can be no question.*

From the standpoint of the philosophy of experimentalism, there are
at least three theories of the unity of experience corresponding to the
three theories of the other features of experience already considered.
In educational authoritarianism the degree to which the various aspects
of experience are emphasized depends upon the relative emphasis
attached to their correlative factors in the environment to which they
correspond, and the weighting of these factors to maintain desirable
unity is the responsibility of those in control of the educational influ-

ences of the school and other educational agencies. In educational laissez faire desirable unity is conceived as an incidental by-product of the realization, actualization, development, or unfoldment of human impulse, which is often called purpose. In educational experimentalism desirable purposes are derived through reflective operations, and desirable unity is the cumulative effect of purposeful activity in which aims are intelligently chosen and pursued.

THEORY OF EXTERNAL UNITY
(EDUCATIONAL AUTHORITARIANISM)

Educational authoritarians assume that those responsible for the guidance and direction of educative experience can keep it unified and integrated by maintaining a balance among the various elements of the environment. The authoritarian conception of this feature of educative experience is therefore here designated as the theory of external unity. According to this theory, certain aspects of the environment correspond respectively to the various aspects of experience. Whatever affects the aspects of the environment, such as science, corresponding to thoughts, art, corresponding to the emotions, and social institutions, corresponding to will, affects the character of experience itself. It thus becomes the obligation of those who assume responsibility for influencing themselves and others constantly to control their environments. With respect to the problem of unity, they should so influence the environment that the various phases of experience maintain harmony, balance, and unity in the process of their development.

The phenomena of experiencing, which historically have been considered the subject matter to be investigated in psychology, are interpreted in various ways. In fact, the various explanations of these phenomena are what constitute the so-called psychologies or theories of psychology.

The authoritarian theory or principle of external unity assumes that experience as a process consists entirely of the aspects or phases of experience which constitute the subject-matter content of psychology. As we have already pointed out, some phenomena such as action, feeling, and thought — including perception, memory, imagination, and reasoning and other processes — are recognized as topics to which psychologists everywhere direct attention. From the standpoint of many educational authoritarians, these factors are not merely definable aspects of experiencing, but they constitute experiencing. According to this point of view, experiencing itself is nothing but the phenomena of experiencing which the psychologist subjects to study and investigation. Consequently, one way, perhaps the best way, of maintaining the proper balance, proportion, measure, and unity is to keep the various aspects of experience working harmoniously with one another.

In faculty psychology, thought, feeling, and action are explained as the operations of certain invisible powers of the mind usually called faculties. In association psychology, they are explained as the association, combination, and collocation of certain invisible and unchangeable impressions and ideas. In structural psychology, they are explained as conscious activities arising from the reactions of the individual to certain stimuli. In behaviorism, they are conceived in terms of responses to external stimuli, without reference to the factor of consciousness. In functional psychology, they are explained as conscious activities of the individual in adjusting to certain special demands of practical experience. In Gestalt psychology, they are explained as operations of certain configurations involving the interaction of individual and environment in the process of adjustment on the social level of experience.

The educational authoritarian may adopt some one of the psychological theories or he may adopt certain aspects of different theories; but whatever explanation of the psychological processes he adopts, whatever his psychological theory may be, he assumes not only that the different aspects of experience are distinguishable in thought, but that they are fundamentally different from one another as a matter of fact and occur at different times in response to different conditions. Even when he admits that ideational elements, affective elements, and active elements are inextricably interwoven and intertwined, he assumes that any given experience is predominantly intellect, feeling, or action. With respect to intellect he is convinced that perception, memory, imagination, and reasoning are separate and distinct experiences. These different types of experiencing, of course, involve one another in the sense that the quality of any given kind of experience, such as perceiving, affects the quality of other kinds of subsequent experiences, such as reasoning and imagining, but every experience is still predominantly some one type.

Since the relationship of the psychological functions in the process of development are conceived in various ways, the exemplification of the theory or principle of external unity in educational theory and practice assumes various forms. For instance, the educational doctrine that early childhood is the time for habit-forming, later childhood the time for exercise of memory and imagination, and adolescence the time for reasoning, harks back to the time when mental powers were supposed to appear, develop, and mature at different age levels. On the basis of this psychological conception the adherents of the authoritarian theory of external unity emphasize habits when the psychological capacity for habit-forming is present, memory work and imagination when these capacities are present, and reasoning when the capacity for reasoning is present. Actual requirements must correspond closely to the capacities present; otherwise the evil of arrested development is sure to result. Likewise, the conception that some scientific subject, some art subject, and some sociological subject should be studied in every year of one's educational career harks back to the old notion that mental functions correspond closely to the faculties of thought, feeling, and will, which were thought to be present in everyone. If these powers are present, the authoritarian exponents of the theory of external unity who are responsible for education are under obligation to provide the subject-matter materials on which they may be exercised.

But perhaps the best examples of the operation of this principle of unity are to be found in (1) certain technical conceptions usually adopted in the field of professional education; and in (2) certain conceptions that seem to be common assumptions held both by many members of the teaching profession and by the public. For convenience of discussion the technical conceptions of professional education will be considered first, to be followed by a consideration of the general conceptions which members of the profession and the public hold in common.

1. *The professional technical conceptions* to which reference is made are: (*a*) that there is a limited number of psychological types of educational aims to be sought in educational practice, and that these aims must somehow receive the proper emphasis and be properly related; (*b*) that there is a limited number of psychological techniques of teaching, each of which should be used at the proper time; and (*c*) that the values attributed to different subjects are so different that a proper balance must be maintained among the subjects included in the program of studies.

a. The tendency to think in terms of the types of experience and the effort to maintain a balance among them seem implicit in the discussions and formulations of educational aims in authoritative statements, as well as in official courses of study. Usually such psychological types of aims are distinguished as understanding or knowledge, appreciation or attitude, and skill or ability. It is quite clear that understanding or knowledge corresponds to the intellectual processes; appreciation or attitude corresponds to feeling; and skill or ability corresponds to habit-forming, involving both memory and overt activity. In practically all discussions of educational aims attention is given in one way or another to all three types, and often an effort is made to indicate their relationship to one another. In current practice all three types of educational aims are recognized, and in some instances their relationship is considered.

In recent years, although the threefold classification of knowledge, appreciation, and skills is recognized, some one type is often considered primary. For instance, Bobbitt calls all aims *abilities*, the term that is used by others to designate skills as one of the three types. But in listing aims he recognizes different types of ability, such as ability to perform certain acts, ability to appreciate certain things, and ability to understand certain things. Other educators consider *appreciation* the primary factor in stating educational aims, and knowledge and skill are conceived as aspects of appreciations. In the Virginia state courses of study, the threefold classification is recognized and designated as emotionalized attitudes, understandings or generalizations, and abilities. It is pointed out, however, that the emotionalized attitudes are the inclusive aims and that the understandings and abilities to be sought are contributory to them.

The importance of maintaining some kind of balance among the aims representing the different types of mental processes is thus widely recognized in the formulation of educational aims. There are different ways by which such a balance is sought; but everyone seems to consider it important. The educational authoritarian usually differs from other theorists by considering the question of balanced aims from a quantitative standpoint. He seeks to give sufficient emphasis to knowledge, sufficient emphasis to skill, and sufficient emphasis to appreciation. In other words, logically he should have about the same number of aims of each type. He might place special emphasis on one type when he thinks the other types have been overemphasized. If he thinks that knowledge has been overemphasized in the past, he will place greater emphasis on some other factor, such as skills or abilities. If he thinks that too much attention has been given to the mechanical skills and factual information, he may emphasize understanding. If he thinks that too much emphasis has been given to knowledge and understanding, he may emphasize appreciation and abilities. At this particular time, when there is a reaction against over-intellectualization in education, he seems to have become especially interested in placing the emphasis on appreciation and attitude. Perhaps the most extreme illustration of this reaction against intellect is to be found in the recent educational program of national socialism in Germany, where intellect and the intellectuals were subjected to the contempt and derision of the powers in control.

b. With respect to general methods or general techniques of teaching, similar aspects of experience are also recognized. For instance, the problem-solving techniques correspond to knowledge as one kind of aim and reflective thinking as one aspect of experiencing; the appreciation techniques correspond to appreciation as another kind of aim and feeling as one kind of experiencing; the drill techniques correspond to skills as one kind of aim and memorizing and habit-forming as aspects of experiencing; and, finally, the construction techniques correspond to abilities in the production of articles of objective achievement as still another kind of aim, and overt activity as an aspect of experiencing.[2] Everyone recognizes such distinctions or similar ones. The educational authoritarians, however, think of them as being separate procedures, one adaptable to the achievement of one kind of aim and the use of one kind of subject matter and others adapted to the achievement of other kinds of aims and the use of other kinds of subject matter. Since they wish to maintain proportion and balance in the kinds of aims to be sought and the kinds of subject matter to be used, they wish to utilize also the various types of techniques in the proper proportion. They wish to have enough problem-solving, but not too much; enough appreciating, but not too much; enough drill, but not too much; enough construction work, but not too much. The same applies to even the newer techniques, such as the socialized recitation. They wish to have enough socialization, but not too much. They seek to maintain a balance among the aspects of experiencing that are recognized as important whatever they may be.

c. Like aims and techniques, the values often attributed to school subjects correspond closely to the types of experiencing. As already

---

[2] National Education Association, *The Third and Final Report of the Committee of the Department of Classroom Teachers on Evaluation of Instruction.* Presentation at the Philadelphia Convention, July, 1926. Pp. 6–8, 25, 49–53, 74.

John P. Wynne, *General Method: Foundation and Application.* D. Appleton-Century Company, New York, 1929. Pp. 488–508.

suggested, science, art, and sociology, including political science and government, correspond to the three types of experience recognized in one variant of educational authoritarianism, but it is common practice for people to think of some subjects as good for some things and others as good for other things. Mathematics and Latin, for instance, may be good for the reasoning, history good for the memory, fairy tales good for the imagination, poetry good for the feelings, and industrial arts good for motor development. There is, of course, no unanimity of agreement as to which subject is best for what, but there seems to be a general feeling that the different subjects have their primary function in serving the needs of some particular psychological factors to which they primarily correspond.

2. *Certain conceptions widely held by people in general, including many members of the teaching profession, also exemplify the principle of external unity.* Many people, perhaps most people, who seek some justification for current practices in many fields assume that: (*a*) play serves a secondary and contributive rather than a primary and constructive function; (*b*) only the study of certain subjects can produce the most desirable character and personality; and (*c*) desirable unity is possible only in the case of individuals belonging to certain social classes.

a. Everybody thinks he knows the difference between work and play. Perhaps no other classification of human activities is better established in the minds of people everywhere. Their meaning and relationship have been considered in psychology, sociology, and educational theory for many years. The importance and significance of both are now widely recognized, but there is a wide difference in conceptions concerning their functions and how they should be related to each other to secure the most desirable results. The theory of external unity seems to be assumed in the attitude of those who think of the function of play as primarily a relief from work.

From this point of view, there are two kinds of activities — work and play. Work is generally considered naturally disagreeable and play naturally agreeable. Play is thought to serve as a means of repairing the damage for which work is invariably responsible. The primary values of life are secured through work and the primary value of play is to prepare one for more work. Like other types of activities thought to correspond closely to the different psychological factors of memory, imagination, reasoning, and the like, work corresponds to some human impulses and play corresponds to others. In the practical affairs of life, as well as in the activities of the school, enough play must be provided to secure good work. "All work and no play makes Jack a dull boy" seems to mean that some play is necessary to make us more effective. But from the standpoint of many who are in control of business and industry as well as the schools, the primary function of play is to make work effective.

It is necessary, therefore, to have play periods interspersed with work periods. It is now generally agreed that people do better work when they have vacations. It is admitted that pupils do better work when they have some recesses and vacations. As to how long the vacation should be and how long the recess should be depends upon how much play is required for the rehabilitation of one's physical and mental capacity for work when one returns to the line of duty. If the primary function of play is relaxation, the play periods should be of sufficient length and frequency to supply the relaxation desired. The character of the play should also be such as to secure the necessary reparation of functions that have been exhausted in work. There is no problem of supplying sufficient work to balance over-indulgence in play. If a person does not have to work and lives a life of recreation, that is his own business. Work is not a good in and of itself. It is merely a means of securing the necessities and luxuries of life. If one already has them, it is not necessary to work. But even for one who has riches, there is no royal road to education. Those who possess riches do not need to work, but those who do not have an education will need to play in order to facilitate the work required to get an education. In school everybody has to work and, therefore, should have an opportunity to play. In life outside the school some people are completely balanced because they spend a life of leisure, while others should have vacations and leisure sufficient to keep them fit for work.

b. The theory of external unity seems to be implicit in the conviction of many people that desirable education and personality are the effects derived from the study of certain kinds of school subjects. For instance, in the minds of many people the so-called intellectual subjects supply the kind of experiences that produce the highest types of moral character, whereas the so-called practical subjects produce the routine personalities of the so-called laboring classes. This principle is also assumed in the classification of school subjects as intellectual and utilitarian. The intellectual subjects are considered good for the intellectual functions, whereas the practical and utilitarian subjects that do not require much thought are good for the physical and mechanical functions. Theoretically, everyone should study some practical subjects as well as intellectual ones in order to maintain a proper balance of personality. However, the intellectual functions of most people are naturally so weak, so most authoritarians think, that they cannot deal with the intellectual subjects. The intellectual studies, therefore, should be limited to those who can handle them effectively. It may be admitted that these intellectuals should have some of the practical subjects, but only for the purposes of maintaining a balance. These practical subjects for the intellectual class serve the same function as play for the laboring class outside the school.

There are many play farmers and gardeners, and in some communities flower gardening is considered more wholesome and less menial than vegetable gardening. For such gardeners practical work is mere play and the further it is removed from the productive arts the better. In many places, there are people who would not be caught doing the relatively light work of picking beans or gathering turnip salad for personal use but do not hesitate to hoe and dig laboriously in flower gardens. On the whole, intellectual individuals should engage in activities which require thought and artistic feeling. It may be unfortunate, so authoritarians think, that the common run of people are by nature debarred from the higher things of life, but there is no disputing the fact. All we can do for these common, ordinary people is to provide for them a measure of balance and integration on a lower level. At best they are mere imitators in the fine arts and serve as mere sounding boards in fields requiring reflective thought.

This attitude is perhaps responsible for the current tendency in many quarters to segregate the intellectuals from the more practical-minded. It is suggested in the tendency to separate children on the basis of their ratings on intelligence tests. It is indicated by the disposition of some to demand vocational schools, vocational curricula, and vocational subjects for the non-intellectuals, who are thought incapable of success in the usually accepted educational program. It is exemplified in the attitude of many of the so-called intellectual students who look upon those who attend the more practical schools and pursue the more practical curricula and courses as somehow inferior to themselves. This distinction between the two types of courses may be accepted even by the students who seek this so-called practical education. But such an attitude is not confined to students. Faculty members in our high schools and colleges, as well as many people in all walks of life, rate the character and personality of those who attend the so-called intellectual schools, take the intellectual curricula, and elect the intellectual courses, a little higher than they do those who attend the vocational schools, take the practical curricula and elect utilitarian courses. Some are convinced that only partial credit, if any, should be recognized for the so-called practical subjects in the requirements for graduation from our high schools and colleges. Some consider the best qualified instructors in the intellectual fields superior to the best qualified instructors in the practical fields.

c. Finally, in the minds of many people, as already implied in the consideration of the relationship of work and play, and the intellectual and practical subjects, desirable unity is possible for only the naturally gifted. They recognize the importance of maintaining a balance by emphasizing properly the environmental factors corresponding to the different aspects of experience. They recognize the importance of giving everyone an opportunity to develop what intellectual power he has. They emphasize the importance of the beautification of parks, playgrounds, and public places for the purpose of developing the sense of beauty. They recognize the importance of having everyone conform to certain moral standards revealed by the moral sense. They recognize the importance of some kind of recreation to offset fatigue. But they are quite sure that after every effort has been made to maintain a proper balance of all the environmental forces affecting individuals, the variations in human capacity are such that the unity desirable for all can be attained only by few.

As long as the so-called psychological functions of the individual are conceived as relatively independent, people will be classified into relatively distinct types. The powers which all have in common are unevenly distributed, and some people are so superior in some respects and so inferior in other respects that they constitute a social class. For instance, Plato attributed to each individual only three powers — appetite, courage, and reason. In his theory of the state, those in whom appetite was dominant were to be the laboring class; those in whom courage was dominant were to be the soldiers; and those in whom reason was dominant were to be the rulers.

The principle operates the same way today when the psychological functions are considered in terms of thought, feeling, and action, or in some similar way. The so-called motor-minded individuals constitute the laboring classes; the so-called emotional individuals constitute the artists; and those in whom reason is dominant constitute the superior class who are by nature capable of leadership and control. It thus becomes the business of the schools and other social institutions to preserve and develop what nature has supplied. In practice the emphasis is placed upon the distinction between the intellectual-minded and the motor-minded. Just as the intellect should control the individual, so the intellectual class should control society. The problem of desirable unity thus consists in securing such quantitative balance as is possible in individuals of the so-called lower class and a higher type of quantitative unity in those of the so-called higher class. The integration, balance, and unity of society as a whole depend upon the development of the lower powers of the lower classes and the higher powers of the higher classes. In social activities we must always look to the intellectual class for leadership and to the motor-minded class to carry out their instructions in the production and distribution of goods. The theory of external unity thus reflects itself not only in professional education and school programs and the disposition to separate peoples into distinct social classes, but also in giving such tendencies intellectual justification in the inherent psychological nature of man.

From the standpoint of the philosophy of experimentalism the theory of external unity is inadequate because: (1) the isolation of the functions of experiencing which it assumes is psychologically unsound; (2) the practices which exemplify it are unacceptable; (3) the atomistic theory of learning which it assumes is inadequate; and (4) the results of the application of the theory of external unity have been unsatisfactory. These objections will now be considered in order.

1. *The isolation of the functions of experiencing is psychologically objectionable for two reasons. First*, the mental functions, such as perception, imagination, and reasoning, do not develop in any chronological sequence in the growing individual. The best psychological evidence available today indicates that all these processes are inextricably intertwined and emerge and develop together. There is no particular age, therefore, when educational activities should place special emphasis on habit-forming; when they should place special emphasis on memory and imagination; or when they should place special emphasis on reasoning.

Second, it is now almost universally admitted that the so-called mental functions, although they represent useful classifications and distinctions in psychology, are stages of experience and not separate and distinct from one another. They do not represent the operation of separate faculties of the mind. They are not isolated processes. They represent important points of emphasis to take into account in educational programs and activities, but they are not independent. In other words, one may be forming ideas, appreciations, attitudes, and skills all at the same time. Any so-called general techniques of teaching, such as the problem-solving method, the appreciation method, the drill method, the construction method, the socialization method, or any other procedure corresponding to any other psychological function, are not applicable to particular situations without reference to each other. To deal with an educational activity as if it involved acquiring skills or any one type of educational product without reference to others contributes to disunity and disintegration rather than to unity and integration. If unity is to be secured, the different psychological functions involved and implicated in concrete experiences must operate harmoniously with one another. It is not enough to seek proportion, harmony, and balance among different experiences. The particular experiences themselves should be balanced. Particular things are not learned in isolation from other things. For instance, ideas, generally called knowledge and understanding, are not typically learned in isolation from appreciation, skill, motor abilities, and social attitudes. In other words, *no educative experience is limited in its effect to any one type of psychological aim, such as knowledge, appreciation, attitude, or skill.*

2. *The practices which exemplify the theory of external unity are undesirable.* In the *first* place, arrested development, instead of being overcome by the application of the older conception of chronological, or longitudinal, development, is, as a matter of fact, more often caused in this way. If all functions are present at every period of life, arrested development must result from the neglect of any of them at any stage. For instance, to neglect reasoning in early and later childhood is a good recipe for arrested development. On the basis of the long recognized laws of habit this function becomes weakened through disuse. If the function of reasoning is in fact present from the beginning, it may be very much arrested by the application of any quantitative theory of unity which ignores its existence.

Second, the effort to balance the different types of aims, such as knowledge, appreciation, and skill, and the means by which they are realized, seems to contribute to disunity and disintegration rather than to unity and integration. When only one type of effect is considered, the other types of effect are neglected. Instead of rendering the experiences developed in accord with some particular type of technique harmonious, balanced, and integrated, such a program tends to cause experiences to be more unbalanced than they otherwise would be. The special emphasis which the so-called type techniques require forces in each given experience an emphasis on some one kind of effect out of proportion to other effects that are implicit and implicated.

To be more explicit, if skill is sought through the drill technique, attention should be given to appreciation, knowledge, social attitude, and physical development. But to consider these other types of outcomes and their corresponding processes requires, according to the theory of external unity, the use of their corresponding techniques. To employ the different techniques at the same time signifies the abandonment of the conception that experience is to be balanced through the operation of different techniques in the development of different types of experience. In other words, maintenance of balance among the so-called elements of experience signifies that every experience in so far as possible should be balanced. The employment of general techniques corresponding to the different elements prevents maintaining such a balance. The only way to secure unity is to develop whatever unity may exist. It is as difficult to break experiences up into their component parts and then combine them into a unity as it is to break the body into fragments and recombine them into a living personality. *Any desirable unity of experience that may be achieved must somehow involve an integration of the various aspects of particular experiences.* It is doubtless helpful to consider the different types of procedure; but any adequate theory of unity must take all of them into account in every experience. No balance of unbalanced experiences secures a balanced experience and a balanced personality, as the theory of external and quantitative unity seems to assume.

Even the constant attention to the different aspects of experience such as the reflective, emotional, executive, and social, is insufficient. No man is wise enough to tell in what proportions the various elements should be combined. Are they all equal in importance? Are they all unequal? Are some more important at one time, and others at other times? Who can tell? Even to ask such questions indicates the futility of trying to secure desirable unity through external quantitative control, and suggests the importance of discovering some unifying factor operating within experience itself.

Third, the implications of the conception of play as relaxation from work are very undesirable. The distinction between work and play is quite justified, but the assumption that the only function of play is its contribution to efficiency in work is not justified. From the standpoint of education play is as important as work. Play does serve the purpose of relaxation, but this is not its only function. It may be as educative in its effect as work is. Work is educationally most desirable when it is pervaded with the spirit of play, and play is most educative when some organization and control, which characterize work, are in evidence. Both work and play are desirable, but a desirable balance cannot be maintained between them by reducing the one to the other or making the one dependent upon the other. When play becomes merely relaxation, life loses its meaning and significance for those who have to do the world's work, labor becomes routine drudgery, and recreation, emotional indulgence. In the school and the home play should serve the constructive function of keeping the young physically and mentally fit and producing lasting educational effects. It should not serve merely as a means of overcoming the damage which work has already done, and thus as a preparation for more work. Vacations should not be conceived only as a means of overcoming fatigue resulting from more serious business. They should be conceived as a means of preventing such fatigue from occurring in the first place because vacations are in effect positively and constructively educative. In a word, there must be some unifying and integrating factor common to experience in both work and play, if experiences are to be as desirable as they might be. Work and play can never be quantitatively balanced, as the theory of external unity seems to imply.

Fourth, the usual contrast of the functions of different school subjects is not only psychologically unsound but socially and morally undesirable. Psychologically, there is no reason to believe that one subject is inherently any more intellectual or practical than any other. All depends upon what is done with the subjects. Socially and morally the idea that some subjects are intellectual and others practical not only maintains the gap between social groups but even widens it. Everybody cannot engage in the same occupation and everybody should not take the same curriculum, the same subjects, and the same courses in our educational institutions. Moreover, there is no valid reason whatever for one occupation to be considered inherently intellectual and cultural while other occupations are inherently manual, practical, and utilitarian. *The so-called intellectual and cultural occupations must be practical if they are to be really cultural and liberal, and the so-called practical occupations must be intellectual if they are to be meaningful and significant.* But here again the practical vocational occupations cannot be the same in every respect as the so-called cultural ones. Although neither can be reduced to the other, one should not be conceived educationally as primary and the other secondary, any more than work and play should be so conceived.

Likewise, the so-called intellectual and the so-called practical courses, subjects, curricula, and institutions of our educational system cannot be reduced one to the other. One is no better and no worse than the other and should not be so conceived. *Any practice that produces feelings of superiority or inferiority in students and in teachers should be eliminated.* There is need for some integrating factor common to all courses, subjects, curricula, and schools. It is impossible to secure artificial and external unity in any one field, to say nothing of securing it in all fields.

The separation of people into sharply distinct groups, which the theory of external unity seems to justify, is entirely unwarranted. The presence of class distinctions is familiar enough, but the fact that they exist is no reason for seeking to perpetuate them. Moreover, the fact that class distinctions exist does not warrant the conclusion that they are inherent in human nature, as the isolation of the aspects of experience seems to suggest. As already shown, there is no scientific evidence to indicate any such isolation of mental functions, or to signify that some functions belong to one class rather than to another. It is not true that some men are born to be leaders and others to be followers, as Plato thought and many still think. All men may be leaders in some things and all should be followers in some things. If the individual cannot secure desirable unity through a quantitative balance of the various functions of his experience, certainly society cannot secure desirable unity by weighting differently the various aspects of experiences of individuals constituting different groups. What is needed is some unifying and integrating factor to be found in the experience of everybody, regardless of race, nationality, and natural endowments.

3. *The atomistic theory of learning assumed in the theory of external unity is inadequate.* As already indicated, this theory assumes that the process of experience consists of the psychological functions which can be isolated and logically analyzed. The underlying assumption is that any conception and, by implication, any pattern of experience is no more than the elements into which it may be reduced through logical analysis. In mathematical terms, the whole is equal to the sum of its parts. When carried over into psychology and stated in terms of learning, this principle signifies that the way we acquire our patterns of thought, feeling, and action consists in learning the elements into which these patterns have been logically analyzed. Thus in the theory of external unity the so-called atomistic theory of learning is assumed. From the standpoint of the philosophy of experimentalism, the whole in psychology and learning is always more than its parts. One may

learn all the so-called logical divisions and still not learn the conception or habit, or any psychological pattern from which such elements are logically derived. Just as the so-called aspects of experience do not constitute the whole of experience, so the psychological outcomes of experience, such as knowledge, appreciation, and skill, do not constitute the whole effect of experience. Consequently, no effort to maintain a quantitative balance among the aspects or effects of experience can secure a desirable unity of experience. *No balance of parts which do not constitute the whole can ever produce a balance of the whole.* The unifying and integrating factor required must be found in experience itself and not in any quantitative treatment of the parts into which it may be analyzed. Unquestionably, the proper procedure is for one to maintain the integrity of experience and develop whatever unity already exists.

4. *The results of the application of the theory of external unity have been unsatisfactory.* In spite of the fact that the theory of external unity has been widely accepted and extensively applied, conditions which its use should remedy are becoming worse rather than better. Mental ailments, including complexes and conflicts of all kinds, are continually increasing in number. Individuals and groups are becoming mentally more and more isolated from one another in spite of the fact that physically and mechanically they are getting closer and closer together. The renewed emphasis everywhere on the importance of balance, unity, measure, and integration is sufficient evidence that the age-old struggle of man to find harmony and peace in himself and with his fellows is not yet realized. The disposition of educational authoritarians and others to emphasize all the aspects of the environment corresponding to the various aspects of experience and to provide a variety of activities in order to effect the operation of the different functions of experience is successful to some extent, but as a theory of desirable unity it is insufficient and inadequate.

Theory of Impulsive Unity
(Educational Laissez Faire)

Purpose usually designates the factor to which proponents of educational laissez faire look for balance, integration, and unity. But a purpose as they conceive it is at best a conscious urge, drive, or "toward-whichness," which experimentalists may call impulse in order to distinguish it from a purpose which has been selected through intellectual operations. For this reason, the laissez-faire conception of unity is here designated as the theory of impulsive unity, and "purposeful unity" is reserved for designating the theory of unity to which educational experimentalists subscribe. Impulse is broadly conceived to include desires, wishes, wants, and even uncriticized purposes. In the principle of impulsive unity, life and education, in the practical, existential, and psychological sense, is a process of development from within, and desirable life, desirable education, consists in the unfoldment, actualization, or realization of the inner nature of man. Human impulses represent the manifestation of the urge of inner life to realize itself. Such impulses are, therefore, good and should not be repressed, restrained, or inhibited. It should be the business of those interested in a better life for all to provide the conditions under which natural impulses may be manifested and be developed to the full.

Since the typical educative experience under consideration is on the mental and social level, the impulse to which attention is directed is not only purposive in the sense of mere toward-whichness, seemingly characteristic of all behavior, but it is also purposeful because it is conscious of the end toward which it moves. It is good, however, not because it has been reflectively chosen from among alternative ends suggested. It is not a mere proposal to be rejected or pursued on the basis of probable consequences. It is a command of nature that must be obeyed. It is the end of nature revealed in human desire, thought, and action. Its very presence warrants our every effort to provide for its fullest development.

Mental processes are invariably involved in the manifestation, expression, and realization of these natural ends that should control the destiny of the individual and the race. They are permeated with feeling from beginning to end. Intellectual processes, such as perception, memory, imagination, or reasoning, are typically present. The number and quality of these processes vary from time to time. For instance, perception may be pronounced at one time, memory at another time, and imagination at another time. Their functions vary also. For instance, perception, memory, imagination, or reasoning may be conceived as merely attending the activity involved, without serving or aiding the process directly or indirectly. However, these mental processes may be conceived also as serving their proper functions when they, each in its own way, aid in the realization of those natural ends in whose existence and selection they have no part. At best, the mental processes, even reflective thought, are servants in the development of a course of action for which some active force, immanent in the individual, is entirely responsible.

Apparently such impulsive activity provides a basis of securing the desirable unity suggested in such a conception as balance, proportion, measure, and integration. If all mental functions participate, each according to its special qualification, in the promotion of courses of action prompted by impulse, they must be properly balanced, proportioned, and integrated. The questions of how much, to what extent, and how long, which confront the theory of quantitative unity, do not have to be faced when the theory of impulsive unity is adopted. If each mental process, such as feeling, perception, memory, imagination, and reasoning, does what is required of it in each particular situation, each is balanced and integrated. It is not necessary for some outside agency to allocate to these functions different kinds of subject matter, provide them with a time schedule, and supply each one with a technique of procedure consistent with its own nature. Each now takes hold at the proper time, does just enough and not too much, and proceeds in the right way. The natural impulses that direct the process of experience control it in all of its phases. The desirable unity required is inherent in the process itself if it is given an opportunity to operate in accordance with its own nature.

Like the theory of external unity the theory of impulsive unity is exemplified in current practices and in the principles used to justify them. *In the theory of external unity the importance of giving sufficient emphasis to all mental functions to keep them working harmoniously with one another is recognized; in the theory of impulsive unity the variety of activities is emphasized so as to provide for the actualization of whatever impulses may emerge and thus exercise the different functions of experience.* According to the theory of external unity, the psychological types of aims, such as knowledge, appreciation, and skill, and their corresponding techniques of problem-solving, appreciation, and drill, must be given proper consideration; according to the theory of impulsive unity, no specific psychological aims should be formulated in advance nor formal techniques used to secure them; for in the variety of activities that provide for the immediate development of whatever impulses emerge in experience the various aspects of experience receive whatever emphasis they should receive, and in the proper proportion.

The theory of external unity seems to be exemplified in the current tendency of many people to look upon play as a means of securing more and better work; the theory of impulsive unity seems to be exemplified in a counter tendency to reduce all work to play. If the authoritarians desire only such play as will contribute to increased production, the adherents of educational laissez faire desire only such work as is felt to be play. The authoritarians so control the extra-curricular activities of the school as to make them almost indistinguishable from the curricular activities, and the exponents of educational laissez faire so remove control from the curricular activities as to make them almost indistinguishable from the extra-curricular activities. The authoritarians in business and industry so intersperse and control vacations and holidays as to facilitate the production of economic goods; the exponents of laissez faire so remove the mechanical routine involved in production as to cause all work to seem like play.

The theory of external unity seems to justify a current disposition to classify people as the intellectual and the motor-minded, to be treated quite differently; the theory of impulsive unity seems to justify the disposition to remove this distinction and treat every individual as unique. From this point of view the old authoritarian classification of individuals and subject matter must be abandoned. There is no intellectual class destined to lead, and there is no motor-minded class destined to follow. One individual is as important as another and is so unique that his activities defy advance classification. As for the subjects, they represent classifications of subject matter that must be abandoned as schemes of organization. Whatever intellectual and practical patterns of thought, feeling, and conduct are desirable are achieved incidentally by every individual who is free to engage in such a wide variety of activities that all his unique impulses have an opportunity to realize and actualize themselves.

From the standpoint of the philosophy of experimentalism, the theory of impulsive unity seems to overcome the objections that have been leveled against the theory of external unity. It does not involve bridging gaps between different mental functions. There are no gaps to be bridged. Every function, however specific or however general, has its functional or operational place in a more inclusive whole. There is no conflict among functions that are thus working together in the development of a program to which they all owe their existence and allegiance. The importance of developing schemes and techniques for the proper promotion of this process of unification has disappeared. The mental processes are no longer separated and independent, each with its own ways requiring special conditions for its proper growth and development. Desirable unity now does not have to be super-imposed upon experience from the outside; it is already there. All we have to do is to provide the kind of environmental condition required for human impulses to actualize, develop, or realize themselves. Such impulses are the source, the means, and the measure of the desirable unity of experience now so widely demanded. Why should we become so eager to provide artificial unity involving all kinds of labor when natural unity is already ours if only we will accept it?

According to the philosophy of experimentalism, the theory of impulsive unity has certain advantages over the theory of external unity but it also is open to question. It avoids the impossible attempt to bridge gaps of unknown dimensions by the proper weighting of the exercise of isolated mental processes that cannot be measured. In providing for a variety of activities necessary for the manifestation of different impulses the principle of impulsive unity provides also for the effective operation of the various functions of experience which the principle of external unity emphasizes. It contains the suggestion that if desirable unity is to be secured it must embody the unity that already exists. However, it is not self-evident that whatever exists is on that account desirable. How do we know that the natural impulses are desirable? If they are not desirable, how can the unity which their development provides be desirable? What are the practical implications of this principle? In practice is it satisfactory? It seems necessary to consider such questions as these before committing ourselves to the principle of impulsive unity.

With respect to the desirability of natural impulse there certainly is room for doubt. Ordinary, common observation indicates that some impulses, if given right of way, would lead to the destruction of individuals and the society to which they belong. All of us have impulses which, if immediately expressed, would prove detrimental to ourselves and to others whose welfare we normally wish to promote. The old conception that every impulse is bad — the more natural it is, the worse it is — is not now widely accepted by the rank and file, nor even by students of psychology and morals; however, the opposite conception that every impulse is good — the more natural the better — is equally unacceptable. More reflective individuals are quite aware that all impulses to action are not good, and students of psychology and morals agree with them. The reverse of a bad principle is not necessarily a good principle. It is perhaps practically more often a bad principle; it may even be worse than the one it is designed to replace. All impulses are certainly not good.

If we assume that the good impulses are to be selected from the bad, the principle of impulsive unity, as we have defined it, is by implication rejected. If good impulses are to be selected and the bad ones rejected, some factor other than the impulses themselves must do the rejecting and selecting. Whatever factor is responsible for this differentiation of impulses must be itself responsible for whatever unity may exist among those selected.

On the other hand, if impulses are unmoral rather than moral or immoral, good or bad, the logical position of the principle of impulsive unity is not improved. If impulses are neither good nor bad, desirable nor undesirable, they constitute the raw materials that must be reworked before they should be permitted to actualize or realize themselves. Not the impulses themselves but whatever factor is responsible for this remaking and reconstructing of the original impulses is the factor to which we must look for desirable unity.

With respect to practical implications, the principle of impulsive unity seems highly questionable. It suggests that existing experience be the starting point for further experience. This much seems psychologically sound. There is no place for anyone to start but where he is. But this principle requires more. It signifies that the structural basis of experience, whether it be mental or physical, or something else, contains within itself the unactualized reality that is to be expanded, elaborated, and developed. In other words, the process of actualization does not signify the production of a new individual and through him a new world. It signifies that the old mental powers, ideas, interests, habits, or what have you, are merely to be filled in through experience. In beginning with existing experience, we are to take it for what it is and make all of our work conform to the requirements of the structure that already exists. The old ideas and habits are not to be remade. They are to remake the world in their own image.

Those who adopt the principle of impulsive unity must, of course, discover the impulses which they are to serve. They do not, however, have any instrument by which they can detect these impulses inside the body. They must wait for their manifestation. When such entities fail to reveal themselves, the protagonists of this principle must resort to whatever means may be available to bring them out in the open. They may ask individuals what they wish to do, send out trial suggestions, or set the stage so to speak. But from this viewpoint, they must, of course, refrain from telling children in the home, pupils in the school, or others for whose constructive guidance they are responsible what to do. To give orders or to make assignments would be a dangerous procedure, because some natural impulse, which is inviolable, might be thwarted, repressed, restrained, or inhibited. The so-called purposes that constitute the integrating factor of all aspects of experience, from this point of view, emerge as ready-made wholes to be elaborated through the activities they demand for their actualization. The purposes that are fundamental in the direction and control of experience are to be derived from forces outside of it — not from those inside of it. From the standpoint of the philosophy of experimentalism, to accept impulsive purposes as guides to action is morally objectionable and practicably impossible, for people have to meet the demands of a world that does not conform in all respects to human desires.

Only a casual examination of the activities of many people and the maxims and shibboleths they use in their justification indicates that the applications we have suggested as possible logical implications of the principle of impulsive unity are no exaggeration of the possibilities of the operation of this interpretation of the feature of unity when employed systematically over a wide front. All of us are acquainted with people who proceed to work for whatever they desire, wish, or want, without regard to whether they should, under the circumstances, wish, want, or desire such things. The same people, and those who supply intellectual support for such practices, readily tell us that this is a free and open world; every man in trying to fulfill his own desires, wishes, and wants is doing the best in the long run for all. We all know individuals both old and young who seem to think that the world was made for them. They are constantly seeking things that others need; hoarding things that others want; displaying things that others desire. Their justification for their actions is that they want to do these things and that what they want to do is their own business. Many of us have never grown up. We are still children, even spoiled children — who cry and pout when we cannot do as we please.

The "have" nations and the "have" individuals do not hesitate to take from the "have not" nations and the "have not" individuals, and then to dangle their trophies before longing eyes. The "have not" nations and the "have not" individuals, without reflecting upon the justice of their methods, seek by hook or by crook to deprive others of their goods, opportunities, and freedom merely because they have the impulses to do so. Any effort to control or to direct the activities of the "have nots" is immediately confronted with the proposition that they are merely exercising the right to do what they please in a world where everyone is by nature guaranteed the same privilege. They take this position and proceed in the same way without stopping to realize that the conditions of life have long since rendered obsolete the conception of natural rights and privileges. On the other hand, the "have nots" point out that the "haves" have secured their possessions, privileges, and opportunities by the conquest and exploitation of others, and that they in turn have the same right to conquer and exploit. On the basis of the theory of impulsive unity, everyone is justified in doing in so far as he can whatever seems to give him pleasure and satisfaction. When systematically applied, such a principle must disrupt balance, proportion, and integration — every nation would then be against every other nation, every group against every other group, and every individual against every other individual. According to the philosophy of experimentalism *a world in which some people remain children, and seek to fulfill the demands of their impulses directly and immediately, is bad enough, but a world in which everyone does so on the basis of a principle accepted by all cannot for long endure.*

Those who endorse the theory of impulsive unity in the schoolroom supply concrete illustrations of its operation. They tell us that it is the teacher's business to follow the lead of the child. The pupils are the only ones who have educational aims. The aim of the school and the teacher is to aid pupils in the realization of their aims. The school where the child controls everything is designed to aid the pupils in the realization of their purposes. The school must not provide a preliminary plan of curricula, subjects, and courses; the teacher must not organize the content and the materials of his courses in advance. Such advance planning, so it is believed, will prevent the manifestation of the impulses which are usually called purposes. The school and the teacher must practice a policy of watchful waiting. Only as the pupils reveal what they want to do can the school and the teacher know what content to select, what materials to provide, or what methods to use. Such statements as these are applicable to much current practice that they are often used to justify. They are clearly implicit in the principle of impulsive unity and other allied conceptions embodied in the still more inclusive point of view of educational laissez faire of which subjective contingency, inherent sociality, and immediate interest, creative self-expression, and free choice, already considered, constitute other principles.

According to the philosophy of experimentalism, children brought up in the home or in the school where such a philosophy of life and education prevails may fit into a world where everybody is for himself and against everybody else. They may be better qualified to take the initiative and be more persevering in their effort to secure what they want; but in the larger life of the world as it actually exists they must soon be quickly disillusioned or else be subjected to many severe stresses, strains, and conflicts. Instead of becoming balanced and integrated, they must become unbalanced, confused, and disintegrated. They may contribute somewhat to the tendency already present in many quarters to do whatever one wishes until prevented by forceful measures. The practices which such a theory justifies must be restrained, either by force or by intelligence, if civilization itself is to survive. The theory of external unity may not secure the ends it is designed to achieve; but the theory of impulsive unity when deliberately applied contributes systematically to the conflicts, confusions, and tendencies to disintegration that it is intended to reduce. It must inevitably make bad matters worse. It has been said that without a vision the people perish. Without the light of intelligence there can be no vision. In the principle of impulsive unity intelligence is a mere servant or attendant of impulse and desire. Only an interpretation of the feature of unity that frees intelligence in theory can provide the principle required for the liberation of intelligence in the practices of the home, the school, the church, and all institutions whose existence can be justified educationally on the basis of the qualities of experience they foster in the people.

THEORY OF PURPOSEFUL UNITY
(EDUCATIONAL EXPERIMENTALISM)

The conception of desirable balance, integration, or unity to which educational experimentalists subscribe may be designated as either purposeful unity or reflective unity, for they consider reflection a fundamental factor of purposeful activity and purpose a fundamental factor of reflective operations. The emphasis is placed on the reflective factor, because failure to do so might cause some to take conscious impulse as purpose. To do so would signify that the interpretation we here have in mind would be essentially the same as the laissez-faire principle of impulsive unity that has just been considered. Reflective thought is recognized in that principle, but it serves a mere secondary role of attendant or servant, whereas in the experimentalist theory of purposeful unity to which attention is now directed reflective intelligence serves a primary role. It assumes the function of control, direction, and guidance, which impulse itself assumes in the theory of impulsive unity.

It is not unusual in educational theory for interest, impulse, and desire to be used interchangeably. As a matter of fact, definitions of such conceptions that distinguish them satisfactorily for everyone are doubtless impossible, but to distinguish reflective purpose from any and all of these other conceptions is not difficult. Reflective purpose embodies both interest and impulse, but it involves more. In the course of experience impulse precedes interest in point of time and both precede purpose. Mere impulse or even conscious impulse, sometimes called purpose, is initial in experience, whereas purpose as here conceived is eventual.

The initial stage of an activity that becomes an experience is the effect of a state of affairs that we have seen fit to designate as the need of experience. As we have already pointed out, it is a more complex and involved level of the condition known as loss of equilibrium or balance. On the distinctly human level, we call such loss of equilibrium experience need or need of experience, not because of any awareness of the loss of equilibrium, although such awareness is often present, but because the equilibrium or adjustment required can only be achieved through experience. Experience is thus needed. The need may be conscious or unconscious, but the need is a need of experience independent of consciousness. It is experience that is required to fulfill the need and to restore the equilibrium, and that involves consciousness. The need is initial and lies outside of the experience, although it is reflected in the experience and endures as long as the experience. It is the initiating and sustaining condition of experiences, which come to a close when it disappears.

The existence of the need causes movements, as does the loss of equilibrium or lack of adjustment. But mere movement, or even multiple and diffuse movement or multiple and varied reaction, is not sufficient to overcome the stress or strain involved. A particular qualitative kind of movement is required that simply cannot be discovered by accident. Experience is necessary. Conscious experience begins to emerge when obstructions to activity are met. When obstructions are met, the individual becomes aware of what he is doing and takes time out to think. He is consciously interested in what he is doing, and does not just do, without thought, first one thing and then another. He examines the practical conditions and probable consequences and considers whether or not it will pay to do this, that, or the other. He acts out in imagination the various suggestions that occur to him, and takes the course of action that seems to be the most promising, all things considered.

There is a world of difference between this kind of activity and mere impulsive behavior. The course the individual actually takes is a purpose. It is the outcome of operations involving reflective thinking.

Unity as a quality of such experiences differs widely from the quality assumed in both the theory of external unity and the theory of impulsive unity. The balance and proportion among the various aspects of experience are not superimposed from the outside. Such balance and proportion are not inherent in the nature of impulse. Unity is achieved in the process of experience in consequence of operations which reflection performs. Needs that lie outside of experiences and initiate them may be satisfied on the social level in many ways, but they are blind. The impulses that are aroused are also blind. Reflective thought surveys the situation and selects the course to follow — the purpose.[3]

The purpose selected may turn out to be wrong — it may not meet the need — but whether it is successful or unsuccessful, it is different from the original impulse or even from the purpose as understood by some. It is no mere wish, desire, or want immediately expressed. It has been subjected to reflection and chosen because of its promise in the light of the evidence at hand. Consequently, it is flexible and capable of change. The reflective intelligence that selected it continues to direct the activities involved in developing it. Reflective thought continues to survey the field, noting possibilities, checking results, and constantly reconstructing purposes to meet the requirements of a dynamic and changing situation.

In this conception of purpose reflectively achieved we seem to have the principle of balance, measure, proportion, and integration required. As in the theory of external unity, the importance of a balanced emphasis on the various aspects of human experience is recognized, but unlike the principle of external unity, the method of securing such emphasis is not limited to external and quantitative measures prescribed by forces from outside of experience. As in the theory of impulsive unity, the functional relationship of the various aspects are conceived as mutually involved in the more inclusive experience to which they belong, but unlike the theory of impulsive unity, the intellectual factor in the theory of purposeful unity is no mere spectator, attendant, or servant. It is a participant, not merely in carrying out a program that is determined before it arises. The program itself is modified and transformed by reflective, critical thought, and the

[3] William H. Burton, *The Guidance of Learning Activities.* D. Appleton-Century Company, New York, 1944. Pp. 101–105.

purposes that guide and direct it are initiated, selected, and adapted to requirements in the process of experience. The purpose here under consideration does not arise outside experience to cause it. It arises within experience to guide, direct, and control it.

All the functions of experience that may be differentiated and defined are involved in experiences in which such reflective purposes emerge. Some vague feeling of satisfaction or annoyance is present at the origin of impulse, which precedes every experience in point of time, and continues to operate in reporting favorable and unfavorable conditions. Perception is involved in checking and analyzing observable factors. Memory is involved in recognizing the significance of present factors on the basis of past experience, and in recalling pertinent information previously acquired. Imagination combines the data derived from the past with the data supplied by the immediate objective conditions. The will consists of the driving force of the original impulse that has been transformed into intelligent purpose. In reflection, all factors co-operate in executing a program that has been initiated by one factor known as impulse, and they participate, each according to capacity, in initiating, planning, and developing a process in which all are mutually involved.[4]

The theoretical objection of some that we are overemphasizing the role of intellect is not difficult to refute. The present-day emphasis on feeling in morals, education, and politics is not the result of overemphasis of intellect. It is the result of the separation of intellect from the rest of life. Even in national socialism, once dominant in Germany, the intellectualism against which complaint was raised was not the result of the overemphasis of thought and intelligence. As a matter of fact, it was the result of an underlying assumption of the principle of external and quantitative unity that the various features of conscious experience are at bottom relatively independent and must somehow be harmonized from the outside.[5]

When the various aspects of experience are conceived as separate processes and effort is made to allocate each to its proper sphere without any functional unity among them, overemphasis of one or another aspect is almost inevitable. Any overemphasis of one will almost certainly lead to a reaction and possibly to an overemphasis of another.

[4] William H. Burton, *The Guidance of Learning Activities*. D. Appleton-Century Company, New York, 1944. Pp. 5–13.

[5] George Frederick Kneller, *Educational Philosophy of National Socialism*. Yale University Press, New Haven, 1941. Pp. 142–153; 241–253.

Since the intellectual processes are more easily defined and studied in psychology, the danger of their receiving too much attention in economics, morals, politics, and education is always present. That the intellectual is usually over-stressed has long been recognized by reformers in the field of education as well as in the field of morals. The recent emphasis on feeling and emotion in this country and on the physical and the irrational in Germany is nothing new. It represents an accentuation of a demand for balance and unity that is the inevitable result of the separation of intellect from the other phases of experience, and of education from life.

A permanent solution of the problem, however, does not lie in a mere quantitative adjustment. The attempt to divide the world and assign one sphere to the intellect, another to the feeling, another to the body, and still another to the will, probably will accentuate the one-sidedness it is designed to remove. Such a conception caused the work school and work instruction, as they were developed in Central Europe after the first World War, to be confined in the minds of some educators to physical activity. It resulted in the effort to limit the "project method" to construction work and the activity curriculum to activities involved in the production of objective things, such as bird houses, post offices, and rabbit boxes. The extension of the time devoted to the emotional and physical education of the people may render the masses irrational and confine intellectual control to a chosen few. The extension of the time devoted to merely physical activities decreases the time devoted to intellectual pursuits and, correspondingly, will tend to render the activities of the multitude less intellectual. Likewise the withdrawal of the intellectuals from practical affairs which they are unable to influence will render their activities impractical and irrelevant.

The danger does not lie in the overemphasis of intellect in experiences in which activity, feeling, and thought are equally and mutually involved. The danger lies in separating the fields of operation and confining each function to its own province. *The experiences of men cannot be broken down into pieces and then reassembled in such a way as to produce measure, unity, and balance.* If balance, integration, and proportion are to be achieved and improved, the functional unity that exists must somehow be maintained. The problem is not one of deciding where physical activity should dominate, or where will should dominate. It is a problem rather of seeing that all factors are recognized in all fields. It is not solely a problem of spending the proper proportion of available time in intellectual pursuits, artistic pursuits, and physical pursuits. It is a problem of utilizing the intellect, the feelings, and overt activity in the same activities. Of course, it must be admitted that in the material world of affairs some fields require more intellect, some require more feeling, and others require more physical activity than others. The problem is not, however, to place an interdict on any field or circumscribe it in favor of another. The problem is to recognize all aspects of experiences in every province of life and give them an opportunity to co-operate in a functional relationship in which reflective thought continuously controls the direction.

Such a conception does not require the impossible, as is sometimes suggested in many current slogans and shibboleths. It does not signify that the intellectual, the physical, and the artistic are invalid distinctions, and that work and play must be reduced to a common denominator. There are no fields in which intellect should be squeezed out, no fields in which the physical should be eliminated, and no fields in which the artistic should be neglected. All fields cannot be reduced to a dead level. Different fields of experience exist because they represent concentrations of energies that nature provides. They represent points of emphasis that have not been artificially controlled by men; they correspond to the very nature of man and therefore cannot be artificially eliminated. On the other hand, the activities in each field should be functionally related to activities in all fields. Work should include play, and play should include organization which suggests work. Nevertheless, there must remain in the very nature of human life two kinds of activity — play and work. Recreation is not to be conceived as merely a relief from work and a preparation for it.[6] Recreation cannot be reduced to work and work cannot be reduced to recreation. On the other hand, work may be morally, artistically, and intellectually constructive. Extra-curricular activities and curricular activities cannot be legislated out of existence by changing terms. Educative experiences under school conditions involve the extra-curricular activities as well as the curricular activities, but this fact does not mean that the distinction between the two is to be abandoned. In our world there is a time for work and a time for play, and both may be suffused with qualities of desirable experience, by even reflective unity, without the reduction of either to the other. Neither is good or bad solely with respect to its influence on the other. The experience of each may be good in and of itself, although contributions to each

---

[6] John Dewey, *Human Nature and Conduct.* Modern Library, New York, 1930. Pp. 156–168. (Henry Holt, 1922.)

other must be realized. *Reflective purpose integrates particular experiences, aids in maintaining a balance among different types of experience, and facilitates measure and proportion among different fields of experience.*

In the theory of purposeful unity the policy of watchful waiting that seems logically implicit in the theory of impulsive unity is no longer required. The purposes that supply the integration and unity required are not to be discovered by the mere observation and manipulation of the minds of those whom we undertake to guide and direct. For instance, the teacher in the school need not hesitate to ask pupils to do things for fear their budding purposes will be repressed or restrained. He does not expect to find immanent in them any ready-made purposes in which the various aspects of experience are properly integrated. He does not engage in soliciting or prodding as a practical measure when the policy of watchful waiting breaks down. He is not concerned as to how activities are initiated; but he is particularly concerned that they be of the kind and character that will provide for the selection of purposes through intelligent reflection. He is not afraid to make plans in advance, involving attention to aims, content, materials, and methods, for fear he will deprive pupils of an opportunity to actualize, unfold, or develop existing purposes. He usually does not wish them to actualize or realize purposes that are inherent in them. He recognizes such purposes, which, as a matter of fact, are mere conscious impulses, as the raw materials out of which the purposes required in the theory of purposeful or reflective unity are developed in the process of experience itself. He believes in organization and systematic arrangement as a means of getting under way those activities in which pupils will construct purposes through reflective operations.

The theory of purposeful unity conceives all aspects of experience as functionally related to reflective purposes that emerge within the process of experience itself. It recognizes the distinctions of the mental functions that have been developed in psychology and the corresponding classifications of experience in the world of affairs. It does not admit, however, that any mental function in any field develops independently and that it therefore has to be artificially balanced. The different fields require attention because they are fundamental in the individual and in the physical and social world, but they cannot be adequately balanced by weighting, according to any formula, the emphasis to be given different phases of experience. All schemes, devices, and techniques for maintaining a balance among separate fields may well be considered in dealing with any field. Purposeful unity recognizes the aspects of experience that external and quantitative unity emphasizes, and involves the impulsive purposes that impulsive unity emphasizes. Purposes reflectively chosen integrate the phases of experience and transform original impulse or purpose into balanced programs of action.

The theoretical and practical implications of the principle of purposeful unity are very significant. On the theoretical side, the principles of functional contingency, widening sociality, pervasive interest, creative originality, and intelligent choice are combined into a single unifying conception. Adequate purposes can be developed only where individual and environment are conceived as functional factors that change in meaning and significance in terms of the more inclusive process of experience. Reflective operations involved in the selection of such integrating purposes can occur only in a social situation, and consideration of their educational significance includes their direct effect upon the individual and their indirect effect upon the wider community. Although not every experience in which purposes are reflectively selected may be acceptable, those which are otherwise educative and desirable are acceptable. The operations in such purposeful activity involve creative originality or the creative reconstruction of experiences, which signifies the remaking not only of the individual but of the social order itself. The principle of intelligent choice is a quality of every experience in which purposeful unity is achieved through reflective operations. In fact, purposeful unity is another way of designating the presence of intelligence.

On the practical side, as already suggested, the effective application of the principle of purposeful unity signifies the abandonment of the theory of external and quantitative control of human activities as the sole method of securing desirable integration and unity. The consistent application of the theory of purposeful unity would counteract the negative doctrine which, in its reactions against external control, relies on uncriticized impulses and desires to supply the only worthy aims of educational and social policies, programs, and activities. Its adoption would mean the rejection of the conception of two distinct classes of people, the leaders and the followers, as well as the rejection of the counter proposal of the adherents of the laissez-faire philosophy that individuals are so unique that no common requirement can be justified for particular groups. Every individual who selects his own purposes through reflective operations must be a leader in some things as well as a follower in other things. The school program that reflects the historical policy of maintaining a sharp distinction between a ruling class and a servant class will be so modified that all occupations and all subjects, as well as the students who pursue them, the teachers who teach them, and the schools that provide them, will be equally respected.

The adoption of the theory of purposeful unity might check the current tendency, accelerated in consequence of war conditions, to isolate certain individuals in certain schools, curricula, and courses, as suggested in the present movement for vocational education. Where separations are necessary for efficiency or breadth of scholarship for those enrolled in the so-called practical programs, and where wider practical experiences are necessary for those enrolled in the so-called liberal programs, the adoption of this principle would make invidious distinctions irrelevant in fact as they are in theory. Where people, whether in the school or in the affairs of life, are responsible for the intelligent selection of their own aims, they become free. When they do not have such responsibility, they become slaves. *The question to be asked in regard to the character and personality of people is not what are their vocations or what subjects have they studied in school, but what qualities of experience have they had.* An essential quality, perhaps the primary quality of desirable experience, is purposeful reflection.

PART II

Theories of School Practice

CHAPTER 9

Education and the School

As ALREADY INDICATED in the first part of this book, philosophy of education should be a recognized study in general education because it is of concern to everybody. Furthermore, it is a recognized subject of professional education and should therefore be of special interest to those directly in charge of schools. Although education is as broad as experience itself, although most of our experiences are a part of our education, although all of us are engaged in education throughout our lives, although everyone is constantly educating other people and they in turn are constantly educating him, and although every social institution is an educational institution, the school is an educational institution in a special sense. Such institutions as the home, the church, the government, and business and industry are also educational agencies, but for them education is a secondary consideration while for the school it is the primary consideration. Since education is the vocational and professional occupation of those directly responsible for the activities of the schools, philosophies of education to be rendered most directly and immediately significant for this professional group must be stated not only in terms of experience but also in terms of school practice.

FUNCTIONS OF THE SCHOOL

The school along with other social institutions has a method function and a training function. Its method function is to influence the qualities of experience; its training function is to teach certain specific things. Most institutions have some primary function other than education; but the school exists solely for the purpose of education through method — the way it treats people — and through subject matter — the specific things it teaches. Other educational institutions often engage in education unconsciously and incidentally, but the school must always engage in it consciously and deliberately. It is important that those responsible for other institutions become conscious of their educational significance and responsibility, but it is especially important that the school recognize and understand the philosophy that controls its practice.

The school is often called a residual institution because it assumes necessary educational obligations which other social institutions have become unable to perform satisfactorily. It emerged historically in response to practical demands. Among primitive people the young were steeped in the traditions of the people quite incidentally through their participation in the activities of everyday life, supplemented by certain ordeals and ceremonies conducted by the elders and those responsible for the religious welfare of the tribe. With the advancement of civilization, however, it became increasingly difficult to teach incidentally the facts and skills that were considered indispensable. Gradually, the school emerged to assume the obligation of teaching these things.

At first the method function, influencing qualities of experience, was neglected by the schools. The personality and character of the people were shaped by the customs, traditions, and mores that prevailed in the life of the community. The school confined its efforts largely to training — that is, teaching the essential facts and skills which could not be adequately taught by other social institutions. Finally, we reached the stage when other social institutions were unable to accept full responsibility for the method function of education — namely, of so influencing the qualities of experience that individuals develop personalities and characters that are most desirable. The school as a residual institution had to assume some responsibility for the method function along with its traditional training function.

Those directly responsible for running the school should be interested, even primarily interested, in theories concerning the desirable qualities of experience which have been considered already, but they should not on that account neglect the traditional training function, the teaching of certain facts and skills. Philosophies of education stated in terms of school practice might be very meaningful to them when stated in terms of qualities of experience. Still they might understand better the requirement of these philosophies if both their method function and their training function were stated in terms of the responsibilities of members of the teaching profession. Therefore, those who write books or teach courses in philosophy of education for teachers and other schoolworkers should state the philosophies they recognize not only in terms of experience but also in terms of school practice.

More specifically, we shall discuss the philosophies of educational authoritarianism, educational laissez faire, and educational experimentalism in terms of the school just as we have discussed them in terms of experience.

FEATURES OF SCHOOL PRACTICE

We are thus confronted with the problem of selecting some adequate method of defining these philosophies in terms of school practice. We could proceed to criticize, appraise, or evaluate descriptions of school practice, using the sets of principles derived from defining these philosophies in terms of experience, but to do this would require detailed descriptions of practices that are not readily available. Moreover, we are not so much interested in applying principles of experience to school practice as we are in finding in school practice other principles that correspond to the principles of experience. *If the theories of school practice and the theories of experience logically support one another, they may be conceived as different statements of the same underlying philosophies.* In other words, we are interested in studying philosophies of education that actually prevail in the school rather than in applying philosophies of education to the school. We might restate and elaborate whatever principles and theories have been applied to the schools, taking them just as we find them, but this procedure is not so easy as it may at first appear to be. We must have some way of selecting the important from the unimportant. The only method that seems feasible is to proceed as we did in stating these philosophies in terms of experience. Just as there are certain widely recognized features of experience that embody important points of emphasis, so there are also certain widely recognized features of school practice that embody important points of emphasis.

If we could determine the features of school practice which all schoolworkers consider important, or with respect to which they assume theoretical positions, we should perhaps be able to formulate general theories with regard to them just as we have in the case of certain features of educative experience. However, there are so many features of school practice that we cannot consider them all. We must be selective. *School practice consists of educational activities for the guidance and direction of which those in charge of schools, including the colleges and universities, are responsible. Features of school practice are classifications of such school activities.* The classifications or features of school practice which seem most important to schoolworkers depend somewhat on the kind of educational service they perform. There are some factors which seem especially important to teachers, others which seem especially important to supervisors, and still others which seem especially important to administrators. Likewise, there is some difference between the interests of teachers in the elementary school and in the high school, and in the high school and in the college. Moreover, there is some difference in various fields of study, such as science, social studies, and the fine arts. It is impossible in a book or course in philosophy of education to consider every special interest. The point of view here adopted is that every topic to be considered should be of interest to every professional schoolworker; not that some topics should be of interest to some and other topics should be of interest to others. We must think not merely of teachers in the elementary school, in the high school, or in the college, or of teachers in general education or in some particular field, but of every kind of teacher in every field and every kind of education, every kind of supervisor, every kind of administrator, and everybody else who has any part in the immediate control or direction of the activities of the school. It is necessary, therefore, to deal with problems that at one time or another confront all members of the teaching profession.

The same thing may be stated somewhat differently. There are certain school topics with respect to which all those responsible for the activities of the school often have to take some kind of stand. The particular topics with respect to which the three philosophies of education under consideration are to be stated and elaborated are as follows:

1. Educational Aims
2. Subject Matter
3. Educational Organization
4. School Curriculum
5. General Method
6. School Training
7. Educational Research
8. Devices and Techniques
9. Improvement Programs
10. Educational Leadership

Members of the teaching profession assume toward these features of school practice attitudes comparable to those people in general assume toward the features of educative experience. These attitudes, whether consciously or unconsciously maintained, represent different philosophies of education. They may be defined as theories or principles just as similar theories of the features of educative experience have been defined and named. Like the theories derived from different interpretations of the features of experience, they are easily classifiable into three more general theories or philosophies of education.

For convenience of discussion, it is necessary to name both features and theories. Some people may prefer other names, but those used here seen to be most acceptable, all things considered. What they are called may be important for purposes of communication, but their existence is a far more important consideration. As we shall point out in the subsequent discussion, the features and theories to be defined represent actual school practice.

In the chapters that immediately follow, we shall consider the different theories entertained not only by philosophers but by practical schoolworkers themselves concerning the foregoing ten features of school practice. In doing so, it seems to be quite in order to take, at least in some instances, the sayings of recognized experimentalists in the field of education as the starting point. However, as in the case of the theories of the features of educative experience, the explanations and elaborations of them will not be confined to a documental study of educators who accept the experimental outlook. We shall take into account also the theories stated or suggested by recognized students of education representing other philosophic positions. For instance, the writings of different kinds of authoritarians and of the proponents of different laissez-faire doctrines are considered along with the materials which the educational experimentalists themselves have provided.

Although the information thus secured is indispensable, there are also other resources available. Some of the most valuable data for the author or instructor, as well as for the student interested in these philosophies of education, are to be secured through observation in the schools and through participation with school people in the discussion of their practical educational problems. In this way we are able to secure concrete evidence of the operation of the three philosophies of education. Any qualified observer of how people in general deal with their social and moral problems can discover from their assumptions the different theories of experience considered in the preceding chapters. Likewise, any qualified observer who is interested in school problems can, through observation and discussion, discover the theories to be developed with respect to the features of school practice in the chapters that follow. It is from observation of practical educational situations in the schools and from the discussion of practical school problems that evidence of the influence of these theories has been secured.

Through such observation and participation many inconsistencies are revealed. Some individuals assume elements of different theories with respect to the features of school practice just as they do with respect to the features of experience. For instance, one may adopt an authoritarian theory of aims, a laissez-faire theory of research, and an experimental theory of general method. One may hold at one time a position with respect to any feature, such as aims, which is inconsistent with the position he may hold with respect to it at some other time. A mixture of these three philosophies of education may thus be found in current school practices, as well as in the assumptions and principles used to justify them. Those in charge of school education, however, like people in general, tend to favor one or another of these philosophies of education. As Dewey suggests, the schools are authoritarian most of the time and laissez-faire for very little of the time. But some individuals tend, on the whole, to support one philosophy, some another, and some the third, although everybody at one time or another adopts some elements from all three of them.

It is the purpose of the chapters that follow to render these philosophies of education, which may often consist of only general attitudes unconsciously held, more explicit and, in the explanation and elaboration of the theories of school practice, to draw the lines between them as sharply as possible. Perhaps such an examination of the three philosophies of education as they actually operate in school practice and in reflective discussion of school practice will enable those responsible for formal education to see more clearly just which philosophy of education they assume in dealing with school problems, as well as to see more clearly what other philosophies of education they might adopt. If they do not improve their practice, they at least may discover the intellectual foundations of it, and then act with more understanding of their own attitudes as well as of the attitudes of others.

Special Questions Anticipated

Some readers may raise a question as to the relationship of the theories of educative experience and the theories of school practice. There must, of course, be some logical relationship between them. Otherwise, both could not consistently be called educational authoritarianism, educational laissez faire, and educational experimentalism. For instance, the three theories of any particular feature of school practice, such as aims, should be consistent with the theories of the relativity of experience, and likewise with the theories of any other feature of experience or school practice. As a matter of fact, any careful analysis of the theories developed with respect to these two kinds of topics reveals considerable consistency; but the presence of such logical consistency does not mean that the sets of theories stated with respect to the different kinds of features were derived solely one from the other.

The experience of the author in stating the theories of the features of educative experience doubtless has influenced his statements of the theories of the features of school practice. Perhaps it would be possible to derive the theories of school practice from the theories of experience, or even to derive the theories of experience from the theories of school practice. *The plan of the study is to derive the theories of school practice from an examination of school practices and attitudes toward them rather than logically from the theories of experience that have already been developed.* In other words, the theories of school practice to be explained and elaborated are actually operating in the minds of those in control of school education, whether they have considered the philosophies of education implicit within them or not. This study in large measure is reportorial. It consists of a systematic and logical statement of theories that people in responsible school positions actually entertain with respect to their own problems.

The arrangement of the features of school practice, like the arrangement of the features of educative experience, is not intended to suggest the relative importance of topics. For instance, the feature of aims to be considered first is no more important than the feature of leadership to be considered last. Any one topic is as important as any other. The order in which the different topics are treated is one which we have found through trial and error to facilitate most the discussion as a whole. Some other arrangement might prove just as satisfactory.

Some readers may feel that certain topics of common interest to teachers and school officials have been neglected; however, they should understand that all topics of common interest cannot be considered. Life is too short. It is sufficient if the theories developed are presented clearly enough for the reader to understand the philosophies of education which they represent and clearly enough for him to apply them in the consideration of other problems as they arise. For instance, at first sight, it may appear that such topics as moral education, religious education, and general education as well as elementary education, secondary education, and college education have been neglected. True, they have not been considered as separate topics, but they have all been included logically in the consideration of school training. Many may miss planning and evaluation. They are not considered because aims, subject matter, organization, and devices and techniques, which are included, are themselves the more important features of planning and evaluation. If the theories developed with respect to these topics have been sufficiently explained and elaborated, they doubtless can be applied to problems of planning and evaluation.

Perhaps some readers will note that several of the topics have not been discussed, or have been only incidentally considered, by the widely recognized experimentalists. It is true, for instance, that devices and techniques have not been discussed systematically by any experimentalist. Nevertheless, it could be shown that James and Dewey have expressed themselves rather clearly with respect to various aspects of the topic. This topic has been selected not merely because the experimentalists have considered it, but because it is a topic with respect to which the philosophies of education which they recognize can be clearly stated. Widely recognized experimentalists may not have stated the three philosophies of education with respect to the improvement program and educational leadership. These topics have emerged as features of school practice only in recent years. Since the experimentalists have always been interested in the practical implications of philosophy, they are almost sure some day to give these topics their attention. Dewey says it is the business of philosophy to enlighten men's minds about the problems of their own day, and as the improvement program and educational leadership increasingly command the attention of practical school people, they should increasingly command the attention of the experimentalists.

Moreover, the topics selected are not just those which the educational representatives of the philosophy of experimentalism have considered from the standpoint of the authoritarian, laissez-faire, and experimental philosophies of education, nor even merely those which the experimentalists or any other recognized students of education have heretofore considered. The topics selected are the ones in which experimentalists have shown an interest in the past or should logically be expected to evince an interest now. In a word, some of the topics here treated as features of general school practice have not previously been specifically considered, at least not under the same heads as they appear here. There are perhaps some important features of school practice to which the experimentalists have not yet had time to devote their attention, at least not sufficiently to indicate the theories which the adherents of the three philosophies of education adopt. The features of school practice to be discussed embody general points of emphasis with regard to which these philosophies of education may be so defined as best to serve the function of philosophy as experimentalists conceive it — namely, to enlighten men's minds about the problems of their own day. In other words, it is the business of students of educational philosophy to consider the features of school practice that are problems to those directly responsible for school education, and it is just these topics that we have developed in the chapters immediately following. In selecting the features of school practices, in stating theories with respect to them, and in appraising such theories, the general outlook of the movement in philosophy known as experimentalism, pragmatism, instrumentalism, and humanism has been accepted as a basis of orientation, just as it has been so accepted in explaining and criticizing the theories and the features of educative experience.

CHAPTER 10

Educational Aims

PERHAPS EVERY SCHOOL OFFICIAL at one time or another has asked himself just what the value or worth of some program or activity was. He may have also compared the ends that were actually sought with other ends that might have been sought. Individuals or groups that put such questions to themselves are face to face with the problem of educational aims. The topic of aims, also called values, objectives, or purposes, has long been recognized as an essential feature of school practice, and is usually treated in professional courses and in books for teachers. Aims are generally considered in curriculum programs and constitute an important feature of most courses of study. They are often considered by school faculties and accrediting agencies in evaluating school programs and activities. Competent students of education and authoritative educational commissions and committees have from time to time given attention to the formulation and elaboration of aims for the use of schools and teachers in planning, teaching, and evaluating their own work in practical school situations. It seems necessary, therefore, that the topic of aims should be given some attention in any effort to state philosophies of education in terms of theories of school practice. Although it is generally agreed that aims are an important factor in school policies, programs, and activities, there is no unanimity among conceptions of the nature and function of aims. From the standpoint of the philosophy of experimentalism, there are at least three general attitudes towards aims — the authoritarian theory, the laissez-faire theory, and the experimentalist theory — that have been defined already in terms of the theories of educative experience.

THE EXTERNAL-ENDS THEORY
(EDUCATIONAL AUTHORITARIANISM)

The attitude of the authoritarians toward aims may be properly designated as the external-ends theory because, according to them, the objectives, values, or purposes that govern educational programs and activities are determined outside the actual situation itself. When so conceived aims do not indicate what is possible or desirable under specific conditions, all things considered. Usually they consist of ends formulated by recognized authorities to be used by schoolworkers as standards of direction in practical situations in some community, school system, subject, or course. They are considered by some authoritarians as objectives to be achieved and by others as goals toward which some contribution is to be made. All who adopt this theory, however, think of authoritative aims as supplying direction to school activities of all kinds.

Authoritative aims vary considerably in their origin, scope, and form. They may be stated by authoritative educational commissions or committees, by students of education, by administrative authorities, and even by teachers. An authoritative educational commission or committee consists of a group of recognized students of education usually appointed or selected by some important professional organization, such as the National Education Association, to define the aims which should guide the activities of the schools. Some of the more important of the recognized authoritative groups that have defined educational aims are the Committee of the National Education Association, which formulated the Cardinal Principles of Secondary Education in 1918; the Committee of the National Education Association, which formulated the Socio-Economic Goals of America in 1934; and the Educational Policies Commission, which formulated the Purposes of Education in American Democracy in 1938.[1] Similar sets of aims have been defined by students acting independently, among the best known of which are the analyses by Herbart, Herbert Spencer, David Snedden, Franklin Bobbitt, and Chapman and Counts. Such authoritative aims are not, of course, external ends from the standpoint of those who formulate them. They are real *aims* developed within the practical situation which confronts these students of education and the groups they represent. They become external only when they are used uncritically by others as standards of direction. They are external to school systems, to schools, or to teachers who accept them ready made and make their aims conform to these authoritative pronouncements.

The administrative authorities who are responsible for authoritative aims may represent a school system, a particular school, or some particular department, such as home economics, agriculture, or physical

---

[1] See pages 68–71 for a summary statement of these different sets of aims.

education. They may consist of school officials, committees, or other authoritative groups and individuals who may be commissioned by administrative officials, as in the case of many groups responsible for curriculum programs. The aims formulated by such officials are not external from their own point of view, unless perhaps they take aims already formulated by others, such as those of the authoritative students of education, to whom we have referred, or even, perhaps, the aims that have been set up for other school systems and special fields. Nevertheless these aims are external to all those who adopt them uncritically as their objectives in practical school situations. The school faculty or the teacher who accepts, for a particular situation, the aims of others outside that situation, even if those others are the most capable people within the school system, is adopting the external-ends theory.

Often school faculties and individual teachers formulate their own aims. It is obvious from what has been said that such aims represent the external-ends theory in so far as they are aims taken ready made from authorities, educational or administrative; that is, from students of education, from school officials, or from their delegates. They are actual aims of the faculties and individual teachers who defined them for their own guidance, after taking into account the whole practical situation. Still they represent the external-ends theory when considered from the standpoint of others upon whom they may be imposed. For instance, the individual teacher, even a member of a group responsible for formulating the aims for his school, adopts the external-ends attitude to the degree that he accepts unconditionally aims formulated outside the practical, specific situation as the sole standards in dealing with his own pupils. Moreover, the teacher who sets up aims in advance for his own guidance is accepting the external-ends theory in so far as he fails to take into account the whole situation or fails to modify his aims as actual learning-teaching activities emerge and develop.

Variation in the scope of aims has already been suggested. They are as broad as the interests of those who formulate them. They may be world wide in conception, as are natural development, social efficiency, and complete living and similar formulas which great thinkers have defined from time to time as the all-inclusive aims of education. Currently in the minds of most people, educational aims consist of certain specified values formulated with respect to some particular frame of reference, such as a nation, a school system, a school, or some particular school group. They are not external ends in consequence of their scope, but solely in consequence of the function they are thought to serve. In so far as aims place a limitation upon those who are expected to use them, they are external ends.

The form in which aims are expressed varies considerably. Aims may be defined and elaborated in essay form, in a tabulated or outline form, or in a combination of these. For instance, in *The Purposes of Education in American Democracy*, developed by the Educational Policies Commission, four general aims are stated. These are then elaborated in outline form into ten or twelve items. Each item is then further elaborated in some detail.[2] Aims are also usually defined in terms of the psychology prevailing at the time they are formulated, or in terms of the psychology most congenial to their authors. Herbart defined his aims as ideas, corresponding to the elementary units of which experiences psychologically were thought to be built. Herbert Spencer thought of his aims in terms of "what knowledge is of most use." Some students of education have formulated aims in terms of abilities, understandings, appreciations, or attitudes; others have formulated them in terms of interests, or needs. Perhaps the most common attitude of those who construct courses of study and develop curriculum programs is that there are several psychological types of aims, and so the aims formulated for the guidance and direction of schools and teachers are usually classified as abilities, corresponding to habit and memory in psychology; knowledge and understanding, corresponding to thinking in psychology; appreciation, corresponding to feeling in psychology; and attitudes, corresponding to emotions and tendencies to action in psychology.[3]

But the form in which aims are stated does not indicate whether or not they are conceived as ends to be sought. Rather it indicates the psychology of the formulator and his conception of what is the best way to make his ideals intelligible to those who are expected to use them. The form does not indicate how the aims are to be used, for they are external ends, it matters not how they are expressed, if they are used uncritically as standards of direction in the development of practical school policies, programs, and activities. Any approval or disapproval of the form in which aims are stated must be based upon considerations other than the attitude toward the function of aims.

---

[2] See pages 70–72 for a more detailed discussion of *The Purposes of Education in American Democracy*.

[3] See pages 196–198 for a more detailed discussion of the psychological types of aims.

Up to this point, the discussion of the external-ends theory of aims has been merely reportorial and descriptive. Now we must face the problem of appraisal or evaluation. What are the advantages and disadvantages of this authoritarian external-ends theory of aims? Our criticism, as in the case of the authoritarian theories of educative experience, is made from the standpoint of the philosophy of experimentalism.

The external-ends theory of educational aims arises from the need which many people feel for some standards of direction other than those which experience itself supplies. Such a need expresses itself in the form of a demand for some authoritative ends or values to be sought through educational activities. It is not enough, so many people think, for pupils to engage in learning activities. They must accomplish, in terms of changes in behavior, certain results. From this point of view, the attitude that teachers and schools do not know where they are going but are on their way is not satisfactory. It is necessary for them to have a very clear notion about where they are going. Educational aims are supposed to supply the desired standards of direction.

Aims thus seem to meet an essential need of experience. We must have some ends in view to guide our activities. Without such standards of direction, educational policies, programs, and activities cannot be justified. The standard used in evaluating an educational undertaking is generally found in the ends toward which it is directed.

The objection to the external-ends theory of aims does not arise from a denial of the need for direction; it arises from the conviction that the direction should come from inside rather than from outside individual experience. There is no objection to having students of education state their aims for the country and even for the world. There is no objection to having educational officials state their aims for school systems, schools, and special fields. There is no objection to having teachers of various subjects state their aims for these subjects. In fact, everyone should have aims.

The difficulty arises when one group or one individual undertakes to state aims for the guidance and direction of others. According to the external-ends theory, educational authorities should supply the aims to be sought by those who are involved directly in the learning-teaching relationship. Administrative officials should adopt the authoritative aims developed by students of education, and teachers should adopt the aims of the administrative officials. In the words of Thorndike, "It is the problem of the higher authorities of the schools to decide what the schools should try to achieve and arrange plans for the school work which will attain the desired ends. Having decided what changes are to be made, they entrust to the teachers the work of making them. The special problem of the teacher is to make these changes as economically and as surely as is possible under the conditions of school life. His is the task of giving certain information, forming certain habits, increasing certain powers, arousing certain interests, and inspiring certain ideals.

"But the problem is always fundamentally the same: Given these children to be changed and these changes to be made, how shall I proceed? Given this material for education and this aim of education, what means and methods shall I use?" [4]

According to this point of view, educational aims are hierarchical, the higher authorities always determining the aims for the lower. The administrators of the school system define the aims for the school, the school for the teachers, and the teachers for the pupils. Of course, school administrators should have their own aims; there is no objection on this score. Everybody should have his aims, and the more clearly he has defined them, the better. The trouble arises when the aims of one administrative level are conceived as the legitimate and exclusive aims for a lower administrative level. Aims that are taken ready made from others are not aims at all. As Plato said, those who take their purposes ready made from others are slaves. In so far as students of education and school administrators seek to have others take their aims as the sole ends of schoolwork, they are exponents of intellectual slavery. In so far as individuals adopt uncritically ready made aims as they are handed down from authorities, they are enslaving their own souls.

We also face serious practical difficulties in the application of this theory of educational aims. An aim, to be an aim at all, must be flexible; that is, capable of being changed as conditions change. Those who adopt the external-ends theory conceive educational aims as fixed and unchangeable. Some contend that aims represent values immanent in the very nature of the world; others, that they represent the generalizations of competent students who sense the demands of the social situation prevailing at some particular time and place. In either case, however, the aims that are stated must remain fixed until competent students see fit to revise them in consequence of new insight into nature or reality, or of their recognition of changes in social condi-

---

[4] Edward L. Thorndike, *The Principles of Teaching.* A. G. Seiler, New York, 1920. Pp. 3–7.

tions. Those responsible for the actual learning-teaching situation must seek the same aims, year in and year out, until the authorities see fit to change them.

To be an aim at all, an aim must be an outgrowth of practical conditions. The aims that are handed down by authority do not take into account the demands of specific situations. It is not enough that teachers seek, as Thorndike suggests, to achieve aims in so far as possible under the conditions. It is highly desirable that the aims themselves should be the aims that the conditions require. The aims of the teacher should be the ends which seem desirable to him in consequence of the ability, disposition, and experiences of pupils as individuals and as groups, the availability of materials and equipment, the attitude of the community, and his own capacity. Aims handed down by authority do not take such conditioning factors into account.

It is as important for pupils to have aims as it is for anybody else to have aims. If the teacher takes his aims ready made from administrative or educational authorities over him, it seems inevitable that the pupils must take their aims ready made from the teacher. If the teachers are enslaved by the imposition of aims by authority, so are the pupils.

The theory of aims as external ends to be sought seems to be consistent with the authoritarian theories of the features of educative experience. It assumes the theory of objective contingency since the environment, structurally considered, is the primary factor determining what the schools shall teach and what the pupils shall learn. It assumes that proper socialization of the individual consists in his adjustment to, or incorporation of the social ideals of those in power. It assumes that interest as a quality of educative experiences is merely a means to the realization of ends and not an end itself. It assumes that the products of experience are embodied in the minds, hearts, or bodies of pupils without regard to the quality of originality. It assumes the theory of selective choice since it limits the intelligence of teachers and pupils to the achievement of ends selected by those in authority. Finally, it assumes that desirable unity of experience can be achieved in some external and quantitative way without the presence of purpose. Those who accept this theory of educational aims logically accept also the philosophy of educational authoritarianism stated in terms of the theories of the features of educative experience. In fact, the external-ends theory of aims may be considered either as an elaboration or as an application of this philosophy of education.

THE IMMEDIATE-ENDS THEORY
(EDUCATIONAL LAISSEZ FAIRE)

The laissez-faire attitude toward aims may properly be designated as the immediate-ends theory because the ends to be sought by the teacher and by the school are discovered primarily through direct and immediate observation of the activities of pupils. It is perhaps more often implied in certain school practices, and in statements made to justify these practices, than it is expressed in terms of definite aims or principles. Those who adopt the immediate-ends theory of aims look to the pupils themselves to reveal the proper aims of education rather than to the outside world of nature and the social order. They usually designate the aims on which they center their attention as pupil interests, needs, or purposes. From this point of view, the ends of education are to be discovered through a direct study of childhood and youth. The studies involved in such surveys are of two kinds. First, experts in child study, child psychology, or child development, undertake to discover, list, and define the interests, needs, or purposes of all children. Second, teachers discover the interests, needs, or purposes of particular pupils through direct inspection.

The first kind of study makes available to teachers aims which may serve as standards of direction. In fact, some seem to think that such inherent values attributed to children in general by qualified students constitute the all-inclusive aims of education. However, they would be willing to encourage committees of teachers and even the individual teacher, to supplement the specific objectives included in authoritative lists with other objectives that they may discover. Such a conception of educational aims places the emphasis on the pupil as contrasted with most authoritative formulations of aims. It is the interests and the needs of the individual in the present rather than the interests and the needs of society in the future that are conceived as important. Furthermore, such sets of values are not fixed. They may be modified through use.

Nevertheless, from the standpoint of the philosophy of experimentalism, there are serious objections to any such conception of educational aims. First of all, it is extremely doubtful that such a list of interests or needs can have any universal validity. At least, they represent abstractions from evidence secured from observation, and cannot represent the interests and needs of particular individuals and groups under varying conditions and circumstances. So long as such ends are conceived as suggestions of what to look for in concrete situations, they should be helpful, but the moment they are taken as the aims of education and used uncritically as ready-made standards, they become external ends, subject to all the objections that have been raised to other authoritative aims that seem so important to some students of education. The aims of education, whether defined as powers, interests, needs, or something else, cannot be determined by inspecting children apart from current situations any better than by inspecting the social order without reference to particular children.

Teachers may, however, abandon authoritative aims of all kinds and rely entirely on their own powers of direct observation and inspection. They consider aims reliable that are discovered in the immediate learning-teaching situation. The teacher studies his pupils day in and day out to determine their needs, wishes, interests, and desires, all of which usually are called purposes, and so he does not burden the pupils with any preconceived notion of what they shall learn or do. His all-inclusive aim is to give their natural tendencies free play to reveal and express themselves. His problem is to find out, and to make provision for, what his pupils wish or want to learn or do.

To determine what interests pupils, the teacher uses any available technique at his command. He prepares a situation, known as "setting the stage," that will call out suggestions: he tells stories, asks questions, and enters into general discussions; he asks the pupils what they wish to do; or he may even himself make proposals as a last resort. By this method, purposes for a day, for a week, or for a term are listed and defined, and become the working-aims for the group.

Working-aims for the group, determined in this manner, are conceived as valid merely because they represent the needs, interests, or desires of the pupils themselves in a concrete situation. They have an advantage over the so-called typical interests or needs of pupils in general. A least, they take into account the environment to which the children are responding during their selection. They are not conceived as values immanent in the children apart from conditions; they represent values experienced by children under specific conditions.

According to the philosophy of experimentalism, such a theory of aims represents a natural reaction against the inadequacy of the theory of external aims imposed by authority; but such aims do not provide the social direction which authoritative aims are designed to supply. It is difficult to see why pupils should be encouraged to learn or do what they wish merely because they wish it. From this point of view, one thing is as good as another only if it satisfies immediate needs, interests, or desires. In the minds of many people, such a conception is contrary to common sense. Almost everyone believes that pupils should devote themselves to learning what will be useful to them in the future and what will improve the social order to which the school is responsible. Most people are not convinced that merely because an activity seems good to us in·the present the result will be good. They are not convinced that what pupils are inclined to learn and do immediately is sufficient to maintain and advance the interest and welfare of society, which sustains and supports the school.

If we undertake to reply that the wishes, desires, and wants of children are part and parcel of the social situation and, thus, must reflect the needs and interests of society, we are faced with the fact that there are undesirable as well as desirable factors in the social situation, and that children are as immediately responsive to the one as to the other. It must be admitted that immature pupils who need education are not capable of distinguishing the desirable from the undesirable. The school and the teacher should not be expected to take their aims uncritically from their pupils any more than they should be expected to take them uncritically from their official superiors. Somehow or other, *the teacher must adjust, integrate, or combine the demands of authority with the interests and needs of the pupils.* He must somehow discover aims in the situation, but any aims, however defined, that are taken directly from the pupils themselves are inadequate. They do not include the social direction required.

As already suggested, the immediate-ends theory of aims is most congenial to those who accept the laissez-faire theory of the features of educative experiences. It is consistent with the theory of subjective contingency since the individual supplies the ends which the schools should seek. It is consistent with the theory of inherent sociality in its reliance upon the social nature of the individual to provide the reliable standards of social direction. It is consistent with the theory of immediate interest in advocating the acceptance of the immediate interests, desires, wishes, wants, or purposes of the pupils as desirable ends. It is consistent with the theory of direct creative self-expression in so far as the pupils are thought to reveal new factors that will signify social progress and advancement. It is consistent with the theory of free choice in so far as the aims of the pupils are accepted as sufficient without critical evaluation, and with the theory of impulsive unity in so far as the aims of the pupils are uncriticized impulses, wishes, or wants.

The immediate-ends theory of aims should, therefore, be acceptable to all those who accept the laissez-faire theory of educative experience. By the same token, this theory is rejected by the educational experimentalists, although it is often attributed to them by both authoritarian and laissez-faire spokesmen.

THE EMERGENT-MEANS THEORY
(EDUCATIONAL EXPERIMENTALISM)

According to educational experimentalism, aims are not supplied directly by authority or by pupils, nor do they exist ready made outside of experience. They emerge in experience and serve as a means of controlling and directing it. Such a conception of aims may therefore properly be called the emergent-means theory. From this point of view, everyone should have real aims that arise in the practical situations with which he is confronted. Such aims cannot be taken ready-made from others. They are an outgrowth of changing conditions. Students of education, administrative authorities, teachers, and pupils should all have aims or purposes that are meaningful to them. The aims of one group or one individual should not determine, in all respects, the aims of other groups and of other individuals. In education, as in politics, some people cannot be free while others remain slaves. Those who take their aims ready made from others are slaves. We do not wish our teachers to be slaves to the aims either of educational authority or of children. If students of education and administrative authorities should have their own aims, children should have their own aims, also. Moreover, if educational authorities and children should have their own aims, teachers should also have their own aims.

In the consideration of purposeful unity as a desirable quality of educative experience (see Chapter 8), the meaning of aims or purposes, which are derived from an empirical analysis of experience, was indicated. It was shown that desirable aims are quite different from interests, desires, wishes, or even purposes as they are often conceived. An aim of any kind is, of course, a foreseen end that one desires. Not every foreseen end desired, however, is desirable. Only those aims that are intelligently selected are desirable. Intelligent selection involves dramatization in imagination of alternative courses of action. It includes an evaluation of prevailing conditions and probable future consequences. Only aims or purposes which emerge from such operations are desirable.

The aims of students of education doubtless satisfy these requirements. Their aims seem desirable to them only after considerable reflection. On the other hand, their aims do not represent reflective consideration on the part of others who take them as aims just as they are given. The same is true of aims formulated by administrative authorities and by those commissioned to prepare aims for teachers and schools. Their selection of aims may involve reflection and intelligence, but their adoption of ready made aims without critical appraisal does not involve the operation of intelligence, and therefore, such aims are unsatisfactory. The aims which teachers have for pupils should not invariably be identified with the aims of pupils. The pupils should have opportunity to select reflectively their own aims, and so should teachers. The teacher's aims should be what, under the circumstances, intelligent reflection indicates to him that the pupils should learn or do. The pupils' desirable aims consist of the ends that emerge in the activities which they project or in which they are actively engaged. *The only aims that are desirable for anybody are those that he himself selects intelligently from among the alternative ends that emerge in actual experience.*

If desirable aims embody both desire and intelligence, the question naturally arises as to what is the proper relationship of authoritative aims and the interests and needs of pupils to the aims of the teacher. The answer is implicit in what has already been said. The aims of the teacher should take into account the whole situation in so far as possible. From the standpoint of their quality, aims are desirable in so far as all pertinent factors are considered in their projection. The situation includes, of course, available formulations of aims, such as the Cardinal Principles, the Socio-Economic Goals of America, and the Purposes of Education in American Democracy,[5] and any official aims that may have been provided by the administration or the school. It includes any available lists of the needs and interests of childhood and youth that may have been defined by experts in child study, child psychology, or child growth and development. It includes also any other sets of aims or needs that may be available. It may include the whole background in social and economic conditions which supplies the frame of reference that has conditioned the formulation of various lists of aims. Especially important, however, are the needs, interests, purposes, and powers of the particular pupils for whose direction the teacher selects his aims.

---

[5] See pp. 68–71 for various formulations.

From this point of view, we may repeat, with respect to sets of aims, what Dewey said long ago relative to such all-inclusive aims as culture, social efficiency, and natural development — the more aims, the better.[6] Each set of authoritative aims reflects the demands of some particular set of conditions as they are analyzed by responsible students. Any critical formulation represents certain important points of emphasis that provide balance and perspective for the school and for the teacher who examines them and the conditions under which they are developed. The same may be said of the lists of interests and needs of pupils which are now often conceived as aims. The more we have of such formulations, the better. Every list represents an emphasis that the school and the teacher should by all means take into account. There are those who are very much interested in having schools seek religious and moral values corresponding to values for which the home and the church have in the past assumed responsibility. From the standpoint of the philosophy of experimentalism and of the emergent-means theory of aims, these people would do an important educational service if they would render these values available in some definite form corresponding to other available formulations of aims. Whereas aims are conceived as desirable to the degree that they take into account the whole situation, all those who can make available any unknown factors in the situation should by all means do so. The more pertinent suggestions, the better. The school and the teacher should not accept without question the aims offered them, but they should consider any formulation of values that represent important points of emphasis.

The emergent-means theory of educational aims seems to meet the requirements of the educational experimentalists' theories of the features of educative experience. The theory of functional contingency is assumed since desirable aims must be an outgrowth of conditions involving a consideration of all important factors. The theory of widening sociality is assumed since both doctrinaire sociality and inherent sociality are rejected and the way left open for the constant selection of those values that widen the areas of common interests and concerns. The theory of pervasive interest or acceptable experience is implicit in the emergent-means conception of aims as embodying interests, needs, and desires. The theory of creative originality is assumed in the conception that any aim is considered an emergent in some actual situation. The theory of intelligent choice is assumed in the reflective opera-

[6] John Dewey, *Democracy and Education*. The Macmillan Company, New York, 1916. Pp. 128–129.

tions required in weighing various ends. The theory of purposeful or reflective unity is assumed in the conception that intelligence must be employed in the selection of needs, desires, and interests before they can be accepted as aims. The emergent-means theory of aims thus seems to be another way of indicating the meaning of the philosophy of educational experimentalism.

QUALITIES OF EXPERIENCE AS AIMS

In concluding this chapter, perhaps some consideration should be given to a question that may arise in the minds of some with respect to what has been called the theories of desirable experience and the qualities of experience they imply. The theories of educational experimentalism that have been designated as functional contingency, widening sociality, pervasive interest, creative originality, intelligent choice, and purposeful unity, as well as the theories of educational authoritarianism and educational laissez faire, may be called aims from time to time. In the light of what has been said about aims, the question naturally arises concerning the sense in which such theories or principles can properly be conceived as aims. Are they aims which everyone should adopt? Are they aims for students of education, for teachers, for pupils? Are they external ends, inherent values, or emergent means?

With respect to the qualities of experience endorsed by educational experimentalists the answers to such questions are not difficult. Such qualities are the aims of the author. They are values he has kept in mind in criticizing and appraising other theories of experience, and they are values he will keep in mind throughout his criticism of the different theories of the features of school practice. They are the qualities of experience that he has found, through an extended investigation for many years, to be desirable to many people, whether they recognize the fact or not. He believes that everyone who takes the trouble will find those qualities that educational experimentalists idealize. They may, then, seem at first to be fixed aims. From the author's point of view, they are not to be imposed upon anyone. However, he does recommend them to others for consideration, with confidence that some such values will be found very desirable. Even if they were external and fixed in quality, the author would not be imposing his aims on anyone, and he does not wish to have anyone impose them on others. Moreover, since they are qualities of experience without fixed content, they are not fixed aims. The activities in which these qualities are to be found vary from individual to individual and from one occasion to another. They contain within themselves the ingredients of their own reconstruction in every situation.

If the qualities of experience are values, then some qualities are more valuable than others. The test of these values is always experience itself. The qualities suggested are simply those that the author has found most valuable. To those who believe that the qualities of experience are values, the results of his efforts should at least be suggestive. If the author's selections are not adequate, everyone has the same kind of sources of information for further study that the author has used, as well as the ever-widening vistas of human experience. If such qualities are the greatest of all values, they are worth seeking. If there are some to whom no qualities of experience seem valuable, they are under no obligation to accept this formulation or worry about securing a better one.

Those who consider the qualities of experience the most important of all things will want for themselves the most desirable ones. They will want them for their children, their pupils, their teachers, and their employees. They will want them for everybody. They will give attention to these qualities in both church and state, in business and industry, in war and peace. They will find a place for them in work and play, at home and abroad, in dealing with one's self and with others. But these qualities should not be received uncritically and ready made. Each person has the opportunity and the privilege of considering what his own experience and the common experience of men everywhere testify as to the validity of the theories proposed, and also the opportunity and privilege of making such modifications as his findings require. If qualities of experience are the most significant kind of values, everybody should have those qualities which are most desirable. The qualities that the author has selected are the ones which seem to him most desirable, and they are used as standards of evaluation and appraisal throughout this study. It is upon the basis of these values that he has taken a stand on aims as a feature of school practice. Those who adopt the theories of educational authoritarianism and educational laissez faire as aims may use them as standards of criteria and appraisal; however, from the standpoint of the philosophy of experimentalism, such theories are very inadequate for reasons already given.

CHAPTER II

Subject Matter

THERE IS SOME TRUTH in the saying of some teachers to the effect that they teach pupils rather than subject matter. It means that they give special consideration to the needs and interests of pupils in deciding what subject matter to teach. But subject matter is just as essential to both learning and teaching as are pupils. Without subject matter there is no learning, no teaching. In fact, subject matter is widely recognized as an essential feature of school practice. It is a familiar topic in professional books and professional courses everywhere. It is a conception of long standing in educational literature and scarcely any one doubts its importance and significance. It is usually considered in curriculum programs and other educational improvement programs. Subject matter occupies some place in every official course of study and in every phase of instruction. Its significance is sometimes emphasized and sometimes minimized as contrasted with other features, such as aims and method, but everyone in some way admits its importance without question. The three different philosophies of education may be revealed in the different attitudes toward subject matter, and an analysis of these theories should be of interest to all who are responsible for school policies, programs, and activities.

TYPES OF SUBJECT MATTER

Historically, subject matter is an abbreviated term for subject matter of study. It consists, then, of whatever it is that we study when we are seeking an education. There are two different types of subject matter to which teachers devote considerable attention. These are: (1) subject-matter content; and (2) subject-matter materials.[1]

1. *Subject-matter content* consists of topics, problems, propositions, questions, issues, activities, or whatever central factors determine the scope of educational practices in the school. Subject-matter content

[1] John Dewey, *Philosophy of Civilization.* Minton Balch and Company, New York, 1931. Pp. 264–265.

for a school or for a course may be defined in terms of one or more of these factors, which may be organized into courses, subjects, branches, fields, or other classifications. The subject-matter content, then, consists of these subject-matter units, whatever they may be and into whatever system they may be organized.

Perhaps such a general conception of subject-matter content may be rendered more concrete by reference to the content of specific fields. For instance, the subject-matter content of psychology consists of such topics as perception, memory, imagination, and reasoning, rather than of the books and chapters in which these phenomena of experience are treated. These content units contain the psychological issues, problems, or questions to be studied or investigated, rather than the subject matter employed in their study and investigation. It is the subject-matter content that constitutes the scope of any field or any subject and differentiates it from other subjects. For instance, new fields of study, such as general science, general mathematics, social science, and philosophy of education, must have some distinctive subject-matter content if they are ever to be established on a firm foundation. A so-called fused subject, such as general science, does not have any real existence in fact so long as it consists of content units that are treated as central units in chemistry, physics, biology, astronomy, any other natural science, or any combination of them. It must consist of peculiar units of its own that are not considered in other subjects. When this subject-matter content is justified, the subject matter employed in dealing with it may be secured from any of the sciences or from any other available source.

What is true of the subject-matter content of any given field is true in regard to subject-matter content in general. It consists of the content units, whether they are designated as topics, issues, propositions, questions, problems, activities, or something else. The subject-matter content of any subject, fused subject, broad field, core curriculum, activity program, or any other classification, consists of subject-matter units to be studied, investigated or developed The content of any particular field consists of some series or sequence of content units that seem to belong together.[2]

2. *Subject-matter materials*, the second type of subject matter, consist

---

[2] John P. Wynne, *The Teacher and the Curriculum*. Prentice-Hall, Inc., New York, 1937. Pp. 117–128.

of the data and the sources of data which research workers, educated adults, teachers, and pupils use in dealing with subject-matter content — phenomena, questions, problems, or issues that seem to them important. If subject-matter content may be classified under content units consisting of topics and subjects, the subject-matter materials may be related, in discussion and organization, to these content units. If the subject-matter content consists of the areas or fields in which study and investigation take place, the subject-matter materials consist of the data and things used in their study and investigation. For instance, if perception, memory, imagination, reasoning, feeling, emotion, and learning are the subject-matter content of psychology, the data secured from biology, neurology, psychological experiments, and general observation are the subject-matter materials of psychology. What is true of psychology is true of mathematics, economics, general science, or any other field. The subject-matter content consists of the particular content units considered, and the subject-matter materials consist of those facts and principles, from whatever source they may be drawn, that are used in dealing with the subject-matter content. Subject-matter content defines and delimits the field of operation, but subject-matter materials supply the means of dealing with it.[3]

Subject-matter materials may be conceived in terms of data derived from various human activities in dealing with things, or they may be conceived in terms of the things or activities themselves. Perhaps they may be most conveniently classified as data secured from observation and memory, reading and listening, and research and experimentation. While engaged in the study of any feature of content units, the student or investigator gets suggestions and evidence from direct observation, from recalling his past experiences, from reading books and listening to discussions by qualified students in the field, and from engaging in research and experimentation. Of course, he may use all these means or only a few of them. As a matter of fact, he usually employs several at once. For instance, it is practically impossible to secure data from reading or listening without using one's memory. It is impossible even to secure adequate data through observation without the use of memory or without imagination and judgment. In the process of research and experimentation one must observe, remember, and often

---

[3] John P. Wynne, *The Teacher and the Curriculum*. Prentice-Hall, Inc., New York, 1937. Pp. 155–165.

read and listen to what others have to say.[4]

Subject-matter materials are often classified in terms of two types of experience through which data are derived. Some data are secured from first-hand contact with things and concrete situations, while other data are secured through indirect experience. Materials of the first type are called direct experience and materials of the second type are called vicarious experience, in consequence of the different sources from which the student is supposed to draw. For instance, concrete objects of sense and data derived from them are materials of direct experience, and books and data derived from them are materials of vicarious experience. As a matter of fact, both the direct and the vicarious experiences are often employed simultaneously. Nevertheless, more attention may be given to one of them than to the other. When we speak of a person as bookish, academic, or impractical, we are thinking of the individual who trusts largely to second-hand sources for his subject-matter materials. Similarly, when we speak of the book-learning or listening school, we are thinking of schools in which children spend most of their time in reading and listening and the teacher spends most of his time in talking and lecturing.

When the distinction of direct experience and vicarious experience is once made, students of education and teachers may consider one superior to the other. In many of the more recent educational movements, such as the Work School in central Europe, the Heuristic Method in England, and the project method and the activity curriculum in this country, direct experience has been emphasized. In curriculum programs direct experience is usually emphasized; attention is often called to the importance of raw materials and environmental materials as contrasted with vicarious materials derived largely from books. Such an emphasis results in a counter-emphasis on the part of some students of education who sense the possibility that teachers may be so eager to have pupils deal directly with things that they will neglect important subject matter of vicarious experience and of our rich social heritage. Most students of education do not like to see either direct experience or vicarious experience slighted. They prefer to use data derived from both sources. When pupils do not have an opportunity to secure considerable first-hand experience, even the most valuable vicarious experience is meaningless and insignificant to them. If they do not have an opportunity to deal with considerable vicarious

---

[4] John Dewey, *How We Think*. D. C. Heath & Company, New York, 1934. Pp. 247–259.

experience, they are unable to perceive the wider meaning and implications of things directly experienced.[5]

SELECTION OF SUBJECT MATTER

Although the distinction between a subject-matter content and subject-matter materials seems to be practical and useful, they are closely related. If subject-matter content is conceived as an essential feature of school practice, subject-matter materials also may be so considered. Just as the general topic of subject matter is always considered in professional books and courses, so both subject-matter content and subject-matter materials are considered in conducting curriculum programs and in constructing courses of study. Nevertheless, they are so closely related that at times one may be taken for the other. For instance, the teacher who identifies a chapter in a textbook with the topic that is treated in the chapter fails to make the distinction between content and materials. Furthermore, when the distinction is systematically maintained, the principles involved in the selection of content seem to be essentially the same as those involved in the selection of materials in dealing with it. As a matter of fact, materials, when distinguished from content, are always subsidiary to content. The attitude a person assumes toward the selection of content determines the attitude he assumes toward the selection of materials. For instance, if the unit of content is acceptable, the materials which are most useful in dealing with it are usually satisfactory. Consequently, the different attitudes assumed toward the selection of subject matter have reference to both content and materials.

According to the philosophy of experimentalism, the three attitudes often assumed toward the selection of subject matter correspond somewhat closely to the three attitudes often assumed toward educational aims which we have already considered. According to the first attitude, educational authoritarianism, subject matter should be determined in advance; according to the second attitude, educational laissez faire, it should be determined in the immediate situation; and according to the third attitude, educational experimentalism, its selection should be continuous. Stated in more concrete terms, the teacher may definitely decide upon his subject matter before approaching the

[5] William H. Burton, *The Guidance of Learning Activities*. D. Appleton-Century Company, New York, 1944. Pp. 61–70; 74–81; 89–94.

John P. Wynne, *The Teacher and the Curriculum*. Prentice-Hall, Inc., New York, 1937. Pp. 158–165.

pupils in the learning-teaching situation; he may wait until he meets them in the actual situation before making any effort at its selection; or he may engage continually in its selection, beginning long before he meets the pupils and continuing to make modifications and adjustments so long as he works with them. Students of education, teachers, and school administrators seem to favor some one of these attitudes.

THE ADVANCE-DETERMINATION THEORY
(EDUCATIONAL AUTHORITARIANISM)

Those who assume the theory of advance determination wish to have a very definite course of study indicating the specific content units to be considered and the materials to be used in their treatment. They may differ considerably with respect to how specifically the content units should be defined and elaborated, and how definitely the materials should be related to the content. They may also differ somewhat as to who should select the subject matter — authors of textbooks, official curriculum-makers, administrators, or teachers. But that the subject matter should be determined fairly well in advance of the actual educational situation they all are agreed. Perhaps the best way to indicate the meaning and significance of this theory is to state the practical educational effects implied in the different means by which subject matter may be determined in advance.

The first means of determining subject matter that naturally suggests itself is that of the textbook. Despotic rulers in both church and state have controlled the minds of the people by controlling the materials they read. Of course, they sought, first of all, to control the ideas and beliefs which men might entertain. The most available means was to control the materials in which such ideas were embodied. Consequently, only the books and documents which embodied ideas, beliefs, and suggestions that favored the maintenance and extension of the control of those in power were to be used. Only books and parts of books that contained the "right" ideas from the standpoint of the authorities were allowed in the schools. Materials containing subversive religious, moral, economic, and political conceptions were scrupulously kept out of the schools.

The belief that educational material forms the opinions of the people has been so well established in church, state, and home that it is still one of the most pervasive educational conceptions in the minds of the rank and file. The peoples of democratic countries have learned too well what the masters of the past taught them — if you want people to believe right, have them read only the right things. Legislatures, school boards, lawyers, teachers, and even statesmen and scientists have engaged in controversies as to the kind of biology or history textbook that should be used in a school or school system. Libraries have expurgated magazines favorable to evolution. The National Manufacturing Association, the American Legion, and even the faculty of a large university have become involved in a controversy over the content of social science books. Such instances as these, which can be multiplied many times, show beyond question that the people of even a great democratic country still consider the advance determination of subject matter desirable and believe that the best way of controlling it is to determine the character of the materials contained in the books used in the schools. Such a conception seems self-evident perhaps to the majority of people throughout the civilized world. Doubtless it is more pronounced in the totalitarian than in the democratic states, but it persists in the minds of many people everywhere. No wonder, then, that many students of education, administrative officials, and teachers accept the theory that subject matter should be determined in advance and seek to use the textbook as a means of exercising such control.

The textbook is one of the most effective means of making desirable information available to youth. Textbooks can be so written as to include essential and reliable information. They can also be written within the range of the capacity and interests of particular groups. As contrasted with oral lectures, they contain a permanent record for constant review. They are indispensable instruments in the hands of teachers, who are limited in their resources in knowledge and information, and they must long remain, many of them, in a world committed to universal education at comparatively small expense. The textbook properly used is certainly an effective means of school education.

From the standpoint of the philosophy of experimentalism, although the textbook must be recognized as a desirable, even an indispensable, means of instruction, there are serious objections to using it as means of determining subject matter. First of all, when it is used, subject-matter content and subject-matter materials sometimes are not distinguished by either teachers or pupils. The textbook includes not only the content units but all the data used in dealing with them. The teachers and pupils not only deal with the topics that are in the textbook and those alone, but they may use only that information which the book supplies. Although a permanent record is very important from the standpoint of instruction, the content and materials that are most significant from the standpoint of society and most interesting from the standpoint of childhood and youth are not permanent. Changes in social and economic conditions, the corresponding interests of people, including children, and the advancement of knowledge require that both content and materials be constantly revised and reconstructed. Therefore, teachers and pupils alike should consult other sources of subject matter rather than limit themselves to the content of one book. Of course, it may be said that authorities responsible for the content of books and the school officials responsible for selecting them should make the changes as they are required. It must be admitted that more help could be rendered in this way than is provided at present. However, it matters not how well the authorities do their work, at best books can be revised only periodically. On the other hand, *the conditions to which the public, the teachers, and the pupils should be responsive are continually changing. They should not have to wait for the incorporation of a new topic in a revised textbook before dealing with it, and they should not have to wait for new subject-matter materials, already available in the immediate environment, to be incorporated in textbooks.*

Of course, to determine subject matter in advance in this way is practically impossible in democratic countries. It may be used effectively by totalitarian despots who determine not only what goes into the books that children read but what goes into those that the teachers read; who determine not only the character of school books but the character of the whole school environment. In democratic countries teachers and pupils simply cannot remain insensitive to what goes on outside the school. They must bring content and materials into the schools that are not contained in the textbooks. But, it may be asked, why worry about the content of the textbook if its control cannot be effective? The question may be parried with another question: why undertake to do the impossible thing of controlling subject matter? The more important consideration, however, is the attitude of the public and of the school toward the textbook. Students of education everywhere are convinced that reliance on textbooks is too heavy. Teachers should not be encouraged to chain themselves to a mere tool, which the textbook obviously is. They are too much inclined to do so, anyway. Furthermore, such reliance on textbooks overemphasizes indirect experience at the expense of direct experience; neglects the living present for the dead past; accentuates the tendency to rely on the authority of the written word, even when contradictory evidence lies everywhere before the very eyes. The conclusion seems to follow that, *although the textbook may be used to great advantage in rendering subject matter available, it should not be used to determine in advance the content with which teachers and pupils deal or the materials they use in dealing with it.*

The second means by which subject matter may be determined in advance consists in prescription by authorities of the course of study or the curriculum. The political authorities of the country, or the administrative authorities, or their delegates, may prescribe the subject matter to be taught in the schools. There does not seem to be any objection to the disposition of political authorities to compel the study of certain subjects in response to popular demand. There does not seem to be any objection to the disposition of administrative authorities to set up certain minimum standards, such as those for reading, writing, arithmetic, and health education. In fact, the establishment of such requirements seems to us an indispensable means of extending popular education.

But the advance determination here under consideration is of another kind. It is both positive and negative. It may include what must be studied as well as what must not be studied. For instance, some of our state legislatures have passed laws compelling schools to teach the Constitution and prohibiting them from teaching evolution. Such requirements as these have met with serious objections from the teaching profession, and the resulting instruction has been very ineffective and unsatisfactory. The means frequently used by school authorities to control the subject matter in advance is the official course of study. In times past courses of study were prepared by school administrators themselves, who decided upon topics and books, and who even assigned page references, which different age groups of pupils were to study. In more recent years the official course of study has been developed through curriculum programs enlisting the interests of students of education, the teachers, and the public. In some of the programs, perhaps in most of them, the notion of determining subject matter in advance still prevails in varying degrees. In most courses of study the distinction between subject-matter content and subject-matter materials is recognized. In many the materials are conceived as suggestive, although in some courses, textbooks are definitely prescribed. However, there is seldom any intention to limit the material to be used by teachers to that contained between the covers of prescribed books. Nevertheless, the mere fact that certain books are prescribed and must be used, often forces teachers to neglect more appropriate and helpful books. **If** inferior books must be bought, it is not always practical to buy better books, also. Only the more enterprising teachers are able to secure other materials which they recognize as desirable. Many give up and limit the activities of pupils to the study of the prescribed books.

Prescribing the subject-matter content of courses of study in advance is more common than prescribing subject-matter materials in advance. The difficulties involved in the assignment of content to schools, grades, and courses is not so impractical as is the assignment of specific materials. It is almost impossible to keep subject-matter materials other than those listed from finding their way into the learning-teaching situation. However, content that sets the limits of the educative process can be, and usually is, much more definitely prescribed. It may assume the form of subjects, units of study, centers of interest, major functions of social life, areas of culture, or whatnot. There is no unanimity as to what content should be prescribed or how it should be designated. Nevertheless, the tendency of official curriculum-makers to determine in advance the fields of operation for schools, grades, and courses to some degree seems well established in most communities. The degree to which content is prescribed varies considerably from place to place. Some officials prefer to state in only very general terms the ground to be covered, whereas others prefer to state it in considerable detail. In a sense, those who define the scope of schoolwork in general terms allow more room for choice in particular situations. Such general prescription also exemplifies the theory of advance determination.

From the standpoint of the philosophy of experimentalism, the criticism of this attitude which prevails in curriculum-making in many quarters is of the same kind as that which we made of the external-ends theory of educational aims. It is all well and good for official curriculum-makers to indicate the subject-matter content which they consider important and which seems to be adaptable to the interests of various groups. They should by all means supply help. They have more time and are often better qualified to survey whole situations. Obviously, however, the state authorities are unable to predict several years in advance exactly what content units should be considered in particular localities, particular schools, and particular schoolrooms. They cannot determine intelligently the demands of immediate conditions and particular situations with which they are unfamiliar. Only the teachers themselves in these practical situations can do this. The very fact that curriculum-makers are constantly revising the content of courses of study indicates that no analysis is satisfactory for all times and for all situations. Moreover, since there is no unanimity among recognized students of education, or among specialists in the various fields, as to what should be prescribed, any particular prescription must represent little more than a compromise. The constant controversy as to what content is important and how it should be organized and stated is sufficient to indicate that there is no fixed content that is satisfactory for any school system, any school, grade, or course.

From the standpoint of the philosophy of experimentalism, however, the controversy as to what should be the content for any educational group in general cannot be settled. No selection that is best for all can be decided upon in advance. Subject-matter content, like subject-matter materials, to be satisfactory must take into account the conditions that prevail in situations which are constantly changing. The trouble does not arise from the scope of the prescription or from the authority which assumes responsibility for it. The difficulty lies in the very idea of advance prescription. No kind of advance determination can be satisfactory for particular situations which cannot be foreseen.

Up to this point we have had in mind political and administrative effort to prescribe in advance the subject matter which schools and teachers shall use. According to the philosophy of experimentalism, the same reasoning applies to the planning of the teacher. If he should not be expected to take his subject matter ready made from the administrative authorities or from the official curriculum-makers, he should not, by the same token, expect pupils to take their subject matter ready made from him. *The teacher, like the administrator and the official curriculum-maker, can be too rigid in his requirements with respect to ground to be covered or materials to be used.* There is no reason why the ground and the materials that the teacher considers satisfactory in advance should be entirely satisfactory in fact for the pupils. Adjustments to changing conditions must be made in the actual educational situation, which involves both the individual and his environment. No one can justify the advance determination of subject matter for any other individual or for any group on the basis of the desirable qualities of experience as the experimentalists conceive them, although perhaps one could justify it on the basis of other principles.

In fact, this attitude toward subject matter seems quite consistent with the philosophy of educational authoritarianism as it has been stated in terms of educative experience. It assumes the principle of objective contingency since subject matter determined in advance represents the environment without reference to the individual in the ever-living present. It assumes the principle of doctrinaire sociality because prescribed content and materials are designed to indoctrinate. It assumes the principle of provisional interest since prescribed subject matter, however much one may be devoted to interest, must take precedence over interest in certain situations where fundamental essentials must be secured. It assumes the principle of creative embodiment since education is thought to consist in learning certain subject matter to the exclusion of other subject matter. It assumes the principle of selective choice since the subject matter actually studied is limited by authoritative prescription. It assumes the principle of external unity in so far as it takes into account the problem of unity at all. The only way that unity can be secured when subject matter is determined in advance is to supply the proper quantity of the different types of materials at the proper times. Like the external-ends theory of aims, the advance determination of subject matter with respect to school practice seems to be a restatement of the authoritarian philosophy of education already defined in terms of experience.[6]

THE IMMEDIATE-DETERMINATION THEORY
(EDUCATIONAL LAISSEZ FAIRE)

The laissez-faire theory of immediate determination of subject matter represents, perhaps, a natural reaction against the logical difficulties and practical objections to the theory of advance determination. It is difficult to appraise the implications of the idea of prescription without also considering the rejection of all effort at advance selection. The rejection of prescription is the essence of the theory of immediate determination.

From the laissez-faire point of view, it is the pupil, in the last analysis, who must cover the content and who must use the materials. Why should they be determined for him in advance? In fact, how can adequate subject matter be selected without reference to the pupils? The notion that legislative bodies, school administrators, or official curriculum-makers can properly prescribe the subject matter for the schools is preposterous. They cannot know the individual pupils who are to be educated. Only the teacher has an opportunity to know them in the actual educational situation. Apparently, then, the teacher is

---

[6] William H. Burton, *The Guidance of Learning Activities*. D. Appleton-Century Co., New York, 1944. Pp. 81–94.

the only one who can select satisfactory content and materials, and even he cannot do so outside the actual situation.

In consequence of this attitude, some students of education, as well as some teachers, object to planning in advance. They do not favor selecting important subject-matter units and elaborating upon them through topical analysis, questions, and activities, or in any other way. Neither do they favor the selection and arrangement of materials to be used with subject-matter content. Such advance planning is conceived as a means of imposing the teacher's conceptions upon the pupils. The only way, so it is thought, for the pupils to assume their full share of responsibility in selecting their activities and their materials is for the teacher to refrain from making any selections of materials until the pupils are engaged in the development of undertakings. The undertakings themselves either constitute the content or else suggest it. Each undertaking is doubtless related to some content unit, but the unit cannot be properly selected until the activities related to it have emerged. Likewise, the subject-matter materials are not to be planned in advance. Pupils should first decide upon what they propose to do and then decide upon the materials they will use. For instance, teachers sometimes congratulate themselves on being unaware of the availability of essential materials at the time they encourage pupils to engage in certain undertakings.

Perhaps few teachers in their actual practice would go to these extremes in order to avoid imposing subject matter upon their pupils; but that there is a tendency in this direction in certain quarters is unmistakable. Even when it is impractical to do so, many teachers still think they must refrain from any advance planning involving the selection either of content or of materials. They hesitate to mention content and speak of subject matter as if it were something to be avoided like poison. They teach children rather than subject matter. Why should they plan this contemptible subject matter in advance? The more attention they give to content and materials, so they seem to think, the less attention they must give the children. To give considerable attention to subject matter in advance would, therefore, be preposterous to those who are actually interested in children.

From the standpoint of the philosophy of experimentalism, the difficulties confronting the laissez-faire theory of immediate determination of subject matter are tremendous. As a reaction against the overemphasis upon subject matter conceived in isolation from the child, the laissez-faire theory overemphasizes the child in isolation from the subject matter. Such shibboleths and slogans as "the child-centered school," "teaching the child rather than teaching subject-matter," and "engaging in activities" as contrasted with "learning subject matter," call attention to defects in current school practice. However, they fail to suggest an adequate positive program. The fact that existing practice neglects the interests, powers and needs of the pupil does not justify the neglect of subject matter, the school's only means of adequately serving these interests, powers, and needs. *The teacher who keeps his pupils in mind thinks of his subject matter from the standpoint of its possibilities in dealing with them. He selects subject matter in advance to aid pupils in their study.*

Another difficulty confronting this laissez-faire attitude is the sense of superiority and self-sufficiency it engenders. Logically, there is no place in the implications of this theory for the positive contributions of students of education, school administrators, and official curriculum-makers. Their function is to remove all obstacles in the way of the teacher, just as his function is to remove all obstacles in the way of the pupils. Advance planning of subject matter by recognized educational authorities and officials has no place in this program. It should be the business of educational authorities to supply the teacher with the materials he needs, and the authorities should find out what the teacher needs by consulting him, just as the teacher has to find out what his pupils need by consulting them. Neglect of the contributions of recognized students and authorities is impractical, to say the least. They make mistakes and often place undue restraint upon teachers, but they will not abdicate their educational function. As they see it, they have a job to do, and they will do it. No theory of subject-matter selection that fails to recognize the positive services of educational leaders can be satisfactory.

Finally, the practice which exemplifies this laissez-faire theory conflicts with plain common sense. Many people object to the inefficiency, the waste of time and energy, the procrastination, and the uncertainty that often prevail in the school due to the failure of teachers to select their subject matter in advance. Before building a house, planting a crop, or conducting a military campaign, materials to be used must be decided upon; and so, similarly, before conducting a class, why shouldn't the teacher, at least tentatively, select his materials. *Much of the criticism that has been directed at the progressive schools arises from the fact that certain schools and teachers fail to give adequate attention to the advance selection of the subject matter they use.* Common sense contains a practicable reasonableness that cannot be neglected with impunity by those who are working for progress and advancement, even in educational theory.

In practice the immediate-determination theory is consistent with the principles of educative experience in terms of which educational laissez faire has already been defined. It assumes the principle of subjective contingency, for, in isolating the child from subject matter and giving exclusive attention to the former, it emphasizes the individual to the relative neglect of the environment. Moreover, in neglecting in advance the importance of selecting socially important subject matter, it relies on the social impulses of the individual for desirable direction, which the principle of inherent sociality requires. It assumes the principle of immediate interest since the interest of the pupils is assumed to be indispensable at all times. In relying on the impulses of pupils to indicate the desirability of subject matter, this theory assumes the validity of the principle of direct creative self-expression. In postponing the responsibility of selecting subject matter until confronted with the pupils in the educational situation, this theory adopts the principle of free choice as a desirable quality of experience. It seems to assume the principle of impulsive unity since the immediate impulses of the pupils determine the subject matter to be selected by the teacher. In fact, this theory of selecting subject matter is another way of stating the philosophy of educational laissez faire, which has already been stated in terms of these very principles.

THE CONTINUOUS-SELECTION THEORY
(EDUCATIONAL EXPERIMENTALISM)

The attitude toward subject matter which is most acceptable to educational experimentalists is called the continuous-selection theory because it emphasizes the need for constant attention to the problem of selection. The experimentalist attitude recognizes the importance of selecting subject matter prior to its use in the educational situation, as well as the importance of considering its adaptability to the demands of the actual situations in the learning-teaching relationship. From this point of view, subject matter — both content and materials — is so important that it should receive constant attention from all those responsible for educational programs and activities; and its effect on the lives of pupils is so significant that their powers, interests, and needs must always be considered in its selection. The closer one is to the practical activities and the closer one is to the situation where subject matter is used, the less difficult it is to tell just what materials will be needed. But some contribution to adequate selection can be made long before the time of its use, and the final selection should not be terminated until the activities to which it is related, or in which it is involved, come to a close.

Subject matter that is not determined in advance or on the spot must be selected continually. Students of education who are constantly engaged in research and investigation to determine what subject matter is socially useful within the range of the interests and capacities of pupils are contributing in a desirable way to the selection of content and materials. Those who make available the findings of research are also doing their part, as are the authors who embody the results of such work in the preparation of textbooks for school use. The administrators and the official curriculum-makers who help place within reach of the teacher books and materials that include the findings of research and the research studies themselves are contributing to the selection of subject matter in an important way. Likewise, the teacher who selects in advance subject matter that he thinks will meet the requirements of his pupils is making his contribution. The more fully he takes into account the available evidence as to the social usefulness and function of content and materials, the greater his contribution. The fact that he does not have all the evidence at hand, however, does not signify that he should not begin on this work as soon as possible. Even the prospective teacher still enrolled in college should, by all means, begin planning for the pupils he expects to teach long before he teaches them. If he knows them, so much the better. If he does not know them, however, he can still make tentative selections of both content and materials. The more fully he takes into account the findings of research, official courses of study, and available textbooks, so much the better. *But the time for the teacher or the prospective teacher to begin to select his subject matter is now. There is no time to lose, and those responsible for either the pre-service or the in-service education of teachers should assist them in this respect as much as possible.*

Doubtless most of those who adopt the theory of advance determination would subscribe to the foregoing doctrine. The difference between the authoritarian theory and the experimental theory does not lie in the fact that one of them favors the advance selection of subject matter and that the other does not. It lies rather in the degree of rigidity assumed in the selections that are made. In accord with the theory of advance determination, there is a tendency to consider subject matter selected in advance as fixed and complete. According to the theory of continuous determination, the more in advance the selection is made, the better, but every later study should reconstruct, readjust, and remake what has gone before until the subject matter is actually utilized in the immediate educational situation. Even here the teacher should learn something new that will improve his selection of content and materials for subsequent activities and programs.

The consideration of subject matter in the practical situation is as important as the exponents of immediate determination of subject matter contend, but its consideration before the final selection is made is much more important than they think. In fact, its proper selection during the final stages depends in no small way on the attention that has already been given to it by the teacher himself, by students of education, by authors of textbooks, by school administrators, and by official curriculum-makers. Constant attention to the selection of subject matter in the immediate educational situation is indispensable, but attention to it then alone is inadequate. *The selection of content and materials cannot be completed once and for all.* With respect to any particular activity or program, it must continue as long as the program lasts, and with respect to the school and the professional career of the teacher, it should never end.

From this point of view, school administrators and official curriculum-makers should not hold schools and teachers rigidly to any prescribed subject-matter units and materials, however defined. They have done their part if they have placed within reach of the school and the teacher all the information. There is no best subject matter for every individual, independent of conditions. All advance selection of content and materials, as in the case of educational aims, when properly conceived, should be considered as suggestions only. But the more attention is given to the selection of subject matter in advance, the more effectively can its selection be completed in the immediate situation, provided only that no subject matter is ever taken uncritically as stuff to be taught without regard to conditions.

This theory of subject matter, like the emergent-means theory of aims to which it corresponds, seems to be consistent with the experimentalist principles, which we have stated in terms of the desirable qualities of educative experience. It assumes the principle of functional contingency since subject matter, representing the environment, is conceived as functionally related to the activities of the pupils, representing the individual. It assumes the principle of widening sociality since a continuous selection of subject matter implies the constant extension of the areas of common interest and concern, without endorsing either doctrinaire or inherent sociality. It assumes the principle of acceptable experience or pervasive interest since the selection of subject matter is never completed until the attitude of the pupil is taken fully into account. It assumes the principle of creative originality since provision is made from beginning to end for the incorporation of new factors as they arise and justify themselves. It assumes the principle of intelligent choice, for the selection of both content and materials requires the operation of critical intelligence on the part of both teachers and pupils. It assumes the principle of purposeful unity since everyone who has any part in the selection of content and materials should do so as part and parcel of a continuous co-operative program in which each participant chooses the subject matter which the pursuit of his own purposes requires. Thus, the theory of continuous selection of subject matter, like the emergent-means theory of aims, is another way of stating the philosophy of educational experimentalism.

CHAPTER 12

Educational Organization

ORGANIZATION IS ONE of the most controversial issues in the whole field of education. Two conditions seem to be largely responsible for the clash of opinion in regard to this topic. In the first place, organization is a universal feature of school practice. It must be considered by the teacher who guides the pupils in the organization of their experiences and the effects of these experiences. It must be considered by the official curriculum-maker who prepares preliminary arrangements of subject-matter content and materials for the use of teachers in dealing with pupils. It must be considered by school administrators, including superintendents, college presidents, principals, and department heads, who must assume responsibility for the relationship of different aspects of the educational program under their control. In the second place, educational workers are primarily interested in the organization of some particular feature of the school program, such as the school system, the school, the department, the course of study, or the work for some specific grade or other group for a year, a semester, a month, a week, or even for a day. They are seldom conscious of the underlying comprehensive problems as to just how subject matter — the effect of experience — is organized in the minds of those who learn it. Thus, when different practical schoolworkers are discussing organization, they are usually considering the organization of the particular aspect of the program of most concern to them at the time. It is difficult for people to avoid misunderstandings when they are applying the same term to different things. All of us must think of organization, but we are likely to be thinking of different things. One function of the philosophy of education is to clarify the issues involved in the consideration of such controversial problems.

Perhaps the proper approach to the subject of organization is to determine, if possible, the underlying theories of educational organization which those primarily interested in the more immediate problems take for granted, for their position in regard to this deeper question determines how they consider the more specific problems of organization with which they are directly concerned. From the standpoint of the philosophy of experimentalism, organization in this inclusive and deeper sense is not the organization of the school system, the school, the department, the course of study, or any other preliminary arrangement preparatory to the actual development of the curriculum in the practical educational situation. *It is the organization of the effects of experience, the subject matter learned by the pupil.* The theory we consciously or unconsciously adopt toward organization in this sense determines the attitude we take toward the more immediate practical problems of preliminary arrangement. If such underlying theories so vitally affect our decisions with respect to advance organization, it seems that an understanding of the meaning and significance of these underlying theories reflected in our practices should be very helpful. It is our task in the remainder of this chapter to describe, explain, elaborate, and appraise th~se theories. There seem to be three such theories of organization corresponding to the theories of other features of school practice that we have considered, which, for convenience of discussion, may be designated, respectively, as: (1) the separation theory; (2) the incidental theory; and (3) the continuity theory.

THE SEPARATION THEORY
(EDUCATIONAL AUTHORITARIANISM)

The separation theory adopted by the educational authoritarians assumes that the organization of subject matter in the experience of the learner is separate from and antithetical to the logical organization of subject matter found in the various school subjects. The long historical tendency of the teacher, the school, and the curriculum-maker to impose logical forms familiar to authorities in the various fields of study upon the minds of the immature and inexperienced has its theoretical justification in the separation theory. According to this authoritarian theory, perhaps more often implicitly assumed than deliberately applied, the mind of the child or the neophyte in any field is a heterogeneous mass of impulses, habits, and ideas, with no logical arrangement among them. The only way the mind of the inexperienced individual can be logically organized is by impressing upon it certain logical conceptions into which human knowledge has been classified or organized. These conceptions are embodied in the minds of experts, authoritative students, and teachers in the various fields, in authoritative textbooks, and in the minds of educated adults.

According to the proponents of the separation theory, this problem of educational organization consists in incorporating in the minds of the immature and undeveloped the logical conceptions constituting the fields of organized knowledge. The first step in the program required usually consists in analyzing these conceptions into their logical parts, ranging from the most general to the most specific. When this operation is adequately performed, the arrangement for teaching purposes is reversed. The simplest elements are taught first and the more complex elements last in an ascending logical scale. The neophyte in any field learns the simplest elements first, the less simple next, and so on, up the logical ladder.

From this point of view, education, as the process of learning, proceeds from the logical part to the logical whole. The more detailed the analysis of a conception is, the better it can be learned. In fact, the parts always come before the whole in learning. It thus becomes the business of those responsible for educational programs and activities to analyze the conceptions, habits, appreciations, or whatever the general outcomes of education are expected to be into their component parts. These parts are then arranged in the order of their logical simplicity and difficulty so that the easier ones may be learned first and the more complex and difficult ones next, in an ascending logical order.

According to this theory, the general aims of education, whatever they may be, represent general traits that have been analyzed into more specific objectives. When they are so analyzed they may be organized into subjects or courses and assigned to the grades or school years in which they can best be learned. The aims of general education may be the same for all; but the aims for any given grade are different from the aims of other grades since the allotment of particular objectives into which the general aims have been analyzed are different for each grade. As the child proceeds up the educational ladder, he is supposed to proceed from the particular to the general, from the simple to the complex, from the concrete to the abstract. In this way, he comes step by step to realize, in the forms of habit, appreciation, knowledge, the general aims of education.

Dewey describes the operation of this theory in this way: "It assumes that logical quality belongs only to organized knowledge and that the operations of the mind become logical only through absorption of logically formulated, ready-made material. In this case, the logical formulations are not the outcome of any process of thinking that is personally undertaken and carried out; the formulation has been made by another mind and is presented in finished form, apart from the processes by which it was arrived at. Then it is assumed that by some magic its logical character will be transferred into the minds of the pupils.

"An illustration or two will make clear what is meant by the foregoing statements. Suppose the subject is geography. The first thing is to give its definition, marking it off from every other subject. Then the various abstract terms upon which depends the scientific development of the science are stated and defined one by one — pole, equator, ecliptic, zone — from the simpler units to the more complex that are formed out of them; then the more concrete elements are taken in similar series — continent, island, coast, promontory, cape, isthmus, peninsula, ocean, lake, gulf, bay, and so on. In acquiring this material the pupil's mind is supposed not only to gain important information, but, by accommodating itself to ready-made logical definitions, generalizations, and classifications, gradually also to acquire logical habits.

"This type of method has been applied to every subject taught in the schools — reading, writing, music, physics, grammar, arithmetic. Drawing, for example, has been taught on the theory that, since all pictorial representation is a matter of combining straight and curved lines, the simplest procedure is to have the pupil acquire the ability first to draw straight lines in various positions (horizontal, perpendicular, diagonals at various angles), then typical curves; and finally, to combine straight and curved lines in various permutations to construct actual pictures. This seemed to give the ideal 'logical' method, beginning with analysis into elements, and then proceeding in regular order to more and more complex syntheses, each element being defined when used, and thereby clearly understood." [1]

The foregoing quotation is not, of course, selected to indicate Dewey's theory of organization. It is selected because it supplies an excellent analysis of the operation in practice of the authoritarian theory of educational organization that has been designated as the separation or logical analysis theory. As a matter of fact, Dewey has developed an entirely different theory of organization. The selection of this quotation is not intended to show that most schools adopt the practices described in all fields in this extreme form; but there is sufficient tendency in this direction for us to see instances of its operation in almost any school. As Dewey has pointed out, "Even when the method in its extreme

---

[1] John Dewey, *How We Think* (Revised Edition). D. C. Heath and Company, New York, 1933. Pp. 79–80.

form is not followed, few schools (especially of the middle or upper elementary grades) are free from an exaggerated attention to forms supposedly necessary for the pupil to use if he is to get his result logically. It is held that there are certain steps, arranged in a certain order, that express preëminently an understanding of the subject, and the pupil is made to 'analyze' his procedure into these steps; i.e., to learn a certain routine formula of statement. While this method is usually at its height in grammar and arithmetic, it invades also history and even literature, which are then reduced, under plea of intellectual training, to outlines, diagrams, and other schemes of division and subdivision." [2]

Considerable experience in teaching and observation seems to justify the conviction that this same theory of organization is the most pervasive theory exemplified in both college and high-school teaching. It is used and sometimes endorsed in courses in the field of education even in dealing with the topic of organization. The teaching habits which it justifies are often so fixed in the mind of the professor of education that it is next to impossible to overcome them, even though he verbally endorses some other theory.

From the standpoint of the philosophy of experimentalism, this authoritarian theory of organization is confronted with serious practical and theoretical difficulties. Pupils learn the words in which the logical patterns are supposed to be embodied, but they often, perhaps usually, miss their meanings. They learn all the logical elements from grade to grade but fail to grasp the fundamental principles. Sensitive to current educational slogans, such as "articulation," "unity," and "integration," and realizing the failure of the traditional subject scheme to meet current educational demands, many authoritarians have undertaken to develop some better scheme without surrendering the fundamental principles of logical analysis and the impression of logical forms or conceptions on the minds of the uninitiated. These authoritarian reformers are sharply divided among themselves as to the proper approach to the problems of isolation, compartmentalization, and scrappiness, which the critics of school practices are constantly calling to their attention.

They have made so many approaches to the problem that it is impossible in a study like this to describe them all. In general, there are three different kinds of plans, depending upon three clearly dis-

---

[2] John Dewey, *How We Think* (Revised Edition). D. C. Heath and Company, New York, 1933. Pp. 80–81.

tinguishable authoritarian attitudes. *According to one faction, the problem of organization can be solved by properly relating the school subjects to one another; according to a second faction, it can be solved only by the discovery of some integrating scheme that cuts across all subject lines; while according to a third faction, the problem can be solved, at least on some levels, by following the organization of the best books without reference to subjects or to integrating topics.* For convenience of reference, these three general types of approach may be designated as: (1) the subject-reform method; (2) the integration method; and (3) the best-books method.

1. Those who adopt the *subject-reform method*, which has been most extensively applied in the elementary school, assume that the whole problem of organization can be solved by properly relating the school subjects to one another. As they see the situation, the subjects as they have been developed historically must somehow be maintained, although they should be more effectively co-ordinated, related, or adjusted to one another. They thus proceed, some in one way and some in another, to work out methods of relating the traditional subjects.

In times past, the separate-subject organization was known as "co-ordination." According to this plan, each subject consists of a body of logically arranged subject matter separate and distinct from every other subject. The more independence and separation maintained among the different subjects, the better. Such a position is assumed in some quarters even today. It is exemplified in the colleges and universities wherever professors are inclined to resent the use, in other departments, of textbooks which, according to the title, belong in their fields. At least some of the criticism of overlapping that has been made of courses on the college level arises from the conviction of some that the same subject-matter materials should not be used for different purposes in different subject fields. Nevertheless, the proponents of subject reform have sought to break down this traditional isolation, especially on the elementary school level.

To achieve this end they have proposed several different schemes of selecting and arranging subject matter in the different school grades. Some advocate the correlation plan, according to which the logically related topics in two or more subjects are taught during the same day, week, month, or term. Often topics in history, geography, and literature are correlated in this way. Others advocate what is known as the plan of concentration, according to which some one subject, known as the core subject, is analyzed into its component parts and allocated to the different grades on the basis of some such principle as recapitulation. The topics of other subjects are then allocated to the different grades on the basis of their logical relationship to the topics of the core subject that are allocated to each grade. For instance, if history is the core subject, then certain selected topics of history are allocated to the different grades. Then the topics of other subjects to be allocated to any grade are logically related to the history topics for that grade. Still others advocate what is known as the fusion of subjects, according to which such subjects as physics, chemistry, biology, and geology are combined into general science; such subjects as arithmetic, algebra, and geometry are combined into general mathematics; and such subjects as history, government, sociology, and economics are combined into social science or social problems.

Of course, not everyone who advocates the fusion of subjects contemplates such a mechanical mixture of different fields as suggested in the foregoing discussion. Some do not think of subjects such as general science, general mathematics, and social science merely as mixtures, nor even as combinations of elements of the older established subjects. They think of them as actually new subjects because they have their own subject-matter content. For instance, the central topics, issues, or problems constituting general science may be quite different from those which constitute the older subjects. They need not even represent common elements found in the different sciences. They may consist of new topics, issues, or problems that have their own meaning and significance. The same is true of other so-called fused subjects. *Any new subject, whatever subject-matter materials are adopted from other fields, has its own subject-matter content*, that is, its own topics, issues, or problems. Otherwise, it is no subject at all but merely a mixture of many subjects, and it is even less satisfactory than the separate subjects themselves. Many who advocate fusion adopt a still broader conception. They think of the whole subject-matter offering of the school as classifiable into a few broad fields, such as the humanities, mathematics and the natural sciences, and the social sciences.

2. Those who adopt the *integration method* refuse to see any good in any kind of subject organization. The members of this group contend that all traditional subjects should be eliminated. They insist that some more fundamental approach must be made to the problem of organization. Some advocate the selection of *centers of interest*, one or two for each school grade. These centers of interest, however they may be analyzed or elaborated, constitute the scope or content of the curric-

ulum for the school. For instance, some such topic as community life may constitute the center of interest for the second grade. When analyzed or elaborated into topics, questions, or activities, this general theme constitutes the subject-matter content for the grade. Likewise similar centers of interest constitute subject-matter content for all grades of the elementary school, and, in some cases, for high-school grades as' well. Others advocate what is known as the *social-functions plan*, according to which certain major aspects of social life, such as economic life, recreational life, religious life, and educational life, constitute the subject-matter content of the school from the first grade of the elementary school through the high school. Various aspects of such topics or of similar ones are elaborated for various grades according to some principle of grade placement, such as the center-of-interest theory. For instance, in one course of study, where educational life constitutes one of the social functions and where "effects of inventions and discoveries upon our living" constitutes the center of interest for the fifth grade, the aspect of the function allocated to the grade is: "How do inventions and discoveries influence education?" In this manner, aspects of the various functions are allocated to the various grades according to their centers of interest.

From the standpoint of the philosophy of experimentalism, any scheme of organization that can provide some perspective in the general confusion which prevails should be welcomed. *But as long as the separation theory is assumed, there cannot be any fundamental improvement in the organization of the effects of experience in the minds of the pupils.* The effort to develop different plans of organization has, of course, called attention to needed points of emphasis and, perhaps, has supplied the teacher with new perspectives, although the same defects persist in the actual experience of the pupils. Verbalism, lack of interest, inattention, procrastination, and aversion to effort are still prevalent in the schools employing the new plans of organization.

Meanwhile, the debate continues as to whether this or that particular scheme of preliminary organization of content is the more satisfactory. Many of the so-called progressives logically are assuming the same underlying theory of organization as do those whom they consider conservative and reactionary. They differ with them in regard to what scheme of preliminary organization is most satisfactory. However, so long as they both think of the method of organization as impressing on the minds of pupils, conceptions derived through logical analysis, they themselves are faced with the same practical difficulties.

No amount of argument or even experimentation can discover a uniform universally accepted method of preliminary organization. Even if such a method could be discovered, the old difficulties of inattention, procrastination, flagging interest, dependence on mere *memoriter* learning and on routine performance would continue as long as teachers and curriculum-makers were bent upon impressing on the minds of pupils logical forms broken down into small doses. In fact, the presence of the same conditions where the so-called new schemes of organization have been introduced indicates that the difficulties are beyond the reach of any particular plan of organization, such as the fusion of subjects, core curriculum, area of experience, or even the so-called experience organization itself.[3]

The real problem does not lie in the development of some new scheme of preliminary organization, although the use of any new plan calls attention to factors which might otherwise be overlooked. The fundamental problem is that of the relationship of the subject matter already embodied in the experience of the neophyte to the logical conceptions embodied in the minds of the expert and the educated adult. Whatever this relationship may be, it is not the relationship that the simplest logical elements of complex conceptions bear to these same conceptions. *When an individual learns only the logical elements derived from the analysis of a general conception, he simply has not learned the conception.* Any scheme of organization that assumes such a theory is doomed to failure, whether it be some form of subject organization or some form of the so-called integrating schemes of organization. The mind simply does not work that way. The logical organization represents the end of learning and not its beginning. The experts do not learn the so-called logical elements in an ascending scale. What they do, however, is to reorganize the logical elements in an ascending scale. They begin with actual concrete situations involving various factors that are later systematically organized. No logical analysis will ever reduce the final conceptions of the expert to the elements with which he actually began. The neophyte will have to begin with the elements in his own experience and not with elements derived through logical analysis of final generalizations or conceptions.[4]

3. Those who adopt the *best-books method* have so far been active only in the field of higher education. In advocating a scheme of organiza-

---

[3] L. Thomas Hopkins, *Interaction: The Democratic Process.* D. C. Heath and Company, New York, 1941. Pp. 17–92.

[4] L. Thomas Hopkins, *Interaction: The Democratic Process.* D. C. Heath and Company, New York, 1941. Pp. 164–165.

tion that differs from the other schemes advocated by the proponents of the separation theory the best-books method neglects the first step of analyzing conceptions to be mastered into their logical elements. The sponsors of this plan seem to have abandoned subjects and all other forms of logical organization except the materials themselves. The materials consist of what is known as "the hundred best books." The organization of subject matter for teaching purposes does not involve any analysis; the organization required is just that which is found in these hundred so-called best books.

From the standpoint of the philosophy of experimentalism, these books are not a record of the concrete experiences of the authors but a reorganization of the conceptions they developed through concrete experience. Aside from the fact that the subject matter contained in these selected volumes is inadequate, the arrangement is impossible for the average student. The organization of the subject matter in these books is just about as far removed from the way subject matter must be organized in the mind of the student as one can imagine. It is difficult enough for the average student to grasp the full significance of the conceptions of some of history's great thinkers. It is possible for students to develop many of these conceptions if they approach them gradually and progressively through the reorganization of their own ideas. Some of these concepts, perhaps most of them, will eventually be achieved by many students in dealing with materials much closer to their own experience. If they cannot secure them in this way, it is doubtful whether they can secure them at all. Furthermore, conceptions developed in any other way, for most people, remain mere verbal statements.

The assignment of the so-called best books to all college students without discrimination is one of the best examples of the authoritarian theory of organization. The mind of the student is not only to be filled with certain ideas, many of which are of doubtful value, but it is to be rendered logical through the absorption or appropriation of logical forms embodied in prescribed materials logically arranged. The concepts are not arranged according to the intellectual growth and development of the student but according to the final intellectual organization of mature scholars. According to the experimentalists, such an organization of the curriculum, which neglects the present experience of the student, is reactionary in character. Such a plan has little to recommend it on the college level, and it is impossible on the lower levels.

THE INCIDENTAL THEORY
(EDUCATIONAL LAISSEZ FAIRE)

The attitude of the exponents of educational laissez faire toward organization is called the incidental theory because they assume no responsibility for its direction and control. Like the authoritarians, they consciously or unconsciously assume that logical order and development is foreign to the development of individual experience. They minimize, in their practices and in the principles used to justify them, the importance of logical order and arrangement of subject matter in the education of the young. Since many of the uninitiated and inexperienced rebel at the various systems of knowledge presented in certain formal courses and textbooks, the adherents of educational laissez faire do not take this problem of organization very seriously. They seem to assume that if only free play is given to impulse and desire, intellectual development will take care of itself. In other words, the best organization of the effects of experience consists in that arrangement which is incidental to the expression of impulse and the fulfillment of desire.

Those who adopt this theory of organization are sensitive to the verbalism, mind-wandering, and routine performances resulting from the effort of the authoritarian to impose external logical elements on immature minds. As already pointed out, some of those who are sensitive to these defects in current practice seek to remedy the situation by discovering some better way of organizing in advance the ground to be covered. But adherents of the laissez-faire theory of incidental arrangement do not rely on any mere scheme or device for doing better what they consider to be impossible, namely, for imposing logical systems of knowledge on the minds of the uninitiated and inexperienced. They agree with the authoritarians that the mind is naturally averse to the forms of logical order; but where the authoritarians recognize the need for bringing order out of chaos, *the exponents of the laissez-faire theory of incidental arrangement are content to let nature take its course.* Whatever organization occurs is satisfactory to them. Their favorite mottoes are, as Dewey says, such slogans as "freedom," "interest," "spontaneity," and "self-expression." They exert no effort to cause children to organize logically the effects of their experience.

Any preliminary arrangement of content and materials to facilitate logical organization is to these modernists preposterous. They do not, as the authoritarians do, differ among themselves as to which is the best preliminary arrangement or scheme of organization. They do not prefer one arrangement to another. They do not have, and they do not wish to have, any preliminary arrangement at all. From their point of view, the chief business of the teacher is to stimulate pupils to express their capacities in the order of their natural development. Whatever pupils learn in the process of such natural unfoldment and whatever form of organization such learning happens to take are both incidental to direct self-expression.

From this point of view, for educational workers to acquaint themselves with such formal schemes of organization as the authoritarians advocate is worse than a mere waste of time and a needless expenditure of energy. The use of such plans of organization cramps the spontaneity of both teacher and pupils. For instance, the teacher who makes an advance preliminary plan for a year, a quarter, a month, a week, or a day to guide him in dealing with a group of pupils is, from the laissez-faire viewpoint, incapacitating himself for good teaching rather than preparing himself for such a goal. No scheme of advance planning should be considered because no advance planning should be done. Not only is the curriculum made on the spot, but any effort to develop it in one way rather than in another is to do violence to the nature of the young and inexperienced, whose impulses and inclinations, which are inviolable, should be trusted to unfold themselves properly without external control and without authoritative restraint implicit in any preliminary form of organization.

From the standpoint of the philosophy of experimentalism, this laissez-faire theory of incidental arrangement is very unsatisfactory. In spite of the fact that some of the authoritarians have imputed such a theory to the experimentalists, widely recognized experimentalists have never advocated it. Dewey, Bode, and Kilpatrick have consistently rejected this theory, even as they have the separation theory. As they see the situation, good planning is just as much a necessity in preparing for teaching as it is for anything else. Furthermore, they deny that the mind of the young and inexperienced is averse to logical forms, and contend that to conceive psychological organization and logical organization as opposed to one another, as the exponents of educational laissez faire tend to do, is to misunderstand the nature of organization.

Psychological organization refers to the organization of the *process* of experience and logical organization refers to the organization of the *effect* of experience. They are complementary rather than antithetical.

Logical organization is just as indispensable to education as is psychological organization, for educative experience is both a process and a product. As Kilpatrick says, "the psychological order is the order of experience, of discovery, and, consequently, of learning. The logical order is the order of arranging for subsequent use what has already been learned." [5] Just as the scientist organizes the results of his experiments and investigations to make them available for subsequent experiments and investigations, so should the very young child organize the results of his experience to render them available for subsequent experience. The exponents of educational laissez faire in adopting this theory of incidental arrangement not only misconstrue the nature of psychological organization but reject logical organization, which is indispensable to effective learning in subsequent experience.

THE CONTINUITY THEORY
(EDUCATIONAL EXPERIMENTALISM)

The principle of educational organization developed by the educational experimentalists is here designated as the *continuity theory* because the organization of subject matter in the mind of the beginner is continuous with that which specialists have developed. It rejects the fundamental assumption underlying both the separation theory of educational authoritarianism and the incidental theory of educational laissez faire. These two latter theories assume that the mind of the learner is lacking in any logical arrangement whatever. According to the proponents of the continuity theory, first-hand knowledge of children is sufficient to contradict any such belief.

In criticizing the authoritarian and the laissez-faire schools of thought with respect to their attitudes toward organization, Dewey says: "Thus the basic error of the two schools is the same. Both ignore and virtually deny the fact that tendencies toward a reflective and truly logical activity are native to the mind, and that they show themselves at an early period, since they are demanded by outer conditions and stimulated by native curiosity. There is an innate disposition to draw inferences, and an inherent desire to experiment and test. The mind at every stage of growth has its own logic. It entertains suggestions, tests them by observation of objects and events, reaches conclusions, tries them in action, finds them confirmed or in need of correction or rejec-

---

[5] William Heard Kilpatrick, *Foundations of Method*. The Macmillan Company, New York, 1925. P. 302.

tion. A baby, even at a comparatively early period, makes inferences in the way of expectations from what is observed, interpreting what it sees as a sign or evidence of something it does not observe with the senses. The school of so-called 'free self-expression' thus fails to note that one thing that is urgent for expression in the spontaneous activity of the young is *intellectual* in character. Since this factor is predominantly the *educative* one, as far as instruction is concerned, other aspects of activity should be made means to its effective operation." [6] In other words, according to the theory of continuity, even the beginner has the indigenous logical factors that constitute the proper starting point for the progressive intellectualization of the subject matter of experience and for its organization into logical systems.

The theory of continuity also rejects the assumption of the incidental theory of educational laissez faire that psychological organization is antithetical to logical organization. We have already indicated Kilpatrick's position on this point in our appraisal of the incidental theory. With respect to the same issue, Dewey says: "Any teacher who is alive to the modes of thought operative in the natural experience of the normal child will have no difficulty in avoiding the identification of the logical with a ready-made organization of subject matter, as well as the notion that the way to escape this error is to pay no attention to logical considerations. Such a teacher will have no difficulty in seeing that the real problem of intellectual education is the *transformation* of natural powers into expert, tested powers: the transformation of more or less casual curiosity and sporadic suggestion into attitudes of alert, cautious, and thorough inquiry. He will see that the *psychological* and the *logical*, instead of being opposed to each other (or even independent of each other), are connected as the earlier and the terminal, or concluding, stages of the same process. He will recognize, moreover, that the kind of logical arrangement that marks subject matter at the stage of maturity is not the only kind possible; that the kind found in scientifically organized material is actually undesirable until the mind has reached a point of maturity where it is capable of understanding just why this form, rather than some other, is adopted.

"That which is strictly logical from the standpoint of subject matter really represents the conclusions of an expert, trained mind. The definitions, divisions, and classifications of the conventional text represent these conclusions boiled down. The only way in which a person can

[6] John Dewey, *How We Think* (Revised Edition). D. C. Heath and Company, New York, 1933. Pp. 83–84.

reach ability to make accurate definitions, penetrating classifications, and the comprehensive generalizations is by thinking alertly and carefully on his own present *level*. Some kind of intellectual organization must be required, or else habits of vagueness, disorder, and incoherent 'thinking' will be formed. But the organization need not be that which would satisfy the mature expert. For the immature mind is still in process of gaining the intellectual skill that the latter has already achieved. It is absurd to suppose that the beginner can commence where the adept stops. But the beginner should be trained to demand from himself careful examination, consecutiveness, and some sort of summary and formulation of *his* conclusions, together with a statement of the reasons for them." [7]

Thus, according to the continuity theory, elements of important subjects and general conceptions common to many subjects and areas of experience that have been organized into logical systems are found in the experience of pupils in the elementary school. Nucleuses of mathematics, social science, literature, and natural science are already present in the experiences of children when they first come to school, and even the experiences of pre-school children are not without some logical order. The problem for the teacher as a curriculum-maker is to do systematically and deliberately what out-of-school life does unconsciously and incidentally. He must teach children to weigh evidence, observe logical sequence, summarize, and draw conclusions. The logical results of such thinking may be inadequate from the standpoint of the mature, educated adult, but the immature and uninitiated neophytes must start with the logical contents of their own experiences. The conceptions of educated adults and experts constitute the completing logical stage in the direction of which the psychological organization followed by the pupil should move.

Perhaps an analysis of the procedure which a young child follows in learning the meaning of a simple conception would render the foregoing formal statement more concrete and significant. The concept of "dog" — not just some particular dog but "dog" in general — is, for instance, pretty well established in the mind of the educated adult. But take a child born in a home where there is a little black terrier that is the pet of the family. At first the child knows nothing about "dogs," nor anything about "the family pet." Gradually, however, he adopts the terrier as a companion. They play together and the child

---

[7] John Dewey, *How We Think* (Revised Edition). D. C. Heath and Company, New York, 1933. Pp. 84–85.

gets some idea about a dog, and about dogs in general. But so far his idea concerning the wide variety of dogs to be found in the community, to say nothing of all dogs everywhere, is very incomplete and inadequate.

According to the continuity theory, the child's conception of "dog" had its beginning in his dealings with his own black terrier. But since this one dog is very different from many other dogs, the child's notion of "dog" must be very inadequate when applied to other dogs. There are white dogs, brown dogs, spotted dogs, large dogs, small dogs, unfriendly dogs, and many other kinds of which the child is ignorant. The only way he can acquire a conception of dogs in general is to reconstruct the meaning of "dog," which he has learned to associate with the family pet and to include other dogs in addition to the family pet. As the child becomes aware of other dogs, step by step his concept of "dog" broadens until it approaches the meaning held by his parents, and perhaps even the meaning developed by canine experts.

Now this first concept of "dog," which the child developed in daily contact with his own pet, is continuous with all his subsequent experiences in which dogs play any part. After each such experience the child has a clearer understanding of "dog" in general as distinguished from "dog" in particular. Such a conception is not just a composite of sensory impressions secured from observing different dogs. It is the culmination of a long process of reconstruction of experience.

According to the continuity theory, the way a young child learns the meaning of "dog" is the way all of us learn every conception that we ever develop. We build concepts, not mechanically by adding logical part to logical part, as the authoritarians assume, but we learn them only in situations where the effects of past experience undergo reconstruction. No arrangement of the logical elements of important conceptions can be satisfactory for learning purposes.

It is equally clear, however, that the learner should not be left to make his own organization without guidance or direction. It seems perfectly clear that the parent, if he takes the trouble, can guide the child in developing his concept of "dog" by directing his attention to essential factors after each experience involving "dog," either some particular dog, or even the idea of "dog." In the same way, the teacher may guide pupils in the development of any concepts he considers important. When he causes the pupil to analyze, summarize, and review the effects of each experience in which such a conception is involved, he is giving logical organization his attention. The pupil develops conceptions because of the part they play in his experiences, but how he organizes the concepts after each experience determines their usefulness in subsequent experience. The teacher and the school have the responsibility of so directing pupils that the effects of their experiences are organized to point logically to conceptions that exist in the minds of the teacher, the expert, and the educated adult, and in the systems of established knowledge.

To provide for such continuous and progressive organization of subject matter in the mind of the beginner, two conditions are essential. The teacher must discover in the experiences of pupils the elements of the more general logical patterns toward which organization is to be directed. He must also direct the activities and experiences of the pupils so that the elements thus discovered will gradually approximate the conceptions that are understood and used by mature educated adults. Three kinds of study should characterize every effective teaching program. First, the experiential background of the pupils must be constantly and continually surveyed, analyzed, and studied. Second, the experiential background of the mature educated adult, the teacher, and the expert must also be surveyed, analyzed, and studied to discover the conceptions or patterns which constitute the final stage in educational organization. Third, activities must be discovered through which the vital elements in the experiences of the young and uninitiated may be psychologically deepened, broadened, expanded, and transformed until they approach the conceptions of the mature educated adult.

Such studies as the foregoing which the application of the continuity theory seems to suggest, far from rejecting preliminary planning and organization on the part of the teacher, emphasize its importance. It is not enough to know the minds of the pupils and the minds of the authorities. Not only must they be seen as two stages in the same process, but the connecting links between them must also be seen. The final logical patterns are relatively stable but the beginning stages vary considerably from one group to another and from one individual to another. This fact means that the intervening connections vary widely in consequence of the previous experiences of those to be educated. In other words, the road leading from the mind of the uneducated to the mind of the educated is not a well-graded highway along which modern road signs are properly located. The road to be traveled is different for every individual, and it has never been traveled before. In fact, everyone has to make his own road. The teacher cannot know the road of every traveler, but he can know approximately the location of the individual and the direction of his destination. He also knows something of the lay of the land through which everyone has to travel. He does not know exactly which way any individual will go at various points, but he should know when someone is going in the wrong direction.

If he knows where his pupils are and where they should eventually go, the teacher is in a position to do some real planning. He makes tentative plans that embody the present experiences of his pupils and that look toward the ultimate goal. With such plans he can go over mountains and hills, and into swamps and rivers, and still keep in mind the general direction. Only with such plans can he direct his pupils from day to day and from week to week.

Principles of child development, of course, should be studied, but they are insufficient themselves. The techniques of child study must be learned. Then these techniques must actually be applied by the teacher in studying the very children he is teaching. The logical conceptions of the mature, educated adult, of the teacher, and of other authorities in different fields may be studied by classifying and organizing them in different ways. It is just here that the so-called schemes of curriculum organization have a real office and function. The teacher should arrange the logical patterns toward which his pupils progressively move in as many ways as possible. He may organize them by subjects, by centers of interest, by units of work, by occupations, and in other ways. There is no one best scheme of advance organization. The teacher should use all schemes to gain perspective with regard to the pupils. Although he should keep his pupils in mind while reconstructing his advance organizations from time to time, any such organization should be conceived as an instrument of teaching and not as an order to be followed in learning.

This theory of organization, which has been developed by students of education who accept the general outlook of the philosophy of experimentalism, is always implicit in the practices of good teachers and has far-reaching implications. It means, first of all, that there is no one best scheme of organization to be used, and that the method of organization used by the pupils never takes as its point of departure the so-called logical elements derived through the logical analysis of the patterns most satisfactory to recognized authorities in the various fields. It means that the problem of organization should not be solved by denying its existence, and that the organization of the effects of experience should not be left to mere chance. It means that students of education should continue to describe different schemes of organization as they have done in the past, but it means also that they should give up the notion of some universal scheme preferable to all other schemes. It means that educational administrative officials should not prescribe single uniform schemes of organization to be followed by whole school systems and by whole schools, but instead should describe different schemes which teachers might use. It means that each teacher should develop his own plans in the light of his knowledge of the field and his information in regard to his pupils, and that such plans should be continuously reconstructed in order to guide pupils in their progressive intellectual development.

CHAPTER 13

School Curriculum

THE CURRICULUM HAS LONG BEEN CONSIDERED an important feature of school practice. It has always been one of the central topics in educational literature. In recent years it has received more consideration than any other factor to which professional workers direct their attention. There are many courses in our teachers colleges and schools of education devoted to it; and in practically all professional courses and books at least some attention is given to it.

People do not, however, always mean the same thing when they use the term *curriculum*. The different meanings of the term as now used in education are all derived from, and analogous to, the different meanings of the Latin word *curriculum*. Cicero used the word in a figurative sense to signify the race of life or a vocational career. Analogous to this meaning, the curriculum in an administrative sense consists of an arrangement of courses leading to some occupation or to some occupational interest. Analogous to other meanings of the Latin word, the curriculum in an educational sense has two meanings. The word signified to the Romans literally a race course, or the ground over which contestants competed in chariot races. Corresponding to this meaning, the curriculum as the chief factor of the educative process consists of subject matter to be studied or learned. The Latin word in a metonymical sense also signified not the race course but the race or the running itself, the sum total of the activities or experiences of the contestants. Similarly, the curriculum as the most important factor in the educative process consists of the activities of the pupils in the race of life.[1]

THE EDUCATIONAL CURRICULUM

Now it is the curriculum in the educational sense that commands most widespread attention. When the educational profession took for granted that subject matter was the most important feature of the

[1] John P. Wynne, *The Teacher and the Curriculum.* Prentice-Hall, Inc., New York, 1937. Pp. 1–2.

educative process, it was confronted with the problem of what combinations of subject matter, consisting of courses and subjects, were best for the people in general and for special groups; and the question conceived in a somewhat different way is still with us. The recent extended interest in curriculum-making arose when leading students of education conceived the educational curriculum — curriculum in the broadest sense — in a new way. When they began to think of curriculum in terms of activities analogous to the metonymical meaning of the Latin word *curriculum*, a new movement in curriculum development was initiated. At first there was some confusion as to exactly what people were talking about when they discussed curriculum. However, *as now understood, curriculum refers to the activities of the pupils under the direction of the school.*[2]

Educational representatives of the philosophy of experimentalism, therefore, think of curriculum in terms of the activities of pupils, and the main problem as they see it is not whether we shall have an activity curriculum or some other kind of curriculum. There are not some schools in which the curriculum consists of activities and other schools in which it consists of subject matter. Pupils in all schools engage in activities. The curriculum problem is not whether pupils shall have activities but what kind of activities shall they have.

As the experimentalist sees the situation, there are three general theories of the nature of a desirable activity, or, perhaps better, of how those in control of school education should select desirable activities. According to one theory, desirable curriculum activities are those that involve the proper handling of prescribed subject matter; according to a second theory, they are those activities that involve an elaboration or expression of impulses, wishes, wants and desires of pupils, usually called purposes; and, according to a third theory, they are activities in the development of which pupils have desirable experiences. For convenience of reference, these curriculum theories, which in much current discussion are often assumed or taken for granted, may be

---

[2] The discussion in this chapter is equally applicable to both curriculum and guidance. Curriculum has reference to all the activities of the pupils under the direction of the school, and guidance is now conceived by some to consist of the management of the curriculum. The term *curriculum* is here given preference because we have in mind primarily the activities of the pupils rather than the activities of those who manage them. One's theory of guidance depends upon the theory of the curriculum which he assumes. For a brief historical statement, see John S. Brubacher, *A History of the Problems of Education.* McGraw-Hill Book Company, Inc., New York, 1947. Pp. 315–317.

designated as the subject-matter theory of curriculum activities; the expression theory of curriculum activities; and the experience theory of curriculum activities.

THE SUBJECT-MATTER THEORY
(EDUCATIONAL AUTHORITARIANISM)

From the standpoint of the experimentalists, the heart of the curriculum problem is not whether we shall teach subject matter or pupils, or whether pupils shall or shall not engage in activities, but what kind of activities they shall engage in. According to the authoritarian subject-matter theory the only desirable curriculum activities are those in which pupils deal with prescribed subject matter in some prescribed way, which may be definitely defined or clearly assumed. With special reference to the way pupils are to deal with subject matter, there seem to be at least three variants or forms of the subject-matter theory of selecting curriculum activities.

As already pointed out, subject matter may be conceived in terms of the issues, questions, or problems to be investigated, studied, or taught, or it may be conceived in terms of the materials used in the investigation, study, or teaching of such issues, questions, or problems. Subject matter of the first type may be designated as subject-matter content and subject matter of the second type may be designated as subject-matter materials. We thus have two conceptions of the subject-matter curriculum — the content curriculum and the materials curriculum. But the possibilities of interpreting subject matter are not yet exhausted. In recent years, the facts, skills, and principles, or whatnot, to be learned in dealing with content and materials have been conceived as the most inclusive and important factor of the educative process — the aims curriculum. Therefore, there are three different conceptions of the subject-matter curriculum: (1) the materials curriculum, (2) the content curriculum, and (3) the aims curriculum.

1. Historically, the *curriculum* was first conceived in terms of subject-matter *materials*. The distinction between content and materials had not been clearly made. Certain subjects in the trivium and the quadrivium, constituting the two divisions of the seven liberal arts, had been differentiated, but in practice the books in which these subjects were developed constituted the most important factors of the educative process. They constituted the curriculum. Even today many people think of curriculum in terms of the materials, usually in terms of the

textbooks that are used. The sensitiveness of certain people to the subject matter contained in textbooks is sufficient evidence that the materials conception of the curriculum is still effective. Both parties in the well-known Scopes case, which involved the legislature of Tennessee, William Jennings Bryan, and Clarence Darrow, and enlisted the interest of people throughout the civilized world, assumed that the subject-matter material is the most important factor of the educative process, and that the curriculum consists of subject-matter materials. Such a conception of the curriculum seems implicit also in the recent controversy, involving the American Legion, the National Association of American Manufacturers, and the National Association of Educational Administrators, over the subject matter contained in certain social science books.

But however important and influential the materials conception of the curriculum may be in certain quarters and in the minds of certain individual teachers, it has been largely abandoned by recognized students in the field of curriculum-making. Materials are, of course, considered essential in curriculum development everywhere. Nevertheless, their role is secondary rather than primary as it formerly was. The materials selected, recommended, and used are conceived as contributory and secondary to some other factor, such as subject-matter content, aims, or activities, which are considered primary. Subject-matter materials no longer occupy a central position in the reports of authoritative curriculum committees and in the official courses of study prepared for the use of schools and school systems. Although some teachers still let prescribed materials determine the activities of the children, many teachers today think primarily in terms of topics, aims, or activities rather than in terms of specific materials. *This conception of the curriculum is of historical interest only*, but it paves the way for an understanding of another variant of the subject-matter theory of the curriculum that is perhaps much more widely held.

2. The reference is, of course, to the *content curriculum*. As already suggested, the fact that the distinction between content and materials was not clear tended to emphasize the importance of materials. However, the materials conception of the curriculum was undermined by the constant increase in the variety and quantity of materials. When the subject-matter materials were no longer contained within the covers of a few books, something else besides books became the central points of reference in dealing with curriculum. The subject-matter content, consisting of topics, issues, questions, or problems, was dis-

tinguished from the materials used in dealing with these topics. The content rather than the materials thus became the primary factor of the educative process. The curriculum was conceived in terms of the topics, issues, problems, and questions to be considered regardless of what materials were to be used in their investigation and study.

Many authoritative committees and official curriculum-makers have been governed by this conception of the curriculum. They have devoted considerable attention to the materials which are primary in the older conception of the curriculum that has now, for the most part, been discarded. They often gave some attention to textbooks, chapters, and pages, but these were considered as secondary to the selection of the right subjects and topics. Such committees and official curriculum-makers proposed or prescribed the subjects and the topics to be covered, the materials proposed or required being selected according to their supposed usefulness in dealing with the content. However, other materials might be used, even in the state systems, provided that the prescribed books were also used.

This conception has considerable advantage over the materials conception of the curriculum. *Distinguishing between subject-matter materials and subject-matter content, making the latter primary, provides for some choice in materials on the part of the teacher and pupils.* The teacher may still have to use the state-adopted textbook, but he is not limited to it. Such a conception also places more emphasis on reflection and understanding than did the *memoriter* learning, apparently inherent in the materials conception. In the content theory of the curriculum, however, teachers and pupils are given an opportunity to deal with more comprehensive topics, issues, questions, and problems than they had under the older conception. Attention is shifted somewhat from books, chapters, and pages to the more important subject-matter content with which they deal.

Today, however, this content theory of the curriculum has many implications that seem quite unsatisfactory to most students of curriculum-making. In the past, the content proposed by authoritative committees has often been selected without reference to the needs and capacities of particular pupils. Usually authoritative committees represented subject fields and selected content whose mastery logically signified a well-rounded scholar in each subject. Furthermore, many subjects which contained content of vital concern to the pupils and to the communities in which they lived were neglected because those subjects were not recognized by committees representing the well-known and respected subjects. The official course of study, which often incorporated the content of the authoritative committees, was identified with the curriculum. The teachers were expected to have pupils cover the ground prescribed. With the increase in school population it gradually became clear that, *although all covered the ground required, only a few mastered it to the degree expected.*

3. Realization of this fact paved the way for the development of the *aims curriculum.* According to this view, the most important factor in the educative process consists of the things pupils are expected to learn rather than the ground they are expected to cover, whether defined in terms of subject-matter materials or of subject-matter content. This conception of the curriculum is quite in line with the scientific movement in education and justifies scientific students of curriculum-making in their effort to define just what pupils should learn. Some curriculum specialists devote their attention to the school subjects, such as spelling, arithmetic, handwriting, and reading. Others take in more territory and seek to determine what everyone should learn in order to engage successfully in all the activities of life. They state the new objectives, as they are called to distinguish them from the more general aims which philosophers have formulated, in terms of abilities, appreciations, understandings, and attitudes. Official curriculum-makers, schools, and teachers proceed to define the curriculum in terms of the new aims in line with the scientific movement in education.

The resulting program is an improvement over the ground-to-be-covered conception. It calls attention to the fact that what pupils learn is more important than the content they cover. It calls attention also to the inadequacy of vague general aims and to the need for clearness on the part of the teacher in regard to specific things pupils should learn. It emphasizes the importance of scientific research in the field of curriculum-making as well as in other fields.

But the results are not entirely satisfactory. In the first place, the experts select the specific things which they prescribe in total ignorance of the interests and needs of the very pupils who are expected to learn them. It is less difficult to define facts and skills than it is to define understandings, appreciations, and attitudes. Consequently, teachers seek the specific objectives that are easily defined, and neglect those that are difficult to define. When this conception of the curriculum is combined with another phase of the scientific movement in education — the measurements movement — the resulting effect is subjected to severe criticism. The curriculum experts determine the information and skills that should be learned and the experts in tests and measurements provide the instruments with which such outcomes can be adequately measured. The more general traits, such as initiative, responsibility, and co-operation, are often — perhaps usually — neglected. The curriculum is still conceived in terms of subject matter confined largely to school subjects. The specific items of subject matter to be learned without reference to the qualities of experience through which they are learned constitute the most important factor of the educative process. Consequently, the students of education and the teachers who consider these desirable qualities the primary and all-inclusive aims of education can never accept the aims theory of the curriculum as satisfactory.

From the standpoint of the philosophy of experimentalism, *the activities constituting the curriculum cannot be adequate when they are determined by prescribed subject matter in any form.* Teachers are to be found everywhere who adopt one or another of these theories of curriculum-making. In spite of the obvious objections to the materials conception, many teachers today in so far as possible limit the activities of the pupils to learning the prescribed facts and principles contained inside the covers of the official textbook. Some college teachers even hesitate to adopt a new text because they are almost sure to have to study it to determine how to teach it. Many other teachers try to limit the activities of their charges to dealing with content topics prescribed by official courses of study. Some try to confine the activities of the pupils, in so far as possible, to the achievement of the specific aims prescribed by the school authorities for the grade, subject, or school. Experimentalists reject all these variants of the subject-matter theory because they see that adequate curriculum activities cannot be prescribed in advance, and that any subject-matter curriculum prescribes them in advance.

From this point of view, the activities of pupils that are determined in advance must neglect their interests, result in indoctrination, limit the operation of intelligent choice, paralyze originality and creativeness, lack integrating purposes, and contribute to making individuals dependent upon external authority. *It is not desirable for school authorities or even for the teacher to decide in advance just what materials are to be studied.* In the first place, such a program is impractical. There is no way of telling in advance what everyone can do. It is useless to decide that any individual should do what he cannot do. *The opportunity to do what one cannot do is no opportunity at all.* The requirement to do what one is indisposed to do and cannot become disposed to do is not educative, whatever else it may be. The subject-matter theory of the determination of the curriculum is thus both theoretically and practically unsatisfactory.

THE EXPRESSION THEORY
(EDUCATIONAL LAISSEZ FAIRE)

The expression theory of selecting curriculum activities is the very opposite of the subject-matter theory. Whereas those who adopt the subject-matter theory of selection are disposed to determine everything in advance, those who adopt the expression theory are disposed to determine nothing in advance. The activities in which pupils should engage are not those in which teachers may think they ought to engage, but rather those in which pupils are disposed to engage. Many who adopt the "activity curriculum," or the "activity program," assume the expression theory of the curriculum. They mean that the curriculum consists of the activities of pupils, but they have their own notions about what activity means. To them any curriculum activity is one in which pupils should engage because it is desirable. In consequence of variation in the meaning attached to the term *curriculum activity*, there are at least these three variants of the expression theory, which may be designated as: (1) the overt-activity conception, (2) the center-of-interest conception, and (3) the purpose conception.

1. According to the *overt-activity conception*, almost any kind of overt or manual activity is a desirable curriculum activity. It consists of such operations as making a dress, constructing a rabbit-box, or building a miniature house, as contrasted with such intellectual operations as memorizing, imagining, and reasoning. Moreover, reading, writing, solving mathematical problems, or studying history and geography are not considered activities. Consequently, in many schools the production of articles of objective achievement becomes for a while the dominating factor of the curriculum. A few years ago, the author visited a rural elementary school which had a wide reputation for its progressive practices, and which was credited with the adoption of the so-called *activity curriculum* or activity program. In every room in the school the pupils were engaged in building a miniature house of some kind, and practically everything else said or done in the school was conceived as closely related to this construction work. This program illustrates the overt-activity variant of the expression theory of curric-

ulum-making. Although it was called the activity program to distinguish it from the program in which the activities are determined by prescribed subject matter, psychologically the curriculum in both kinds of schools consists of activities. But the only kind of activities the progressive authorities considered curriculum activities were those which involved doing things with the hands. In this kind of activity the pupils were thought to be expressing their wishes, wants, desires, or purposes. They had, so to speak, the real activity program.

2. According to the *center-of-interest conception*, another variant of the expression theory, curriculum activities are related to certain topics, usually called centers of interest.

Although a center of interest means different things to different people, it usually is conceived as some kind of comprehensive topic that cuts across the ordinary school subjects and includes other things as well. It is supposed to be a topic to which many interests of the pupils are related. One or more such topics may constitute the subject-matter content for a whole grade. For instance, in the *Farmville State Teachers College Course of Study for the Elementary School*, published in 1914, the following centers of interests were recognized.

Kindergarten.	Rhythm, Games, and Songs
Grade I.	Children's Home Life Homes of Other Children
Grade II.	The Surrounding Occupations
Grade III.	Sources of Our Food Our Clothing
Grade IV.	The World We Live In
Grade V.	How Some of Our Ancestors Lived Where We Americans Came From North America Today Home and Community
Grade VI.	Our Heritage and the Nations to Which We Are Indebted The Beginnings of Our Nation Home and Community
Grade VII.	Growth of Our Nation into a World Power Other World Powers of Today Group Activities

In the Virginia Courses of Study published in 1934, the following centers of interest were recognized.

Grade I.	Home and School Life
Grade II.	Community Life
Grade III.	Adaptation of Life to Environmental Forces of Nature

Grade   IV. Adaptation of Life to Advancing Physical Frontiers

Grade   V.   Effects of Inventions and Discoveries Upon Our Living

Grade   VI. Effects of Machine Production upon Our Living

Grade   VII. Social Provision for Co-operative Living

Grade VIII. Adaptation of Our Living Through Nature, Social and
              Mechanical Inventions, and Discoveries

Grade   IX. Agrarianism and Industrialism, and Their Effects upon
              Our Living

Grade   X.   Effects of Changing Culture and Changing Social Insti-
              tutions upon Our Living

Grade   XI. Effects of a Continuously Planning Social Order upon
              Our Living

The teacher who accepts or assumes this form of the expression theory naturally adopts the so-called activity program, and sometimes takes the position also that only activities related to the centers of interest are curriculum activities. It is quite possible that many things of interest to pupils may be related to such comprehensive topics, at least in the mind of the teacher. When teachers get the idea that the only activities to be recognized as curriculum activities are those related in their minds to such comprehensive topics, they easily get their own notions about the subtopics into which these so-called centers of interest may be analyzed and about the particular activities that are satisfactory. Such topics and the activities related to them are often described and published in books for teachers. They are called "projects," "activities," "enterprises," "units," or whatever the latest slogan happens to be. They are incorporated in courses of study and in professional books for teachers and recommended as the kind of thing that constitutes the activity curriculum.

In many places the activity curriculum thus conceived is formalized. Teachers speak of the research work of little children who actually engage in the study of such topics as pioneer life, the eye, and the ear. Often a so-called project, activity, or unit consists in finding out everything the children and teacher can find out about some topic in which the children have very little interest. The situation becomes still more serious when supervisors adopt this conception of the activity curriculum and build up their own stock of activities, which they consider the activity curriculum. Their teachers not only must seem to adopt this conception of the curriculum but, to save face, they have to guess what particular patterns the supervisors have in mind. Teachers have to conform blindly to programs contained only in the heads of those to whom they are responsible. The situation is all the worse because everything is done in the name of the activity curriculum or the activity program, which is thought by many to provide considerable freedom for both pupils and teachers. *There is no formalism that is so deadening and enslaving as what one recent author has called the "formality of informality."*

It is doubtful if many exponents of the activity curriculum have wished to confine the activities of the pupil to such all-inclusive integrating topics. Few, if any, of them have sought to formalize the activity program. They have sought to overcome the formality that certainly existed in the so-called traditional school with which they have been accustomed to compare the activity school.

Nevertheless, such a tendency toward formality in informality is clearly visible in many places. If teachers, supervisors, and curriculum-makers get the idea that there is some psychologically right kind of activity that constitutes the activity curriculum, which is the only conception acceptable in many quarters, they must inevitably seek to bring this kind of activity into the school. They may be mistaken as to the right kind of activity, but so long as they think there is some right kind, they should not be condemned for trying to find it. Even those who adopt the expression theory of curriculum-making feel the need for some standard of selection that will indicate activities through which pupils express themselves.

3. According to the *purpose conception*, a third variant of the expression theory, a curriculum activity is a purposeful activity. Now the conception of purpose is as variable as the conception of activity. There is little doubt that purpose in some sense is fundamental in educative experience. Still, people may mean quite different things when they use the term. Once they have adopted the expression theory of the curriculum, however, and are convinced that the only real activities are purposeful, they are logically required to confine the curriculum to purposeful activity.

Some curriculum-makers, supervisors, and teachers seem to think that anything an individual pupil proposes is on that account a purposeful activity not only for him, but also for the group to which he belongs. On the other hand, it appears obvious to most recognized students of education that the mere suggestion by a pupil need not be a purpose either for the individual himself or for the group to which he belongs. The more socially minded and alert pupils will usually suggest something if they have nothing else to do, especially when such suggestions are solicited by the teacher. However, as Dewey has pointed out, such suggestions are at best mere "hunches." They are certainly not desirable purposes. Furthermore, the fact that a group of pupils votes to engage in the study proposed does not necessarily mean that they have any well-defined purpose in mind. They usually are merely conforming to a pattern that has come to prevail in initiating activities. However, if the teacher adopts the purposeful activity variant of the expression theory of curriculum-making, he naturally thinks that all curriculum activities are purposeful activities, and that any purposeful activity is a curriculum activity. He naturally seeks to make the curriculum on the spot, according to the suggestion of certain students of education, by discovering the purposes of pupils and translating them into activities.

Other curriculum-makers, supervisors, and teachers adopt a broader conception of purposeful activity. To them all behavior is purposive. All activities serve some need, desire, wish, or want. Whenever and wherever such activities become conscious they are purposeful. The teacher or the pupils may propose undertakings. The only requirement is that they embody the desires, wishes, or wants of the pupils. It may seem obvious to most students of education that other things must be considered in selecting curriculum activities besides the wishes, desires, wants, or even purposes of the pupils. Still, if it is assumed that pupils can express themselves only through activities, and if all curriculum activities are purposeful, it is logical not only to include purposeful activities in the curriculum but to limit it to them.

From the standpoint of the philosophy of experimentalism, the expression theory of the curriculum in all three forms is logically and practically unsatisfactory. Dewey has shown that activities cannot be confined to overt activities, such as those required in making things with the hands. The pupil who is apparently the most quiet is often the most active.[3] The progressive rural school to which we have referred, for instance, was soon compelled, in order to care for the interests of the pupils, to place less stress on manual activities.

The conception that all curriculum activities should be related to specified centers of interests may become just as authoritative as the subject-matter theory. The activities related to the so-called centers of interest may not even be interesting. They may have to be motivated. For instance, one summer in the Farmville State Teacher's College Demonstration School the activities of one group were all supposed to

[3] John Dewey in *Thirty-Third Yearbook* of the National Society for the Study of Education. Public School Publishing Company, Bloomington, Ill., 1934. Pp. 81–86.

be related to "how the weather affects our living." The demonstration teacher had the children note the headlines in the daily papers every morning to learn the effects of the drought and the difficulties that the people in the Dust Bowl were having that year. One morning everybody came with his paper indicating the number of people that had been killed in Virginia in automobile accidents during the year. The demonstration teacher said with some show of pain that she simply could not stand to talk about killing people and things like that. She had a very pleasing personality and the children liked her very much, so they did not talk about the dreadful subject any more. As a matter of fact, some of them may have thought she had already talked about matters in connection with storms and the Dust Bowl that were much worse. Some may even have "caught on" that the teacher was merely trying to hold them to her center of interest, which was not at the time interesting to them.

The difficulty with the purposeful activity form of the theory, from the standpoint of the philosophy of experimentalism, is not that purposeful activity is undesirable. It lies rather in the misconception of purpose that the adherents of the laissez-faire philosophy of education usually adopt, and further, in the fact that all desirable curriculum activities cannot be purposeful from beginning to end. Purposes of the right kind are not merely foreseen ends, things that the pupils wish to do. They are foreseen ends that arise out of the dramatization in imagination of alternative courses of action. In response to some proposal or suggestion different possibilities are developed in thought, and the best undertaking that can be decided upon by the group, taking all pertinent considerations into account, is chosen. Such an activity is, of course, satisfactory from the standpoint of purpose. However, it is quite clear that all the activities of the curriculum cannot be initiated in this fashion. It seems more reasonable to believe that purposes of the kind here suggested emerge in educational activities that have already been under way for some time. It is certainly true that some of the more desirable educative experiences are not immediately and directly interesting and purposeful from beginning to end.

Purposefulness as the single qualification of curriculum activities is confronted with the same difficulties as any other variants of the expression theory. *A conception of some particular psychological type of activity places a limitation on practical experience. Some curriculum activities are related to the so-called centers of interest or integrating topics. But all desirable curriculum activities are not related to them* and some that are related to them are undesirable. Pupils may suggest some of the curriculum activities, but they cannot suggest them all, and some they do suggest are not desirable. Some curriculum activities may be purposeful from beginning to end, but they cannot all be this purposeful. And some of them that are purposeful are not desirable. *The desirable curriculum must include activities of many kinds, and any effort to limit it by definition to any particular kind must fail.*

Stated in a different way, a limiting factor is implicit in all forms of the expression theory, which leads straight back to the subject-matter camp of the authoritarians. It resides in whatever mark is used to distinguish a curriculum activity from any other activity. Such activities do not typically represent inherent tendencies or purposes residing in the individual independent of experiences. Typically, they consist of factors derived from experience under narrow, circumscribed, fixed conditions. They are usually symbols of habits, customs, and mores rather than innate tendencies, propensities, or dispositions. Engaging in the activities which their expression requires leads to authoritarian imposition rather than to freedom and emancipation. As Bode has pointed out, the reformer in adopting an absolute may easily be betrayed into the camp of the authoritarians. In many situations this is what seems to happen to the adherents of educational laissez faire. The difficulty with the idea of expression as a theory of the curriculum, implicit in the philosophy of educational laissez faire, is that it requires some concrete and tangible sign of which course to take in selecting activities, and whatever sign is adopted as a part of the very definition of an activity leads straight into the camp of the authoritarians, where imposition, not expression, is the ideal.

THE EXPERIENCE THEORY

(EDUCATIONAL EXPERIMENTALISM)

The experience theory of the curriculum is adopted by professional students of education and by professional workers in charge of the schools who assume the philosophy of experimentalism as their general outlook on the world of nature and man. As students of the curriculum problem they accept the current definition of the curriculum — that it consists of the activities of pupils under the direction of the school. As exponents of educational experimentalism, *they adopt the theory that the only desirable curriculum consists of those curriculum activities that supply desirable experiences.* Every curriculum, whether called the subject-matter curriculum, the activity curriculum, or something else, is, as a matter of fact, an activity curriculum. There is no other sort of curriculum. But *every curriculum is not a desirable one.* All depends upon the qualities of experience considered desirable.

When the curriculum is conceived in terms of the activities of pupils, we no longer have any problem of distinguishing the activity curriculum from the non-activity curriculum. We no longer have any problem of distinguishing which of the school activities are curriculum activities. They are all curriculum activities — even the extra-curricular activities. But we do have two problems — the problem of defining the qualities of experience which are desirable and the problem of selecting activities in which pupils have experiences with such qualities.

The qualities of experience assumed to be desirable or educative in the experience theory of the curriculum of educational experimentalism are indicated in the theories or principles of desirable experience that experience itself approves. These principles have been suggested in the first part of this study. An educative experience in the constructive and approved sense not only involves both the individual and his environment; it involves them in such a way that the standard of direction is to be found in neither the one nor the other but in the situation which includes them both. Hence, activities conducive to the development of desirable experience cannot be determined in advance as the authoritarians assume, and they cannot be left entirely to the inclination of the individual, as the adherents of educational laissez faire assume. They must take into account the individual as he is both at the time and under the conditions to which he is subjected. In other words, the general situation, including both the individual and the conditions, must supply the standard of direction.

First, the curriculum activities initiated and developed when all the pertinent factors are taken into account have the quality of contingency. Things are looked upon as relative; that is, they get their meaning and significance in their relationship to other things, and whatever is learned in such activities is flexible and capable of modification as conditions change.

Second, a desirable curriculum activity in the approved sense involves not only socialization but socialization of a special quality. Unless it involves widening the area of common interests and concerns, it is unsatisfactory, no matter how social it may be. Widening sociality signifies social sensitivity, participation, and appreciation. Whatever contributes to these characteristics is socially desirable, and an activity that involves them is socially desirable.

Third, a desirable curriculum activity in the approved sense must be acceptable on the whole to the individual who engages in it. It need not be emotionally exciting, but it should be mildly satisfying. It need not be satisfying from beginning to end, but it should be the kind of thing that the individual does not regret having done by the time it is completed.

Fourth, a desirable curriculum activity involves creativity or originality. It provides for learning new things in new ways. It allows curiosity and wonder to operate, and suggests and encourages experimentation with new ideas.

Fifth, a desirable curriculum activity involves intelligent choice and requires selection among alternatives on the basis of profitable consequence. It permits possibilities of error and uncertainty in making decisions, and requires systematic organization of facts and principles.

Sixth, a desirable curriculum activity typically reflects purpose. The emergence of purposes is eventual rather than initial. They constitute the integrating agencies of desirable experience and necessitate a psychological variety of activity.

From the standpoint of the philosophy of experimentalism, the only way to compare theories of the curriculum is to compare the qualities of the experience which the activities they suggest provide. The qualities of experience which the experience theory suggests are indicated in the foregoing criteria. These qualities and those which the subject-matter and the expression theories emphasize have been more fully defined in Part I, where the three different philosophies of education were stated in terms of experience. Those who object to the use of the proposed qualities as criteria of desirable experience should think of them as only one possibility. Other suggestions may be found in the analyses of educational authoritarianism and educational laissez faire. No one is under obligation to accept any of these analyses, but everyone who thinks of the curriculum in terms of activity should define the general qualities of experience to be used as criteria in the selection of curriculum activities.

CHAPTER 14

General Method

GENERAL METHOD, whatever else it may signify, has reference to the general ways of teaching. But these general ways are conceived differently, depending upon the general philosophic position assumed. Educational authoritarians usually think of general method in terms of some general techniques of general application; adherents of educational laissez faire think of it as a set of general principles of education, without reference to techniques of any kind; and educational experimentalists think of it in terms of a systematic elaboration of general principles involving the analysis and evaluation of standard techniques. These different attitudes toward general method are reflected in method textbooks and method courses for teachers. In some instances general method is conceived as some one general technique or set of techniques of general application, with or without reference to a philosophy of education; in some instances it is conceived as some general principle or set of principles with little reference to formal procedures of any kind; and in other instances it is conceived as systematic elaborations of general principles with special reference to procedures in learning and teaching. For convenience of discussion, these attitudes may be designated as the formal-techniques theory; the general-principles theory; and the systematic-elaboration theory.

THE FORMAL-TECHNIQUES THEORY
(EDUCATIONAL AUTHORITARIANISM)

Perhaps most authors of textbooks and teachers of method courses, as well as students preparing for teaching positions and teachers in service, assume the formal-techniques attitude toward general method. They think of it as a single general procedure applicable in all fields, as a few general procedures applicable in all fields, or as many general procedures, each applicable in some one field. In general, then, the formal-techniques theory of general method assumes three forms:

(1) the single-technique conception, (2) the multiple-techniques conception, and (3) the special-methods conception.

1. *The single-technique conception*, one form of the formal techniques theory adopted by the authoritarians, is clearly exemplified in the formal steps developed by the Herbartians from Herbart's analysis of the process of educative experience. The great German philosopher and student of education, Johann Frederick Herbart, during the first half of the nineteenth century, developed an all-inclusive conception of educative experience. With this conception of the educative process in mind, he distinguished these four steps of experiencing or learning: clearness, organization, system, and method. In *clearness*, the individual absorbs or appropriates particular sense impressions derived from his contacts with the environment. In *organization*, he organizes these impressions into more comprehensive wholes. In *system*, he integrates these comprehensive wholes into still more comprehensive wholes or systems. In *method*, he interprets, on the basis of these systems of ideas, particular concrete cases. For instance, the individual acquires the conception of fruit in the following way: In Step 1 (clearness), he receives from an orange the impressions of sourness, sweetness, yellowness, roundness, and the like. In Step 2 (organization), he organizes these impressions into the percept of an orange. In like manner, he organizes other impressions received in Step 1 (clearness) into the percept of apple, and still others into the percept of peach. In Step 3 (system), he generalizes the percepts of orange, apple, and peach into the concept of fruit. In Step 4 (method), he thinks of pear as fruit. In this way the individual builds up his experiences and educates himself. Such a pattern was thus proposed as a general method of experiencing to be used as a basis of teaching in all fields. Later it was formulated from the standpoint of the teacher, and then it was known as *the general method of teaching*.

This general method as a technique of teaching usually is known as the five formal steps of the recitation. *Preparation*, the first step, involves preparing the mind of the pupils for receiving the materials that are to be presented. *Presentation*, the second step, involves presenting detailed facts and principles for the reception of which the pupils have been prepared during the first step. *Comparison*, the third step, involves the various activities of the teacher to get the pupil to compare the facts and principles presented during the second step in such a way as to classify and organize them under different heads. *Generalization*, the fourth step, involves the problem of getting the pupil to draw some generalization or conclusion from the comparisons and organizations suggested during the third step. *Application*, the fifth step, involves having the pupil apply the generalization developed during the fourth step to particular cases.

For instance, let us assume that the teacher wishes to teach the pupil the meaning of honesty. In the first step, *preparation*, he might begin with "truth-telling" or some other general idea that the pupil already understands. In the second step, *presentation*, he would put before the pupil in some way various activities illustrating "honesty" and "dishonesty." During the third step, *comparison*, comparisons would be made between cases of honesty and cases of dishonesty, and perhaps even general cases of truth-telling. During the fourth step, *generalization*, some general conclusion as to the meaning of honesty on the basis of preceding comparisons would be stated; for instance, honesty means taking possession of only the things that belong to us, or some other such general idea. Finally, during the fifth step, *application*, the teacher would present a hypothetical case in which somebody took something that belonged to somebody else, or perhaps a case in which someone refused to do so, and in this way test the pupil's understanding of the general idea of honesty developed during the preceding steps.

According to the Herbartian philosophy of education, desirable experience, educative experience, consists in learning the right ideas in the right way. It was assumed that those in charge of the schools knew what ideas were important, and the technique of the five formal steps was the general method to be used in teaching them. In other words, the five formal steps were conceived as the general method of teaching everything to everybody, for everything was considered an idea, whatever else it might be.

If the five formal steps were to be used exclusively, the older methods in common use had to find their place in this new general method. Before the Herbartians used the five formal steps, several general methods had been recognized. Such procedures as the lecture method and the question method, the reading method and the writing method, and the oral method and the book method had been described in textbooks and education courses. Even the so-called object lesson and the techniques of teaching by objects were well known. These older methods were now conceived as devices or techniques to be used in the steps of preparation, presentation, comparison, generalization, and application. They were not considered by the Herbartians as different general methods co-ordinate with the five formal steps; they were considered as different means available for use in connection with the various steps. For instance, during the step of presentation the teacher might tell the pupils things — the lecture method; he might have them read certain things — the book method; or he might ask certain questions — the question method.

At the time the five formal steps were developed democratic countries had already developed the class system in which pupils were organized into classes and taught during a set period known as the recitation period. The Herbartians spoke of the new general method as the formal steps of the recitation, and teachers generally thought of the formal steps as all taking place during a single class or recitation period. They also thought of them as sequential; that is, during the class period, they tended to follow the steps in the order of their statement, beginning with preparation and ending with application.

The development and general use of the five formal steps as the method of the recitation seem to emphasize two different ideas in regard to method that were already taking form. According to one point of view, there was some one formal procedure by which everything worth teaching could be taught; whereas, according to another point of view, different kinds of subject matter required the use of different methods of teaching. This difference of opinion in regard to general method prevails in the minds of teachers and students of education to this day. Some deny the importance of general method entirely and think only in terms of the methods of teaching different subjects, the so-called special methods. Others, while admitting the importance of general methods, reject the notion of any one all-inclusive general method. According to this conception, there are several general techniques, some good for one thing and others good for other things, but no one all-inclusive general method. Even such a so-called general method as the formal steps is thought to be useful in teaching one thing, knowledge, as contrasted with other general techniques useful in teaching appreciation, problem-solving, and skill.

From the standpoint of the philosophy of experimentalism, there is no one all-inclusive formal technique of teaching every desirable thing to everybody. Any such steps as the five formal steps should not be conceived chronologically; that is, to follow one another in a sequential order. Moreover, they should not be conceived as confined to any limited period of time, such as a given recitation period. Although the experimentalists recognize the idea of formulating a theory of educative experience into logical steps as a means of suggesting its implications for teaching, they insist that the steps represent only important aspects of learning and teaching that should be taken into account. They reject the five formal steps not only because they have been misused by the Herbartians but because they consider Herbart's theory of educative experience inadequate, it matters not how its implications for teaching are indicated. This theory of educative experience emphasizes the importance of the authoritarian principles of doctrinaire sociality, and the five-formal-steps method is one of the most effective schemes for indoctrination.

As Bode points out, "the whole scheme then becomes a device for indoctrination. The conclusion to be reached is determined in advance, and the successive steps are so arranged as to culminate in this conclusion. The method makes indoctrination the normal aim of teaching." [1] The experimentalists are, therefore, opposed to the formal steps for several different reasons, but they are also opposed to any single formal technique of teaching, regardless of the theory of experience from which it is derived.

Most authoritarians, as already suggested, also have abandoned the idea of any all-inclusive general method. The foregoing discussion of the formal steps of the recitation is here conceived, therefore, mainly as preparatory to the discussion that is to follow. It paves the way for a consideration of the multiple-techniques theory acceptable to most educational authoritarians, as well as for a later consideration of certain objections of authoritarians to the formulations of general method which the experimentalists themselves have developed in order to apply their theory of educative experience to procedure in teaching.

2. *The multiple-techniques conception*, the second form of the formal-techniques theory, like the single-technique conception, can perhaps be best explained by reference to the formal steps. The authoritarians adopting this attitude toward general method not only have revived the old general methods in use before the days of the Herbartians, but have reduced the Herbartian formal steps of the recitation to a general technique conceived as co-ordinate with those older techniques, and have treated subsequent analyses of theories of educative experience in the same way.

In spite of the fact that the older general methods were conceived by the Herbartians as general techniques to be used as needed in connection with the different steps of the formal pattern which they conceived

---

[1] Boyd H. Bode, *How We Learn*. D. C. Heath and Company, New York, 1940. P. 157.

as the all-inclusive general method, it was impossible to keep these old general methods reduced to such a secondary and incidental function. The widespread recognition of the formal steps as the method of the recitation for a time minimized the importance of these older procedures. But when James defined education as the organization of habits of conduct and stated the laws to be followed in learning habits, there was, in fact, another general method of learning that might be translated into a general method of teaching. Stated in summary form, these laws contained three important points of emphasis. According to the first law, *focalization*, the attention should be focalized upon the act to be made habitual. According to the second law, *repetition*, the activity should be constantly repeated. According to the third law, *opportunity*, the act to be made habitual should be performed every time an opportunity presented itself. Logically, one of two things should have happened to the formal steps of the recitation. They might have been replaced by the laws of habit-forming as the general method of the recitation, or the field might have been divided between them. As a matter of historical fact, both things happened.

The students of education who sought to divide the field between them had the advantage. They defined the laws of habit-forming as the method of teaching habits and recognized the formal steps as the method of teaching ideas.[2] Herbart doubtless thought of ideas as working themselves out in practice, and James certainly thought of habits as arising from the conscious activities in which ideas were involved. He thought of his conception as including the same facts as the Herbartian conception.[3]

Nevertheless, the rank and file of teachers thought of ideas as one kind of thing and of habits as another kind of thing. Consequently, they could see no inconsistency in having one method for teaching ideas and another method for teaching habits. Moreover, students of education who had never recognized the formal steps as all-inclusive had an opportunity to develop a whole set of general methods co-ordinate with the kind of general methods in use before the popularization of the formal steps. They called themselves eclectics, condemned any all-inclusive general method, and defined every so-called general method as simply a general technique of teaching. They divided the five formal

---

[2] Stuart H. Rowe, *Habit Formation and Science of Teaching*. Longmans, Green and Company, New York, 1909. Pp. vii–viii, 37, 60–68, 94, 277.

[3] William James, *Talks to Teachers*. Henry Holt and Company, New York, 1903. P. 83.

steps into two methods of the recitation, of which the first four steps became the inductive lesson and the last step the deductive lesson.[4]

These authoritarian eclectics were the students of education who prepared textbooks for teachers in the public schools and for departments of education and who taught most of the method courses. They were not interested in the elaboration or application of any all-inclusive theory of educative experience. They were teaching general methods as general techniques of limited application. Every effort on the part of the leading educational thinkers to develop an all-inclusive theory of educative experience into a general method of teaching seemed doomed to very limited success. These thinkers might be understood by some students of education and by a few teachers, but the eclectics taught the courses in methods in which students preparing to teach were enrolled, and wrote the books in methods that students in training and teachers in service read.

In 1909 Dewey analyzed his theory of educative experience in still another set of steps. In the first step, *difficulty*, the individual feels some difficulty. In the second step, *definition*, he locates and defines the difficulty. In the third step, *suggestion*, he entertains some suggestion as to a way out or a possible solution. In the fourth step, *reasoning*, he develops some tentative hypothesis as to the peculiarities of the situation. Finally, in the fifth step, *testing*, he determines, through observation and experiment, the validity of the proposed solution.[5]

In 1918 Kilpatrick analyzed his theory of educative experience into another general method. In the first stage, *purposing*, a purpose is selected as a guide to the process of learning. In the second stage, *planning*, plans are made for guidance in executing the project proposed. In the third stage, *executing*, plans for the attainment of the aim projected are executed. In the fourth stage, *judging*, results are estimated with respect to the specific situation and to the general lessons to be derived from the experience.[6]

So well established was the authoritarian eclectic way of thinking about method and teaching method that Dewey's analysis of reflective thinking — designated as an all-inclusive general method of learning and teaching — was immediately incorporated in books on general

---

[4] W. C. Bagley, *The Educative Process*. The Macmillan Company, New York, 1905. Pp. 284–315.

[5] John Dewey, *How We Think*. D. C. Heath and Company, New York, 1909. P. 72.

[6] William Heard Kilpatrick, *Foundations of Method*. The Macmillan Company, New York, 1925. Pp. 203–206.

method and in courses on method as the technique of problem-solving, co-ordinate with the inductive lesson and the deductive lesson, into which the Herbartian steps had been split, and with the drill lesson into which James' laws of habit-forming had been reduced. Likewise, Kilpatrick's analysis of purposeful activity, which was also designed as a general method, soon had its pretentions curbed. It was recognized by the authoritarian eclectics as a technique to be used in construction work or in the development of "articles of objective achievement," and was incorporated in courses and books in the field of method on an equal basis with the other general methods whose scope of application had likewise been reduced. Any general method, technique, device, or procedure became just so much more grist for the eclectic mill. Every new system that came along meant another chapter in method textbooks or perhaps another lecture in method courses.

From the standpoint of the philosophy of experimentalism, the authoritarians who adopt the multiple-techniques attitude toward general method are more disturbing than those who adopt any single formal technique, as the Herbartians did. The Herbartians at least clearly put forth an intelligible theory of educative experience, as perhaps anyone does who undertakes to develop a single all-inclusive general method. It is possible to criticize such a theory of educative experience and point out its inadequacies and defects in its formulation as a general method. However, it is impossible to criticize or appraise any theory of educative experience that the authoritarian eclectics apply to procedure in teaching, inasmuch as they say very little about philosophy of education, and inasmuch as they seldom, if ever, show any connection between the various general techniques they advocate and any all-inclusive theory of experience.

Moreover, the authoritarian eclectics seem to be unable to understand the difference between a single formal technique to be slavishly followed and an attitude toward life stated in terms of its logical aspects for the purpose of suggesting important points of emphasis. To them any single general method is a rigid formula, conceived as universal in its application, to be followed chronologically step by step in teaching any kind of subject matter determined in advance. In other words, although they consider any such general formulation a valuable analysis, it is not in reality what its originator and its sponsors take it to be. It is, in fact, nothing but another device or technique very useful in teaching some specified kind of subject matter authoritatively determined in advance.

Perhaps this narrow interpretation of every general method that has been prepared, from the object lesson and the formal steps to the analysis of purposeful activity, has been facilitated by the different types of experience emphasized in popular textbooks in psychology. The laws of habit developed by James were readily conceived as the method of developing habits, as contrasted with the Herbartian formulation of thinking, which was associated with the development of ideas. Similarly, Dewey's analysis of reflective thinking was readily associated with thinking in psychology. It was not taken by the authoritarians as a general theory of the process of educative experience, as Dewey considered it, but as a separate factor of consciousness corresponding to the association of ideas, to habit-forming, and to other psychological processes, such as feeling and overt activity. Consequently, when the formulation of purposeful activity appeared it was perhaps inevitable that it should be associated with overt activity or with constructive work of various kinds. It seemed literally impossible for many people, even teachers and students of education, to see that Herbart, James, Dewey, and Kilpatrick intended to include all aspects of experience in their respective theories of desirable experience or educative experience, and in their respective formulations of a general method of learning and teaching.

Nevertheless, it matters not what factors facilitate the eclectic attitude of most authoritarians toward the problem of general method, for it seems inherent in their philosophy of education to think of any general method as just another way of getting some particular sort of prescribed subject matter learned. As they see the situation, every kind of subject matter has its own methods. In criticizing Kilpatrick's analysis of the theory of experience developed by the experimentalists into the general method of purposeful activity, some informed him that everything could not be taught in the same way. For instance, Professor Ernest Horn in criticism of the wider conception of method commented that "the way to learn to spell a word is not the way to learn to play on the piano. Even the motivation is not the same in any but a rhetorical sense." [7]

People who think of method only in terms of prescribed subject matter and ways of getting it embodied into the minds, hearts, or muscles of children and youth simply do not seem to be able to under-

---

[7] Ernest Horn, quoted by William A. Maddox, in I. L. Kandel (Editor), *Twenty-Five Years of American Education*. The Macmillan Company, New York, 1924. P. 166.

stand the educational experimentalists, who are interested primarily in the quality of the experiences of those who are learning subject matter. Authoritarians do not see that the general method which the experimentalists have in mind has reference to the quality of experience. What is worse, from the standpoint of the philosophy of experimentalism, the eclectic attitude toward general method which authoritarians assume and the educational program which they thus support nevertheless emphasize qualities of experience. Furthermore, the qualities that the authoritarians are thus emphasizing are the very qualities that many of them actually do not wish to emphasize. At least some authoritarians living in democratic countries do not sincerely wish to idealize the qualities that have produced the fanatics who have set the world on fire twice in a generation. Yet those people who neglect the qualities of experience in their dealings with themselves and with others are almost sure to emphasize unconsciously the very qualities that have produced the kind of people who make a war of conquest repeatedly inevitable until they are destroyed or else led to change their natures through experiences of a different kind. When teachers fasten their attention entirely on external ends, prescribed content to be covered, specified materials to be mastered, and formal procedures to be used, their pupils' experiences are pervaded by the same qualities of mechanical routine, subservient dependence, and blind obedience as are the experiences of pupils in autocratic societies, where teachers deliberately cultivate such qualities. After all, it is conforming to fixed forms and procedures that generates these qualities of conformity, whether those in charge fix their attention on them or on the means by which they are generated.

From the standpoint of the philosophy of experimentalism, teachers have been systematically indoctrinated far too long with the so-called general techniques by means of which they indoctrinate children. Any device or technique designed merely to secure outcomes in terms of ideas, habits, appreciations, or what not, while neglecting the qualities of experience, is an instrument of indoctrination. Unless we work for those qualities of experience that we idealize, we are almost sure to get those we do not wish. Through our general techniques we have too often secured the very qualities that autocrats and despots have always desired for their subjects.

The experimentalists are always ready to raise a voice of protest against any program that emphasizes, even unconsciously and unintentionally, the qualities of experience idealized in despotic and autocratic societies. The qualities of experience and personality unconsciously and incidentally secured through the application of the authoritarian theory of general method may be only a little more desirable than those which the leaders in autocratic societies and the leaders of certain social groups in democratic countries deliberately cultivate. If it is possible to develop Fascists by the deliberate idealization of the Fascist qualities of experience, it may be possible to develop Fascists by incidentally emphasizing in the learning-teaching relationship the Fascist qualities of experience. When educational procedures are controlled by standard techniques, they are just as much pervaded by the qualities of conformity as they are when procedures are deliberately selected for the purpose of securing such qualities. For instance, when teachers mechanically follow a routine formal technique in order to realize appreciations, skills, or ideas as outcomes of instruction, the qualities of routine inflexibility and conformity pervade their own experiences and those of their pupils to virtually the same degree as they would if procedures were consciously selected to secure those qualities.

From another angle, the constant accumulation of general techniques, many of which are only syncopated general methods, is not satisfactory — not even to the authoritarians themselves. In other words, they may have too many methods. The tendency toward pedagogical verbalism had been noticed in Europe even before the popularization of the Herbartian formal steps in this country. Referring to a manual of pedagogy that was very popular in Germany, Gabriel Compayré said: "What good can come from this leader's analysis, from this complicated enumeration, from this purely verbal science, in which hundreds of words are employed, and yet teach nothing of the things themselves? Teaching would become a very laborious art, were it necessary in order to be a good instructor, to have lodged in the memory all these definitions of pure form, all these insipid abstractions." [8] In this country the difficulty of realizing the meaning of the different methods considered in method books for teachers was already recognized even before Kilpatrick popularized his analysis of purposeful activity as the project method.[9]

In 1926, after the controversy over the project method got under way, the author had a group of graduate students in education define

---

[8] Gabriel Compayré, *Lectures on Pedagogy,* edited by W. H. Payne. D. C. Heath and Company, New York, 1887, 1893. Pp. 270–271.

[9] Chauncey P. Colegrove, *The Teacher and the School.* Charles Scribner's Sons, New York, 1910, 1922. Pp. 365–366.

what authorities meant by a number of methods, such as the inductive lesson, the deductive lesson, the appreciation lesson, the drill lesson, and the socialized recitation. After they were sure they knew what each method signified, they were asked to keep in mind the meanings of these methods while they listened to descriptions of actual lessons by the author of a well-known textbook in the field of method which he designated as respectively exemplifying these techniques. After reading a description of each lesson, the instructor asked for a show of hands as to which method each description represented. As might have been expected, there was no unanimity. As a matter of fact, a lesson which five or six called an appreciation lesson, several called something else, several more still something else, and so on. In 1932, after the popularization of several new general methods of teaching, Leonard V. Koos had this to say about the method situation revealed in the high schools by the National Survey of Secondary Education: "A startling fact about the long unit assignments, individualized instruction, contract plan, laboratory plan, problem method, and project method is that detailed analyses of practices in schools purporting to use them with unusual success find these practices to be essentially identical, no matter what name is applied. A significant implication here is that terminology is needlessly elaborate and complex and that the educational world will be better off if it discards most of this jargon." [10]

The so-called eclectics, who think of general method as a variety of procedures for teaching different kinds of subject matter, now have more methods than they know how to handle. Teachers do not know one from another and many are disgusted with the whole pedagogical business. Some authorities resort to classification, combining two or more methods into one, while others argue for "a composite of methods." The latter are returning to something like the Herbartian formula, perhaps to be designated as the unit method. To most teachers who have been indoctrinated with conceptions of different general methods for different things, the new composite unit method probably will seem good for some things while the older methods will seem good for other things — unless, perchance, teachers are already disgusted with the whole method business. *The problem of method in the wider sense, which the experimentalists emphasize, is always the problem of securing the qualities of desirable experience.* Method can never be confined to the problem of

---

[10] Leonard V. Koos, in *The North Central Association Quarterly.* 7:210–211, September, 1932.

subject matter. It always involves something far more significant — the qualities of experience that determine personality and character, and which many authoritarians neglect. By neglecting desirable qualities, authoritarians are almost certainly securing other qualities they do not wish.

3. *The special-methods conception* is a third variant of the authoritarian formal-techniques theory. According to this point of view, the general principles and general techniques of teaching the so-called psychological types of school subject matter, such as knowledge, appreciation, skill, and the like, are different for every school subject and are often different for different grade levels. Consequently, the only methods that need be considered by teachers are the standard methods consisting of the principles, devices, and techniques of teaching the various subjects. In his discussion of the project method Professor Ernest Horn said in effect that the way to teach one to spell is not the way to teach one to play on the piano. This statement exemplifies the special-methods conception. If there are no general methods except in a rhetorical and figurative sense, as he says, obviously students of education, as well as teachers, should confine their attention to a study of special methods.[11]

At the present time there are many volumes on the teaching of the different school subjects, such as reading, spelling, writing, arithmetic, language, English, and history. Usually the principles, devices, and techniques recommended for use in teaching school subjects represent a combination of materials derived from many sources. They include suggestions from the experience of teachers, from controlled experiments in teaching different subjects, and from laboratory experiments in psychology. When the materials are secured primarily from experimental educational psychology, methods are often designated as the psychology of school subjects.

There is, of course, considerable variation in the special methods recommended by authorities in the same field in consequence of the variety of data they employ in the development of principles and procedures as well as of the variety of interpretations they place upon such data. For instance, the methods of teaching language vary not only in consequence of the experience in this field but in consequence of the interpretation placed upon experiments in the teaching of grammar

---

[11] Ernest Horn, quoted by William A. Maddox, in I. L. Kandel (Editor), *Twenty-Five Years of American Education*. The Macmillan Company, New York, 1924. P. 166.

and language. According to some authorities, grammar should be emphasized in the teaching of language, and according to others, it should be minimized. In other words, there is no certainty about what is the best way to teach anything. Still, many believe that the only way to teach methods of teaching is to teach the methods of teaching the different school subjects.

From the standpoint of the philosophy of experimentalism, the methods of teaching various school subjects should be recognized, but they should be recognized for what they are, not for something else. First of all, no best devices, techniques, or forms of teaching anything can be derived directly from tradition, experience, research, or scientific experiment in psychology or in the field of teaching. All that can be discovered through such research are sources of suggestions that teachers should consider in situations where they are relevant. No authoritative discussion of the teaching of any school subject can inform any teacher exactly what procedure should be used in any concrete learning-teaching situation, for the simple reason that whenever one has to deal with people, there are always variable factors that no advance scheme, device, or technique can adequately take into account. Pupils and teachers not only vary in general, but they vary as circumstances and conditions change. Therefore, *no single best method of teaching reading, arithmetic, history, biology, or any other subject, has ever been found or ever can be found.* Every so-called new method, for instance, the functional method of teaching shorthand, makes a contribution in the new suggestions it provides, but it tends to generate qualities of conformity in the experiences of both pupils and teachers when it is so conceived and employed as to prohibit the use of other valuable procedures.

Like other exponents of the formal-techniques theory of general method, the exponents of the special-methods variant of this theory usually pay little or no attention to the qualities of desirable experience. In other words, the qualities of experience that they emphasize are all incidental to the mastery of the specific subject matter contained in the different fields. The neglect of the qualities of experience does not mean, however, that qualities are not present in every learning-teaching situation. It means rather that the qualities present are not always the qualities which those in control would like to have present if they had given any thought to the problem of quality. From the standpoint of the philosophy of experimentalism, there is no objection to the organization of evidence from many sources in terms of teaching the various school subjects. Students of education should use whatever means they have at their disposal to keep teachers informed on the findings of educational research; but they should not interpret the so-called special methods for teaching, or even the psychology of school subjects, as ways to do things in specific situations. At best, in the teacher-pupil situation, any such special methods should be conceived by both teachers and authorities in the special field as suggestions to be considered when and as they are pertinent to practical situations. But this is not the way special methods are usually considered. They are considered as things to do rather than as things that may be done. When they are so considered, the qualities of experience which the experimentalists consider indispensable aspects of desirable experience are neglected. When they are so considered, the authoritarian qualities which the experimentalists condemn are consciously or unconsciously emphasized under cover while attention is devoted to more direct and immediate considerations that are secondary in importance.

Two factors ever present in the educational situation tend to emphasize the importance of special methods. Just as the counter reaction of the authoritarians against the "lunatic fringe" of progressive education directs attention almost exclusively to subject matter, the constant demand for the teaching of more subject matter puts a premium on rapid learning procedures. One emphasis calls for more subject matter and the other for teaching it faster; but neither of them includes any recognition of the importance of the qualities of experience. From the standpoint of the philosophy of experimentalism, the criticism directed against progressive education is difficult to justify. Those who refer to the failure of a large percentage of American youth to meet educational qualifications for war service should remember that very few of them had ever attended a progressive school. They should also recognize the fact that the personal qualities of the youth of democratic countries have been more than a match for the authoritarian qualities deliberately instilled in the youth of other countries. The so-called rapid learning methods developed during World War II may have been successful in teaching certain specific things in the shortest possible time, but they have not been responsible for producing the qualities of personality which made our youth superior to the youth of the enemy. These qualities represent the cumulative effect of our way of life, and are not the result of any special methods of teaching subject matter, whether in school or in the nation's service. The truth is that these qualities of personality have been developed outside the school almost in spite of our neglect of them in the school. They are the very qualities which the special methods neglect and which the experimentalists idealize.

From the standpoint of the philosophy of experimentalism, the mastery of subject matter and the use of economical methods of learning and teaching it are always to be welcomed. *Nevertheless any general theory of method which, merely to save time, neglects the qualities of experience indispensable to the democratic way of life, is short-sighted. Qualities of some kind are always present in learning and teaching anything, and failure to emphasize the qualities that experience finds desirable cannot be justified.* Our way of life has been sufficient to develop the desirable qualities of personality in the past, but the changes in social and economic conditions justify the conviction that if they are to be satisfactorily secured in the future the school must not neglect them. What does it matter how efficient our methods of teaching subject matter may be if the qualities of experience that pervade the school and other social institutions are such as to develop a Fascist rather than a democratic people?

It is, of course, important that we consider the qualities of experience that have been idealized in the first part of the book. But it is important that those in direct charge of our schools and colleges recognize the significance of desirable qualities of experience as soon as possible. They should not be carried away by the current criticism of progressive education for not doing a job for which authoritarian education assumed responsibility in almost all fields, and they should not adopt the superficial idea that mature scholarship can be developed almost overnight in any field. To this end those who teach in the colleges should learn as soon as possible the difference between method in the wide and in the narrow sense. Special method courses should be either eliminated or taught by those who know the importance of method in the wider sense. If our teachers in service and our students in college are not warned against the authoritarian propaganda for achieving quick results through the use of special methods without reference to the qualities of experience which such methods engender, though we have won the war and perhaps the peace, we may lose our own souls. The objection is not to special method courses as such, but to special method courses which neglect the consideration of desirable qualities of experience, and which in doing so may give emphasis to other qualities in conflict with the qualities that experience itself finds desirable.

THE GENERAL-PRINCIPLES THEORY
(EDUCATIONAL LAISSEZ FAIRE)

The situation which the eclectic attitude toward general method in its practical application has produced paves the way for the adoption of the educational laissez-faire theory that any systematic elaboration of a theory of educative experience with respect to the learning-teaching situation is undesirable. The proponents of this philosophy of education say much about the importance of interest, needs, purposes, integration, socialization, and self-expression, which they conceive as principles or theories of experience such as have been attributed to them in the first part of this study. They say much about the "whole child," the "child-centered school," teaching the "child rather than the subject," "variety of experience," and similar slogans with which all of us are familiar. They seem to have obtained such ideas in part from the theories attributed to Rousseau and to certain so-called Romantic philosophers, from Bergson and Freud, and from certain theories attributed to the experimentalists, such as F. C. S. Schiller, William James, and even John Dewey.

As a matter of fact, however, these principles seem to be little more than a negative reaction to an unsatisfactory situation. Many people, tired of rigid formality, turn for guidance to nature as it manifests itself in the child. However, they are always pleased to discover a statement by some recognized authority, whoever he may be, that justifies their negative reaction to all kinds of formality. They abandon not only the so-called traditional education but everything associated with it. If any general method of teaching has been employed in the traditional school, that is, for them, enough to justify its rejection.

They not only reject the five formal steps and the various general techniques popularized by the authoritarian eclectics, but refuse to spend much of their time on such formulations of experience as those developed by Dewey and Kilpatrick. They give some attention to such formulations, but they do not analyze them sufficiently to understand them. For instance, they usually mean by "purpose," "project," or "unit" whatever some child proposes to do. Moreover, they reject as outmoded any such thing as a class period involving assignment, study, and recitation. The consideration of methods of making assignments, guiding study, and conducting recitation during the class period seems futile to them. So far as they are concerned, there is no such thing as assignment, study, and recitation. Such procedure as the question method, the book method, and the drill method deserve no advance consideration. There is no reason for teachers to spend any time studying such formal techniques. As a matter of fact, *as they see it, the less the teacher knows about any kind of formal procedure the more spontaneous he will be and the more spontaneous his pupils will be.*

About the only thing these exponents of educational laissez faire will do in the way of considering general method is to discuss with one another such general principles as those mentioned above and activities of pupils directed by teachers according to such principles. They are prolific contributors to educational periodicals, which publish descriptions of school practice. They state their general philosophy of education in such terms as we have already suggested and indicate its meaning in terms of activities and statements which they attribute to their pupils. But concerning a systematic consideration of different methods of teaching of any kind they have little or nothing to say.

From the standpoint of the philosophy of experimentalism, this attitude toward general method is as bad in one direction as that of the authoritarians is in another. As already indicated, the qualities of experience that the exponents of educational laissez faire idealize are objectionable. Unlike the authoritarians, who in their concentration on subject matter usually neglect the quality of experience, these radicals in their concentration on the child usually neglect subject matter and emphasize qualities of experience that enslave the pupils to their own impulses rather than to external authority.

There are also more specific objections to this attitude toward the application of general theories of experience to education. In the first place, one way of indicating the meaning of a theory of experience is to state it with respect to some kind of procedure. Only in this way can teachers come to understand what it means. In the second place, it is necessary to live in the world as we find it. For instance, we may not like the usual ways of making assignments, guiding study, and conducting recitations, but as long as these features of the class period are recognized in our schools, the problem of dealing with them must be faced. A definite obligation of those who wish to make a theory of educative experience intelligible to teachers is to state it in terms of problems with which teachers are confronted. In the third place, this attitude toward general method tends to reject everything that is old merely because it is old, which, according to the experimentalists, is just as bad as rejecting everything new just because it is new. There is some value in almost any device or technique of teaching if properly applied at the right time. To neglect the true heritage of the past, even our pedagogical heritage, is not merely to show a lack of proper regard for authority but to deny ourselves a mine of suggestions indispensable in good teaching, as in every other realm of human endeavor.

THE SYSTEMATIC-ELABORATION THEORY
(EDUCATIONAL EXPERIMENTALISM)

The attitude of educational experimentalists toward the problem of general method, which for convenience of reference has been designated as the systematic-elaboration theory, emphasizes the importance of general techniques, to which the authoritarians devote their attention almost exclusively, as well as general principles, to which the laissez-faire devotees give their attention. They consider the principles of general method as a more detailed elaboration of a theory of educative experience with respect to the learning-teaching situation and of general techniques as a means of elaborating such principles. The theory of educative experience that seems most satisfactory has been discussed in Part I of this study. The theories or principles there defined are conceived as applicable not merely to methods of teaching but to every feature of school practice, to every feature of our social institutions, and to all the activities of life everywhere that affect the experience of people.

Typical devices and techniques of teaching consist of typical things that teachers do and the way they do them in dealing with pupils. General method consists of the application of the principles of educative experience to the things teachers do and to the ways they do them. The problem of general method, then, from the standpoint of the teacher, becomes the application in the learning-teaching situation of the principles constituting a theory of educative experience. From the standpoint of the student of education, it consists in such elaboration and application of the principles constituting a theory of educative experience that teachers may use it as a guide in directing the learning activities of pupils in all types of schools and in all fields. The educational experimentalists, therefore, have not hesitated to elaborate and to apply their theory of educative experience to teaching in any way that appears feasible.

In the discussion of the authoritarian attitude toward general method, the logical-analysis method of applying theories of educative experience to method in teaching has already been indicated. This method of elaborating general method was used by Herbart and the Herbartians in their application of their theory of educative experience to procedure in the recitation as it existed in the school of that time. In elaborating the theory of educative experience the experimentalists followed the example of Herbart. James may not have followed it in stating his laws of habit-forming; but there is no doubt that Dewey followed it in making his analysis of reflective thinking and that Kilpatrick followed it in making his analysis of purposeful activity. In the first edition of *How We Think*, Dewey not only distinguished five steps of reflective thinking, the same number as the Herbartians distinguished, but in elaborating them pointed out their advantages over the steps in the Herbartian pattern. In his *Foundations of Method* Kilpatrick showed the relationship of his analysis of the complete purposeful act to the analysis of the complete act of reflective thinking.

However, although the experimentalists employ logical analysis as a means of elaborating general method, they are well aware of the difficulties involved. They have pointed out repeatedly that the steps are not chronological, but logical; that is, they are aspects of experience that must be considered in desirable activities. They are not to be followed one at a time in the order of their formulation, as was done by many teachers in the case of the formal steps. These steps are not confined to any prescribed period such as the recitation. They are conceived as the principles of desirable experience definitely applied to the learning-teaching situation in general. They constitute a general method.

James once said that teachers might think of experience in terms of association of ideas, as Herbart suggested, or in terms of the laws of habit, as he suggested, for both sets of laws cover the same facts. It seems equally feasible for teachers to think of experience as applied to the learning-teaching relationship in terms of the steps of reflective thinking according to the pattern Dewey defined or according to the pattern Kilpatrick defined. They both cover about the same facts. Which pattern one prefers is, of course, a mattter of personal choice. The main thing is that the steps constituting the analysis must be conceived as principles and not as specific things to do in any definite order, and that each set of principles is general in its application and not merely useful in teaching some particular kind of subject matter.

The experimentalists have not, however, limited their efforts to this method of developing a general method consistent with their theory of educative experience. They have used other procedures as well. For instance, even in the first edition of *How We Think* Dewey compared the implications of the pattern of reflective thinking with the implications of the Herbartian formal steps for conducting the recitation as it then prevailed in the schools. In the revised edition of *How We Think* Dewey stated the implications of his theory of educative experience with respect to the recitation or class period as it then prevailed. In like manner, the present writer, in *The Teacher and the Curriculum*, has tried to indicate the implications of the same theory of educative experience for making assignments, for guiding study, and for conducting recitations, which are the features of the class period or recitation now generally recognized.

The educational experimentalists have also stated the implications of the theory of educative experience for the use of the so-called general devices and techniques of teaching. In the revised edition of *How We Think*, Dewey gave considerable attention to the art of questioning as a technique employed by teachers everywhere. The present writer has likewise attempted to state the considerations involved in the use of many general procedures in common use, such as the telling technique, the textbook technique, the questioning technique, the demonstration technique, and the discussion technique. In dealing with such devices and techniques, however, the experimentalists are not primarily interested, as are the authoritarians, in indicating which procedures should be used in getting the different kinds of subject matter learned. They are interested in indicating what is involved in using available techniques in such a way as to contribute most to the development of desirable experience. The experimentalists' attitude has been suggested in their limited attention to the drill technique, the problem-solving technique, the appreciation technique, and the construction technique, which, for the most part, represent syncopated general methods of the type that the educational authoritarians have considered so useful in teaching different types of subject matter.

On the other hand, the experimentalists have not neglected the general subject-matter techniques entirely. For instance, Kilpatrick not only has elaborated the experimental theory of educative experience into logical steps after the example set by Herbart and Dewey, but he recognizes four types of purposeful activity which he calls, respectively, the *producer project*, the *consumer project*, the *problem project*, and the *drill project*. These different kinds of purposeful activity correspond to the different types of techniques correlative to different types of subject matter of which the authoritarians thought so highly. In fact, since they had contended that Kilpatrick's analysis applied only to *the production of articles of objective achievement*, it was necessary for him to show that the same principles applied not only to producer projects but to all other kinds of projects as well. In this way, the wider meaning of purposeful activity was indicated, and more and more this theory of educative experience has influenced even the authoritarian discussion of the different kinds of subject-matter techniques.[12]

In recent years, in consequence of the confusion resulting from the accumulating multiplicity of methods and names of methods, students of method representing the authoritarian outlook on life and education, as well as those representing the experimental outlook, have sought to determine what general features of an educational undertaking or unit must be used under practical school conditions, and to indicate procedures useful in dealing with each of them. At least three such features — the initiation, the development, and the culmination — are now widely recognized. The experimentalist has sought to elaborate his theory into a general method through a systematic discussion of features of the undertaking, usually called a unit.

But there is a vast difference between his treatment of such features and the way the authoritarian deals with them. The authoritarian usually thinks of the unit as something that he wishes the pupils to learn or some topic he wishes them to study. He may even contrast this unit with what he calls the activity unit, of which the adherents of laissez faire make so much. He sometimes considers his unit as the kind necessary under present conditions, whereas the activity unit is suited only for ideal conditions. But as the experimentalist understands the situation, every unit is an activity or experience unit. There cannot be any other kind. Just as children have experiences in laissez faire schools where little or no attention is paid to subject matter or to systematic organization, so they have experiences in any other schools. *The problem is not whether or not pupils shall have experiences, but what kind of experiences they shall have.*

The features of the unit are thus conceived by the experimentalist as stages in the development of a pupil undertaking, which he hesitates to call a unit because of its association with some logical topic or pattern of thought, feeling, and action with which pupils are to be indoctrinated. He therefore prefers to use such terms as "undertaking," "enterprise," or "activity," which place the emphasis on

[12] John P. Wynne, *General Method: Foundation and Application.* D. Appleton-Century Company, New York, 1929. Pp. 493–497.

things to do. The initiation consists in getting the enterprise under way, the development consists in the process of realizing the undertaking, and the culmination consists of the activities involved in bringing the enterprise to a close. The experimentalist does not undertake to indicate how such undertakings are to be initiated, developed, and culminated. He merely indicates, from the standpoint of his theory of educative experience, the considerations involved in using different procedures in dealing with the three features. He feels it important to apply his theory of educative experience to the recognized features of pupil undertakings not only to overcome the current tendency of the authoritarians to popularize another formal technique reminiscent of the Herbartian formal steps, but in order to apply his theory of educative experience to procedure in teaching. General method is the teacher's application of some theory of educative experience. Unless experimentalists constantly apply the theory of educative experience that seems to them fundamental in life and in education, teachers generally will adopt unconsciously the theory of experience that the authoritarians assume but which they seldom definitely relate to the methods they advocate for use in initiating, developing, and culminating units of a different kind.

The problem of general method consists in the proper selection and direction of learning-teaching activities in which both teachers and pupils are involved. Any theory of educative experience is definable in terms of qualities of experience assumed to be desirable. *Any general method consists of all the things the teacher does to foster desirable qualities of experience.* What he should do in any particular situation depends upon what is required to secure the qualities of experience he seeks. From general-method courses conducted by the educational experimentalist, the teacher can learn of typical devices and techniques and can evaluate their different uses in the light of the qualities of experience that seem most desirable from the standpoint of experience itself. He is using general method whenever he considers such qualities of experience in selecting ends and means while planning, teaching, and evaluating the activities of the learning-teaching relationship. General method and the curriculum are aspects of a single process for which the teacher is directly responsible. If he relies on fixed standards, whether determined by tradition or by recognized authority, he is an educational authoritarian; if he relies on his own sensitivity to the impulses of his pupils, without reference to authoritative and traditional standards, he is a laissez-faire reformer; and if he uses traditional and authoritative standards and spontaneous impulses as means of securing qualities of experience which experience itself finds desirable, he is an educational experimentalist.

CHAPTER 15

School Training

THROUGHOUT OUR STUDY we have thought of education in two ways — as a function of method in the broad sense and as a function of subject matter. Method in this sense, as contrasted with methods of teaching specific things, has reference to the way people are treated whatever the subject matter may be. Method thus understood determines the personal qualities of people. Subject matter has reference to the things studied and is an abbreviation of the expression "subject matter of study." Subject matter in this sense determines the specific things learned, often defined in terms of knowledge, appreciation, and skill, or in some similar way. The desirable effects of method and the desirable effects of subject matter constitute two kinds of educational outcome. *Method determines the kind of people that are developed and subject matter determines their future careers.*

In describing the education of the old Germany before the first World War, the late James Earl Russell, Dean of Teachers College, emphasized this distinction between subject matter outcomes and method outcomes in this way: "In the making of Germans little weight is attached to the control of the curriculum. What one studies may have an important bearing on one's future career. The peasant attends one kind of school, the businessman another, and the future soldier still another, but all must be made first of all Germans. It follows, therefore, that the secret of training for the common good is to be found in the methods of instruction within its control. The principle that methods of teaching and modes of discipline make the man while what he learns determines his career will surprise some Americans who have delighted to describe methods as a hobby of those who have nothing to teach." [1]

It is the function of the school to develop people, but it is also a function of the school to teach specific things. The teaching of specific things without reference to method in the broad sense is, *in its intent,*

---

[1] James Earl Russell, "Education for Citizenship." *Teachers College Record*, 17: 120–121, March, 1916.

training. As contrasted with the emphasis on the effects of method, we can here designate the purposeful emphasis on subject matter as training. Education involves both the effects of method and the effects of subject matter, although those who have control of education may consider one and neglect the other. Training is universally recognized as a feature of school practice. Since up to this point we have placed the emphasis on method, it seems important that some attention be given now to training.

Types of Training

Many so-called types of education are widely recognized. Among the more familiar of them are general education, vocational education, moral education, and religious education. It has long been customary in courses and books on philosophy and on principles of education to consider separately at least some of these different kinds of education. Perhaps the reader would like to have some of them considered here. However, to do so would require several chapters and thus extend much further a volume which is already growing too long. If we can state the three philosophies of education developed in this study in terms of theories of some one topic that combines the various types of education into a single conception, perhaps sufficient attention to satisfy most readers can be given to the different types of education. The feature of training seems to be the topic required.

Perhaps some will feel that the term *training* is too narrow, and that we should not reduce the so-called types of education to acquisition of subject matter. The reply is that we are not reducing the types of education to training; the distinction of types itself in the minds of most people has reference to definable effects of different kinds of subject matter rather than to the different methods; that is, different ways of treating people. They think of education as training without regard to method in the broad sense. But we here recognize the fact that how people are treated affects their training. In fact, our comparison of the three philosophies of education which we have been explaining and elaborating in this study is based primarily on the different attitudes assumed in the various departments of life as to how people should be treated. According to each of these philosophies, different types of education can be distinguished. Such distinctions, according to any one of the three philosophies, are based primarily on difference in subject matter. Hence, the difference between one kind of education and another is due to training rather than to method.

The problem that thus confronts us is to explain the different theories of training which seem to exemplify, respectively, the three philosophies of education we have under consideration. Their explanation must involve a statement of (1) the different conceptions of the relationship of training to method, and (2) the different conceptions of the relationship of the various types of training to one another. In educational authoritarianism, training and education are identified; in educational laissez faire, training is incidental to education; and in educational experimentalism, it is relative to method on the one hand, and to practical conditions on the other.

THE IDENTIFICATION THEORY
(EDUCATIONAL AUTHORITARIANISM)

According to the identification theory of training, education is conceived primarily in terms of the mastery of subject-matter aims, and the different types of education consist in the mastery of the different kinds of subject-matter aims. Authoritarians in autocratic societies often emphasize method aims as well as subject-matter aims. But typically in democratic societies they devote their attention exclusively to subject-matter aims. In a word, education is reduced to training.

As we have already indicated, there are many different kinds of authoritarians, and they all agree that everyone should be trained; that is, everyone should learn the right things, definable in terms of subject matter. However, they often, perhaps usually, disagree as to what these things should be. When authoritarians agree on what things should be learned and on how they should be stated, they may disagree on what materials and procedures — methods in the narrow sense — should be used in learning and teaching them. Even when they agree in specific instances, their theoretical justifications vary widely. For instance, various pressure groups may insist on teaching certain historical facts for entirely different reasons. Such agreements and disagreements arise from different underlying philosophies of life, from different social and religious traditions, and from different psychological conceptions, which influence learning and teaching. But, however they differ in other respects, authoritarians assume that education is a matter of proper training — learning the proper specific things. Since we are interested here not in how the authoritarians differ from one another but in how they differ from the proponents of educational laissez faire and from the proponents of educational experimentalism, we shall neglect these distinctions in dealing with the different theories of training, just as we have in the consideration of the other features of school practice. We shall here confine our discussion to the position that all authoritarians hold in common.

With respect to general education, the authoritarians hold that there are some patterns of thought, feeling, and action, however defined, that are indispensable to everybody. These patterns, whether stated as ends to be sought, ground to be covered, or material to be studied, constitute general education, which we have called "general training." Typically, the requirements for every type of school, such as the elementary school, the secondary school, and the college, often, even for particular grades or years, are definitely prescribed. The same curriculum conceived in terms of subject matter is usually required of all. Variations in time allotments, arrangements of courses, and methods of procedure may be allowed, but all pupils are expected to learn the same things in so far as they can or will. Usually, however, it is necessary for an individual to meet grade and school standards for admission to a higher grade or school. Completion of requirements must be met also before a pupil may be graduated from elementary school, high school, or college.

In vocational education the requirements are varied according to prospective occupations. Those who expect to enter a particular occupation are specially trained for it. Prospective lawyers, physicians, ministers, engineers, and teachers are given specialized training, which varies according to the demands of these respective professions and which also varies with respect to specialized services to be rendered within these different general fields. Those who expect to enter the various trades are also specially trained for the work they plan to do.

Likewise, in the case of moral education certain subject matter is recognized as indispensable. In some cases, the subject of morals, like any other subject, is definitely prescribed. Prescribed courses in morals are typically required in certain European countries. Usually in this country there are no prescribed courses, yet moral lessons, ideals, attitudes, and beliefs are given some attention in connection with other courses and subjects. Only in the colleges and universities are separate courses in morals, usually called ethics, offered, and they are seldom required. Nevertheless, educational authoritarians generally think of moral education in terms of training in subject matter that is different from the subject matter in other fields.

In certain European countries religious instruction, like morals, is provided in definitely prescribed courses. In this country, in line with our tradition of the separation of church and state, definite religious instruction is seldom provided in the public schools. In some communities provision is made for a specially qualified teacher to teach religious education, the subject matter of which is prescribed by mutual agreement among recognized representatives of the different denominations of the community. Such instruction is provided at private expense. Only pupils who have the consent of their parents are enrolled. In some other communities the various churches offer religious instruction during school hours. In private schools, especially in church schools, definite courses in religious education are provided. But whatever arrangements are made for religious education, it is typically conceived in terms of specified kinds of subject matter. There is considerable disagreement among authoritarians as to how religious training should be provided. Some insist that it should be given by the public schools, some believe that it should be left to the churches, and some believe that because of its importance the churches should assume full responsibility for all education. Some are convinced that it can be handled in some way by the various denominations during school time. But they all seem to be unanimous in their belief that religious education is nothing but religious training in some specified kind of subject matter. Although most educational authoritarians in this country are not satisfied with religious education, they are satisfied that it would be effective if the proper training in certain subject matter could be provided. In other words, the separate-subject-matter or identification theory is assumed with respect to religious education.

From the standpoint of the philosophy of experimentalism, the authoritarians are right in recognizing the importance of different types of training, but they are wrong in neglecting the qualities of desirable experience as criteria to be used in the selection and use of subject matter. It is essential that people everywhere have the conceptions, appreciations, and skills that enable them to function as members of society. General training is necessary for all. It is necessary for individuals to have specific training to prepare them for various professions and vocations. They should also have moral and religious training. Such distinctions represent important emphases that should not be neglected.

On the other hand, if education is conceived as mere training, the qualities of desirable experience are neglected. The method effects are just as important as the subject-matter effects. In fact, they cannot be separated. It is, of course, possible to aim at only subject-matter effects, but method effects are always present. It is difficult enough to secure desirable qualities when we deliberately seek them, and to leave them to chance is almost certain to result in securing those that are undesirable. Moreover, when we make training the primary consideration, the qualities must be those which authoritarians in autocratic societies idealize. The reason why authoritarian qualities are secured when attention is given only to subject matter is that *subject matter without reference to qualities of experience requires in its mastery qualities which self-conscious authoritarians idealize.* From the standpoint of the philosophy of experimentalism, such qualities are just as undesirable when they are secured unconsciously as they are when they are consciously and deliberately emphasized.

According to experimentalists, it is typically desirable to limit training to those experiences whose qualities are desirable. The qualities of desirable experience are never to be considered as mere means. They constitute the criteria for selecting aims, subject matter, and methods of teaching. The qualities of experience are what distinguish education from mere training. When they are not considered, education may be reduced to mere routine performance. *Of course, training is necessary at times, whether the qualities of experience secured are desirable or not.* There are times when people must be taught certain things even if their experiences cannot be desirable in all respects. But, if we know what qualities of experience we wish, we can conduct training in essentials, whatever the curriculum may be, in such a way as to adjust the demands of method aims and subject-matter aims to one another. In the event that training must be given priority over method, we should so direct the process as to do as little harm as possible to the qualities we wish. *The qualities of experience must never be surrendered as an ideal, even when they cannot be fully realized under certain conditions.*

Moreover, when the qualities of experience are not considered, there is a tendency to isolate the different types of training from each other. Not only does general education become mere training, but its relationship to vocations, morals, and religion is neglected. Vocational education becomes mere routine training without reference to the broader training — general education — implicit in vocational fields. Moral education becomes training in prescribed standards and habits without reference to morals as an aspect of all education. Religious education is confined to the absorption of prescribed subject matter ignoring other religious values of personal experience not confined to any prescribed materials.

Stated somewhat differently, the experimentalists object to the method — the way of treating people — implicit in the authoritarian identification theory rather than to the specific subject-matter ends which it idealizes. It is desirable for all to have general training in order to become good citizens, to have vocational training to become self-supporting, to have moral training to develop good character, to have religious training to further religious ideals. There is little objection to be found in such ends. But from the standpoint of the experimentalists, the method of securing these ends colors the quality of the ends themselves as the outcomes of experience. In neglecting method, the identification theory in concrete programs permits, if it does not require, all kinds of formal prescriptions, compartmentalizations, and systems that are very objectionable, especially because these conditions make inevitable the qualities of experience which authoritarians in autocratic societies idealize.

Perhaps reference to certain specific doctrines implicit in the identification theory will be helpful. Some people contend that all general education should be completed before professional and vocational education begins. Some contend that vocational education is a function of vocational subjects and general education is a function of general subjects. Some contend that each lower level is preparatory to some higher level, it matters not what type of training is under consideration. Some contend that moral education should be confined to specific courses. Finally, some contend that religious education is a function only of specified subject matter and courses. Some even contend that the more definitely the various types of education are separated from one another, the better. These doctrines may not be inherent in the identification theory; but they are not inconsistent with it. When only subject-matter training is sought, the only problem in practice is how the training can be done best. All of these doctrines may emphasize efficiency, but, from the standpoint of the philosophy of experimentalism, efficiency so narrowly conceived entails prescription and isolation, which accentuate the very conditions, individual and social, that a comprehensive educational policy should alleviate. Sharp separations lead to the development of separate schools, curricula, subjects, and courses to maintain and accentuate class distinctions. When such sharp separations are made intellectually, they are often translated into distinct programs, and inevitably some are prescribed for some people and others for other people. They may even be so separated in time and place that not only are they isolated from one another but those assigned to them are unable to associate with each other. Members of different educational groups which become sharply differentiated, such as those preparing for college and those preparing for some trade, not only study different things but they do not mingle with one another socially. When different religious denominations assume responsibility for religious training, some pupils learn some things and others learn other things, and some do not have any religious training at all. When a special teacher is provided at private expense, some pupils have religious education and others have none. *All such separations accentuate method effects inconsistent with the qualities of experience which experience itself finds desirable.*

THE INCIDENTAL THEORY
(EDUCATIONAL LAISSEZ FAIRE)

According to the incidental theory of training, the mastery of specific things to which the so-called types of education call attention is a by-product of experiences whose qualities are desirable. Desirable experiences have no direct reference to what specific things should be learned or to how well anything should be learned. They involve such learning, and only such learning, as the impulses and desires, usually called purposes, require. Whereas in the identification theory subject-matter aims are the primary, if not the sole, consideration, in the incidental theory the method aims are the primary, if not the sole, consideration. According to the former, attention is focused upon the specific things to be learned, which Kilpatrick has designated as primary learnings, to the almost total neglect of the qualities of experience, which he has designated as attendant learnings. According to the latter, attention is focused upon the interests, needs, desires, and purposes of the pupils to the almost total neglect of the learning of specific things. What the authoritarian exponents of the identification theory consider primary, the laissez-faire exponents of the incidental theory consider secondary.

Like the authoritarians, the proponents of educational laissez faire recognize such distinctions as "general education," "vocational education," "moral education," and "religious education." But they conceive of them as inherent aspects of education, rather than as distinct kinds of education that require special emphasis by the school or by the teacher. From the laissez-faire point of view, pupils must realize their own needs, interests, wants, wishes, desires, and purposes. In the process of such realization, sometimes called growth, development, unfoldment, or actualization, pupils must deal with different aspects of the environment. These different aspects of the environment include the subject matter of general concern, and activities involving this subject matter constitute general education. They provide for learning what is of concern to the various vocations and professions, and activities providing for such learning constitute vocational education. They include materials with which morals are concerned, and activities involving these materials constitute moral education. They include the things with which religion is concerned, and activities involving these things constitute religious education. Therefore, it becomes desirable, on the basis of this theory, for the schools to provide a rich and varied environment so that individuals may engage in a wide variety of activities that will satisfy their needs. Only as the conditions for the development of such a variety of activities are provided can the individual secure a balanced education. Only so can he learn those things that are typically conceived as general education, vocational education, moral education, and religious education.

No artificial separation of the different types of environmental materials or subject matter can be established in advance. The various subjects and classifications of subject matter represent artificial distinctions. They should be abandoned as rapidly as possible until the ideal of the *activities curriculum* is realized. *An adequate general education does not require learning certain specific facts, skills, appreciations, and conceptions rather than others.* Of course, many such outcomes will be realized; but no deliberate effort should be made to determine what they should be. If pupils are permitted to engage in the activities that satisfy their needs and fulfill their desires, they will learn the things that the general demands of life in the future will require. Moreover, these things will be learned sufficiently well. There is no need for drill and review beyond satisfying the demands of immediate needs. If principles, facts, appreciations, and skills are mastered sufficiently well to satisfy these needs, further effort in the interests of efficiency and mastery is superfluous. In fact, the extent to which schools and teachers overemphasize drill and review determines the degree to which the qualities of experience become undesirable.

As for special types of training, such as vocational education, moral education, and religious education, much less differentiation is required than most people suppose. On the lower levels, many activities require learning principles, appreciations, and abilities that may properly be considered aspects of the so-called special types of education. For instance, pupils in the elementary schools can learn many things that will be useful to them in various vocations. In fact, if permitted to engage in special activities, the elementary school pupil will learn many things that, for the most part, he usually would not have opportunity to learn until his last years in high school or even until his first years in college. Nevertheless, the vocational needs of the high-school junior or senior, or of the college freshman or sophomore, are sufficient to justify providing for vocational courses in our secondary schools and colleges. In these courses, as in the undifferentiated program of general education, it is necessary to learn only such things as the satisfaction of immediate needs and the fulfillment of immediate desires require. Additional practice or drill is unnecessary for vocational efficiency and is objectionable from the standpoint of desirable experience. Moreover, pupils should be enrolled in such courses only as their special abilities and interests emerge.

With respect to moral and religious education, there should be little, if any, differentiation of courses, certainly not before the college level. In fact, moral and religious education may be properly conceived as aspects of general education. Nevertheless, refusal to divide them into separate courses does not mean that their importance is minimized. Pupils at all educational levels have moral and religious needs in addition to other needs. Moreover, some needs may arise in connection with the satisfaction of other needs. In fact, the same activities may be required to satisfy these needs as are required to satisfy other needs. Even when needs require different activities for their satisfaction, they are insufficient in number to necessitate separate courses before the college level. When needs are thus differentiated, they may be conceived as general education or as vocational or professional education for those who are specializing in these fields.

For pupils in the lower grades, moral and religious education for all practical purposes may be conceived as aspects of general education. Morals and religion should not be dragged in to meet some external requirements. They are whatever they happen to be in a varied and rich environment where moral and religious needs, along with other needs, manifest themselves. They do not require any special and deliberate emphasis. No effort is required to see that pupils engage in the study of any special subjects, whether moral or religious. When they do face moral and religious problems as they arise, no effort is made to have pupils master specific materials beyond what the satisfaction of immediate needs requires. For instance, if the question of honesty, keeping promises, or telling the truth comes up in some connection, a decision is made that meets the demands of the situation, but no effort is made to have pupils study these problems further unless perhaps they wish to do so.

From the standpoint of the philosophy of experimentalism, the proponents of the incidental theory are right in placing the primary emphasis on method rather than on training, but they are wrong in limiting training to learning in such quality and quantity as is required for the satisfaction of immediate demands. The qualities of experience that experience itself finds desirable, as we have indicated already in many connections, are quite different from the qualities that are idealized in educational laissez faire. Even if we should assume that these laissez-faire qualities are desirable, still the incidental theory and its underlying philosophy do not attach sufficient importance to training. The fact that authoritarians emphasize the mastery of subject matter only for future use is not a good nor a sufficient reason for limiting learning to the requirements of immediate needs.[2]

Practical people of common sense everywhere are convinced that there are certain things boys and girls should master while they are still in school. They are further convinced that some of these things cannot be learned sufficiently well unless those in direct charge of schools make a special effort to have them mastered. They are not willing to leave the learning of such things to chance. If these things cannot be learned as means to ends in activities arising out of immediate needs, they should, nevertheless, be learned. The experimentalists are inclined to agree with the spokesmen of common sense. Most of them would be willing to subscribe to this statement from Bode: "Perhaps children may learn a great deal about numbers from running a store or bank, but this alone does not give the insight into mathematics that they need to have. They may learn a great mass of historical facts from staging a play, but this is not a substitution for a systematic study of history. Learning for immediate progress or incidental learning is too much of a hit-and-miss affair: it dips in here and there, but it gives no satisfactory perspective, no firm hold on fundamentals."[3]

---

[2] William H. Burton, *The Guidance of Learning Activities.* D. Appleton-Century Company, New York, 1944. Pp. 81–89.

[3] Boyd H. Bode, *Modern Educational Theories.* The Macmillan Company, New York, 1927. Pp. 150–151.

The experimentalists recognize need as the initiating and sustaining condition of all educative experience, but they are unwilling to admit that the activities involved in the satisfaction of every need are desirable. Not all immediate needs supply the basis of desirable experience. Moreover, it is quite possible for those directly responsible for school education to provide conditions which will provoke needs requiring desirable activities for their satisfaction. The experimentalists also think that the school and the teacher should have definite ideas about what will be good for particular pupils in the future, as well as about what will be good for them in the present. In deciding upon what will be good for them, teachers should think of the various demands of life, which such distinctions as general education, vocational education, moral education, and religious education suggest. *They should not hesitate to suggest, propose, and even as a last resort, require activities through which things that are known to be essential are to be learned, and learned sufficiently well.*

Implicit in the foregoing objections to the tendency of the laissez-faire incidentalists to neglect the mastery of specific things unrelated to the so-called natural activities of pupils is an objection also to their disposition to reject any kind of differentiated organization. If specified kinds of subject-matter outcomes should be sought, then whatever organization or arrangement best facilitates their achievement through desirable experiences should be provided. We can agree with exponents of laissez faire that the formal and isolated courses that the authoritarians provide often do violence to the method aims of education, *but still we insist that there are times when some differentiation in organization is necessary to secure essential training.* Moreover, there is no objection to a separation of pupils into different courses and even into different schools provided the qualities of desirable experience are always considered primary. In fact, there are times when such separation and differentiation are necessary, not only for training purposes but also for securing the desirable qualities of experience. The tendency of the authoritarians to overemphasize forms, schemes, and devices does not justify rejecting them entirely. The fact that the curriculum consists of activities and that the approved curriculum consists of activities which provide desirable experience does not mean that all preliminary forms of organization involving a differentiation of courses, departments, curricula, and schools are to be abandoned. Forms of organizations are not the ends of education, but they may be used as means and should be used in such ways as to facilitate the generation of the desirable qualities of experience and the attainment of adequate training.

THE RELATIVITY THEORY
(EDUCATIONAL EXPERIMENTALISM)

In educational experimentalism the emphasis to be placed upon training is relative to the qualities of desirable experience on the one hand and to the demands of practical conditions on the other. For convenience of reference, therefore, this attitude toward training may be designated as the relativity theory. It does not minimize the importance of the desirable qualities of experience as does the authoritarian identification theory, and it does not minimize the importance of subject-matter achievement as does the laissez-faire incidental theory. It assumes that the method function of securing desirable qualities of experience and the subject-matter function of securing desirable training are both necessary and indispensable. Under normal conditions the method function is considered primary, but in particular situations training should be given special emphasis.

In this theory of training the residual function of the school is recognized. Historically, the school has assumed those educational functions which other social institutions have been unable to perform satisfactorily. Under conditions of primitive life there were no schools as we know them in most civilized communities today. As civilization advanced it became more difficult for the family, the religious leaders, and the community to teach children and youth the appreciations, understandings, and skills that were deemed essential to the welfare of the group and to the future of the individual. To meet this new demand the school emerged as a distinct social institution. As civilization continues to advance, more and more formal training seems to be required in the interests of both the individual and the community to which he belongs. The period of childhood is constantly lengthened and the period of time spent in school is constantly extended.

The chief function of the school, almost until our own time, has been training. As a residual institution it taught formally the indispensable subject matter that other institutions were unable to teach incidentally. Training became more and more a secondary function of other institutions, and more and more the primary function of the school. The other social institutions continued to share in training while serving the primary functions of rearing, feeding, clothing, sheltering, and inspiring, and also in consequence of their method — the way they treated their members — they developed the general qualities of personality assumed to be desirable in their common way of life. So far as the school was concerned these traits were at most a secondary consideration. The primary function of the school was conceived to be the teaching of specific subject matter that other educational agencies could not teach or could not teach satisfactorily.

But the very fact that the school requires more and more time for training the individual in subject matter indicates to the experimentalists that it must also assume responsibility for the achievement of desirable qualities of personality. So long as the conditions of life produce these qualities, the effort of the schools may be focused upon training in subject matter. But with the change from an agricultural to an industrial civilization, the personality traits usually designated as initiative, responsibility, independence, self-control, and the like, which the experimentalists idealize, receive less and less emphasis among people of school age. They do not share directly in the life of the industrial community in such a way as to develop these qualities as did the young people of the generations that shared in the agricultural communities. Moreover, the schools supply the chief occupation of more and more people for a longer and longer period. Besides, the home, the church, and the other social institutions emphasize less and less the desirable qualities of personality. *Responsibility for the achievment of these traits thus increasingly becomes a residual function of the modern school* in the same way that the achievement of certain subject-matter aims became increasingly a residual function of the traditional school. In other words, method outcomes as well as subject-matter outcomes should now command the attention of those responsible for school education.

The acceptance of the method function, through which these desirable qualities are to be realized, raises the question of how the change in emphasis in the school programs thus required should affect its recognized responsibility for specific training in subject matter. The educational experimentalists have not hesitated to face the problem squarely. They are not only willing to assume considerable responsibility for the method function; they are willing to assume responsibility for the traditional function of training. The very fact that responsibility for the outcomes of method is accepted signifies also that some adjustment must be made in the training program. First of all, the experimentalists distinguish clearly between the training function and the method function. They consider both indispensable, and in practice inseparable. Neither can be used as a substitute for the other, however. We must not think in terms of subject matter and let method take care of itself. Neither must we think entirely in terms of method and let the mastery of subject matter take care of itself. Both must be considered at all times.

For proper balance in emphasis we must provide some criteria for selecting both experiences and subject matter. The criteria proposed consist of the principles into which the experimentalists translate important features of educative experience. Experiences that meet the requirements of these principles, will, we believe, secure the desirable qualities of experience, which in their cumulative effect produce the desired traits of personality now recognized as the function of method. Such experiences, under normal conditions, also require sufficient mastery of subject matter, recognized as the function of training. In other words, both the achievement of desirable traits of personality and the mastery of essential subject matter are phases of a more inclusive process of desirable experience. In a word, both the outcomes of method and the outcomes of training may be minimum essentials. As Kilpatrick says, "There are certain things so useful for future progress in school and life, both immediate and more remote, that we should use compulsion if need be to get them, so important that if they are not got otherwise there would eventually come a time when we should, if need be, drop practically everything else." [4] Bode's objection to this recognition of minimium essentials as an inconsistent compromise of principles seems to assume that Kilpatrick would be satisfied with the qualities of experience under such conditions. If so, he would be surrendering principles and leaving the logical gates open for the authoritarians. It seems more likely, however, that Kilpatrick is simply recognizing the fact that the school has a training function as well as a method function, and that there are times in the kind of world in which we live when we have to limit education to training as a necessity of special conditions rather than as an ideal.[5]

The desirable qualities of present experience thus become the primary aims of all school education as well as of education in general. The development of desirable personality traits and the mastery of essential subject matter are both the effects of such experiences. There are times when it may seem necessary to place the primary emphasis on subject matter. For

---

[4] William Heard Kilpatrick, *Foundations of Method.* The Macmillan Company, New York, 1925. Pp. 365–366.

[5] Boyd H. Bode, *Modern Educational Theories.* The Macmillan Company, New York, 1927. Pp. 159–164.

instance, when a child seems to have the traits of personality that we so much desire but does not have the principles, facts, and skills which he needs or which he will need, we must somehow or other get him to engage in activities through which these things can be learned. Review and direct drill may both be required. Moreover, there are times when pupils must be forced to learn things in order to safeguard them against immediate dangers or future embarrassment. But whatever compulsion is required, it should be required with due regard to the desirable qualities of experience. When it is necessary to compel people to do things or to learn things for their own good, we should, above all, be reasonably sure that such things are really for their own good. We should also, in so far as possible, cause the required activities to culminate in experiences which are desirable. When some principle, such as acceptability, has to be violated, it should not be violated to any greater extent than is necessary to achieve the training thought to be essential.

The mastery of subject matter, considered by all to be essential, probably requires fewer experiences whose qualities are undesirable than at first sight might be expected. But, as already indicated, there may be times when we simply must do some things even if some quality or all qualities of the experiences involved are not desirable. Under such circumstances, we should not consider ourselves educators in the full sense. Education is not complete when attention is confined only to training. Nevertheless, *there may be times when training is more important than education.* It is more important when a choice has to be made between experiences whose qualities are desirable and experiences such as those which involve safeguarding individuals against physical handicaps and contagious diseases. It is more important when a choice has to be made between desirable experiences and training for war against enemies who idealize qualities of experience which experience itself finds undesirable. It is more important when a choice must be made between desirable experiences and learning things without which either the individual or society will be handicapped in some important respect. Such exceptions are not, however, exceptions to the principles of desirable experience as the all-inclusive standards of education. These exceptions simply mean that there are times when we have to quit education and engage in training, just as there are times when business and industry must cut down on the production of consumer goods to produce instruments of war.

The relativity theory of training thus places first things first. The desirable qualities of experience come first. Experiences lacking in such qualities are not educative in the approved sense. They constitute training and possibly even undesirable education. Nevertheless, they may be used, not because they are educative, but for other reasons. However, undesirable qualities of experience are to be avoided where possible, and when they cannot be avoided they should be used in such a way as to provide, in so far as possible, for subsequent experiences whose qualities are desirable.

This theory recognizes also the importance of the different types of training to which such conceptions as "general education," "vocational education," "moral education," and "religious education" call attention. There are certain appreciations, understandings, and skills that are indispensable to the welfare of the individual and to the stability of the social order. Experiences through which these outcomes and desirable personality traits are achieved constitute general education. The qualities of such experiences should be desirable. But there may be times, as we have already indicated, when the emphasis must be placed upon subject-matter outcomes to the apparent temporary neglect of desirable qualities of experience. Under such circumstances general education becomes mere training. There are certain subject-matter outcomes which must be realized. If they can be realized in experiences that are educative in the approved sense, so much the better; but they must be realized, nevertheless. What such outcomes may be cannot be indicated in general. They must be determined for particular pupils in particular situations, and they may, for the most part, be secured along with desirable personality traits in experiences whose qualities are desirable.

The relativity theory provides for vocational training in the same way. Every individual should be prepared to make his own living by performing some useful social service. Everyone should be permitted to make his own vocational or professional choice. After he has done so, he should learn those things that will enable him to serve effectively in the field for which he is preparing himself. On the other hand, such learning should not be conceived as mere training. The same traits of personality are equally important in all occupations. The subject-matter outcomes designed for specific occupations should be learned along with desirable personality traits in experiences whose qualities are desirable. Otherwise, vocational education degenerates into mere training. However, as in the case of general education, there are times when certain things must be learned whether the experiences through which they are learned are desirable or not. Whatever the demands of particular vocations may be for beginners, they must be met. The essentials must be required, but in so far as possible, they should be secured through experiences whose qualities are desirable.

The educational experimentalist prefers to think of spiritual values as including both morals and religious values. The activities or experiences through which such ends are realized may be conceived as including both moral and religious education. Some of the more important values are "co-operation," "self-denial," "self-sacrifice," "sense of duty," "loyalty," "respect for authority," "freedom," "aesthetic sensations and enjoyment," "persistency," and "tenacity of purpose." [6] There are, of course, many other points of emphasis and they may be classified in different ways. The experimentalist recognizes the importance of such general values and even their classification as social and individual, moral, aesthetic, and religious. It is even important, he admits, to have a clearly defined list of such widely recognized ideals. They are so important that we dare not neglect them. To do them justice requires special emphasis in varying situations. The better such values are defined, the less difficult it is to give them the emphasis they deserve. They should be as clearly defined as the values to be sought in general and vocational education, for without them, general education and vocational education are not as satisfactory as they should be. Still, these values should be given special emphasis on their own account.

Nevertheless, they should not be sought as fixed ends without reference to the qualities of desirable experience. They should be learned at such times and under such conditions that the activities required would contribute to, rather than detract from, these qualities. In fact, these spiritual values are such that they cannot be secured adequately through mere training. They are qualities that are not fixed in character. Unless the qualities of experience through which they are sought are desirable, the values themselves cannot be secured at all. Nor can these spiritual values be adequately secured as by-products of experience without any special attention, as the exponents of educational laissez faire seem to assume. On the other hand, they cannot be secured through methods of direct attack as authoritarians seem to assume. They require constant attention, otherwise important points of emphasis will be neglected. But to direct attention exclusively to

---

[6] John S. Brubacher and others, *The Public School and Spiritual Values*. Harper & Bros., New York, 1944. Pp. 17–25; 124–128.

them without reference to the qualities of desirable experience is to neglect the only process through which spiritual values can be realized.

The relativity theory of training emphasizes the importance of the relationship of method aims to subject-matter aims, but it also emphasizes the importance of the relationship of the so-called types of education to one another. The different types of education are not mere incidental by-products of the process of experience itself. They cannot be secured without direction and control, as the proponents of the incidental theory assume. Their adequate realization requires constant attention to subject matter as well as to method, but they cannot be so sharply separated as the proponents of the identification theory assume. For instance, general education is not the sole function of the old well-established subjects. Vocational education is not the sole function of the subjects usually considered vocational. Moral education has no separate and distinct subject matter. Religious education should not be limited to any prescribed content or materials.

The subject matter typically classified as indispensable to certain types of education is often useful if not essential in other kinds of education. *Some subject matter usually prescribed for vocational education is indispensable in general education.* Certain subjects in industrial education, agricultural education, business education, and home economics are necessary for all, whatever a person's vocation may be. Likewise, some of the subjects usually considered fundamental in general education contribute directly to various types of vocational education. Everyone knows that it is not only possible but desirable to conduct some of the so-called general courses somewhat differently, with an eye to the future occupations of the students enrolled. English, mathematics, science, or any other subjects usually conceived as necessary in general education, may be taught somewhat differently to the students who will go to college from the way it is taught to students who will go directly to work on the farm or in the factories.

The separation of moral and religious education from each other on the one hand and from other kinds of education on the other cannot be justified. A religious education that does not recognize the importance of moral standards is not desirable. By the same token, a moral education that does not secure the dynamic and driving power which religion supplies may be inadequate. Both are inextricably intertwined and should not be divided or compartmentalized on the basis of subject matter. It is quite possible for those in charge of the schools to give direct and concentrated attention to spiritual values from time to time, without organizing them into separate subjects. The current movement to have the public schools assume responsibility for religious education represents an important point of emphasis. Conceived of in terms of spiritual values, the public school should assume responsibility for religious education.

The public school should not assume responsibility for the teaching of isolated courses confined to the traditions of the church. Such a conclusion does not warrant, however, the failure of the schools to use the subject matter of the Christian tradition. That material is certainly as important and essential as the various other traditional materials that are used in the schools. The use of such materials is not only desirable but indispensable for general education and should be used by any and all teachers in the public schools as well as in the private schools. The study of such materials is not merely religious education; it is primarily general education. *The effort to introduce special courses in religious education would better be devoted to emphasizing the proper use of the traditional materials of the Christian religion by all schools and teachers everywhere.* Such a movement is educationally sound. The use of such material does not constitute religious education; moreover, its use is not inconsistent with our national tradition, for the incorporation of such material in the school program does not imply religious training in any narrow denominational sense. On the other hand, the organization of the materials of the Christian tradition into separate courses to be taught by special teachers is usually educationally undesirable from the standpoint of the qualities of desirable experience because it emphasizes subject-matter outcomes to the relative neglect of method outcomes. Practically speaking, it prevents teachers from using materials which they should use and justifies their neglect of spiritual values, which, after all, constitute the foundation of religious education.

In any adequate educational program the outcomes of both methods and subject matter should be considered. The qualities of desirable experience should supply the criteria on the basis of which proper emphasis is given to both. They should also be considered as standards in the selection and organization of material for use in the different types of education. If the qualities that experience itself finds desirable are used as criteria, then the current isolation and separation of various types of education might be overcome. The various forms of education would then be treated as important factors requiring special emphasis on their own account. They would be conceived as different kinds of training which are indispensable to education but which, nevertheless, do not constitute the whole of education. School education involves training, but it should never be reduced to mere training. When the qualities of experience which experience itself finds desirable are conceived as criteria of selection, provision is made for the proper emphasis upon the different types of training and also for the proper emphasis upon the effects of subject matter and of method in each practical educational situation. Then, too, when such criteria are recognized, the current tendency to separate vocational education from general education, or practical education from liberal education, can no longer be justified. *Any education is liberal education which emphasizes the qualities of experience that experience itself finds desirable.* But such qualities become increasingly difficult to secure when schools, departments, subjects, and courses representing special interests are separated and isolated from other schools, departments, subjects, and courses supposed to represent general and liberal education. Training in special fields is most effective when it has its setting in a background of more general interests, and training in general fields is most significant when it has visible connections with practical life.

CHAPTER 16

Educational Research

RESEARCH IS NOW WIDELY RECOGNIZED as an important field of special-ization in professional education. Some research is usually required of all students working for degrees in our graduate schools of education. The findings of educational research usually are supposed to have con-siderable significance for practical school programs and activities. Almost every large school system has its department of educational research. Some recognized students of education insist that every teacher is responsible not only for using the results of educational research but also for engaging in it himself. It appears, then, that one way of elaborating the meaning and significance of philosophies of education is to explain the meaning and implications of different theories of educational research. For convenience of reference, the three theories of educational research often assumed in current theory and practice may be designated as (1) the separate-subject-matter theory; (2) the functional-aspect theory; and (3) the scientific-method theory.

THE SEPARATE-SUBJECT-MATTER THEORY
(EDUCATIONAL AUTHORITARIANISM)

The separate-subject-matter theory of educational research is assumed by most educational authoritarians. There are two forms of this theory: (1) the science form, and (2) the art form. According to some authoritarians, education should be conceived as a science rather than as an art, while according to others, it should be conceived as an art rather than as a science.

1. According to those who adopt the *science form*, we have, or should have, a science of education, just as we have a science of mathematics, physics, chemistry, biology, and psychology. According to this theory, the first step to be taken in the development of a science of education is to stop thinking of it as merely an art and to think of it as a science. The schools could become scientific very rapidly if they would only

abandon the traditional and empirical principles and practices that influence every art. We should look to the educational research worker to determine the aims, subject matter, and methods of teaching, supervision, and administration, as well as the methods of testing results. According to this point of view, the number of research specialists should be greatly increased and the use of the results of scientific studies should be extended as rapidly as possible.

In line with this form of the separate-subject-matter theory of educational research, students of education have insisted that it is quite possible for specialists to determine just what aims or values the schools should seek to achieve. Usually they undertake to discover the abilities, knowledge, and ideals that people will need as adults, not merely in some particular field but in all fields, not merely for some particular occupation but for the general occupation of living as members of society. With such aims, objectives, or values determined, it would become the business of the schools to realize them in terms of changes produced in the thought, feeling, and conduct of pupils. The proponents of this view admit that some of these values can be achieved incidentally without the help of the schools. They insist, however, that the research worker as an educational scientist has the responsibility of determining which values may be secured incidentally and which require the help of the school. The school and the teacher should look to educational research to determine their aims or purposes.

In like manner, they insist that some kinds of subject matter are more useful than others in securing these values. It is possible, they contend, for the educational scientist to select the right subject matter. In fact, it is his responsibility to do so. It is his obligation also to organize it in the best possible way and indicate what materials should be used at different grade levels and even by pupils of varying capacities and interests. Then it is the obligation of the school and the teacher to accept the recommendations of the educational scientist pertaining to the selection, organization, and grade placement of subject matter.

Furthermore, these scientific students of education contend that some methods are best for some things and other methods are best for other things. It is the responsibility of the educational scientist to determine the best methods of teaching the different kinds of subject matter and of securing the different kinds of educational aims. It then becomes the obligation of the school and the teacher to use these methods to secure the scientifically determined objectives by scientifically teaching the scientifically determined materials.

Moreover, this program of educational research should provide methods of testing both the capacities and the achievements of pupils. It should determine the levels of achievement that pupils of varying capacity should accomplish in specific periods of time. It should thus provide for separating pupils into sections and groups on the basis of their abilities. It is the further responsibility of the educational scientist to supply objective methods of testing the results of various methods of learning and teaching. If pupils do not learn what they are supposed to learn through the use of the standard procedures, the educational scientist should even produce the necessary remedial technique to be used in making good the deficiencies. The teacher, the school, the supervisor, and the administrator thus might have at their disposal all the scientific ends and means required for making education a science and removing from it much tradition, opinion, and guesswork.

Those who adopt this form of the separate-subject-matter theory usually think of professional schoolworkers as belonging to two relatively distinct groups. *The business of one group is educational research or the scientific study of education; the business of the other group, often called fieldworkers, is teaching, supervision, administration, and whatever practical work is required in the actual development of policies, programs, and activities of the school.* The educational scientists keep those in direct charge of the schools informed of the ends to be sought and the means by which they are to be achieved. To secure the most satisfactory results, those directly responsible for running the schools must keep themselves informed on the scientific aims of education and the scientific means by which these aims are to be realized. If they seek the ends prescribed by the means prescribed, the exponents of this form of the separate-subject-matter theory contend that education will become a real science like the other recognized sciences.

The foregoing is the ultimate ideal of the so-called scientific movement in education. The proponents of this theory recognize, of course, that, as a matter of fact, in practice many compromises and halfway measures must be adopted for the time being. As an ideal, those directly responsible for the operation of the schools should confine themselves largely to their respective spheres of teaching, supervision, and administration, and leave educational research to the specialists in this field who are qualified by nature, training, and experience, to do this work efficiently. Of course, a teacher, supervisor, or administrator may engage in research, but to that extent he is largely sacrificing his efficiency in his own field of professional service. As a matter of ethical obligation he should do one and leave the other alone, except when circumstances force him to study some service problem in the immediate situation.

In line with this theory of research and its correlative attitude toward those directly responsible for the operation of the schools is the present movement to establish a dualism between research and teaching in our colleges and universities. The distinction between the Master's and the Doctor's degrees in education and the A.M. and Ph.D. degrees emphasizes this separation of functions. It suggests that some students are to be prepared to do a superior quality of practical schoolwork while others are to be prepared for research. Recently, in conferences devoted to the problem of teacher education, the distinction between research and teaching has been sharply drawn. The presidents of some teachers colleges are now developing the belief that they should employ teachers and not research workers. In other words, the universities should do the research work and the teachers colleges should teach the scientific findings of research to their students, who will in turn put them into effect in the elementary and secondary schools.

Perhaps not all authoritarians would be willing to accept the full logical implications of this form of the separate-subject-matter theory. Doubtless, some would admit, as already suggested, the necessity for limited research on the part of practitioners. Obviously, it is necessary for certain individuals responsible for educational programs and activities to secure reliable information in dealing with immediate problems, and they may be able to obtain it only by engaging in personal research. However, according to this separate-subject-matter theory, such practical conditions should be remedied as soon as possible. Every school and every school system should have available research scientists on whom they can depend for reliable information. The necessity for doing a thing under certain conditions is no justification for maintaining the conditions. The conditions in the whole field of education should be changed as rapidly as possible so that each practitioner will have access to the findings of the science of education and the assistance of research specialists as they are needed.

Research should ultimately be of three kinds. First, educational scientists should secure adequate and reliable evidence as to ends and means; second, other students of education should make available the findings of the so-called educational scientists; and third, other research specialists associated with the schools should deal with immediate school problems. If this threefold program were fully developed, those directly responsible for the operation of the schools, so it is thought, would recognize the importance of educational research, and would keep themselves informed on the latest findings of scientific research relative to aims, subject matter, methods of teaching, and methods of evaluation, organization, and administration. They would introduce the results of scientific studies of education into the operation of the schools as rapidly as possible, utilize the services of research specialists in their own schools and school systems, and co-operate in introducing the new measures provided by the specialized experts in the field of scientific educational research. They would not then have to engage in research themselves; their research would be confined to keeping up with the research of others and applying it to school practice.

From the standpoint of the philosophy of experimentalism, this theory of educational research, like other authoritarian theories of school practice, is unsatisfactory. In the first place, there is no science of education consisting of a body of subject matter comparable to that of the well-established sciencies, and no such body of reliable knowledge can be accumulated in the foreseeable future. In the second place, the problems to be investigated cannot be reduced to wholesale aims, subject matter, and methods of teaching, supervision, and administration, as seems to be implicit in the foregoing programs. In the third place, the qualities of experience that such a program engenders are quite different from the qualities which experience itself finds desirable. The first two objections will be considered in connection with the discussion of the theory of research that educational experimentalism supports, and further elaboration is here confined to the third objection; namely, the qualities of experience emphasized.

The exponents of the science form of the separate-subject-matter theory seem to think that the findings of the scientific research workers in the field of education are fixed requirements at least, until they are revised in the light of further research by these scientists themselves. In other words, the aims and methods of whatever kind proposed are the very aims and procedures that should be adopted by the schools. Such a program means that the qualities of flexibility, widening sociality, acceptability, originality, intelligence, and purposefulness, which are of primary importance according to the experimentalists, must be neglected. If those in direct charge of the schools take their ends and means directly from the findings of educational research, they themselves cannot make real discoveries. Many must merely follow directions. The pupils, too, must do what they are told. To be more specific, suppose the schools use the prescribed instruments for measuring the outcomes of instruction and limit their evaluation of results to what the educational scientist prescribes. Then the qualities of experience that the experimentalists emphasize would be neglected. This is just what Kilpatrick had in mind when he made the distinction between "primary" and "concomitant learning," and what he had in mind in "some outcomes yet to be measured." [1]

The concomitant learnings and the outcomes yet to be measured are the cumulative effects of the very qualities of experience that the experimentalists consider primary. Of course, the authoritarian exponents of this form of the separate-subject-matter theory of research may reply that these so-called primary values will some day be measured. But the rejoinder of the experimentalists is that in the meantime the schools must continue to operate, and that to emphasize only what the scientific tests measure signifies the neglect of the very things that are most important. *The only way education can become scientific is for those who operate the schools to become scientific,* and the first form of the separate-subject-matter theory of research seems to prevent rather than to facilitate their becoming so.

2. In the *art form* of the separate-subject-matter theory adopted by the educational authoritarians, education is considered an art rather than a science. The proponents of this theory think of science entirely in terms of subject matter rather than in terms of method. Realizing that there is no separate body of scientific subject matter in education corresponding to that of such sciences as mathematics, physics, or chemistry, they contend that education is an art and must remain an art. Consistent with the logic of their position, they contend that any science of education is impossible. Moreover, as they see the situation, any effort to render it more scientific is futile and must do more harm than good. They are, of course, thinking largely in terms of teaching rather than in terms of administration and supervision, and it is from the standpoint of teaching that this attitude is here considered.

According to this form, those who engage in educational research are deluding themselves if they think they are performing a social service. Education is an art and can never be a science. Any so-called

[1] J. Carleton Bell (Editor), *Contributions to Education.* World Book Company, Yonkers-on-Hudson, New York, 1924. Pp. 86–97.

William Heard Kilpatrick, *The Foundations of Method.* The Macmillan Company, New York, 1923. Pp. 100–108.

rules, procedures, or whatnot, to be derived through educational experimentation and investigation have little or no application beyond the confines of the particular research studies themselves. Such studies may be meaningful and significant to those who engage in them, but they are meaningless and insignificant to those who are directly responsible for the operation of the schools. The best preparation for teaching is a knowledge of the subject to be taught, common sense, and personality. The teacher who has these assets need not worry about any devices and techniques that the educational scientists can provide. With these prerequisites any teacher can teach efficiently. Some individuals are born with good personalities, and others are born without them. Those who are not born with this indispensable essential can never become good teachers. Those who are born with such personalities still have to learn the subject matter which they teach. The born teacher equipped with the right personality and the right subject matter has no use for the findings of so-called scientific research specialists in the field of education. The teacher should, of course, keep informed on the achievements of research in the subject-matter field in which he is teaching. In other words, so-called scholarly or academic research is important; that is, the source of the subject matter to be taught. But keeping informed on what should be taught and on how it should be taught is futile and worthless. According to this theory these matters should be left entirely to tradition and empirical opinion. The personality of the born teacher and the knowledge of the subject to be taught constitute the sole requisites of the artist teacher.

What is true of the teacher is by implication true of the supervisor and the administrator. What should the administrator and the supervisor do but select teachers who know their subjects and have the right kind of personalities? For these officials, as for teachers, personality, academic knowledge, and good common sense are quite sufficient. Moreover, the revelations of the so-called science of educational research should be avoided by those in control of the schools. As these authoritarian artist educators see the situation, any kind of professional education course deals either with things that are perfectly obvious to the born teacher, or with the so-called scientific things that are irrelevant. Those who engage in research to find out what should be taught and how it should be taught are doing great damage to the teaching profession. They deal in "pedaguese." They cannot teach themselves, but they can show others how to teach.

Those who are subjected to the mysteries of this "pedaguese," in which it is thought that the professor of education deals, may be seriously handicapped for teaching. Teaching is an art, and the personality of the born teacher should have free play. If he is loaded down with the so-called rules, devices, and techniques in which the mystical professor of education traffics, then his personality may be routinized and mechanized so that he loses his human touch and spontaneity. The teacher is an artist, and any effort to make him a scientist is not only futile but positively inimical to the teaching profession.

From the standpoint of the philosophy of experimentalism, this form of the separate-subject-matter theory is right in rejecting education as a science conceived in terms of subject matter because there is no available separate body of subject matter that can be called the science of education. But it is wrong in assuming that educational practice cannot become more scientific. There is available much subject matter in such fields as psychology, sociology, biology, physics, chemistry, and philosophy that can and should be used by the schools.[2] Needless to say, the proper use of such materials should render those responsible for school education more intelligent with respect to what they are doing. *To the degree that school people become more intelligent, the art of education becomes more of a science.*

In other words, the antithesis between the conception of education as an art and the conception of it as a science breaks down. A knowledge of recognized schemes and techniques has never been known to affect unfavorably the artist in other fields. As a matter of fact, the artists in all the specialized fields learn the techniques of their art. They utilize all the data that any research renders available in the improvement of techniques. Certainly the educator should do no less. The science of education cannot make teachers, but it can help. It is quite possible that some of the best teachers, like some of the best cooks, cannot explain and analyze what they do. But it would not do them any harm to be able to analyze or explain their procedures as the scientific teacher can do. In fact, the only way the artist teacher can become widely influential is by learning to analyze and explain his art so that others who have not observed him can use, at least as sources of suggestion, the principles and procedures he has emphasized. *To make available such material, the artist teacher must also be a scientific teacher.*

The art form of the separate-subject-matter theory of educational research is effective only in its attack on the science form of this theory.

---

[2] John Dewey, *Sources of a Science of Education.* Horace Liveright, New York, 1929. Pp. 48–57.

It loses its force when compared with the functional-aspect theory and with the scientific-method theory, yet to be considered. In these two theories the science of education is conceived quite differently from the way in which it is conceived in either form of the separate-subject-matter theory. If the science of education is conceived in terms of a separate body of subject matter, the authoritarians who reject education as a science are right. But the science of education may be conceived in other ways.

THE FUNCTIONAL-ASPECT THEORY
(EDUCATIONAL LAISSEZ FAIRE)

For convenience of reference, the attitude toward educational research adopted by the exponents of educational laissez faire may be designated as the functional-aspect theory. According to this theory or principle, educational research is just as important as the authoritarians contend, but it is very different from their conception of it and entails very different obligations for both research experts and practical schoolworkers. The existence of a body of scientific subject matter in the field of education is denied. The need for a group of scientific experts devoted to educational research operating outside the schools and school systems is also denied. The real research is to be done by people in the field of school practice. There is a place for specialists in educational research, but that place is in the field, not in some university separate from the school.

It seems convenient to begin with the actual learning-teaching situation, just where the exponents of the functional-aspect theory of educational research begin. The pupils and the teacher are all engaged in research. The pupils have purposes which they are trying to elaborate, express, realize, or actualize. They must, therefore, study the conditions in order to realize their goals. Such study, from the standpoint of the exponents of educational laissez faire, is educational research. To keep the pupils engaged in educational research, which is their primary business, the teachers themselves must engage in research. They need to know as much about the pupils as they can in order to discover their needs, interests, or purposes. They need to know as much as possible about the community and the school in order to provide the conditions under which the goals of the pupils can be most readily achieved. The *function of the research expert is to help the teacher in his research work in the actual situation.*

The exponents of educational laissez faire think of education largely as removing obstacles and preparing conditions under which pupils can engage in research. Teachers, supervisors, and administrators have an obligation to provide these conditions. The educational research specialists who keep themselves informed about what is going on in certain "progressive schools" should, therefore, be very helpful. They can aid those in charge of the schools in finding means of removing difficulties and of preparing an adequate educational environment in which pupils can realize their own purposes. While the educational authoritarians emphasize the importance of separating educational research from educational practice, the exponents of educational laissez faire emphasize the importance of confining it largely to practical situations.

From the standpoint of the philosophy of experimentalism, the exponents of educational laissez faire are right in thinking that educational research should be functionally related to school practice, but they are wrong in thinking that it is merely an aspect of practice. *The problems of educational research are the problems of those in charge of the operation of the schools. But they are not always merely problems of particular people, schools, and school systems.* They include such problems, but they also include problems common to many individuals, schools, and school systems.

To be more specific, it is the business of educational research specialists to help teachers deal with their immediate problems. They can help them to study the pupils and the conditions under which the pupils work. However, the experts can do these things more effectively if they engage in research of a much more comprehensive kind than is required in particular situations. Even when dealing with the so-called immediate problems, they must take time out for study and investigation. If they are too closely tied to the practical situation where immediate results must be realized, they cannot develop solutions and principles of wide application. Even the teacher, who, according to this theory, is an educational research worker, must take time out for study and investigation if his solutions of problems are to be scientific.

Those who do effective educational research must be interested in more than immediate results. They must be interested in the discovery of principles and procedures of general application. Moreover, they must have time for study and experimentation. If the teacher and the research specialist assume that the aims of education and the methods of learning are to be produced entirely *de novo* in every situation, then, of course the responsibility for educational research consists merely in providing conditions under which pupils themselves engage in research. *The teacher engages in research to help the pupils engage in research.* The research specialist, because of his broader preparation and broader experience, is able to make valuable suggestions to the teacher.

From the standpoint of the experimentalists, however, this kind of educational research is not sufficient. The immediate aims of pupils are not adequate educational aims, and the immediate procedures of pupils are not adequate methods of learning. Educational research specialists should make available materials that teachers can use in selecting aims and methods. Such materials cannot be secured in the immediate situation. Teachers must use these materials intelligently and the scientific expert in education can assist them in doing so. But as a research scientist he has facilities that enable him to do this work more effectively.

From the standpoint of the philosophy of experimentalism, this theory of educational research is unsatisfactory. The qualities of experience of the pupils, whose immediate purposes are taken as the proper ends of education, are not desirable. The qualities of experience of the teacher, who accepts such purposes as aims, are not desirable. There is little place for creativity, widening sociality, purposeful activity, or intelligent choice on the part of either teacher or pupil. Although educational research thus conceived is functionally related to teaching, as it should be, it becomes only an aspect of teaching, which is in turn only an aspect of the activities involved in the development of the so-called purposes of the pupil. These purposes are themselves undesirable because they do not require the operation of intelligence in their selection.

The Scientific-Method Theory
(Educational Experimentalism)

The theory of educational research acceptable to the educational experimentalists may be designated as the scientific-method theory. According to this theory, science is primarily a method rather than a body of subject matter. It is impossible to draw a sharp line between scientific subjects and other subjects. In other words, it is impossible to explain the meaning of science in terms of subject matter. Perhaps there is no definite body of scientific materials. If there were, many fields that we now consider scientific would have to be excluded. In terms of method, on the other hand, *any field is scientific to the degree that it is removed from empirical judgments and routine performance.* Physics and chemistry may be more scientific than biology, psychology, and sociology, and engineering may be more scientific than education. But all of them may be scientific and capable of becoming more so.

Education, like mechanical engineering, may be considered as an art; but just as the science of physics may be more scientific than the science of psychology, so the art of bridge-building as a form of mechanical engineering may be more scientific than school education as a form of man-building. Just as the art of bridge-building becomes more and more scientific through the use of the materials of the sciences on which its systematic improvement depends, so the art of education may become more scientific through the use of the materials of the sciences on which its systematic improvement depends. *The function of educational research is thus to render school education more scientific.* Stated somewhat differently, scientific research in education should remove as rapidly as possible routine performance and empirical opinion from the activities of those in charge of the schools and render educators more intelligent about what they are doing.

To serve the aforementioned end, educational research or science must utilize the materials of science in dealing with school problems. If we may call the topics, problems, or issues that arise in the process of school education the subject-matter content of educational research and the data borrowed from the various sciences the subject-matter materials of educational research, then the science of education does have a subject matter, but a subject matter that is separate neither from school practice nor from the other sciences. The science of education then utilizes scientific methods and procedures, which the authoritarians emphasize, and deals with school practice, which the exponents of laissez faire emphasize. It does not confine itself to general features of education, such as aims, methods, and materials, which the authoritarians seem to advocate. It does not limit itself to the study of immediate school problems, as the exponents of laissez faire seem to advocate. *Educational research becomes a responsibility of both research specialists and field workers.*

The scientific research specialist serves a residual function. He serves the fieldworkers and practitioners in dealing with problems beyond their capacity to solve. The problems with which he deals are not the private, disparate problems of a science of education independent of school practice. They are problems that arise in practice.

They are difficulties that teachers, supervisors, and administrators in the field have to face. They are the difficulties which the practitioners are unable to master because they are too busy with other things and are not adequately equipped to handle such problems. These problems require the assistance of research specialists in the school or in the school system or in the educational research division of the college and the university. Some problems may be solved through the use of these findings and of scientific studies that have already been made, and others may require further original studies and experimentation. Available materials will be useful in proportion to the degree that the problems investigated in previous research are closely related to the problems that arise in the field.

But practitioners everywhere face certain limited problems with which they can deal and to which research specialists do not now have and cannot ever have immediate access. These problems involve deciding what specific groups in actual situations should learn; selecting subject-matter content, materials, and methods to be used at particular times and places with particular groups. These problems are what Waples and Tyler have called "service studies." [3] Such problems arise in specific classes, schools, and school systems where there are no educational research specialists. These local research problems are just as real, important, and significant to fieldworkers engaged in actual schoolwork as the problems of wider application are to the research specialists. Moreover, it is to these more immediate difficulties of actual school situations that the more specialized problems of the educational scientists should be related, and their contribution to the solution of these problems gives their studies meaning and significance. Stated somewhat differently, *educational research, to be effective, must begin and end in school practice.* Practice sets the problems and tests the results of educational research of all kinds.

The practitioner or fieldworker may engage in research of three different kinds. He may participate in the more general and specialized research studies conducted by specialists; he may get so interested in particular problems that they become hobbies for him; or he may consider research an essential aspect of his profession. The first type of research work consists in the co-operation of fieldworkers with experts who are dealing with the more general specialized problems to which attention has been called. If the fieldworker can understand

---

[3] Douglas Waples and Ralph W. Tyler, *Research Methods and Teachers' Problems.* The Macmillan Company, New York, 1930. Pp. 1–28; 75–81.

what the problems are and is interested in their solution, he should by all means lend his assistance. But if he cannot understand them and is not interested in them, he may still provide the information required for their solution. From the standpoint of the philosophy of experimentalism, the fieldworker is not actually engaged in scientific research himself unless he senses the problems and sees the relationship of his contribution to their solution.

When the fieldworker participates in studies of the second type, he becomes a part-time research worker. However, such studies should help rather than hinder him in serving the functions of his particular vocation. Hobbies of this kind serve as an avocational interest and render the individual more intelligent in doing the things which his vocation demands of him. Moreover, the findings that he can apply in dealing with his own problem often may be made available for the use of others confronted with similar problems. From the standpoint of the philosophy of experimentalism, research of this kind is scientific provided that it makes use of available scientific techniques, and it may render the art of education more scientific.

In the third form of research in which the fieldworker may engage, he conceives of research as an essential aspect of his occupation. Whether he is a teacher, a supervisor, or an administrator, he does not accept without thought some prescribed plan, purpose, or scheme to be followed. He develops policies, plans, and programs of his own. The development of such programs requires the use of subject matter which research specialists have provided or may provide. It may involve a study and analysis of previous research; or experimentation to solve specific problems related to the more inclusive ones. Whatever one's specific duties may be, this kind of research, for which many practical school people assume responsibility, is exemplified in the activities of those teachers continually engaged in developing and reconstructing their courses of instruction.

Some teachers in the elementary school, the high school, and the college recognize the importance of developing their own courses of instruction. From the standpoint of educational experimentalism, as everyone knows, official courses of study can be at best only general and suggestive. They all have to be adapted to the demands of the practical situation, involving a consideration of local conditions and the needs of particular individuals and groups enrolled in the schools. The teacher who is constantly studying the powers and needs of his pupils, the materials and equipment of the school, and the instructional resources of the community, should make many and varied modifications of any fixed course of study. If there is no official course of study, he should make his own. In such planning, the teacher takes into account the available official aims, content, materials, and procedures. He thinks of all these in the light of changing conditions in the community, in the school, in the pupils, and even in himself. Some teachers do not think of the making and remaking of such courses of instruction as ever complete. They are a prominent aspect of the teacher's work and grow as the teacher grows. Such planning involves choosing aims, defining content, and selecting materials and procedures in the light of changing demands of particular situations. The construction and use of such courses of instruction require the analysis of various proposed aims of education, the subject-matter content that has been outlined in the field, and the selection, accumulation, and arrangement of materials. The constant making and remaking of such courses of study, including the study of the various factors to be considered, involves research of vital significance to both pupils and teachers.

From the standpoint of the philosophy of experimentalism, this kind of research should receive more and more recognition. It is a type of study in which supervisors and administrators, as well as teachers, should engage. They may not produce a course of instruction, but they can develop a program that will encourage and help teachers in such planning. Such programs require research by supervisors and administrators just as the development of courses of instruction requires research by the teacher. This kind of research will be vital and meaningful to them; it will be as significant for the teacher as the teacher's research in the development of courses of instruction is significant for his pupils.

According to the scientific-method theory, *to separate school practice from research,* as some authoritarians recommend, *is to extract intelligence from practice and significance from research.* To abandon educational research and its findings on the ground that teachers are born and not made, as other authoritarians recommend, is pure nonsense. If the use of science renders other arts flexible and intelligent, it should do no less for the art of education. To abandon advance planning and the utilization of the findings of research as a specialized service merely because practical educational situations are unique is also silly. *It is necessary to plan in order to get others to plan, and it is necessary to engage in research in order to get others to engage in research.* Moreover, materials that the research specialists in the field of education have made available should be used along with those which research in other fields have made available wherever and whenever they are pertinent to the requirements of the situation at hand. Such a theory of educational research emphasizes in practice the very qualities of desirable experience on the part of research specialists, fieldworkers, and pupils that experience itself finds desirable.

CHAPTER 17

Devices and Techniques

IN THE DISCUSSION OF SCHOOL PROBLEMS, devices signify typical forms and procedures that may be used as means to ends in educational activities and programs, and techniques signify the process of using these instruments. For instance, in courses in the methods and principles of teaching, the textbook is a device and the method of using it is a technique; the question is a device and questioning is a technique; the lecture is a device and lecturing is a technique. They are so closely related that they cannot always be distinguished in practice. For purposes of reference in a study like this, perhaps either term may be satisfactory. For example, the distinction between the question and questioning usually does not seem very important. We might use the term *method, form,* or *procedure,* or even *means,* but because all these words have special meanings, their use here might be misleading. Consequently, we shall use *devices and techniques* as a single conception to include both the means and the use of the means, whatever they may be. It must be clearly understood, however, that devices and techniques include much more than materials and procedures in learning and teaching. They include all kinds of means used in teaching, but they also include all kinds of means used in guidance, curriculum-making, administration, and supervision. For instance, they refer to formulations of aims, schemes of organization in both education and administration, methods of conducting improvement programs, and procedures in teaching and curriculum-making, considered in other chapters. Our problem here consists mainly in formulating and elaborating theories or principles of devices and techniques in general, which include the various kinds of devices and techniques already considered as aspects of other features of school practice.

IMPORTANCE OF THE PROBLEM

Some readers may feel that if different kinds of procedures have been considered already, any discussion of devices and techniques is now superfluous and unnecessary. Other more experienced readers may be quite aware that the topic of means, procedures, or devices and techniques in general has been given very little attention in educational literature and, therefore, they cannot see any justification for considering it as a feature of school practice. Still others who are sensitive to the logic of the position so far implicit in this whole study may feel that the topic here under consideration has never been developed by the experimentalists themselves and that its consideration here is logically irrelevant.

At first thought, such objections are understandable, but with a little more reflection it is clear that they miss the main point. According to the position developed throughout this study *it is quite possible for a person to understand the formulation of general theories or principles and still not understand them as aspects of a single, more inclusive theory or principle.* When the various theories of different kinds of devices and techniques already considered are understood as less inclusive phases of a more inclusive theory or principle of devices and techniques, this more comprehensive insight may be seen to have wider applications than all the definable theories or principles which it embodies. The theory of devices and techniques to be developed may be seen as applicable to all forms and procedures consisting of means to ends in all fields of school education, as well as in all the affairs of life where education is considered important.

It is true that devices and techniques as such have been given little attention in educational literature. It must be emphasized, however, that devices and techniques of one kind or another have not been neglected. Courses and textbooks in general methods and principles and techniques of teaching are often devoted largely to devices and techniques. Even courses and textbooks in administration and supervision, like courses in method, are often devoted more to the consideration of schemes, devices, and procedures than to the elaboration of general principles. In school practice everywhere, devices of many kinds are used day in and day out, year in and year out. They include daily reports, blackboards, roll calls, assignment of seats, and literally hundreds of things familiar to us all. In fact, if not in theory, devices and techniques constitute a universal feature of school practice everywhere. They are so common and have to be used so often that the attitudes which students of education and fieldworkers — including teachers, administrators, supervisors, and others responsible for school programs — assume toward them have tremendous practical significance.

As for the failure of the experimentalists to deal with the topic in systematic discussion, it may be said that they nevertheless have not neglected it altogether. William James, in his *Talks to Teachers*, published in 1899, shows conclusively that he does take a definite stand on devices and techniques of all kinds, in the fields of logic and morals as well as in the field of education.[1] Likewise, John Dewey shows conclusively in his *Sources of a Science of Education*, published in 1929, that he takes a similar stand.[2] In fact, there is running through the whole philosophical and educational literature that the experimentalists have developed a clear distinction between devices and techniques and the principles that should govern their use. Moreover, the very fact that students of education and fieldworkers who verbally endorse educational experimentalism, as well as those who oppose it, often do not make the distinction is sufficient reason for emphasizing it in a study like this. To be more explicit, the exponents of experimentalism are both philosophers and practical fieldworkers. The position they take under given conditions usually means using some devices or techniques as, for instance, the adoption of the subject organization, or some procedure in teaching such as the lecture method. Immediately they are accused of talking one thing and doing another.[3] As a matter of fact, they do not ever identify principles with devices and techniques. One purpose of the discussion of the topic here is to render explicit their attitude toward devices and techniques, which is clearly implicit in the whole tradition of educational experimentalism and in its underlying general philosophy.

It is not difficult to distinguish different theories of devices and techniques corresponding to the other theories of experience and school practice constituting educational authoritarianism, educational laissez faire, and educational experimentalism. In the use of terms, however, we must do our best, as we have in the case of designating theories of other features of school practice. For convenience of reference, we shall designate the authoritarian attitude as the best-method theory; the laissez-faire attitude as the direct-suggestion theory; and the experimental attitude as the critical-construction theory. We now turn to the explanation and elaboration of these three theories.

[1] William James, *Talks to Teachers*. Henry Holt and Company, New York, 1899. Pp. 7–11.

[2] John Dewey, *Sources of a Science of Education*. Liveright Publishing Company, New York, 1929. Pp. 14; 32–33; 36–39.

[3] Herman Harrell Horne, *The Democratic Philosophy of Education*. The Macmillan Company, New York, 1932. Pp. 207–208.

The Best-Method Theory
(Educational Authoritarianism)

The best-method theory, constituting an important principle of educational authoritarianism, assumes that best methods in general for doing every kind of thing that should be done can be discovered in advance of the specific situations in which they are to be used. It is readily admitted that few people use regularly the best procedures. The explanation offered for such failure to use the best instruments or failure to use them in the best ways is that the best devices and techniques have not been discovered yet, or that practitioners have not learned them. Still, according to this theory, there is not the slightest doubt about the existence of such best ways. The problem that confronts students of education and fieldworkers alike is how to discover their techniques, and how to use them effectively.

In general, the educational expert and the practitioner are supposed to be responsible for different aspects of the problem. The experts are mainly responsible for discovering the best devices and techniques, and the practitioners are responsible for learning and using them. For instance, there is some universally best way of organizing the school system, such as the 6-3-3 plan, the 6-6 plan, the 6-4-4 plan, or some other method. There is some best method of teaching anything; some best method of teaching each psychological type of thing, such as knowledge, appreciation, and skill; some best method of teaching each subject, such as reading, geography, and arithmetic; some best method of conducting improvement programs, such as the ascending method or the descending method. In fact, from the standpoint of the best-method theory, teachers, supervisors, and administrators alike should use the best methods possible, and it is the function of students of education to make these instruments understandable, although on occasion both experts and fieldworkers may make important discoveries concerning new devices and techniques.

In general, three different methods of discovering best devices and techniques have been employed: (1) the survey method; (2) the intuition method; and (3) the experimentation method.

1. The *survey method* of discovering devices and techniques usually involves one or more of these three types of study: (*a*) the questionnaire study; (*b*) the observation study; and (*c*) the record study. After we have analyzed these different aspects of the survey method of discovering

devices and techniques, we shall devote our attention to the methods of intuition and experimentation.

(a) The questionnaire study, as one form of the survey method of discovering devices and techniques, consists in formulating a series of questions about how things are done or about how they should be done in some specific field, or perhaps more often both, and sending them to practitioners and authorities in the field under consideration. In this way, students of education, and practitioners as well, collect considerable information concerning what things are done and how they are done, and also considerable information concerning what things recognized authorities think should be done and how they think they should be done. Of course, no investigator considers a device or technique good merely because some one has used it or merely because some one thinks it is good. However, those procedures which are generally used in the schools or school systems and which are considered good by recognized authorities are often accepted as good. Some students of education seem to consider the questionnaire method to be the best method of finding out what methods are used in important places and what methods are endorsed by important people in the various fields.

(b) The observation study as a general form of the survey method is very similar to the questionnaire approach. The investigator sees the devices and techniques actually in operation and interviews individuals in regard to these procedures instead of studying them indirectly through correspondence. He looks for the best methods for doing things and not merely for suggestions that may be helpful in dealing with immediate situations demanding attention. A good illustration of this approach to the discovery of best methods is to be found in the attitude of many teachers toward observing the teaching of other teachers. Usually both demonstration teachers and observing teachers are eager to have everything happen just right. The demonstrator appears to believe that it is his function to show others how things should be done. The observer, on the other hand, wishes to see how certain things ought to be done so that he can in turn do likewise in his own school. Some who are responsible for conducting observation courses are very eager that the teaching to be observed be especially good, thus apparently assuming that they are showing the observers how to teach, and not that they are supplying opportunities to see both the good and the bad for purposes of suggestion and appraisal.

(c) The record study as the third form of the survey method of discovering devices and techniques refers to the study of the descriptions and explanations of methods, schemes, and other measures which educators have actually used or recommended for the use of others. For example, one of the best ways by which the teacher can discover the best devices and techniques of teaching, so the exponents of the best-method theory assume, is to study the methods of such famous teachers as Socrates, Jesus, Pestalozzi, Froebel, Herbart, Colonel Parker, and William H. Kilpatrick. Likewise, the best way for practical school administrators to discover the best devices and techniques of school administration, so the exponents of the best-method theory contend, is to study the methods employed by such schoolmen as Horace Mann, William T. Harris, William R. Harper, C. W. Elliott, Henry S. Pritchett, and James Earl Russell. The practices and recommendations of great teachers and administrators, according to this point of view, are to be studied, not to secure suggestions of things that may be done but to find out the best things to do. Apparently those who use this way of discovering best methods believe that individuals endowed with genius have special access to realities in which all the best ways of doing every kind of thing are permanently imbedded.

2. The *intuition method* of discovering best devices and techniques is suggested in the reference to the peculiar capacity attributed to the genius for dealing with undertakings with which the consideration of the record study was brought to a close. It suggests intuition as the best method of discovering best methods. Great educators have not always been highly educated individuals as education is generally understood. In what, then, does their greatness lie? How do they discover the best devices and techniques? The most obvious answer is that somehow they pierce the secrets of spiritual reality by means of intuition, which, in the minds of some people, is the one gateway through which mortals communicate with the eternal. What the great educators have done may be conceived as possible for others. Some practitioners, according to certain exponents of the best-method theory, may secure the best devices and techniques of doing things by just letting themselves communicate with the encompassing spirit that is immanent in the world and also transcends it. Reality thus whispers her ways through the spiritual language of intuition which only the spiritually gifted can understand. Many of the procedures that are recognized as universally best in many fields are thus conceived as merely the record of the peculiar insight and intuition of the genius in the schools and other social institutions.

3. The *experimentation method* of discovering best devices and techniques ranges all the way from common observation and reflection on existing practices to controlled comparative laboratory studies. When recognized scientific procedures are applied by recognized scientific experts in the field of education, the devices and techniques they recommend or suggest challenge the respect of many students of education as well as many fieldworkers. They are inclined to find scientific reasons for thinking one form better than any other form, one scheme of organization better than any other scheme, one method of teaching better than any other. These devices and techniques, according to the best-method theory, are somehow derived directly from the science of education. Surely the methods which scientists have shown on the basis of scientific investigation to be best must be best. At least, many educational workers accept as best beyond question the rules and procedures which they think are derived from experimental studies, and apply them directly without modification to varying situations.

As indicated in the foregoing consideration of the different ways of discovering the so-called best procedures, those who assume the best-method theory of devices and techniques differ widely among themselves as to which are actually the best forms, schemes, and ways of doing things. As shown in various connections throughout this study, recognized authoritarian students of education as well as schoolworkers vary widely in regard to the best methods of organization, the best methods of teaching, and the best methods of dealing with any other feature of school practice. Also, it has been pointed out that, *however much authoritarians disagree as to what particular procedures should be used in any field, they still think there are best ways in general for doing every kind of thing.*

Such difference in belief as to what are the best devices and techniques seems to result in part from the ways of discovering best methods. Some authoritarians rely largely on tradition or some variant of the survey method; others rely primarily on the method of intuition; and others depend almost entirely on the method of experimentation for extracting the best ways of doing things from the secret truths of reality. Still, whatever differences of opinion they may hold in regard to the proper method of enticing nature to reveal her secrets, they see no inconsistency in maintaining that she has secrets. She fails to reveal any best way good for all who seek the best ways of doing things. Still she has secrets to reveal and will do so if properly approached. According to the best-method theory, *there apparently are best devices and techniques for doing everything that should be done except discovering these best ways.*

According to the philosophy of experimentalism, the objections to the best-method theory of devices and techniques cannot be overcome. In the first place, no authoritarian has yet succeeded in developing any device or technique that is acceptable to all other authoritarians, to say nothing of those who hold different philosophies of life and education. As a matter of fact, the only thing about devices and techniques upon which they are agreed is the formal abstract proposition that there are universally best procedures. As already suggested, however, authoritarians not only do not agree on what such a single procedure should be, but do not even agree on the best way of discovering such a procedure.

In the second place, the assumption that there are any formal devices or techniques of universal application in particular fields, without regard to the conditions, fails to take into account the dynamic character of the world of events. Conditions do not remain the same; therefore, procedures must vary. The change in circumstances and conditions is pronounced when people are involved and when problems of education are to be considered. Any formal educational device or technique can never be anything more than a source of suggestion to be used in so far as it is applicable in specific situations. Even the findings of science, which the experimentalists respect above all other sources of knowledge, cannot be directly translated into rules and procedures. As Dewey says: "It is not the capable engineer who treats scientific findings as imposing upon him a certain course which is to be rigidly adhered to; it is the third- or fourth-rate man who adopts this course. Even more, it is the unskilled day laborer who follows it. For even if the practice adopted is one that follows from science and could not have been discovered or employed except for science, when it is converted into a uniform rule of procedure it becomes an empirical rule-of-thumb procedure — just as a person may use a table of logarithms mechanically without knowing anything about mathematics." [4] What is true, he says, of the mechanical arts is even more true in regard to the art of education. According to the philosophy of experimentalism, *there are no universally best forms, schemes, or procedures that can be found outside practical educational situations.* Even experimental science, which is the chief source of knowledge, does not supply the fieldworker in our schools

---

[4] John Dewey, *Sources of a Science of Education.* Liveright Publishing Company, New York, 1929. P. 14.

and colleges with definite rules or procedures. Like other sources of information, the findings of science supply information and suggestion which those responsible for school activities and programs may find useful in dealing with concrete problems.

Previously we mentioned the fact that William James opposed the best-method theory of devices and techniques. He was speaking primarily to teachers, but what he said with regard to teaching is by implication what he would have said in regard to activities of any other schoolworkers. Since James is usually recognized as one of the founders of the general outlook that we have designated as the philosophy of experimentalism, and since his attitude toward fixed procedures is essentially the same as that which Dewey has developed in its wider applications, we shall close this section with a quotation from him. He is speaking about the application of psychology, but certainly he would not have expected more of any other science on which one may draw in dealing with school problems. James said: "I say moreover that you make a great, a very great mistake, if you think that psychology, being the science of the mind's laws, is something from which you can deduce definite programmes and schemes and methods of instruction for immediate schoolroom use. Psychology is a science, and teaching is an art; and sciences never generate arts directly out of themselves. An intermediary inventive mind must make the application, by using its originality.

" The science of logic never made a man reason rightly, and the science of ethics (if there be such a thing) never made a man behave rightly. The most such sciences can do is to help us to catch ourselves up and check ourselves, if we start to reason or to behave wrongly; and to criticize ourselves more articulately after we have made mistakes. A science only lays down lines within which the rules of the art must fall, laws which the follower of the art must not transgress; but what particular thing he shall positively do within those lines is left exclusively to his own genius. One genius will do his work well and succeed in one way, while another succeeds as well quite differently; yet neither will transgress the lines.

"The art of teaching grew up in the schoolroom, out of inventiveness and sympathetic concrete observation. Even where (as in the case of Herbart) the advancer of the art was also a psychologist, the pedagogics and the psychology ran side by side, and the former was not derived in any sense from the latter. The two were congruent, but neither was subordinate. And so everywhere the teaching must agree with the psychology, but need not necessarily be the only kind of teaching that would so agree; for many diverse methods of teaching may equally well agree with psychological laws." [5]

THE DIRECT-SUGGESTION THEORY
(EDUCATIONAL LAISSEZ FAIRE)

The direct-suggestion theory constituting an important principle of educational laissez faire assumes that the best procedures consist of the devices and techniques which each practical educational situation itself suggests. This theory is the exact opposite of the best-method theory assumed by the authoritarians. According to this point of view, there are no universally best ways of doing any kind of thing. Some procedures are relevant to some situations and others to other situations, but they cannot be determined in advance. The practitioner must thus look to each situation to discover not only the ends but also the means of education. The ends are implicit in the pupils and emerge only in specific situations. The possibilities of the environmental conditions in which aims emerge suggest the means, the devices and techniques by which they are to be realized.

If each situation supplies the devices and techniques to be used in dealing with it, knowledge of typical formal devices and techniques does more harm than good. The practical schoolworker who relies on direct suggestion to indicate procedures has no interest in any forms, schemes, or methods that can be described in advance. He looks upon these things as the embodiment of impractical theories or as routine devices and techniques irrelevant to the needs of people like himself who are very much in the thick of things. Those who live each day as it should be lived and take things as they come are sensitive to the demands of each practical situation and are willing to trust themselves to receive direct suggestions about proper procedure, whatever the occasion and the circumstances may be.

This attitude toward devices and techniques is exemplified by certain college presidents and deans, as well as by superintendents, principals, and supervisors, who live from hand to mouth, year in and year out, with little or no study of procedures that have been described, explained, and recommended by students of education and research experts. This attitude is further emphasized by the failure of these officials to

---

[5] William James, *Talks to Teachers*. Henry Holt and Company, New York, 1899. Pp. 7–9.

recognize the importance of a knowledge of such things in connection with the employment and advancement of teachers. Perhaps the best examples of the operation of this theory of devices and techniques are to be found among teachers themselves. All of us are familiar with teachers who give little advance thought to procedures in teaching before they are face to face with their pupils. We know others, especially college teachers, who consider the study by beginning teachers of the methods of administration and teaching as irrelevant and altogether a waste of time. We have heard of teachers, and particularly college teachers, who insist that subject matter is more important than method; that personality is more important than method; and that teachers are born and not made. Apparently these teachers think the less those responsible for school programs and activities know about recognized schemes, forms, and procedures, the better they are prepared to meet their professional obligations in practice. Some of them seem to assume also that the less advance consideration the teacher gives to devices and techniques the better the methods he will actually use in dealing with those for whose education he has a responsibility. According to this point of view, the deliberate employment of the standard procedures that the educational profession has accumulated over the centuries and the data supplied by the sciences which contain subject-matter materials relevant to educational problems reduces the fine art of education to mechanical routine in the name of a science of education, which by the very nature of the case is impossible.

From the standpoint of the philosophy of experimentalism, the direct-suggestion theory of devices and techniques represents a reaction against the unsatisfactory results of the best-method theory. It is a negative rather than a positive approach to an inadequate state of affairs. It seems to assume that the fact that certain uses of formal devices and techniques are unsatisfactory indicates that they have no use at all; if current planning is defective, all planning must, on that account, be futile — even detrimental.

The experimentalist is inclined to agree that the methods of learning, teaching, and using formal devices and techniques are often unsatisfactory, but he cannot, therefore, agree that they are irrelevant nor that a knowledge and use of them tend to reduce the fine art of education to a deadening routine. He agrees that education is best conceived as a fine art, but he does not agree that we have to choose between routine and caprice. Education, like every other art, becomes not only more scientific but even more artistic in proportion to the degree that it uses properly the schemes, forms, and procedures found useful in the past, in addition to those suggested by educational research and by the sciences on which it depends.

Finally, the fact that in both the authoritarian and the laissez-faire camps there are individuals who are always at each other's throats, and who still seem to see eye to eye in regard to devices and techniques, suggests that there must be some inconsistency in the underlying assumptions of both schools of thought. Those who emphasize the spontaneity of personality and who condemn the use of devices and techniques are not all educational reformers. Many educators and fieldworkers, especially college teachers and administrators, are opposed to the study of procedures in administration and teaching. They are, as a matter of fact, both laissez faire and authoritarian; that is, they do not hold any consistent theory. They do not hesitate to impose their traditional routine, mechanical, and rule-of-thumb procedures on others, but they want spontaneity and freedom themselves. Administrators of this type emphasize the importance of personality and spontaneity and at the same time make all important decisions for those whom they are able to hire and fire. Teachers of this type advocate personality and spontaneity at the same time that they reject a knowledge of recognized procedures as irrelevant or detrimental to good teaching and impose their routine methods on helpless pupils. In other words, they are advocates of educational laissez faire in matters that concern them, and practice authoritarianism in matters that concern others.

THE CRITICAL-CONSTRUCTION THEORY
(EDUCATIONAL EXPERIMENTALISM)

The critical-construction theory as a principle of educational experimentalism, like the other two theories of devices and techniques, is assumed by many unconsciously rather than consciously and deliberately. However, it is here offered consciously and deliberately as doing justice to the orderliness and spontaneity emphasized respectively in the other two theories and, at the same time, as meeting the demands of practical experience when reflectively considered. According to educational experimentalism, the best-method theory and the direct-suggestion theory are both right and both wrong. Those who wish to discover the best method of doing each thing or each kind of thing are right in studying available methods that are applicable, but they are wrong in concluding that there is some best way of doing each kind of thing that needs to be done. They fail to take into account many varying factors that arise from time to time and from place to place in consequence of changing conditions. In fact, those who advocate the use of specific procedures for doing specific things must realize that in practice these procedures must often be modified in important respects if they are to be used at all. In advocating any fixed methods, authoritarians provoke an unfriendly reaction in the minds of many who are sensitive to the flexibility required in practical affairs. For instance, the subject organization of the advance curriculum may be unsatisfactory in many situations, but this fact does not mean that some other scheme of organization will be satisfactory in all situations, as some seem to contend.

Those who endorse the theory of direct suggestion are right in wishing to avoid routine and to assure spontaneity; but they are wrong in their implicit assumption that it is necessary always to choose between routine and caprice. It is true that those who know only one way of doing a thing are often, perhaps typically, routine performers. On the other hand, those who do not know any standard procedures are perhaps typically capricious performers. It may be true that capricious performers are spontaneous because they are open to suggestion. *Still, spontaneity which involves nothing more than direct suggestion is not desirable in specific situations except by accident.* Any theory that endorses this kind of spontaneity is not, therefore, satisfactory.

The refusal of the proponents of educational laissez faire and some of the authoritarians to learn available devices and techniques that others have used and recommended places a premium on ignorance rather than on spontaneity. They are unfortunate in choosing the artist as an illustrative example of their theory. The artist does reveal spontaneity in his work, but he does not do so because he is ignorant of devices and techniques that artists in his field have used in the past, nor because he refuses to use procedures which the sciences applicable to this particular form of art suggest. He does so because he uses these methods as means of expressing rather than cramping his personality. Great artists are adept in the use of devices and techniques available in their respective fields. They may use suggestions from sciences applicable to their arts in such a way as to increase rather than decrease their spontaneity. *The knowledge of devices and techniques, as a matter of fact, does not detract from spontaneity but usually facilitates it.* There are differences in the way methods are learned and used. The fact that they lead to undesirable results when they are learned and used as fixed procedures does not mean that they should not be learned nor be used at all. It means that they should be learned and used in some other way. It is the importance of this better way which the theory of critical construction emphasizes.

The proponent of this theory of devices and techniques does not expect to find any one universally best form, scheme, or method of doing anything. He wishes to learn as much as possible about the devices and techniques that have been used in his particular field, and he wishes his teachers, supervisors, and administrators to learn the general forms and procedures which the teaching profession has found useful. He does not intentionally adopt any procedure to be applied universally without critical appraisal and he does not wish others to develop any such fixed methods. He thinks of recognized means, whatever they are, as sources of suggestions and not as forms and procedures to be directly applied. He finds himself using some of the recognized procedures in some situations and others in other situations.

Nor does the proponent of this theory of devices and techniques think of any method as inflexible. Although he may prefer one method to another because he finds it more widely applicable than others, he does not accept the theory that any method is better than another except in the situation where it is intellectually warranted. Some particular procedure may occur to him more often than any others, but this fact constitutes a warning. There will be a time when it will not be effective. It is important, then, that any methods employed, especially those which he is inclined to prefer, be critically chosen. Stated somewhat differently, this theory means that every method used is not just a procedure handed down from the past or a rule directly derived from any source, mystical or scientific. It is a procedure which a knowledge of past methods and the implications of applicable scientific evidence as factors in the immediate situation suggest. However, it is more than any one of these things or all of them together. It is the procedure which reflective consideration of the bearing of all pertinent factors indicates to be best under the conditions. In other words, the procedure actually employed has been constructed through the process of critical reflection. The method may seem to be the same, but it is different in quality because it has passed through the intellectual mill, so to speak. It has been qualitatively transformed, but often the method actually used does not even correspond to any formal procedure of the past. It contains elements from many sources that have been combined into a new procedure.

The proponent of this theory looks upon all forms, schemes, and procedures as human inventions to serve human purposes. They are not, so it seems to him, revelations of reality, by whatever method they may be supposed to have been discovered. Neither are they mere suggestions of particular situations. They are reconstructions derived through criticism. *There is a one best way of producing methods — intellectual criticism.* But this is no device or technique; it is a quality of the good life. It requires suggestion from immediate situations as the proponents of the direct-suggestion theory emphasize, but it also requires suggestions which a knowledge of effective methods and the applications of science make available. A knowledge of the devices and techniques that have been used successfully by great educators is therefore very important. Even intuition properly understood has its place. Some things do seem to reach us through a flash of insight or a still, small voice, although they come most often to those best acquainted with what others have done. On the other hand, these apparently mystical flashes of genius are only hypotheses and suggestions to be considered along with others in particular situations. They are never final.

Experimentation is indispensable to progress in the improvement of forms and procedures in education as in other fields. However, because one device or one technique is found to be better than another in certain experimental situations does not mean that it will be better in every practical situation in which it may be applied. Moreover, a combination of this procedure with some other procedure or some elements of other procedures often may be better than any previously known procedure could be when used alone. A knowledge of standard procedures in any field is no guarantee that right things will be done. Such knowledge does not tell us what to do; it constitutes a source of suggestion as to what may be done. The knowledge of educational research, psychology, and sociology, and other sciences applicable to education, serves the same ends. Nevertheless it is an important means, and in practical situations better suggestions occur to the individual who has learned a wide variety of practices than to the individual who is ignorant of them. Those to whom many practical suggestions occur are even capable of more spontaneity than those to whom they do not occur. If the adoption of one method as invariably best renders the individual a slave to routine, the failure to learn about any method at all renders him a slave to routine or to caprice. In the theory of critical construction, *both standard methods and direct suggestions are recognized as indispensable means of determining effective procedures in practical situations.* They are the materials with which intelligence does the work attributed to standard means and spontaneous suggestions in the other two theories.

The exemplification of this theory in practice is not difficult to detect. Those who adopt it do not argue that one kind of school organization is better than any other. They do not contend that one advance organization of the curriculum is better than any other. They do not insist that some one administrative device is better than any other. They do not contend that there is some one best technique of teaching in general. They insist, however, that there is some best procedure for each particular situation. They insist that the discovery of this best procedure is the function of intelligence — especially the intelligence of those who are responsible for practical programs and activities. They often advocate some procedure, but they do so in the light of a situation to which it is relevant. The exercise of intelligence might require them to advocate a different procedure as the situation changes. In adopting the critical-construction theory of devices and techniques, the experimentalists may seem to be inconsistent in the specific procedures they advocate, but they are always consistent in advocating intelligence as the method of deciding upon what procedure to use. They may readily admit that they were mistaken in advocating any particular procedure, but they are not willing to admit that they have been mistaken in advocating the method of intelligence in deciding what procedure to use. They endorse the supremacy of method, but they always have in mind the method of intelligence; never the method of routine performance or the method of capricious spontaneity.

CHAPTER 18

Improvement Program

THE PROGRAM FOR EDUCATIONAL IMPROVEMENT differs in important respects from the educational program. The educational program is constant and continuous; the improvement program is usually occasional and temporary. The educational program is essential; the improvement program is provisional. Every teacher, every school official, every school, and every school system, as well as the leaders of all social institutions, are regularly engaged in educational work. The schools and all those who have responsibility for them are generally engaged in an educational program, but they may not be generally engaged in a program for educational improvement. An improvement program may, of course, be a private affair which a single individual conducts for himself.

In speaking of an educational improvement program, however, we usually call it a supervisory program, a curriculum program, or a program for the improvement of instruction involving a school or school system. It is the improvement program primarily in this special and limited sense that is here under consideration. The improvement program so conceived has been a common feature of school practice during recent years. The administrative and supervisory staff of a department, school, or school system initiates a program to bring about some definable kind of educational improvement. It may be devoted to the improvement of materials or procedures in some particular field, as in reading, to the improvement of guidance, to the improvement of instruction, or to the improvement of the whole curriculum. Whatever the nature and scope of the undertaking, it represents the effort of some individual or group, such as the state department of education, the superintendent of a local school system, the principal of a school, the supervisor or director of instruction, or even some department head in a high school or college, to enlist the co-operation of others in the improvement of the school activities for which he is responsible. It goes without saying that the attitude which those responsible for an improvement program assume toward their obligations has important implications not only as to the way it is conducted but also as to its educational significance.

As in the case of the other features of school practice, three different attitudes or theories of the improvement program may be distinguished. They may be designated as (1) the domination theory, typically adopted by the educational authoritarians; (2) the indigenous theory, usually adopted by the adherents of educational laissez faire; and (3) the guidance theory, generally adopted by the educational experimentalists. Perhaps some but not many individuals consciously and deliberately conform to any one of these theories. More often they seem to be unconsciously assumed rather than clearly defined and deliberately applied. They correspond to theories of other features of school practice and control different improvement programs. It thus becomes our problem in the pages that follow to explain and elaborate these three theories so that those responsible for educational improvement programs may understand more clearly the philosophy of education to which they practically, if not intellectually, subscribe.

The Domination Theory
(Educational Authoritarianism)

In searching for a term by which to designate the authoritarian theory of the improvement program, we apparently have to make a choice between "dictation" and "domination" as most indicative of the meaning we intend to convey. The latter seems preferable because "dictation" suggests that those in control give direct orders to those whom they direct. Domination may involve dictation, but it is not limited to dictation. The presence of domination is not always realized. It may be entirely unintentional on the part of those who exert it and entirely acceptable to those who are subjected to it. In a word, domination seems to be second nature to some while submission seems to be second nature to others. Perhaps there are few people in the field of school education in democratic societies today who deliberately adopt a policy of domination. Many of those who assume this attitude reject it intellectually, even when their practices constantly exemplify it. At any rate, it does not necessarily consist of formal dictation in any offensive way, although on occasions it may do so. It consists not merely of what those in control of the improvement program decree but of the quality of the experiences they emphasize.

The most obvious form of the domination theory has been described in textbooks and courses in school administration and supervision during the last twenty-five years. It is usually called autocratic administration (or inspection when applied to supervision), which is condemned, in contrast with democratic administration and supervision, which is approved. This autocratic administration and supervision constitutes one form of the domination theory, which expresses itself in the educational improvement program. It is especially well exemplified in certain curriculum programs typical of the past, and it still prevails in some schools and some school systems. In practice it usually takes the form of a descending approach; that is, it works from the top downward.

In developing a curriculum program in this way, the administration prepares a course of study, usually called the "curriculum," setting forth in varying degrees of completeness the aims, content, materials, and procedures to be used, and passes it down for the schools and the teachers to follow according to directions dispensed by authority. If the program is state-wide, then the state department of education prepares the course of study or "curriculum" and transmits it to the heads of the local school systems; and they in turn pass it on to the schools. The heads of the schools pass it on to the teachers who, figuratively speaking, pass it on to the pupils. City, county, and school improvement programs may be conducted in this same way, the only difference being the administrative level on which they originate.

Most of those who assume responsibility for any improvement program would doubtless reject the domination theory stated in such a bold form. Nevertheless, its practice is still quite common. Traditional practices and customs are difficult to dislodge and often circumstances still favor this method of approach. There are still school superintendents, principals, supervisors, college presidents, college deans, and department heads in the high schools and colleges who conduct their own improvement programs without enlisting the participation and co-operation of those whom they control and direct. In fact, they may say little about any improvement program. They study the situation and make definite requirements for changes in curricula, courses, textbooks, and methods of management, and even for the construction and renovation of buildings, with little or no participation in planning and policy-making on the part of those immediately and directly charged with educational responsibilities.

From the standpoint of the philosophy of experimentalism, such changes may be desirable or undesirable, but the qualities of experience which this method of conducting an improvement program engenders are not desirable. Those who use buildings should be consulted in regard to constructing and renovating them. Those who use textbooks should have some part in selecting them. Those who have to teach new courses should be consulted before they are required to teach them. Those who are expected to use new methods should be consulted beforehand. Without such consultation and understanding the quality of domination pervades the experience of the administrators and the quality of submission pervades the experience of those who must accept blindly the decisions of their administrative superiors. But this method of conducting improvement programs is generally rejected in theory if not in practice, and therefore need not detain us further.

However, the domination theory expresses itself in another form which is not so easy to define or appraise. Perhaps it, too, may be illustrated best by the consideration of a method of conducting curriculum programs that has been very popular in recent years. For convenience of reference, this method may be designated as the *ascending approach* as contrasted with the *descending approach*. It differs from the descending approach in taking as its point of departure the reflections of the school staff. If the undertaking is on a state-wide basis, the superintendent assumes responsibility for the program, including the construction and installment of courses of study. Educational leaders from outside the community are employed to advise in the construction and the use of courses of study. The teachers and educational workers of the community engage in a period of co-operative study of curriculum problems under the direction of some representative of the superintendent, usually considered a director of curriculum study. After preliminary surveys and studies, various committees from teachers and supervisors are selected who, with the help and advice of consultants from within and without the community, produce courses of study. In constructing courses of study, all available data are collected from teachers and schools throughout the community. Administrators, supervisors, and teachers, as well as the public, are urged to participate in the program. Any course of study produced actually includes some materials which the various committees and participating teachers of the school system consider highly desirable for the children of the community. As a matter of fact, however, such a course of study is usually produced by a few individuals, in accord with the plans of the administration. There are no orders that any school or any teacher must use it. The course of study is first made available in tentative form for those who by request consent to try it out. After some experimentation, discussion, and criticism, it is revised and published. Again, there are no orders that any teacher or school shall use it. It is simply made available for those who wish to use it.

Of course, the value of the course of study depends, in the last analysis, on the aims, subject-matter content, subject-matter materials, organization, and methods of teaching that it provides. Usually it represents a kind of compromise or composite in respect to all these factors. Inconsistency in point of view very easily gets into such a course of study as a whole and in its use in the classroom, because the principles and philosophy underlying it may be only a compromise and have little connection with practical teaching materials actually provided.

From the standpoint of the philosophy of experimentalism, such programs have undoubtedly done considerable good in many parts of this country. They certainly prompt teachers to learn more about educational problems and enable them to discuss educational questions more intelligently. When emphasis is placed upon knowledge of the child, of the community, and of human culture, such a program must have a far-reaching indirect effect on the curriculum conceived in terms of the activities and experiences of the pupils.

The main difficulty with this approach is that in the minds of teachers the course of study produced represents the purposes and ideals of the administration under which they work. As they see it, the administration has assumed responsibility for all aims, organization, grade placement, subject matter, and procedures. Although there are no regulations that materials be used as they are intended to be used, teachers must, in order to demonstrate loyalty, conform — or seem to conform — to what they deem the expectations of the administration. *It is difficult for teachers, supervisors, or principals to criticize or evaluate seriously any tentative course of study that the administration approves in advance in all fundamental respects.* It is still more difficult for them to criticize and evaluate the final product. Even if they consider it unsatisfactory, every member of the system must follow the prescribed course of study, or, in any event, must seem to follow it. Otherwise, they may have to face in one form or another the resentment of the "powers that be." Furthermore, the authorities themselves soon realize that the enthusiasm they supposed existed during the production of the course of study is waning, and they then are confronted with the problem of sustaining interest. Finally, they are convinced that the course of study is inadequate and needs revision.

When interest can no longer be maintained in the development and installment of new courses of study, which many people consider fundamental factors of any curriculum program, some of the leaders in school education may rechristen the old curriculum program under some new name that has for the time caught the imagination of the rank and file. For instance, it is quite possible that in many quarters we shall now see a number of guidance programs in which the same theories that have already been expressed in programs of curriculum development will again be expressed. From the standpoint of the philosophy of experimentalism, such undertakings should be constantly examined to discover to what extent they exemplify educational authoritarianism, educational laissez faire, and educational experimentalism. The qualities of experience which any improvement program emphasizes are no more indicated in the term *guidance* — or in any other expression that may catch the imagination — than they have been in the term *curriculum*. With respect to the qualities of experience, there may be as many kinds of guidance programs, for instance, as there have been curriculum programs. The authoritarian domination theory may gain control of any improvement program, no matter what aspect of school education it may apparently emphasize.

The obvious intention of the ascending method in the development of the educational improvement program is to embody the needs, interests, and ideals of the pupils, of the teachers, and of the public in all parts of the community in which it is conducted. In actual practice the effects are not typically what they are intended to be. In the first place, there is no way in which the specific concrete interests, needs, and ideals of particular localities, particular schools, and particular individuals can be embodied in a general course of study for a whole state. What applies in the case of a state applies in a corresponding degree, though to a lesser extent, to improvement programs in the city, the county, the school, or the department. At best, the actual standards and materials embodied in the course of study represent generalizations and selections from the wide variety that may have been proposed. Perhaps normally they represent the thinking of the few who actually produced them. Nevertheless, the excerpts from the proposals of various groups who have undertaken to participate in the program are selected mainly to illustrate the controlling conceptions and forms that those responsible for the program consider most satisfactory.

In the second place, the stage is set for what someone has called "formality in informality." In the usual program conducted in this way data are sought from every teacher who has been interested in the program. The course of study is conceived as an indigenous product. The teachers, so it is generally thought, have actually incorporated the interests and needs of the pupils in the materials that are made available. They are, of course, expected to use these materials in teaching their pupils. As a matter of fact, as we have already indicated, such materials are at best a composite and represent the work of relatively few schools and teachers. The aims, the content, the organization, the materials, and the procedures are just as authoritarian as the course of study produced through the method of descending from the top down, but inasmuch as they are proclaimed to be the outcome of the work of the teachers themselves, they are necessarily, so those in charge seem to think, satisfactory to the teachers. The supervisors and principals who are expected to have the materials used develop their own patterns of procedure, whether inherent in the program itself or not, by which instruction is to proceed. Those teachers who do not follow the pattern set by administrative authority are considered either incapable or antagonistic to the program. As a result, teachers may go through the motion of conforming and may seek to secure all projects, problems, units, and undertakings from the pupils, just as the materials of the course of study are supposed to have been secured from the teachers. Whatever the pattern may be, they try to follow it. *An improvement program that in its inception is designed to liberate teachers and pupils from formality and routine performance may culminate in reducing both teachers and pupils to deadening formality and mechanical routine.* This formality in informality may be even worse than the old formality because it is imposed in the name of democracy and progressive education. Those who make a serious attack on grinding routine and pedagogical dry rot may, in consequence of this insidious formality and routine, unconsciously "sell out to the enemy."

Disapproval of such a result should not be considered as a derogatory criticism of the motives and intentions of those responsible for conducting such improvement programs. The difficulty seems to be inherent in the theory of domination, which is assumed despite the asserted allegiance to the democratic theory. However, this procedure may be inevitable and useful in paving the way for a new approach. As magic paved the way for science, so this ascending method of conducting improvement programs may pave the way for a better theory and a better practice. If so, then the energy that has been spent is not entirely lost. Through this procedure curriculum programs have been successful in enlisting the participation of teachers in the study of educational problems. Nevertheless, they never end in the way they begin. In their inception, all ideas, procedures, and materials are supposed to be derived from those who are expected to use them. In their culmination everything seems to be dictated by authority.

The domination theory is not confined to state-wide improvement programs, however. A local supervisor or director of instruction may direct or guide the participation of some local school or school system in the more inclusive program, or assume responsibility for the development of an independent program of comparatively limited scope. If he takes ready made the aims and procedures of the more inclusive program already under way, without enlisting, in policy-making and in planning, the aid of those who are expected to make the changes required, he is adopting the domination theory, it matters not what the aims and practices may be. Moreover, he is not only adopting the domination theory with respect to those under his direction, but he is also submitting to its application on the part of those responsible for the more inclusive program. He may be adopting it even when he solicits suggestions and proposals, just as he does when he makes specific assignments without soliciting such help. All depends upon what is to be done with the advice that is offered. When specific assignments are made to teachers without consultation, dictation and domination are out in the open. Such assignments may at least be accepted or rejected, done willingly or unwillingly. Everyone at least knows what kind of thing to expect, and is not confused by such ambiguous terms as "co-operation" and "loyalty."

Also, the supervisor or director of instruction may solicit information from teachers, not to find out their needs and problems, but to discover what is psychologically and practically possible. If the needs of those under his direction do not become a primary consideration, his improvement program assumes the domination theory, it matters not how much lip service he pays to "democracy," "co-operation," "participation," and other similar slogans. The dictators and the dominators, no less than the liberators and the democrats, want information about the people they wish to control. Furthermore, they usually find democratic practices favorable to their interest, and they do not hesitate to extol the very principles which they are seeking under cover to undermine. However, we are not saying that every supervisor or director of instruction who seeks information for use in developing an improvement program is intentionally dominating teachers, but we are saying that it matters not how democratic he may wish to be, he is still assuming the domination theory if the controlling purposes of his program do not embody the needs of the teachers who are subject to his guidance and direction. Even when every effort is made to secure information from teachers about their interests and needs, the improvement program may still be merely the program of the supervisor or of the director of instruction.

From the standpoint of the philosophy of experimentalism, aims and procedures cannot be determined independently of the actual situation. They must embody the needs of the teachers, but they must also take into account their abilities, the facilities available, and the prevailing difficulties. In other words, aims and methods must be flexible — they must be subject to revision or to modification as the situation changes and as new information is secured, and they must be flexible not only in the light of what is possible but also in the light of what is desirable. Teachers should not be used as mere instruments to further an improvement program that sounds well when one hears its promoters talk about it on special occasions or when one reads about it in the public press or even in some professional periodical. An improvement program that is pervaded with the spirit of domination from start to finish may be described in terms that challenge the respect of those who resent all forms of domination, dictation, and autocracy.

What has been said about the policies and practices of supervisors and directors of instruction applies equally to the policies and practices of college presidents and deans, school superintendents and principals, and heads of departments in the college or in the high school. There is no place in which one can initiate an adequate improvement program except in the specific situation where it is to be developed. The college president or dean who merely dispenses orders to his faculty assumes the domination theory. Those who use information secured from the members of the faculty solely as a means of controlling them adopt this same theory, it matters not how democratic the motives may seem to be on the surface. The principal who solicits the participation of his teachers in policy-making, supposedly in the development of an improvement program, and who is still determined to achieve his original ends without modification, is assuming the domination theory, just as much as the principal who decides in advance what is to be done and requires everyone to do it. The head of a department who, in undertaking to develop an improvement program, holds regular departmental meetings and uses them to secure approval through the force of his ability, his persuasiveness, or the power of his position, is just as much a dominator as the department head who never holds any departmental meeting except for the purpose of assigning new duties which his improvement program demands. Even when a program is adopted with the approval of all, it must be constantly modified in the light of developments about which all should be kept informed. Otherwise, the spirit with which it is initiated will be dissipated, and those who are responsible for its inauguration will dominate those who are faced with actual educational situations.

THE INDIGENOUS THEORY
(EDUCATIONAL LAISSEZ FAIRE)

For convenience of reference, the laissez-faire attitude toward the improvement program has been designated as the indigenous theory. Logically, a systematic improvement program conducted on a laissez-faire basis is, perhaps, impossible. Those who accept this philosophy of education are opposed to any kind of constructive program requiring advance planning. *Nevertheless, many improvement programs seem to be dominated, at least in their early stages, by the indigenous theory.* Paradoxical as it may seem, the form of the state-wide curriculum program that has been selected as an exemplification of the domination theory may also be considered an exemplification of the indigenous theory. If we think of the program as a whole and of its ultimate results, it represents the operation of the authoritarian theory of domination. On the other hand, if we think of the program in its early stages without reference to the form it finally assumes, it is a good example of the laissez-faire indigenous theory.

To indicate the significance of the foregoing paradox, it seems necessary, even at the risk of some repetition, to elaborate what has already been said about the ascending form of the state-wide curriculum program, to which we have referred in our consideration of the domination theory. The leaders in the movement for curriculum reform seem to think that they are enlisting the interest and participation of all. They do not merely hand out a fixed course of study to be used without modifications, as do some who adopt the descending approach. They ask teachers, principals, supervisors, administrators, and even the public, to help organize the kind of course of study they want. In enlisting the services of all to provide materials which all are expected to use, they seem to be starting at the bottom; that is, starting with the actual needs of the teacher in practical educational situations.

Such a program illustrates the indigenous theory inasmuch as those in charge seem to think that the suggestions and proposals of teachers and others interested in concrete educational situations are to be directly translated into the materials and procedures to be used in the improvement program. The aims, scope, materials, organization, and methods are to be none other than those which the practical workers in the field like. They are not to be prepared by the administrative leaders responsible for the program; they are to be prepared by those who are expected to use them. If the leaders responsible for such programs are serious — and we must assume that they are — they adopt, in the inception of the program, a theory that is just the opposite of the domination theory. If the dominators begin at the top, these laissez faire progressives begin at the bottom. Whereas the autocratic leaders in the improvement programs of the past informed the schools and the teachers what they should do, the modern, so-called democratic leaders ask the teachers what they wish to do. The laissez-faire leaders purport to assume the minor role of collecting and arranging the materials which teachers and others directly interested in the schools supply. They really try — if they mean what they seem to say — to develop an indigenous curriculum; namely, a curriculum that emerges out of the actual educational situation. They are not asking those directly responsible for curriculum-making in the actual situation to adopt any fixed aims, schemes of organization, materials, or procedures of any kind. They are merely helping the teachers to understand better what they are doing and to follow the leadership of the child just as they themselves are following the leadership of the teachers.

The reason why we call this procedure an illustration of the indigenous theory is because most of the programs conducted in this way apparently have assumed that every suggestion and proposal must come from the child. The foundation of the real curriculum lies in the immediate needs, desires, and interests of pupils. That is the theory which the exponents of educational laissez faire always assume. On the other hand, inasmuch as those in control of the school system are not in direct contact with the child, the laissez-faire leaders seek to meet this difficulty by the ascending approach. Since they realize their responsibility to overcome the formal and deadening practices that are the result of the long authoritarian domination of the schools, the teachers, and the pupils, and since they simply want to do something about a bad situation, laissez-faire educators begin by building a program from the ground up. Just as they expect teachers to secure all suggestions and proposals from the child in making the actual curriculum, they undertake to get all the materials to be used in the advance curriculum from the teachers, although they usually try to enlist the interest and participation of the public. If teachers were the only ones who could supply such materials, their collection would be unnecessary. The schools and teachers already have the materials, and except for the study and thinking which goes into describing them, nothing new is really added to what they already have. Teachers may, of course, be stimulated to do better work, and that counts. But the materials actually collected could not be very valuable, certainly not so valuable as materials produced in some other way might be.

Furthermore, the materials actually produced are not what they purport to be. They purport to be the very materials the teachers and schools themselves have supplied. Actually, they are the materials that a few teachers have supplied and other materials that those who arrange them have supplied. The materials, then, incorporated in the course of study are not the materials of the schools but materials that those in charge of the curriculum program have provided for the schools. In one aspect, the program is laissez faire, and in another it is authoritarian. From the standpoint of the philosophy of experimentalism, such a program is all the more authoritarian when it is developed in the name of the philosophy of experimentalism.

The indigenous theory of the improvement program is exemplified not only in state-wide curriculum programs but in other kinds of improvement programs in which the ascending approach is adopted. It is revealed in many educational conferences which are supposedly designed to improve some existing situations. Very often such conferences occur without any preliminary study on the part of those who assume leadership in them. Whatever proposals emerge from these gatherings are generated on the spot, so to speak, just as the curriculum is generated in some of the so-called progressive schools. The proposals are indigenous to the experiences of those who are called together for study. Such conferences may include only the faculty of a single school, the teachers, pupils, and supervisors from a local school district, or representatives from all parts of a state or even from every state in the country. If they are designed as a means of improving education in some respects, they are part and parcel of what we have called educational improvement programs. If the leaders responsible for such conferences are unable, after serious study, to make any definite proposals concerning what should be done about some situation, and the only proposals and suggestions that arise are generated in the conference, such conferences assume what we have called the indigenous theory of conducting improvement programs.

From the standpoint of the philosophy of experimentalism, there is no objection to local, state, and even national improvement programs. In fact, such programs are essential in a democratic society. They supply the conditions favorable to the generation of the qualities of experience that experience itself finds desirable. There is no objection to conferences in which the suggestions and proposals of others are solicited. There is a very serious objection, however, to any improvement program which strictly speaking is no program at all. When those responsible for an improvement program have no aims, procedures, or plans that they are willing to propose as a working basis, and when everything is left to those whom they guide and direct, it is doubtful whether much solid achievement can result.

Doubtless, many readers are familiar with so-called improvement programs on various levels and of various kinds that consist primarily of meetings and conferences, the chief outcomes of which are the friendships and *esprit de corps* generated in them. No doubt such conferences are good for us all, and may be very delightful. As a means of socialization and recreation, they are very valuable. *On the other hand, to function most effectively in the improvement program a conference must be preceded by serious study of some real problem on the part of those in charge.* Only in consequence of such study can they make definite proposals, without which little is accomplished. *The conference should not be considered an improvement program, but merely one feature of an improvement program.* It is useful in initiating undertakings and in deciding upon proposed selections at various stages in the development of the program. The overemphasis of polite discussion in large groups to the relative neglect of hard study and reflective thought by individuals and small groups, characteristic of those who assume the indigenous theory, is very objectionable. There is no objection to polite discussion; but when it has no controlling aim and shifts from one thing to another, it contributes but little in the way of concrete improvement.

A general objection to the indigenous theory is that practices that exemplify it typically lapse into practices that exemplify the authoritarian domination theory. For instance, the state-wide curriculum programs to which we have referred as exemplifying both the domination theory and the indigenous theory in most cases are never intended by those responsible for them as a means of dominating those directly responsible for education in practical situations. In most instances, the leaders in curriculum development in recent years have adopted what they thought was the philosophy of educational experimentalism. They have honestly intended to do systematically on a broad scale what they thought the experimentalists would do in specific concrete situations. The philosophy of experimentalism and its leading representatives are very popular in educational circles. But, for the most part, those who have been responsible for the comprehensive programs of curriculum development have not been students of this philosophy for long. They usually have taken as the real educational implications of this philosophy the implications of a certain pseudo-experimentalism which some of the progressive schools have adopted, and which the authoritarians, for the most part, attribute to the philosophy of experimentalism.

Those who adopt this pseudo-experimentalism are not following in the footsteps of Dewey, Bode, and Kilpatrick. They are conforming rather to certain patterns of thought that arise from a combination of influences, such as that of the Romantic naturalists, of whom Rousseau is the most outstanding example, the Romantic vitalists, of whom Bergson is the best known, the spiritual Romanticists, of whom Schelling and Emerson are influential representatives, and the psychoanalysts, of whom Freud is a leader. On the basis of certain conceptions actually derived from these other groups and attributed to the leading experimentalists, even leaders in the field of curriculum development have adopted the indigenous theory of the improvement program. Just as they place a responsibility on the child in concrete educational situations which he is unable to bear, so they place a responsibility on the teacher in preparing the advance curriculum which he is unable to bear. Consequently, when the impractical requirements break down, the leaders fall back on the authoritarian domination theory and attempt to force, directly or indirectly, the schools and the teachers to conform to the requirements of the powers that be. The fact that such domination is unintentional or concealed does not eliminate its presence. What is true of the curriculum program may also be true of the guidance program or any other improvement program, wherever it occurs. *When the indigenous theory breaks down, those in control are forced to fall back on the domination theory in order to produce objective and tangible results.* From the standpoint of the philosophy of experimentalism, the qualities of experience which both the author-itarian domination theory and the laissez-faire indigenous theory generate are undesirable, and any combination of these theories in the development of any improvement program whatever is thus unsatisfactory.

THE ADVISORY THEORY
(EDUCATIONAL EXPERIMENTALISM)

For purposes of discussion, the attitude of the educational experi-mentalists toward the improvement program is here called the advis-ory theory. According to this theory, there is no one procedure to follow in the initiation and development of improvement programs in general. The qualities of experience which such undertakings gener-ate are primary considerations, just as they are in the learning-teaching relationship. The same qualities which are fundamental in the one are also fundamental in the other. The form a program assumes is always a secondary consideration. Much depends upon the scope of the undertaking, the ability and experience of the personnel involved, and the aspects of the on-going educational programs to be modified. For instance, there are several approaches to a general program of curriculum development which may be equally satisfactory. Everything depends on the spirit that prevails at various stages in the develop-ment of the undertaking rather than on the specific things that are done.

As every one knows, the plan of preparing advance courses of study and handing them out to schools for direct use usually exemplifies the authoritarian domination theory, which has already been described and condemned. Nevertheless, there is a modification of this approach that may be used effectively by those who accept the advisory theory of educational experimentalism. A variant of this descending ap-proach, although it has not been popular in recent programs of curriculum development, may provide for real participation of the whole school staff in planning, developing, and evaluating materials, methods, and activities. According to this method, a tentative course of study is produced by a number of experts, supervisors, and teachers selected by the administration because of their special qualifications. They assume full responsibility for the construction of the course of study in all its details. When they have completed it, they submit it to the administration who employed them and to whom they are alone responsible. ·The administration, in the case of a state-wide program, then provides all the local school systems with copies of the tentative course of study to be subjected to analysis, criticism, and experimentation. In other words, the study program on the part of the members of the school staffs follows rather than precedes the construction of a tentative course of study, thus reversing the order of the customary procedure in most of the recent programs of curriculum development. In developing this program the school staffs spend much time in studying curriculum problems and in analyzing the needs of their own varying situations in the light of the different proposals pertaining to aims, content, materials, and methods suggested in the tentative course of study. According to this variant of the descending approach, the proposed course of study itself is the thing that is studied. After it has been studied at considerable length and has been subjected to the criticism and appraisal of every one whose interest can be enlisted, the curriculum-makers who conceived it now reconstruct it, taking into account so far as possible the criticisms and suggestions offered.

The study program of the teachers and other members of the school system is more meaningful and significant when based upon the study of a prepared course of study than when devoted to curriculum principles and practices in general. Furthermore, everyone, including the state administration, feels free to criticize, approve, or condemn the proposed materials. All are able to engage in such criticism and appraisal because they are placed in a position where they can work on something that is of vital concern to them and with respect to which they feel free to say exactly what they think. They have nothing to fear from the administration in evaluating materials for which it is not responsible. This method undoubtedly produces a better course of study than does the customary program in which everyone considers the tentative course of study to be, in the last analysis, a concrete expression of the educational policy of the administration. When it is finally published, it will command the respect of those who are expected to use it to a much fuller degree than a course developed in the customary way.

Of course, an educational improvement program is not limited to a curriculum program in the ordinary sense, and a curriculum program usually is not confined to the construction of courses of study. But in all variants of the descending approach, some kind of material is produced. In the curriculum program, as ordinarily understood, the participation of practical workers often revolves around the construction and use of official courses of study. This second variant of the descending approach deserves more consideration than it has had in recent years.

As already indicated, the educational experimentalist, in adopting the advisory theory of the improvement program, is not committed to any particular form of procedure. As a general rule, he may not even wish to conduct programs of the usual kind. Nevertheless, he is sufficiently familiar with the traditions of school administration and practical school conditions to realize that some such program may be necessary. In some places it may even be demanded. Although he is not committed to any fixed curriculum prepared in advance, he may nevertheless engage in the development of courses of study under conditions which require them. But in doing so, he will emphasize the desirable qualities of experience for both teachers and pupils. He will therefore not only welcome changes in any advance course of study that any group, after due study and reflection, might propose, but he will welcome different kinds of courses. In fact, he will be willing to include in the courses provided the more important sets of aims now available, the recognized schemes of organization, many varieties of materials, and any standard methods of teaching and evaluation that have been found useful. He is not interested in any fixed course of study, but he wishes to use any that can be prepared in such a way as to do as much good and as little harm as possible. He expects real changes to be made in any course prepared. In fact, *he conceives any course of study not as a fixed requirement, but as a constant source of suggestion.* What he seeks first of all is the education of the teachers who alone can actually introduce improvements in curriculum-making, and he is convinced that the variant of the descending approach that has been suggested can be so used as to contribute much to this end.

The educational experimentalist does not object to an intelligent use of the so-called ascending approach; but he is not willing to commit himself to any formal procedure that turns out in the end to be authoritarian rather than democratic. When conditions permit, he will often start at the bottom. But he will not do so in just the same way that the laissez-faire and middle-of-the-road groups usually start. He will actually develop some plan by which those who have superior insight can get to the schoolrooms and to the teachers. He will then work at getting the teachers themselves to plan with one another and with the pupils in the development of the actual curriculum. Teachers will seldom have to collect lists of interests, activities, and the like, to send off to some official committee delegated to make a general course of study. They will be developing curriculum materials for their own use with their own pupils.

This modification of the ascending approach, in certain situations at least, has considerable advantage over the usual form of either the descending or the ascending approach. In fact, it seems to be the kind of approach the laissez-faire exponents of the indigenous theory are actually seeking. They have sought to overcome objections to the hierarchical schemes characteristic of the descending approach in the hands of the educational authoritarians. They seemingly are trying to proceed from the bottom upward, although they often end by proceeding from the top downward. For instance, when a set of general aims is established for a whole school system, each local unit, each school, and each grade must contribute to those aims whether they contribute to other desirable aims or not. Each level must conform to the requirements of the next higher level. The program of the grade must conform to the requirements of the school, and the program of the school to the requirements of the school system. The proponents of the indigenous theory are working to overcome the rigid method of conducting an improvement program. Although they have done some good, as we have already pointed out, they ultimately are compelled to resort to authoritarian procedures in order to complete their undertakings. In refusing to adopt a uniform scheme of development, whether it be considered a descending or an ascending approach, the proponents of the advisory theory avoid entangling association with educational authoritarians.

According to the advisory theory, an adequate program for the improvement of instruction and of the experiences of the pupils cannot be directed by any uniform set of fixed aims, predetermined content, and official schemes of organization. *The actual work of the teacher in the classroom must constitute the proper starting point,* not so much in the development of an over-all plan of procedure as in the actual procedure itself. As a matter of fact, such a program of curriculum development, although not always distinguished as such, has long been in operation in many places. It is now in operation in many schools and school systems throughout the world. In fact, it is present everywhere to some degree. Moreover, we do not necessarily have to choose between this method and any variant of the method which proceeds from the top downward. It is perhaps possible, even desirable, to proceed in both ways at the same time. In proceeding from the top downward, the educational leaders may clarify their own thoughts and gradually begin to look from the bottom upward. Alone, however, this descending method can never produce the desirable qualities of experience that constitute flexible, dynamic, and self-adaptive aims of education until it reaches the bottom and reverses its course of operation. There is reason to believe that in many communities the bottom has already been reached. The time is now ripe for reversing the process and working upward. Moreover, the character of the program contemplated is so different from the ordinary ascending method most congenial to the proponents of the laissez-faire indigenous theory that it should perhaps be given a new name.

In this upward movement the same features need to be considered that are considered in the downward movement. But they are seen from another angle. They are now seen by the leaders and by the teachers from the standpoint of the child in the learning-teaching relationship, whereas, in the usual downward course most acceptable to the authoritarians, they are seen from the standpoint of external authority, system, and order, and in the usual ascending approach advocated by the exponents of educational laissez faire, they are seen in terms of the individual in isolation from the environment. The teacher and the school authorities, from this third point of view, look upon various analyses of aims, schemes of organization, and methods of teaching not as ends to be achieved, forms to be employed, or procedures to be followed, but as sources of suggestion. They examine as many different formulations of aims as possible, because the more aims they understand, the better they are able to maintain a balanced program. They study the various types of organization and experiment with them, because only in this way can they master the important conceptions toward which the experiences of pupils should be directed; and only in this way can they see, from the standpoint of their pupils, the subject-matter content embodied in the school subjects and in other features of human culture. They study the various teaching procedures available, not to learn what must be done, but to learn what, under varying circumstances, may be done. They study the activities and environments of their own pupils to determine their experiential background and to select undertakings in which their pupils can have experiences whose qualities are desirable.

According to this conception, which we have called the advisory theory, a combination of the descending and the ascending methods of conducting the improvement program may be more effective than either used separately. It may be possible, for instance, in the state-wide curriculum program, for state departments of education to provide courses of study that are suggestive only. They may state and elaborate different sets of aims that are increasingly becoming a part of our professional education. They may describe and explain different schemes of organization. They may make available an abundance of instructional materials. They may describe and explain typical methods of doing many different kinds of things, including teaching and evaluating. They may summarize and make available research studies dealing with problems of interest to teachers. Such things may be provided in the form of courses of study or as separate bulletins. The form in which they are presented is determined by practical conditions. The primary consideration is that such materials be rendered available and be submitted as suggestions rather than as requirements.

Such a variant of the descending approach should be considered complementary rather than antithetical to the variant of the ascending approach that has been suggested. These variants of the two approaches are two sides of the same inclusive process. If teachers and pupils, in the last analysis, make the curriculum, as they surely must, then the more help the educational authorities supply the better. There is no one best method of conducting the curriculum program or any other improvement program. *But any procedure which exemplifies the advisory theory must somehow take into account actual pupils in concrete situations.* Furthermore, teachers in concrete situations should not feel that they have to conform to the demands of external requirements or to the demands of immediate impulses of pupils in the development of the curriculum. The curriculum program should thus be conceived as only one form of the improvement program, and the improvement program in all its forms should be conceived as an advisory program.

The foregoing suggestions, for the most part, are stated in terms of a comprehensive curriculum program, but they are applicable to any other kind of improvement program. They should be suggestive to local superintendents, supervisors, directors of instruction, school principals, college presidents, deans, and department heads, who often wish to institute measures of reform. There is no formal procedure that is universally effective. Those who assume responsibility for innovations should always take into account practical conditions. It makes little difference whether they apparently proceed from the top or from the bottom, or whether they proceed in both directions simultaneously. What does make a difference is that the qualities of experience of those who participate in the program and of those who are affected by it be desirable. Those in charge of the program should have their own aims and plans, and so should everybody else, for desirable aims arise in the process itself and change as conditions change. Aims cannot be taken directly without criticism, either from leaders or from followers. The most desirable improvement program depends not on external domination from above or indigenous control from below, but on intelligent direction from within the process itself.

CHAPTER 19

Educational Leadership [1]

SINCE EDUCATION IS MUCH MORE INCLUSIVE than school education, so educational leadership is much more inclusive than school leadership. Other educational agencies, such as the home, the church, the state, business and industry, civic clubs, professional organizations, fraternities, and social organizations of many kinds which exert an educational influence, have their educational leadership. The same theories of leadership assumed by those who control the school are also assumed by those who control other educational agencies. In fact, the topic might be so developed as to include these other agencies in addition to the school. Still, in accord with our general plan, we shall confine ourselves primarily to school leadership. Nevertheless, those who are interested in the different theories of school leadership should also be sensitive to the exemplification of the same theories in other fields. If they are interested in improving the leadership of the schools, they should wish to improve the leadership of other institutions, organizations, and associations. In line with the general plan of our study, we now turn to a consideration of the question of why educational leadership is recognized as an important feature of school practice.

LEADERSHIP AS A FEATURE OF SCHOOL PRACTICE

New ideas seem to emerge and express themselves with disconcerting frequency in the field of education. After the first World War, when uncertainty prevailed with regard to the future of certain defeated countries, and the future of democracy seemed to be assured in the victorious countries, the idea emerged that the qualities of personality were more important than specific things, which had been considered the primary aims of education. It became increasingly clear to many that if the democratic qualities of personality could be developed, then the children in the schools would be able to solve the problems of the

[1] This chapter is an expansion of a talk given by the author at the first Institute on Public Education held at Madison College, Harrisonburg, Virginia, in July, 1944.

future as they arose, regardless of what specific subject matter was taught. It seemed clear also that the traits of personality desired were a function of method in the broad sense. The way people were treated rather than the nature of subject matter was thought to determine the quality of the characters developed. The idea expressed itself in what is known as the method movement.

Eventually, many realized that the specific aims, materials, and methods of teaching are all aspects of method broadly conceived and affect the qualities of personality developed. This idea was soon expressed in terms of the curriculum movement. The curriculum was next conceived in terms of the activities of pupils under the direction of the school. The new movement thus included the method-movement idea in a still broader conception.

At the present writing, two other movements seem to be getting under way simultaneously — the guidance movement and the leadership movement. The guidance movement seems to embody two ideas — the older vocational guidance as well as the curriculum. It is perhaps too soon to tell, but this movement may include curriculum development, just as the idea of curriculum development included the method movement.

The leadership movement, on the other hand, seems to express a conception that has been implicit in the other movements already mentioned as well as in certain collateral movements that have been closely related to them. It seemed quite clear to many that if the democratic qualities of personality were to be developed in pupils, they also must be developed in those in charge of the schools, especially the teachers. Not only the pupils but the teachers too were to be treated democratically. Out of this idea developed the movement for democratic administration, which is often contrasted with autocratic administration, and democratic supervision, which is often contrasted with inspection.

Stated somewhat differently, the idea of leadership has been implicit in a number of movements such as those mentioned. Unless teachers themselves have the democratic qualities of personality, which the method movement emphasized, it is difficult to see how they could develop those traits in their pupils. Unless the teachers are able to develop new aims, use new materials, and employ new methods, which the movement for curriculum development makes available, it is difficult to see how the various curriculum programs can be effective in the actual learning-teaching situation. Likewise, it is difficult to see how the guidance movement can be fully effective unless those who deal directly with pupils are actually capable of supplying the kind of guidance required. In a word, those who deal with teachers must treat them in much the same way as they wish the teachers to treat pupils. Such a conception seems to be embodied in the movements for democratic administration and supervision already mentioned.

This idea of leadership has been given special emphasis in another movement which may properly be designated as the movement for the improvement of teacher education. The five-year program of teacher education just completed under the direction of the Commission on Teacher Education of the American Council on Education exemplified the same spirit in dealing with those directly responsible for teacher education that should be exemplified in dealing with in-service and pre-service teachers. The members of the commission not only were leaders themselves but they recognized teachers and those responsible for teacher education as leaders also. *The movement for the improvement of teacher education thus seems to be in fact a movement for educational leadership.*

Simultaneous with the development of these various movements, the conception of leadership is becoming clearly defined. More and more the newer conceptions of supervision and administration are designated as leadership. The Supervisors and Directors of Instruction and the National Society for Curriculum Study have just consolidated their interests in a new organization. The official organs of the two groups have been combined into a new one entitled *Educational Leadership.* The interests of the groups in method, supervision, and curriculum are thus seen as aspects of the more inclusive conception of leadership. The same idea is receiving increasing recognition in books and periodicals for teachers.

The movement for educational leadership thus seems to emerge as an essential feature of school practice. It is broad enough to include administrators, supervisors, and teachers, and even students who occupy positions of leadership in the schools. It includes those responsible for any form of educational service in any kind of school or school system. It includes both those who have the responsibility for educational leadership and those who have the responsibility of developing leadership. In fact, educational leadership is the responsibility of us all. Thus understood, educational leadership is not only a feature of school practice; it is such an inclusive feature that theories of educational leadership must include much that has been said already with respect to other features. All we have to do here is to combine what has already been said in such a way that theories of other features may be seen as aspects of theories of this new emerging feature.

Although the various educational movements tend to emphasize what some have called "democratic leadership," it is not clear that everyone who uses the term "democratic leadership" means democratic leadership any more than it is clear that every one who says "democracy" means democracy. It is no more difficult to distinguish three theories of educational leadership than it is to distinguish three theories of other features of school practice.[2] One kind of leadership, which for convenience of discussion we may designate as the autocratic leadership, seems to be consistent with and implicit in the theories of certain features of experience and in the theories of certain features of school practice that we have designated as educational authoritarianism. A second kind of leadership, which may be designated as drifting leadership, seems to be consistent with and implicit in other theories of the features of experience and school practice that we have designated as educational laissez faire. A third kind of leadership, designated as democratic leadership, seems to be consistent with and implicit in still other theories of these same features that we have designated as educational experimentalism. The elaboration of these three theories of leadership does not consist so much in stating any new ideas as in stating the same ideas already developed from the standpoint of a new emphasis that is just now taking on definite form in current thought.

THE AUTOCRATIC THEORY
(EDUCATIONAL AUTHORITARIANISM)

The authoritarian philosophy of education is exhibited in the theory of autocratic leadership just as it is exhibited in theories of other features of school practice. The autocratic leader has his own aims, policies, and programs. They embody the values which he prizes, the principles or procedures which he conceives as desirable, and the plans which he considers effective. They may reflect the implications

---

[2] Lewin, Lippitt, and White have expressed in terms of three variations in social atmosphere three theories of leadership very similar to the three theories considered in this chapter; have designated them as the *autocratic*, the *laissez faire*, and the *democratic*; and have tested experimentally their comparative effects on ten-year-old boys.

Kurt Lewin, Ronald Lippitt, and R. K. White, "Patterns of Aggressive Behavior in Experimentally Created Social Climates," *Journal of Social Psychology*, 10 : 271–279, May, 1939.

of fixed standards derived from tradition, from recognized authorities, or from his own deliberations in practical situations. But whatever they are and from whatever source they may be derived, they are considered the proper requirements to meet practical demands at some given time and place. Such aims, policies, and programs may be acceptable or unacceptable to those who are expected to develop them. If they are acceptable, so much the better, but even if they are not, they must nevertheless be accepted. They are not what those directly responsible for results consider important after co-operative deliberation. They may be considered satisfactory or unsatisfactory. If they are satisfactory to the leader in control, there is nothing for those responsible for practical operations to do but to follow directions. The leader may change them at such time and under such conditions as he may see fit; but the institution of changes is his function and not the function of the followers.

The autocratic leader tries with varying degrees of success to enforce his decisions. He may do so by suggestion, persuasion, force of personality, or the power of his position. He may seem dictatorial and domineering, but he need not exhibit such qualities. Of course, the autocratic leader, like the rest of us, may appear dictatorial and domineering at times; but just as it need not be the policy of others to evince such traits, so it may not be the policy of the autocratic leader. If he reveals these qualities on the basis of principles, he realizes, as most of us do, that such exhibition is usually not effective. He perhaps more often uses persuasion or suggestion. Logically, he may be expected to use such means if he can do so with success. If he wishes to get one of his followers to do something he feels that the follower will oppose, he often compliments him for something else or evinces interest in his looks or in something he is doing entirely irrelevant to the matter in hand. Then at the proper moment, he indicates what he wants done. His flattered follower then offers to accept the responsibility for doing something his better judgment, under other conditions, would have compelled him to refuse.

Suggestion and persuasion seem to be second nature with some people. If they have also a pleasing and forceful personality, they usually can get the average person to do what they want done within the bounds of reason. The autocratic leader may also use the power of his position. His followers know that he has power over them, but he may not use that power, nor even seem to use it. On the other hand, he may suggest the use of this power, or in fact actually use it, to hold his followers in line. But autocratic leadership is not confined to any one technique. It exemplifies various techniques in varying proportions. *To the auto-cratic leader, the means justify the ends, and his primary concern is to achieve his ends, to develop his policies, and to execute his plans.* Even freedom of choice is permitted in so far as it does not conflict with his policies and purposes. His ideal is that others shall do what he has decided shall be done. How he gets them to do it is irrelevant.

The autocratic leader is not necessarily a disagreeable person. As a matter of fact, he may be personally very pleasing, courteous, and suave in every respect. If he gets people to do things merely to please him, he exhibits autocratic leadership just as much as if he were to do so by physical force. If he causes others to accept his purposes and plans as their own without reflection, he is an autocratic leader, it matters not how he proceeds. Some of the most beloved teachers, super-visors, and administrators are just as autocratic as those who render themselves disagreeable and reprehensible through the exercise of direct force or threat of force. *Those who become devoted blind followers are just as much subject to autocratic leadership as are those who follow orders and dictation with a sense of compulsion and resentment.* The main thing that distinguishes autocratic leadership is the lack of intelligent partici-pation, on the part of their followers, in the development of purposes, policies, and plans.

All of us are acquainted with autocratic leaders among pupils, stu-dents, teachers, supervisors, and administrators. This kind of leader-ship is more in evidence in some places than in others, but it can be observed almost anywhere. It prevails in totalitarian states, but it is not confined to them. It is evident in some school systems, in some schools, and in some classrooms in the most democratic countries. The pupil who is bent on having his own way, and who can do so only by forcing others to adopt his purposes and plans, is an autocratic leader. The student who forces his fellow students to adopt his program or take the consequences of incurring social disapproval is just as much an autocrat as the student who tries to force his program upon others directly. The teacher who takes his aims, his subject matter, his scheme of organization, or his methods directly from some authority is sub-mitting to autocratic leadership, whatever that authority may be. He is submitting to it no less if he does so willingly than if he does so unwillingly. If he, in turn, by suggestion, persuasion, or force, compels his pupils to adopt his plans directly, that is, without their understand-ing them and believing in them, he is an autocratic leader. The administrator who tries to compel his teachers or pupils to conform through loyalty, devotion, or pressure, to fixed plans of instruction is an autocratic leader. The supervisor or director of instruction, who, through the influence of his position, tries in one way or another to impose his program on teachers is an autocratic leader.

From the standpoint of the philosophy of experimentalism, the presence of autocratic leadership in the world is not sufficient to justify its adoption as a means of controlling the experiences and activities of others. With this point of view, our nation engages from time to time in bloody wars in many parts of the world, and sacrifices our natural and human resources to overthrow autocratic leadership. Still, we must not forget that this kind of leadership exists not only in the countries with whom we have warred in the past, but even in our own land. It exists in almost any community. It has some place in almost every human heart. It plays a larger part in the lives of some than in the lives of others. Nevertheless, it is reprehensible, wherever it may exist. All of us should fight it not only on the battle fields, in the home, in the school, in the church, in the state, in business and industry, but even in our own souls.

The typical argument which authoritarians sometimes employ to justify autocratic leadership is not convincing to the experimentalists. Experimentalists admit that there are times when it is necessary to submit to dictatorial and autocratic leadership, but they insist that such authoritarian control be deliberately chosen by the group, and that its time and sphere of operation be limited. In other words, such leadership may, under certain circumstances, in some fields, be a necessity of the relationship which groups bear to each other. There are times when we must, so to speak, fight fire with fire. Under certain conditions, autocratic leadership seems to be more effective than any other kind of leadership. But all depends upon what we mean by efficiency. If we mean only some direct and immediate end, autocratic control may be indispensable. Very young children have to submit to control at times in order to live at all. Older people have to submit to control in times of war in order to survive.

Such occasions are short, however, and limited in many ways. They do not represent a desirable general policy. The facts of experience seem to indicate that in the long run people who have been subjected to autocratic leadership for long periods of time are unable to compete effectively even in a war with people who have had democratic leaders. Their success in the business of war is limited. They win battles, but they do not win wars. The immediate tangible results which can be secured through autocratic leadership are incommensurate with the correspondingly less desirable qualities of personality, which represent the cumulative effect of the desirable qualities of experience that experience itself finds desirable and which the philosophy of experimentalism idealizes. Any leadership which in its very nature refuses to provide the conditions under which followers as well as leaders can intelligently select and pursue their own purposes is not efficient in the long run. Under these conditions, skill, knowledge, or technique is not very effective. *Those who for the sake of immediate efficiency adopt autocratic leadership permanently and universally and barter away their own souls, will not in the end prove themselves to be efficient,* when efficiency is conceived in terms of the whole race rather than in terms of the first lap.

Moreover, when we get others to accept our purposes blindly, it matters not how we do so, we are in fact making slaves of them. No man has a just right to make slaves of his fellowmen; least of all do educational leaders have a right to make slaves of children and of one another. If intelligent projection and pursuit of purposes are indispensable aspects of desirable experience, they are as indispensable to the followers as they are to the leaders.

The Drifting Theory
(Educational Laissez Faire)

The attitude assumed toward leadership in the laissez-faire philosophy of education has been indicated in the consideration of the theories the proponents of this theory entertain with respect to other features of school practice. It seems to be logically implicit in the laissez-faire theories of certain other features of experience that have been developed. For convenience of reference, this philosophy of education, conceived in terms of leadership, is here designated as the drifting theory.

The practices exemplifying this theory, like those exemplifying autocratic leadership, are often called democratic. In fact, drifting leadership is usually called democratic. It is quite common in democratic countries in both the home and the school. It seems to be idealized in some of the so-called progressive schools. Capable and reflective students of the trend of events preceding the outbreak of World War II defined the political leaders in democratic countries as drifters. The choice of the term was suggested to the author by J. K. Hart's, *Mind in Transition*, in which he contrasted the so-called drifters, who were considered democratic leaders by many, with what the experimentalists consider autocratic leaders on the one hand, and democratic leaders on the other. It seems to be a good name for a kind of leadership which may be distinguished in the school as well as in other social institutions.[3]

Leaders in the schools or elsewhere who adopt this theory are inclined to let things float along, living from one day to the next, from week to week, without doing any long-term planning. They muddle along and meet each situation that comes up with little consideration of the assumptions and implications involved. They patch up a little here and a little there, grabbing at first one device and then another for the purpose of tiding them over realities that they refuse to face courageously. In the schools, as elsewhere, they are inclined to approve those who flatter them, flatter those who offer concrete proposals, and appease those who make specific demands. They oscillate from one course of action to another, following the directions of those individuals or groups who for the time being are able to secure their attention.

In practice this kind of leadership assumes two forms. Some who are autocrats at heart have dominated others so long and have refused so often to enlist their participation and advice in the development of policies and programs that they have lost touch with practical realities. When they suddenly realize their plight, they look to others for direction. They are eager to get suggestions and proposals, and welcome them from whatever source they may come. They are simply confused and want to know what to do. The educational program in any classroom, school, or school system where this kind of leadership prevails, oscillates from one course of action to another, usually following the lead of whatever individuals or groups secure, for the time being, the attention of those in power. Those who are in favor with the powers-that-be today are put in their proper places tomorrow, and others come to the fore. But they, too, will soon have played their role and others who have come into favor will go the same way. Those who adopt this form of the drifting theory of leadership do not do so wholeheartedly. They have been autocrats too long and they fluctuate from one method to the other. They have become drifters not by a change of heart or by deliberate choice, but by necessity. They return to the old ways after each crisis only to fall back on others when a new crisis arises.

---

[3] J. K. Hart, *Mind in Transition.* Covice Friede, Publishers, New York, 1938. Pp. 310–321.

This would-be drifter is not too difficult to discover in almost any school or school system. The most autocratic individual in dealing with some people may be the most submissive in dealing with others. The most autocratic person in the world during the hour of success may be the most helpless in the hour of defeat. So long as pupils learn what the teacher demands of them, the teacher continues to make demands, but when pupils become indifferent, incipiently disorderly, then actively disorderly, and finally undertake to break the teacher, then something must be done. Here is a crisis that the autocratic teacher may have to face at one time or another. He may adopt stringent measures and enforce his decisions. If he does, he maintains his self-respect and continues to be an autocratic leader. On the other hand, he may yield to the pupils and for a while adopt the drifting theory of leadership. He permits those who get his attention for the time being to determine the activities and purposes of the group. Later on he may be following the direction of other individuals and groups who have come to the front. The teacher who is this kind of drifter simply follows the lead of whoever at the time is able to point the way.

What is true of teachers is also true of autocratic administrators. They are at heart autocratic, but by necessity in times of crisis they seek direction from others. They follow the advice of whoever makes himself heard at the proper moment, but they do not hesitate to follow the advice of others when a new crisis appears. They may be autocratic in principle, but they are drifters in practice. They no longer rely on their own decisions as to what is best, all things considered, but depend on the advice of those who are not directly responsible for results.

The drifting theory assumes another form in those leaders who try to please everybody all the time. Some people who are responsible for the guidance and direction of others seem to be entirely lacking in any definite policy or program. They seem to be constitutionally opposed to working out any long-term plans. They let things run along as custom and tradition seem to dictate, are always willing to listen to suggestions and proposals from others, and in fact even solicit them. The teacher who adopts this attitude in dealing with his pupils urges them to indicate what things should be done and how they should be done. He endorses almost any undertaking that seems to be immediately acceptable to the group. As to methods of procedure, the pupils follow whatever course they see fit. The teacher may ask questions, but he hesitates to state his position on controversial questions or to make definite decisions in regard to anything.

The administrator who adopts this attitude has to deal with the public as well as with teachers and pupils. Moreover, he is no more sure of what should be done or what should not be done than the drifting teacher. Often he is very pleasing in manner and agreeable to all suggestions and proposals from whatever source. He really tries to find out what pupils, teachers, and patrons of the school like best. He does not set up definite proposals and try to justify them. He undertakes to put into effect the ideas which please sometimes the majority and sometimes the most influential. Since people in general are inclined to do what they have been doing, very little change in aims, methods, or results occur. Eventually, however, individuals and groups who are sensitive to new demands insist on important changes. The administrator becomes less and less certain about which course to follow. Still he tries to please everybody and offend no one.

The director of instruction or supervisor who adopts this attitude pays proper deference to the administrator, but he deals primarily with teachers, and therefore seeks first of all to gain their favor. He usually proceeds in one of two ways. If he has consciously adopted the philosophy of educational laissez faire, he emphasizes the negative policy of letting pupils have their own way. He takes for granted that all teachers are directly and immediately sensitive to the needs, impulses, and desires of pupils and would give them free rein were the educational conditions sufficiently favorable. He extols the importance of pupil freedom and initiative repeatedly and calls attention to unfavorable conditions under which teachers work. He subjects established practices and procedures of all kinds to criticism and urges their removal. But he does not offer any concrete proposals as to what specific procedures should be used. According to his position, the teachers themselves are imbued with principles of pupil freedom and initiative and can work out new procedures if only the old, established, formal ones are removed.

If, on the other hand, he is by nature the kind of drifter whose controlling purpose in life is to please others at any price, he does not condemn the established order nor advocate important changes. He approves almost everything and everybody. He compliments everything that can be complimented. He seldom if ever raises any objection to any procedure or proposal. Whatever is right and whatever suggestion occurs to those whom he guides and directs is approved in all essential respects. He seems to enjoy discussing school problems with teachers and associating with them socially, and comments favorably upon whatever they are doing. He is often especially laudatory and enthusiastic about almost any form, scheme, or procedure that has become identified in their minds with the most recent slogans of the so-called progressive education, to which he always lends his professional support.

From the standpoint of the philosophy of experimentalism, a *drifting leadership in education scarcely deserves to be called leadership at all*. The only justification it has for being so designated is the fact that some people who actually hold positions of leadership in our schools and colleges or in other social institutions seem to lose all sense of direction and to rely on the impulses, desires, suggestions, and proposals of their followers to point the way. Nevertheless, there are to be found in educational literature certain shibboleths and maxims which actually idealize this kind of leadership. Not only is the school to be child-centered, but the teacher must follow the lead of the child, and those who direct the teacher must follow the lead of the teacher. Drifting leadership is not only a fact but an ideal. In the minds of some, drifting leadership and progressive education mean the same thing. But the experimentalists contend that the fact that some in positions of leadership resort to drifting does not warrant the endorsement of drifting as an ideal.

Moreover, the slogans often used to justify this theory of leadership represent only partial truths. In a sense, it may be proper for the teacher to take cues from children and for administrators and supervisors to take cues from teachers. The attitude of those with whom the leader has to work must be taken into account if he is to work with them effectively. A desire to look at things from the standpoint of his followers does not excuse the leader from having aims, policies, and programs of his own. In fact, he must have a sense of direction, and must even be able to take cues from others.

The drifter who loses his sense of direction and who relies on the shifting interests and desires of others is not typically at heart an exponent of educational laissez faire. He is more often an exponent of educational authoritarianism who has lost his way. He is drifting *de facto*, but in principle he is still an autocrat. The theory or principle of autocratic leadership has been considered already, and the practices to which it often leads are all one with the implications of that form of drifting leadership which is here under consideration.

Just as educational laissez faire represents a reaction and a protest against educational authoritarianism, so the laissez-faire theory of drifting leadership represents a reaction and a protest against the authoritarian theory of autocratic leadership. The drifters seem to think that the direct opposite of whatever the autocrats do is invariably and absolutely right. If the autocrats emphasize the importance of having the followers obey the directions of the leaders, the drifters emphasize the importance of having the leaders take the immediate needs, interests, desires, suggestions, and proposals of the followers as the purposes, ends, and goals of the policies, programs, and activities for the guidance of which they are responsible. If the autocrats insist that the followers should actually obey the orders of the leaders, the drifters insist that the leaders should conform to the wishes of the followers. From the standpoint of the philosophy of experimentalism, this reversal of the whole idea of leadership is logically unsound. The opposite of a bad thing is not necessarily a good thing. Besides, *drifting leadership is the surest way in the world to produce a reaction in favor of autocratic leadership*, against which the drifters themselves — the drifters in principle — are protesting. Available evidence indicates that both pupils and teachers want leaders who have a definite sense of direction. After they have been long subjected to autocratic control, they have a sense of relief from stress and strain when given an opportunity to express their long pent-up desires. If the leaders do not provide direction for their energies, they soon become listless and tired of "doing what they want to do." Then the conditions are ripe for a return to the autocrats, who at least have definite plans and purposes and know where they are going. We are now faced with the danger of just such a reactionary movement in school education.

The drifters are right in condemning the autocrats and their underlying authoritarian philosophy, but they are wrong in their negative approach. The qualities of experience generated under autocratic leadership are bad; but the qualities of experience generated under drifting leadership are no better. The autocrats make slaves of their followers; but the drifters permit their followers to make slaves of themselves. When people make slaves of themselves, they do not hesitate to become slaves of others. As already suggested, when the autocratic leader loses his way, he becomes a drifter; but in becoming a drifter he also becomes a slave to his impulses. As a slave to his impulses, he may become an easy prey to some of his wily followers, at least for a time. Likewise, the followers who are allowed to drift and make slaves of themselves develop a sense of boredom and helplessness and are ready and willing to become, at least for a time, the follower of almost any autocrat who asserts his authority. Both autocratic and drifting leadership are theoretically and practically undesirable. What is needed in education, as well as in politics and business, is an educational leadership that will cause the pendulum to swing neither to the right nor to the left, but in a new direction. This is the only kind of leadership that can find its theoretical justification in the philosophy of experimentalism.

THE DEMOCRATIC THEORY
(EDUCATIONAL EXPERIMENTALISM)

Democratic leadership seems to meet all requirements. Just as educational experimentalism is the educational equivalent of the philosophy of experimentalism — also called pragmatism, instrumentalism, and humanism — so democratic leadership in school education is the equivalent of educational experimentalism in its application to teaching, administration, and supervision. Our approval of the democratic theory of leadership has been suggested throughout the discussions of the theories and principles constituting the philosophy of educational experimentalism. It is necessary here merely to bring together in a more systematic form what has already been indicated.

The democratic leader, like the autocratic leader, has his definite aims, policies, and programs. But unlike the autocrat, he neither takes them ready made from those above him, nor tries to force them ready made on those below him. Like the drifter, he wishes everybody to have his own purposes and plans, but unlike the drifter, he is not inclined to mistake immediate desires, wishes, and wants for aims derived through reflective consideration of alternative courses of action. Like the autocrat, he makes definite plans and knows the direction in which he is going. But, unlike those of the autocrat, his plans are flexible and elastic, capable of modification, not only periodically but gradually, as practical conditions change. He does not keep his head turned in the same direction, regardless of which way the wind blows, until the powers-that-be issue new orders. Like the drifter, he wishes his followers to change their plans as conditions change, and without waiting for him to call the turns. Moreover, he wants his followers to modify their courses of action on the basis of creative intelligence; he does not want them, as does the drifter, to take their impulses and desires as guides to action.

Not everyone who calls himself democratic is democratic. In democratic countries, autocratic leaders as well as the drifters glorify democracy. That is the way they get things done. But, happily, we do not have to rely on what is called democratic. Most of us know a democratic leader when we observe his activities. The democratic teacher begins planning just as soon as he knows his teaching assignment, and he continues to plan *for* his pupils and *with* his pupils. He makes plans for them to plan. The democratic administrator makes definite proposals and encourages others to make definite proposals. He does not wait for the suggestions of others before having ideas of his own. He is not any more afraid to think and act upon thinking than he is afraid of having *others* think and act upon thinking. The democratic supervisor does not impose his own program on teachers, and he does not leave teachers to discover and work out their own problems. He makes definite proposals as to what should be done, but his proposals are conceived, not as things that *must* be done, but as things that *may* or may not be done, after intelligent consideration.

Democratic leadership is the only safeguard against setting back the clock of progress and returning to the authoritative and formal school of the past. Drifting leadership, which some people call democratic, condemns authoritarianism and formality, but it represents only a negative attack and, therefore, has no positive and constructive program. It is responsible, in large measure, for the wide-spread confusion and hypocrisy in educational circles; for the indifference and listlessness of pupils; for unsatisfactory achievement; for the current desire for system and order; and for the tendency to return to the authoritarian and autocratic regime, the leaders of which, under cover of high-sounding phrases, are bidding now for the control of the public schools.

The philosophy underlying the democratic type of leadership does justice to the demand for system and order, which the autocrats idealize, and it also respects the personality of the individual, which the drifters idealize. But it is not a compromise between them; it is not a middle-of-the-road position; it is another point of view. Its translation into practical programs and activities is the hope of the world.[4]

At least, that is the way the experimentalists look upon democratic leadership. In fact, they usually call the ideal of their social philosophy the democratic way of life. Such a philosophy is, of course, a reality

[4] L. Thomas Hopkins, *Interaction: The Democratic Process.* D. C. Heath and Company, New York, 1941. Pp. 102–112; 124–132.

only as an ethical ideal. Why, then, it may be asked, should the experimentalists consider their philosophy in its social aspects the democratic philosophy, even the democratic philosophy of education? Are there not other democratic social philosophies and philosophies of education? The answer is that this is the only philosophy that in all of its aspects idealizes the qualities of experience which experience itself has found desirable. Moreover it idealizes them for no particular social group or social class. It idealizes them for all social groups and for all social classes — for all individuals throughout the world, even for generations yet unborn.

In a word, the democratic way of life, which the experimentalists idealize, is a philosophical justification of that state of affairs in which men may work out their own destiny together, all for each and each for all. The qualities of experience that such a state of affairs might make possible are the very qualities that the historical democratic movement in politics, religion, business and industry, and education has always idealized. *The progressive realization of the democratic way of life depends upon the development of a democratic leadership in all the affairs of life.* A democratic leadership in the schools is indispensable to the development of a democratic leadership in the home, in the church, in the state, and in all other fields. The theory of democratic leadership in education thus becomes another way of stating the ideal of educational experimentalism and its underlying philosophy.

Index

Index

A

Advance determination (theory of subject matter):
  and quality of experience, 261–262
  authoritarian theory, 256–262
  meaning of, 255–256
Advisory theory (of improvement program):
  and quality of experience, 396, 398, 399
  experimentalist theory, 394–400
  meaning of, 394
Aims of education:
  and external unity, 196–198
  as a feature of school practice, 236
  Cardinal Principles, 68–69, 237, 247
  emergent means, 246–249
  external ends, 237–242
  immediate ends, 243–246
  in American democracy, 68, 70–71, 237, 239, 247
  qualities of experience as, 249–250
  scope of, 237–239
  Socio-Economic Goals, 68–69, 237, 247
  ways of stating, 70–72, 196–198, 239
Alcott, Bronson, 46
Aristotle, 100, 203
Authoritarianism (educational):
  advance determination as principle of, 256–262
  autocratic leadership, 405–406
  best method as principle of, 367–373
  creative embodiment as principle of, 142–149
  doctrinaire sociality as principle of, 64–90
  domination as principle of, 381–389
  external ends as principle of, 236–242
  external unity as principle of, 194–208
  formal techniques as principle of, 304–319
  identification as principle of, 329–334

objective contingency as principle of, 28–37
provisional interest as principle of, 111–128
selective choice as principle of, 166–171
separate subject matter as principle of, 348–356
separation as principle of, 270–278
subject matter curriculum as principle of, 290–295
Autocratic theory (of leadership):
  and quality of experience, 408
  authoritarian theory, 405–408
  meaning of, 404–405

B

Babbitt, Irving, 31
Bagley, William C., 2, 3, 310
Barr, Stringfellow, 31
Bergson, Henri, 6, 43, 320, 393
Best method (theory of devices and techniques):
  authoritarian theory, 367–373
  forms of, 367–369
  meaning of, 367
Bobbitt, Franklin, 197, 237
Bode, Boyd Henry, 7, 8, 11, 12, 17, 20, 22, 28, 41, 53, 104, 280, 301, 308, 317, 341, 393
Brubacher, John S., 11, 289, 344
Burton, William H., 24, 126, 218, 219, 255, 262, 337
Byron, George Gordon, Lord, 46

C

Change:
  and curriculum, 294–295
  and educational aims, 241–242, 248–250
  and educational laissez faire, 41–43
  and educative experience, 56–63

419

Religious education, 328–329, 330–331, 334, 336–337, 343, 344–345
Research (educational):
as a feature of school practice, 348
functional aspect, 356–358
meaning of, 348
scientific method, 358–363
separate subject matter, 348–356
Romanticism and romanticists, 9, 38–40, 43–47
Roosevelt, Franklin D., 182
Rousseau, Jean Jacques, 6, 9, 41, 46, 320, 393
Rowe, Stuart H., 309
Rugg, Harold, 10
Russell, James Earl, 327

S

Schelling, Wilhelm Joseph, 46, 393
Schiller, F. C. S., 7, 320
Schlegel, August Wilhelm *and* Friedrich, 44
School, 1–3
and education, 237–335
and other institutions, 227–228, 339–341
and training, 327–347
features of practice, 229–235
functions of, 227–229, 327–328
School practice:
aims, 236–250
curriculum, 288–303
devices and techniques, 364–379
features of, 12, 229–235, 251–256
general method, 304–326
improvement program, 380–400
leadership, 401–416
organization, 269–287
subject matter, 251–268
training, 327–347
Scientific method (theory of research):
and quality of experience, 362–363
experimentalist theory, 358–363
meaning of, 358–359
Selective choice:
and quality of experience, 170–171
assumptions of, 166–168
authoritarian theory, 166–171
meaning of, 166
Selectivity of experience:
as a feature of experience, 22–26
free choice, 171–175

intelligent choice, 175–178
meaning of, 166
selective choice, 166–171
Separate subject matter (theory of research):
and quality of experience, 352–353
authoritarian theory, 348–356
forms of, 349–353, 353–356
Separation theory (of organization):
and "best books," 277–278
and integration, 275–277
and subject reform, 274–275
authoritarian theory, 270–278
meaning of, 270–271
Shelley, Percy Bysshe, 46
Snedden, David, 237
Sociality of experience:
and language, 101–102
as a feature of experience, 22–26, 64
as a level of existence, 97–102
doctrinaire sociality, 64–90
inherent sociality, 90–97
meaning of, 64
widening sociality, 97–110
Spencer, Herbert, 237, 239
Spiritual unfoldment, 30–31
Subjective contingency (theory of relativity):
and change, 41–43
and goodness of nature, 38–41
and quality of experience, 62–63
and romantic idealism, 43–46
criticism of, 49
laissez-faire theory, 37–49
meaning of, 37–38
Subject matter:
advance determination, 256–262
as content, 255–256
as feature of school practice, 251–256
as materials, 252–255
continuous selection, 265–268
immediate determination, 262–265
of direct experience, 254
of vicarious experience, 254
Subject matter (theory of curriculum):
aims conception of, 293–295
and quality of experience, 294
authoritarian theory, 290–295
content conception of, 291–293
materials conception of, 290–291
meaning of, 389–390
Subjects of study, 198–199, 200–202
Supernatural adjustment, 31